Paul's Covert Use of Scripture

Paul's Covert Use of Scripture

Intertextuality and Rhetorical Situation
in Philippians 2:10–16

David McAuley

◗PICKWICK *Publications* • Eugene, Oregon

PAUL'S COVERT USE OF SCRIPTURE
Intertextuality and Rhetorical Situation in Philippians 2:10–16

Copyright © 2015 David McAuley. All rights reserved. Except for brief quotations in critical publications or reviews, no part of this book may be reproduced in any manner without prior written permission from the publisher. Write: Permissions, Wipf and Stock Publishers, 199 W. 8th Ave., Suite 3, Eugene, OR 97401.

Pickwick Publications
An Imprint of Wipf and Stock Publishers
199 W. 8th Ave., Suite 3
Eugene, OR 97401

www.wipfandstock.com

ISBN 13: 978-1-4982-2113-9

Cataloging-in-Publication data:

McAuley, David

    Paul's covert use of scripture: intertextuality and rhetorical situation in Philippians 2:10–16 / David McAuley.

    xiv + 292 p. ; 23 cm. —Includes bibliographical references and index(es).

    ISBN 13: 978-1-4982-2113-9

    1. Bible. N.T. Phillipians II, 10–16—Criticism, interpretation, etc. 2. Bible. N.T. Phillipians II, 10–16—Relation to the Old Testament. I. Title.

BS2705.52 M35 2015

Manufactured in the U.S.A.   10/08/2015

Contents

Acknowledgments | vii
Abbreviations | viii

Chapter 1: Introduction | 1
    The Problem and Need for This Investigation
    Orientation to the Study and Preview of Selected Methods
    Paul and Scripture
    Survey of Previous Approaches
    Procedure

Chapter 2: Theories and Methodologies | 50
    Situational Rhetoric
    Intertextuality
    Allusion
    Conclusions

Chapter 3: The Rhetorical Situation in Philippians | 88
    The Rhetorical Situation in Phil 1:27–30
    The Rhetorical Situation in Phil 2:1–4
    The Rhetorical Situation in Phil 2:5–11
    The Rhetorical Situation in Phil 2:14
    The Rhetorical Situation in Phil 3:1–21
    Conclusions: The Matrix

Chapter 4: Intertextual Allusion in Phil 2:10–16 | 161
    Isa 45:23 in Phil 2:10–11
    Ps 2:11 in Phil 2:12
    Deut 32:5 in Phil 2:15
    Dan 12:3 in Phil 2:15
    Isa 49:4 in Phil 2:16

Chapter 5: Conclusions | 243
    Methodological
    Hermeneutical
    Implications

Bibliography | 253
Author Index | 277
Ancient Document Index | 283

Acknowledgments

THERE ARE SEVERAL PEOPLE to whom I owe a debt of thanks for their guidance, support and encouragement. Special thanks are due to my supervisor, Dr. Marion Carson, for her invaluable guidance and critical evaluation of my work. Her feedback was challenging and always offered with patience and encouragement. I am also extremely grateful to Dr. Andrew D. Clarke for his professional help and indispensable insights and direction. Thanks are also due to my examiners, Dr. Susan Docherty and Dr. Jane Heath, for their helpful suggestions and advice. I want to acknowledge the help given by Rev. Dr. Stephen Chester, Dr. John Dennis and Rev. Eryl Rowlands who reviewed parts of my work at various stages of its development. Their helpful criticism stimulated further study and facilitated improvements. I would also like to thank those who organised the ICC Postgraduate Seminars and the Scottish Postgraduate Seminars for the opportunity to present parts of the work. I am grateful to the ICC library staff (past and present) for their sustained support and flexibility throughout the period of research—Gwenda Bond, Lucy Carroll, Gudrun Porter and Anna Dunipace. I owe much to Gudrun Porter for providing German tutoring and translation. I would also like to extend my gratitude to Dorothy Campbell from the Tron Church for proofreading the dissertation. I am indebted to Cammie and Susie Kennedy for their friendship and support, and to Thomas Sorrentino and George Garcia who sowed the seed of Bible study almost two decades ago in San Jose, California. Finally, I am most grateful for our two children Kirsty and Ben. They have been a constant source of love, comfort and understanding throughout. Most of all, I thank my wife Dawn. She inspired me to keep going, and without her love, encouragement, and support the work would not have started or completed. I dedicate it to her.

Abbreviations

OLD TESTAMENT

Gen	Genesis	Eccl	Ecclesiastes
Exod	Exodus	Song	Song of Songs
Lev	Leviticus	Isa	Isaiah
Num	Numbers	Jer	Jeremiah
Deut	Deuteronomy	Lam	Lamentations
Josh	Joshua	Ezek	Ezekiel
Judg	Judges	Dan	Daniel
Ruth	Ruth	Hos	Hosea
1–2 Sam	1–2 Samuel	Joel	Joel
1–2 Kgdms	1–2 Kingdoms	Amos	Amos
1–2 Kgs	1–2 Kings	Obad	Obadiah
3–4 Kgdms	3–4 Kingdoms	Jonah	Jonah
1–2 Chr	1–2 Chronicles	Mic	Micah
Ezra	Ezra	Nah	Nahum
Neh	Nehemiah	Hab	Habakkuk
Esth	Esther	Zeph	Zephaniah
Job	Job	Hag	Haggai
Ps (*pl.* Pss)	Psalm(s)	Zech	Zechariah
Prov	Proverbs	Mal	Malachi

NEW TESTAMENT

Matt	Matthew	1–2 Thess	1–2 Thessalonians

Mark	Mark	1–2 Tim	1–2 Timothy
Luke	Luke	Titus	Titus
John	John	Phlm	Philemon
Acts	Acts	Heb	Hebrews
Rom	Romans	Jas	James
1–2 Cor	1–2 Corinthians	1–2 Pet	1–2 Peter
Gal	Galatians	1–2–3 John	1–2–3 John
Eph	Ephesians	Jude	Jude
Phil	Philippians	Rev	Revelation
Col	Colossians		

APOCRYPHA AND SEPTUAGINT

Jdt	Judith
1–2 Macc	1–2 Maccabees
3–4 Macc	3–4 Maccabees
Ode	Odes
Sir	Sirach (Ecclesiasticus)
Tob	Tobit
Wis	Wisdom of Solomon

OLD TESTAMENT PSEUDEPIGRAPHA

2 Bar.	*Syriac Apocalypse of Baruch*
1 En.	*Ethiopian Enoch*
4 Ezra	*4 Ezra*
T. Ab.	*Testament of Abraham*

DEAD SEA SCROLLS

1QSa	*Rule of the Congregation*
4QFlor	*Florilegium*

PHILO OF ALEXANDRIA

Leg. 1, 2, 3	Legum allegoriae I, II, III
Sobr.	De sobrietate
Flacc.	In Flaccum

APOSTOLIC FATHERS

Ign	Ignatius of Antioch
Ign.Pol.	Ignatius, *To Polycarp*
Pol	Polycarp
Pol.Phil.	Polycarp, *To the Philippians*

ANCIENT HELLENISTIC LITERATURE

Aristotle
Probl. — *Problemata*
Diod. Sic. — Diodorus Siculus
Dionysius Halicarnassus
Ant. Rom. — *Antiquitates Romanae*
Euripides
Rhes. — *Rhesus*
Hippocrates of Cos
Flat. — *De flatibus (On Breaths)*
Homer
Il — *Iliad*
Plut — Plutarch
Vit. — *An vitiositas ad infelicitatem sufficiat*
Mor. — *Moralia*

PAPYRI

P.Oxyrh	Oxyrhynchus papyri

MODERN WORKS

AB	Anchor Bible
ANE	Ancient Near East
ANRW	*Aufstieg und Niedergang der römischen Welt*
AOTC	Apollos Old Testament Commentary
AusBR	*Australian Biblical Review*
BCE	Before Common Era
Bib	*Biblica*
BBR	*Bulletin for Biblical Research*
BDAG	W. Bauer, F. W. Danker, W. F. Arndt, and F. W. Gingrich. *A Greek-English Lexicon of the New Testament and other Early Christian Literature*
BDB	The Brown-Driver-Briggs Hebrew-English Lexicon of the Old Testament
BDF	F. Blass, A. Debrunner, R. W. Funk. *A Greek Grammar of the New Testament and Other Early Christian Literature*
BECNT	Baker Exegetical Commentary on the New Testament
BFCT	Beiträge zur Förderung christlicher Theologie
BHT	Beiträge zur historischen Theologie
BNTC	Black's New Testament Commentaries
BR	*Bible Review*
BSac	*Bibliotheca Sacra*
BST	Bible Speaks Today
BT	*The Bible Translator*
CBNTS	Coniectanea Biblica New Testament Series
CBOTS	Coniectanea Biblica Old Testament Series
CBQ	*Catholic Biblical Quarterly*
CBQMS	*Catholic Biblical Quarterly* Monograph Series
CBSC	Cambridge Bible for Schools and Colleges
CBSS	Continuum Biblical Studies Series
CCL	Classic Commentary Library
CE	Common Era
ConBNT	Coniectanea Biblica New Testament Series
CRJ	*Christian Research Journal*
CTM	*Currents in Theology and Mission*

DPL	*Dictionary of Paul and His Letters*
EC	Epworth Commentaries
ExpTim	*Expository Times*
GSC	Geneva Series Commentary
GTA	Göttinger theologische Arbeiten
HB	Hebrew Bible
HNT	Handbuch zum Neun Testament
HTKNT	Herders theologischer Kommentar zum Neuen Testament
HTR	*Harvard Theological Review*
ICC	International Critical Commentary
IDB	Interpreter's Dictionary of the Bible
Int	*Interpretation*
ITC	International Theological Commentary
JBL	*Journal of Biblical Literature*
JETS	*Journal of the Evangelical Theological Society*
JSNT	*Journal for the Study of the New Testament*
JSNTSup	*Journal for the Study of the New Testament* Supplement Series
JSOT	*Journal for the Study of the Old Testament*
JTS	*Journal of Theological Studies*
KGS	Kölner germanistische Studien
KJV	Kings James Version
KS	Kölner germanistische Studien
LCL	Loeb Classical Library
LEH	Johan Lust, Erik Eynikel, and Katrin Hauspie. *A Greek-English Lexicon of the Septuagint (Parts I and II)*
LNTS	Library of New Testament Studies
LXX	Septuagint
MM	Moulton, James H. and George Milligan. *The Vocabulary of the Greek Testament Illustrated from the Papyri and Other Non-Literary Sources.*
MNTC	Moffatt New Testament Commentary
MT	Masoretic Text
NA	Nestle-Aland
NASB	New American Standard Bible
NCBC	New Century Bible Commentary

NETS	*New English Translation of the Septuagint*
NIBC	New International Bible Commentary
NIBCOT	New International Bible Commentary on the Old Testament
NICNT	New International Commentary on the New Testament
NICOT	New International Commentary on the Old Testament
NIDNTT	*New International Dictionary of New Testament Theology*
NIDOTTE	*New International Dictionary of Old Testament Theology & Exegesis*
NIGTC	New International Greek Testament Commentary
NIV	New International Version
NovT	*Novum Testamentum*
NovTSup	*Novum Testamentum* Supplements
NPNF	Nicene and Post-Nicene Fathers of the Christian Church
NRSV	New Revised Standard Version
NT	New Testament
NTOA	Novum Testamentum et Orbis Antiquus
NTS	*New Testament Studies*
OG	Old Greek
OT	Old Testament
OTL	Old Testament Library Commentary Series
OTS	*Oudtestamentische Studiën*
Proleg	James H. Moulton. *A Grammar Of New Testament Greek, Vol. I, Prolegomena*
PRS	*Perspectives on Religious Studies*
RB	*Revue Biblique*
ResQ	*Restoration Quarterly*
RevExp	*Review & Expositor*
RSV	Revised Standard Version
SBL	Society of Biblical Literature
SBLSCS	Society of Biblical Literature Septuagint and Cognate Studies
SBT	Studies in Biblical Theology
SHAW.PH	Sitzungsberichte der Heidelberger Akademie der Wissenschaften. Philosophise-Klasse 1927–28/4
SNTSMS	Society for New Testament Studies Monograph Series
SPC	SCM Pelican Commentaries

SPCK	Society for Promoting Christian Knowledge.
Syh	Syrian Translation of Origin's Hexapla
TCGNT	*A Textual Commentary on the Greek New Testament*
TDNT	*Theological Dictionary of the New Testament*
TH	Theodotion
TLG*	Thesaurus Linguae Graecae—A Digital Library of Greek Literature
TLZ	*Theologische Literaturzeitung*
TNTC	Tyndale New Testament Commentary
TOTC	Tyndale Old Testament Commentary
TrinJ	*Trinity Journal*
TynBul	*Tyndale Bulletin*
UBS	United Bible Society
UBSGNT	United Bible Societies' Greek New Testament
VT	*Vetus Testamentum*
WBC	Word Bible Commentary
WTJ	*Westminster Theological Journal*
WUNT	Wissenschaftliche Untersuchungen zum Neuen Testament
ZBNT	Zürcher Bibelkommentare Neues Testament

CHAPTER 1

Introduction

THE PROBLEM AND NEED FOR THIS INVESTIGATION

IF THE POSSIBILITY OF the presence of the OT in Phil 2:10–16 is granted, an immediate problem arises. How do we account for the density and interplay of the tacit references, in seven contiguous verses, to five texts in four books of the OT: Isa 45:23 in Phil 2:10–11; Ps 2:11 in Phil 2:12; Deut 32:5 in Phil 2:15; Dan 12:3 in Phil 2:15 and Isa 49:4 in Phil 2:16? Fee is one of few to recognize the problem in his description of the abrupt way Paul introduces his ministry into the sentence beginning at Phil 2:14:

> [It is perhaps best explained on the basis of its most striking feature]: the sudden and profuse influx of echoes from the OT, which is unlike anything else in the Pauline corpus. So unique is this that one scarcely knows what to make of it.[1]

What has caused a unique passage in the Pauline corpus to have escaped the exegetical net to such an extent given that a scholar of Fee's caliber can claim, "one scarcely knows what to make of it"? The problem is that the presence of the OT in Philippians has not been generally granted, and Phil 2:12–16 has not attracted special interest among scholars,[2] perhaps being overshadowed by its neighboring texts (Phil 2:6–11 and 3:1–21). A *prima facie* interpretation of the passage is that Paul enjoins obedience from the

1. Fee, *Philippians*, 241–42.
2. Weber, "Philipper 2, 12–13," 31–37.

Philippians in his absence and in response to what God and Christ have done and, at best, that the section is peppered with "loose" references to the OT. Thus, although some scholars might admit to some kind of OT "influence" or "reference" in these verses,[3] others account for the presence of the OT as no more than language reproduced by an author steeped in the story of Israel and unconcerned about the contexts of the texts cited or referenced.[4] In other words, the OT, if present at all, is superficial and does not *function* in Phil 2:10–16—essentially, Paul does not use the OT, only its language. A brief survey of the history of scholarship of the New Testament's use of the OT will uncover the reason for, and implication of, Philippians being omitted from this important field of analysis.

The problem of whether or not Paul uses the OT in Philippians can be traced back to Von Harnack. In 1928, he famously claimed that Paul only wrote about the OT in his letters when he was forced to reply to issues raised by Judaizing opponents. Noting the absence of OT introductory formulae (ἡ γραφή and γέγραπται) in Philippians, Von Harnack concluded, "Nonetheless, here the apostle writes as if no Old Testament existed."[5] Philippians has not fared much better in recent scholarship. Moody Smith and Stanley exclude Philippians from their investigations into Paul's use of the OT because it lacks any "quotations."[6] Furthermore, in the *Commentary on the New Testament Use of the Old Testament* (2007), Silva, having proposed several conscious allusions in Philippians, states: "even in these cases, however, it would be misleading to provide extensive comments such as are appropriate in contexts (e.g., Gal 3) where Paul explicitly cites Scripture, for in the latter he evidently expects his readers to take specific OT statements into account."[7] The result is that Philippians occupies the fewest number of pages (five, shared with 1–3 John) in the entire compendium. In the three books of the series, *The New Testament and the Scriptures of Israel*, analyses of Deuteronomy, Isaiah, and the Psalms are offered for Romans, Galatians, 1 and 2 Corinthians. The reason given for the omission of Philippians (in the analysis of the Psalms) is "because overt references to the Psalms in the

---

3. For example, Barth, *Philipper*; Gnilka, *Philipperbrief*; Dibelius, *Philipper*; cf. Pilhofer, *Philippi*, whose investigation lacks attention to OT and Jewish background.

4. For example, Beker, "Echoes and Intertertextuality," 65. He writes: "[Paul] may simply use Scripture to impress his audience with his profundity, while the contours and context of a specific fragment of the Old Testament passage are in fact not the necessary presupposition for the validity of his argument."

5. Harnack, "Old Testament in the Pauline Letters," 31.

6. Smith, "Pauline Literature," 265; Stanley, *Paul and the Language of Scripture*, 37.

7. Silva, "Philippians," 836.

form of marked or unmarked quotations are missing from these writings."[8] The claim, or assumption, that quotation is somehow a superior category to allusion still permeates scholarly thinking, and has retarded extensive investigations into Scripture's presence in Philippians.

Such claims or assumptions have also exerted an influence on broader aspects of exegesis. For example, the composition of the Philippian Church has been described as having no (negligible) Jewish members or influence *because* the text is devoid of OT quotations.[9] In similar vein, the Philippians's lack of familiarity with the Jewish Scriptures is adduced from the absence of the OT in the letter.[10] Although more recent developments have seen an increased focus on "indirect" uses of Scripture in Paul's letters, these invariably occur in letters that also have direct references or quotations.[11] We are therefore indebted to those scholars who persistently "broach the subject" of the OT's presence in Philippians, sensing its latent presence;[12] this investigation is in large measure a response to their promptings. Nevertheless, the possibility of the OT's "indirect" presence in Philippians has been a peripheral issue, acting, primarily, as a preamble to a discussion on terminology and methodology.[13] Furthermore, recognition that Paul's dependence on the OT is *reflected* or *echoed* in Philippians[14] has not prevented the letter from being effectively marginalized as a text capable of shedding light on Paul's use of the OT.

An important implication of this omission is that "Philippians's voice" has not been heard amidst the chorus of proposals about Paul's hermeneutical method. For instance, Philippians was omitted from the compilation of essays covering topics such as: NT authors's respect for OT context, NT authors's treatment of OT authors's intention, NT authors's exegetical method and NT authors's use of typology.[15] Consequently, important conclusions have been drawn about Paul's use of the OT, none of which incorporate findings from Philippians.

---

8. Moyise and Menken, *Psalms*, 2; Moyise and Menken, *Isaiah*; Moyise and Menken, *Deuteronomy*. See also, Moyise, *Evoking Scripture*.

9. See L. Portefaix, *Sisters Rejoice*, 137; de Vos, *Church and Community Conflicts*, 254.

10. Bockmuehl, *Philippians*, 9; Snodgrass, "Use of the Old Testament in the New," 415.

11. For example, Ciampa, *Presence and Function of Scripture*.

12. Hays, *Echoes*; Porter, "Use of the Old Testament in the New"; Porter, "Further Comments," 98–110.

13. Porter, "Use of the Old Testament in the New," 89–94.

14. See Silva, "Old Testament in Paul," 634–35; Hays, *Echoes*, 21–24.

15. Beale, *Right Doctrine from the Wrong Texts*.

For example, Moore argued that Paul follows the tradition of Rabbinic Judaism and interprets the OT independently of its context or historical occasion.[16] Some emphasize Paul's use of the OT as primarily to demonstrate christological relevance by means of a controlled atomistic exegesis.[17] Lindars states that Paul and other NT authors use the OT "in an *ad hoc* way, making recourse to it when and how they find it helpful for their purposes."[18] Limiting his investigation to quotations, Koch divides Paul's use of Scripture into four categories: allegory, typology, midrash, and pesher. He concludes that Paul used Scripture as a witness to the gospel.[19] Sanders has argued that Paul arbitrarily selects OT texts and forces them to fit his argument, in other words he uses the OT for "proof-texting."[20] Dodd famously argued that the NT authors used the OT to elucidate the gospel, that the unit of reference was wider than the quotation and that the NT authors remained true to the intention of the OT authors when quoting them.[21] In none of these works did Philippians contribute to the conclusions drawn about Paul's use of Scripture.

Richard Longenecker, comparing Paul's hermeneutical approach with early Jewish Christian writers, argued that Paul understood the OT christologically, his rabbinic education and background accounting for his midrashic exegetical method.[22] Additionally, Longenecker proposed that Paul interpreted Scripture allegorically (1 Cor 9:9f and Gal 4:21–31). He drew his conclusions from an investigation of 83 quotations in Romans, 1 and 2 Corinthians, Galatians, Ephesians, and 1 and 2 Timothy.[23] Philippians played no part in his analysis. A.T. Hanson, using examples taken from 1 and 2 Corinthians and Romans, claimed that Paul traced the activity of the pre-existent Christ in Israel's history.[24] He also suggested that Paul interpreted Scripture typologically in 1 and 2 Corinthians, Galatians, and Romans and

---

16. Moore, *Judaism in the First Centuries*, 248–49; Michel, *Paulus*, 82; cf. Brewer, *Techniques and Assumptions in Jewish Exegesis*, 222, who points out that pre-70 CE exegesis was varied—while some interpretive techniques respected the context of Scripture, others disregarded it.

17. Longenecker, "Who is the Prophet Talking About?" 7.

18. Lindars, "Prolegomena," 64.

19. Koch, *Schrift*, 92.

20. Sanders, *Paul, the Law, and the Jewish People*, 21–22.

21. Dodd, *According to the Scriptures*, 11–12, 130.

22. Longenecker, *Biblical Exegesis*, 104–5.

23. Ibid., 108–11.

24. Hanson, *Living Utterances of God*, 46.

allegorically in 1 Corinthians and Galatians, and that he respected the OT context.[25] Philippians was not included in his analysis.

Richard Hays argues that typology is a central feature of Paul's interpretive strategy, that he reads Scripture as prefiguring the realities of his own time and that typology is not necessarily concerned with historical facts.[26] Instead, typology is an imaginative trope, all typologies being metaphorical, springing from a perception of likeness between dissimilar entities.[27] Hays accepts Paul's letters as contingent, and sees the contingency rooted in communal self-definition (how were new Gentile-only/Gentile-Jewish communities to interpret their relation to Israel?) Focusing on Paul's use of the OT in Romans and Galatians, but including the Corinthian correspondence also, Hays claims that Paul's pastoral concern for community formation finds expression through the metaphorical strategy of reading Israel's story as a prefiguration of the eschatological community.[28] However, he draws his conclusions without considering what Philippians might reveal of Paul's typological strategy in a letter where it is doubtful that communal self-definition was the contingency.

The need for a detailed, critical examination of the OT in Phil 2:10–16 is supported by several scholars who have recognized the presence of the OT in "allusive" form. For example, Hübner identifies five allusions using verbal agreement of Greek words: Isa 45:23 in Phil 2:10–11; Ps 2:11 in Phil 2:12; Deut 32:5 in Phil 2:15; Dan 12:3 in Phil 2:15; Isa 49:4 in Phil 2:16.[29] Reumann also recognizes that Phil 2:12–16 is "dotted" with LXX phrases. He specifically highlights Deut 32:5 and Dan 12:3 in Phil 2:15; Isa 49:4 and/or Isa 65:23 in Phil 2:16; Ps 2:11 (and several other OT passages) in Phil 2:12; Exod 16:12 and Num. 14:2 in Phil 2:14, and notes that this mosaic of OT phrases is not treated by Hays or others who have investigated Paul's use of the OT.[30] Gnilka describes the passage as "almost a catena of OT citations."[31] Furthermore, UBSGNT[4], NA[27], McLean and Ellis all agree on the presence of three allusions to the OT in Phil 2:10–16: Isa 45:23 in Phil 2:10–11; Isa 49:4 and Isa 65:23 in Phil 2:16; Deut 32:5 in Phil 2:15, with UBSGNT[4] adding Ps 2:11 in Phil 2:12 and NA[27] adding Dan 12:3 in Phil 2:15.[32]

25. Hanson, *Studies in Paul's Technique*, 193.
26. Hays, *Echoes*, 161.
27. Ibid., 101.
28. Ibid., 162.
29. Hübner, *Vetus Testamentum*, 490.
30. Reumann, *Philippians*, 402.
31. Gnilka, *Philipperbrief*, 151.
32. McLean, *Citations and Allusions*, 54, 92–98; Ellis, *Paul's Use*, 154.

The need for a detailed study of the OT in Philippians is not only underscored by Fee's findings (see p. 1), but he also highlights a rationale for limiting the textual evidence studied to Phil 2:10–16. He suggests that Phil 2:14–16 contains echoes of five OT texts: Exod 16:12 (through the use of "murmuring"), Gen 17:1 ("become blameless"), Deut 32:5 ("blameworthy children, a crooked and perverse generation"), Dan 12:3 ("the wise shall shine as luminaries [*phōsteres]*"), Isa 65:23 ("my chosen ones will *not labor in vain*").[33] Admitting the possibility that such a conclusion might be accounted for as his own discovery, rather than Paul's intentions, Fee nevertheless draws attention to the phenomenon of a unique, densely-packed cluster of possible OT references in Phil 2:14–16. To account for this unique concentration of OT texts in such close proximity, he proposes that Paul might be drawing on some former teaching that he weaves into a single, meaningful sentence in order to specify the kind of obedience he is commanding of the Philippians. Thus Fee considers the imperative in v. 14 ("do all things without grumbling") within a larger biblical framework that assures the Philippians of their place in God's story.[34] Fee was not the first to consider a biblical influence in Phil 2:14–16 that went beyond the mere reproduction of OT language. Thielman claims that Paul makes his *argument* with the help of numerous allusions to both the narrative and the legal portions of the Mosaic covenant in Phil 2:14–15. Accordingly, Paul's language appears to have been formulated to echo the wilderness wanderings of Israel whom he uses as a negative example to the Philippians.[35] Others, although recognizing the profusion of distinct OT terms, do not concur that they play a role in Paul's argument. Reed claims that "it cannot be assumed that Paul reflected upon the original context when employing Old Testament language in Philippians (Paul the 'reader'), since the status of these 'allusions' is unclear; hence, I treat them as part of his idiolect rather than his rhetoric."[36] In similar vein, Reumann states that it is unlikely that a story about Israel runs through Phil 2:12–18 because the embedded OT language in the epistolary argument is not in context of the Hebrew Scriptures and would be scarcely perceived by Gentile readers.[37] Not surprisingly then, most scholars recognize the OT language that Paul embeds in Phil 2:10–16. This would be hard to refute, given the profusion of terms, some of which are unusual

---

33. Fee, *Philippians*, 242.
34. Ibid., 242–43.
35. Thielman, *Paul & the Law*, 156–57.
36. Reed, *Discourse Analysis of Philippians*, 291–92. Paul's use of tacit OT references is often explained in these terms and put down to him being steeped in the language of Scripture. See also, Beker, "Echoes and Intertextuality," 65.
37. Reumann, *Philippians*, 402–3.

and only found in the OT.³⁸ Yet few seem prepared to consider this language to reflect an OT framework that might lie behind Paul's *thought* and play a generative role in his *argument*. Even if it is conceded that Paul echoes or draws on the language of the OT to, say, contrast the Philippians with the rebellious Israelites in the wilderness, the idea is not developed with much detail. It must be noted, then, that the possibility of a relationship between the closely-coupled OT texts that make up the supposed "cluster" and how this relationship might define or delimit an OT framework for Paul's argument has not been subjected to a thorough exegesis: neither Fee's nor Reumann's claims have been tested.

Furthermore, the merit of conducting an investigation into this particular OT-text-cluster is underscored by its position in Paul's letter. The ὥστε of Phil 2:12 introduces an hortatory section of the discourse that prompts a response to the climactic death and exaltation of Christ and actions of God described in Phil 2:5–11. This places the passage containing the proposed OT references in the immediate literary context of one of the most analyzed and hotly-debated passages in the Pauline corpus, if not the entire NT. The literary, theological and rhetorical relationships of Phil 2:5–11 to the (alleged) unique concentration of OT references in its immediate literary context have never been probed, despite wide acceptance that Isa 45:23 is reproduced in Phil 2:10–11.

As a consequence of these observations, drawn from the text of Philippians and previous scholarship, this investigation seeks to test the suggestion that Phil 2:10–16 contains a cluster of tacit references (allusions) to the OT. As we shall see, several questions emerge from a survey of previous approaches to the interpretation of allusion in Paul's letters:

1. How are allusions detected?

2. How are allusions defined and interpreted?

3. What special consideration, if any, should be given to the interpretation of a cluster of successive allusions, most of which occur in a single sentence?

4. Given that allusion is a form of tacit reference, how can its interpretation be reasonably (exegetically) constrained?

5. What role should audience recognition and authorial intention play in our analysis of Paul's use of allusion?

---

38. For example, using the Online TLG® database to search Greek literature from the third century BCE through the first century CE revealed that the phrase φανοῦσιν ὡς φωστῆρες only appears in the OT.

6. What role does epistolary argument play in the interpretation of allusions?

From this we will propose several methods which we believe are appropriate for testing the idea that Phil 2:10–16 contains a cluster of allusions to the OT.

ORIENTATION TO THE STUDY AND PREVIEW OF SELECTED METHODS

Several approaches seem particularly well suited to an exegesis of a text containing a cluster of supposed tacit, or covert, references to the OT. Literary critics such as Ziva Ben-Porat and William Irwin have developed theories on the identification, definition and the interpretation of allusion—Ben-Porat from a reader perspective, Irwin from an author perspective. Thus, their methods address questions one, two, and five above. Another literary critic, Michael Riffaterre, has advanced a convention for reading poems that semantically links successive tacit references. His method constrains interpretation of tacit references by considering them to be variants of a single (semiotic) structure which is akin to a text with a single, unifying theme. His ideas might prove useful in testing the suggestion that Phil 2:10–16 contains a cluster of successive allusions which may be variants of a single, unifying theme, if indeed such a theme can be identified for Philippians.

The scholarly search for a central theme that unifies Philippians has been ongoing. Yet, because the letter covers a wide array of themes this search has proved allusive. With no obvious central idea binding the whole letter, Philippians was viewed by some as an informal, personal letter,[39] a family letter whose primary purpose was to strengthen "family" links between Paul and the Philippians[40] or, similarly, a hortatory letter of friendship to strengthen relationships between Paul and the Philippians.[41] However, several traditional, historical exegetes have grappled with the notion of a central theme able to explain the formal and semantic elements of the entire epistle. For example, Lohmeyer famously argued that "martyrdom" is the dominant theme—he was followed by Duncan and Blevins.[42] Swift distinguished the mood of the letter (joy) from a central theme broad enough to

---

39. Hawthorne, *Philippians*, xlviii.
40. Alexander, "Hellenistic Letter-Forms," 95.
41. Stowers, "Friends," 107.
42. Duncan, "Letter to the Philippians," 788; Blevins, "Introduction to Philippians," 311–24.

explain the details of the entire epistle, namely, "partnership."[43] Although accepting difficulties placing chapter 3 within the "partnership" framework, Peterlin developed Swift's idea and proposed "disunity" as the central theme of Philippians.[44] These previous efforts support the choice of Riffaterre's model since a correspondence can be drawn between his central semiotic structure and the central, unifying theme or epistolary argument, and the possibility that the tacitly embedded fragments of other poems or biblical texts are variants (somehow similar) of this argument. Furthermore, the idea that this central theme or epistolary argument can be concisely summarized, or "reduced" to a simple word, phrase or cliché is not new. Thus, Riffaterre's theory addresses questions three, four, and six.

Yet, as we shall see, despite several scholars identifying epistolary argument and rhetorical purpose as necessary for interpreting citations and allusions, there have been few methodologically-oriented approaches to determining the epistolary argument of Philippians. We have already encountered objections to the idea that Paul alludes to the OT in Phil 2:10–16 through the claim of incongruity between epistolary argument and Scripture context (Reumann). But has the epistolary argument of Philippians been proposed or established? Most studies of Paul's tacit use of Scripture (see below) depend upon establishing congruence between NT and OT texts. Indeed, the most important criterion for determining, and interpreting, the presence of tacit references in these studies is "thematic coherence." This is variously defined, but essentially requires the images and ideas of the proposed alluded-to text or intertext to somehow illuminate Paul's argument. The difficulty is how to distinguish argument from theme, motif, idea, image, and casuistically[45] referenced material. For example, Bormann claims that the importance of allusions for the interpretation of Philippians has to relate to four main themes: Paul's imprisonment, his relationship with the Philippians, Christology, and the problem with opponents.[46] Like Reumann, Bormann concludes that Paul's argumentation does not depend on the allusions to Scripture because there is no contextual affinity between the four themes and the proposed OT allusions.[47] But has Bormann correctly identified Paul's argument or merely compared four epistolary themes

---

43. Swift, "Theme and Structure of Philippians," 236, 250.

44. Peterlin, *Disunity*, 3–6. He helpfully distinguishes between questions of immediate occasion (for example, an opportunity for Paul to thank the Philippians for their gift) and immediate purpose.

45. Plausible, but false references.

46. Bormann, "Triple Intertextuality in Philippians," 93.

47. So too, Schoon-Janssen, *Umstrittene 'Apologien' in den Paulusbriefen*, 145; Schmid, "Sinnpotentiale der diegetischen Allusion," 141–87.

to the context of the supposed Scripture references? If any of these four themes is used to constrain the interpretation of any of the alleged allusions, meaning, to control which unstated elements in the alluded-to texts should be evoked in the interpretation, we are hard pressed to find plausible connotations. Perhaps, rather than establishing the epistolary argument, these four themes somehow contribute to it. If themes contribute to argumentation then they cannot, solely, be taken to define the argument of an epistle. Thus, epistolary themes or facticities recorded in the letter (for example, Paul's imprisonment) are not, in and of themselves, the epistolary argument. We suspect that identifying obvious themes and motifs found at the surface-level of the text (other examples are "unity" and "joy") may not be adequate in understanding the role of allusions in Phil 2:10–16. This becomes particularly relevant, as we shall see, when trying to establish congruence between elements of alluding and alluded-to texts. As Fowl rightly points out, "the degree of congruence between OT context and *epistolary argument* provides the basis for arguing that Paul intended to communicate these deeper and wider allusions."[48] We would like to explore the notion that congruence between epistolary argument (and elements of it) and Scripture context might shed light on Paul's use of the OT in Phil 2:10–16. For example, can a consideration of epistolary argument and its relationship to Scripture context provide exegetical constraints in the interpretation of allusion? But how do we determine the epistolary argument of Philippians in order to answer question six above fully?

A promising solution to this challenge is found in Lloyd Bitzer's theory of situational rhetoric. Bitzer developed the idea that rhetoric is designed to constrain (bring certain facts, beliefs, attitudes, traditions, images, interests, motives, and the like, to bear upon) an audience in order to modify a situation by removing or overcoming a controlling exigency (an imperfection or something that is not as it should be). Thus, rhetorical constraints and rhetorical exigencies, recognized in the rhetoric, help to identify the argument and the specific problem which invited the discourse in the first place—the rhetorical situation. With reference to Bormann's first theme above, and using Bitzer's notion of situational rhetoric, we would prefer to say that Paul's imprisonment is an exigency (non-rhetorical) that his letter cannot overcome. *However, an attitude on the part of some Philippians that disdains his imprisonment as a sign of failure is a possible rhetorical exigency that his letter might have been designed to overcome.* An attitude that disdains the suffering-servant paradigm might well account for Paul's prison *apologia* in Phil 1:12–26. If so, the argument of the epistle runs deeper than

---

48. Fowl, "Use of Scripture in Philippians," 13. Italics mine.

the surface-level facticities of Paul's incarceration. Yet the argument is not a merely subjective construct—it can be advanced from the text of Philippians itself. *We therefore believe that rhetorical situation provides the constraint that should be used to interpret tacit references to Scripture in Paul's letter to the Philippians. This rhetorical situation is derived from the text and can be regarded as a textual constraint.*

The principles that lie behind the use of Bitzer's method for analyzing a NT letter are not new. NT scholars have understood Paul's letters as pastoral responses to particular situations rather than abstract theological statements.[49] All of Paul's letters are considered to have been occasional, written to particular churches or individuals in specific situations. The constraints of these situations and their effect on Paul's discourse have led to widely accepted views regarding the nature of Paul's letters as written communication. For example, Aune suggests Paul used letters to communicate what he would have preferred to say, preach or teach in person.[50] Furthermore, Beker uses the idea of "contingency and coherence" to describe Paul's letter form as an emergency measure through which he communicates the gospel in a dialogical situation.[51] In doing so, his thought is geared to a specific situation and his arguments cannot be divorced from the need of the moment.[52] Paul communicates the same coherent gospel in changing situations—the situation determines the expression of his theology. According to Beker, the situational particularity of a Pauline letter is crucial for its correct interpretation[53] since Paul allows the gospel tradition to become living speech (rhetoric) *within the exigencies of the daily life of his churches.*[54] To construct the rhetorical situation, then, by studying Paul's letter as a rhetorical response to those exigencies stands in line with historical, exegetical practice. Moreover, traditional, historical exegetes already treat Paul's letter to the Philippians as functional communication which is a fitting response to the problems in Philippi. For example, although it is not explicitly stated in Phil 4:2 that Euodia and Syntyche are quarrelling between themselves, this is the scholarly consensus.[55] Essentially, exegetes ask the question: why would Paul encourage these two women to "think

---

49. Bruce, "Paul in Acts and Letters," 680.
50. Aune, *New Testament in its Literary Environment*, 197.
51. Beker, *Paul the Apostle*, 34.
52. Ibid., 25.
53. Ibid., 24.
54. Ibid., 33. My italics, intended to highlight the vocabulary he shares with Bitzer (see below).
55. An exception is Tellbe, *Paul between Synagogue and State*, who rightly notes that the text does not convey disagreement between the two women.

the same" in the Lord? Their answer presupposes a disagreement between the women as an explanation for Paul's rhetoric. However, and alternatively, Paul might be asking his true companion (in Phil 4:3) to help both of these women who were somehow neglected by the congregation and were in need of support. In similar vein, Euodia and Syntyche might, jointly, be disputing with others in the congregation as much as disputing with each other. Is Phil 4:2 a fitting response to a quarrel between Euodia and Syntyche, a quarrel between Euodia plus Syntyche and the rest, or a plea for help for two women bearing the burden of conflict? There is no way of knowing for sure, but by asking the question scholars take a rhetorical-exegetical approach that attempts to support their answer from congruent elements elsewhere in the text. Thus traditionally, historical exegetes use a presupposed situation or intertext (material not explicitly stated in Philippians, namely, Euodia and Syntyche disagree with each other) to support their interpretation of disunity in Philippi. This traditional exegetical practice coheres with that advanced by Fiorenza who argues that NT texts were produced in a culture in which rhetoric defined public discourse, including that of Paul: "Since many things are presupposed, left out, or unexplained in a speech/letter, the audience must in the process of reading 'supply' the missing information in line with the rhetorical directives of the [implied] speaker/writer."[56] We are therefore justified in treating Philippians as rhetorical discourse which is a fitting response to the problems in Philippi, and argument as distinct from (although related to or consisting of) theme, motif, idea, and image. We will devote a significant amount of time and space to analyzing Paul's argument in Philippians through a rhetorical-exegetical study of Phil 1:27—3:21. This will enable us to test Bormann's claim that Paul's argumentation does not depend on the allusions to Scripture and Thielman's suggestion that the alluded-to texts might be integral, or even foundational, to Paul's argument.

Although we have argued that both the characteristics of the text of Philippians and the findings of previous scholarship previewed above justify an approach that uses the methods of Ben-Porat, Irwin, Riffaterre, and Bitzer, it might be objected that twentieth-century literary theories, focusing mainly on poetic texts, can be used to analyze a NT letter. Two points are worth considering. Firstly, as Pogoloff observes, poetic and rhetorical discourse rarely exist in pure form: "any text read as poetic can also be read as persuasive and socially situated, just as texts which function rhetorically do so partly through the power of poetic worlds."[57] Both poetic and rhetorical texts prompt for aesthetic responses from their readers (see Irwin below)

56. Fiorenza, "Rhetorical Situation," 387–89.
57. Pogoloff, *Logos and Sophia*, 73.

and, in particular, there seems no good reason why an alluding device in a rhetorical text should function differently from one in a poetic text—although we must be open to that possibility. Secondly, it is not beyond modern scholars to conventionalize ancient reading and writing techniques which could be considered universal. Indeed, this is Kennedy's opinion about Greco-Roman rhetoric.[58] Consequently, using twentieth-century literary theories to analyze a biblical text is not anachronistic; rather, these tools enable the testing of a hypothesis prompted by the text of Philippians and the findings of previous scholarship—in other words, our unique proposal is that Ben-Porat, Irwin, Riffaterre, and Bitzer might just have conventionalized the components of a solution that offers an explanation of how and why a Jewish writer like Paul clustered together tacit Scripture references. Before surveying previous approaches to the problem and sketching out the procedure used in this study, the important preliminary matter of what Scripture meant to Paul must be addressed.

PAUL AND SCRIPTURE

Our investigation, like others,[59] gives priority to Jewish Scripture as the primary source of literary allusion for Paul. This is because Paul was a first-century Jewish writer whose upbringing would no doubt have included considerable instruction in the Scriptures, both at home and in the synagogue. Given his autobiographical reports in Phil 3:5–6 and Gal 1:14, his knowledge of Scripture is likely to have been extremely accomplished: born of the tribe of Benjamin, a Hebrew of Hebrews, a zealous Pharisee, and persecutor of the church, advancing in Judaism beyond many and being extremely zealous for his ancestral traditions. According to Luke, Paul was born in Tarsus and grew up in Jerusalem where he was educated by the esteemed Rabbi Gamaliel (Acts 22:3). Furthermore, Paul was also a diaspora Jew, travelling and living for long periods outside of Palestine. The Hellenistic influence on Paul is obvious from his letters, which he wrote in Greek, and from his use of a Greek translation of Jewish Scripture. Paul's propensity to cite from Scripture justifies a focus on Scripture as his source of allusion. Furthermore, Paul's propensity to create literary allusions to the Jewish Scriptures mandates a focus on Greek Jewish Scripture as his source. However several issues surrounding the nature and text form of what Paul and other NT authors understood as Scripture must be addressed. The authoritative writings of the Jews were translated from Hebrew into other

---

58. Kennedy, *Rhetorical Criticism*, 10–11.
59. Rosner, *Paul, Scripture, & Ethics*, 15–17.

languages and underwent multiple revisions resulting in a variety of text forms in circulation before the common era. In terms of citing from, and alluding to, a Greek translation of Jewish Scripture, Hübner is correct to note that, "After all, this Greek translation of Holy Scripture was considerably more important than the Hebrew Bible for the authors of the New Testament, who wrote in Greek."[60] Consequently, we must address the issue of the Septuagintal sources underlying the Scripture references in Paul's letter to the Philippians.

The LXX—Terminology and Textual Plurality

Although the Septuagint (LXX) referred originally to the translation of the Pentateuch into Greek in the third century BCE, the term is generally employed to refer to the Greek Jewish Scriptures which primarily consist of translations of the books of the Hebrew Bible. But the Septuagint also includes additional books not included in the HB, translations of Aramaic and independently-composed Greek texts. As we shall see, because of the complex historical context in which the origin and transmission of the LXX occurred, it is important to distinguish between general references to a body of texts that witness to Jewish Scripture and the original translation of any individual book. In seeking a more precise terminology, we will use the term LXX to refer to the whole transmitted tradition of Greek texts of the Jewish Scriptures and LXX^{OG} to refer to the earliest stage of Greek translation that can be reconstructed for any book of Jewish Scriptures (OG or "Old Greek"). Revisions to the original Greek translation began immediately and can be discerned in early Jewish scrolls as far back as the second century BCE.[61] These revisions were aimed at improving the Greek style and bringing the Greek into conformity with a proto-Masoretic text since the claims of divine inspiration for the translation were not persuasive within the Jewish community.[62] Evidence of further Jewish revisions of Egyptian papyri dating from the second or first century BCE or first century CE has also been discovered.[63] Moreover, the discovery of a variety of forms of the He-

---

60. Hübner, *Vetus Testamentum*, xv; also Swete, *Introduction to the Old Testament*, 392; Müller, *First Bible of the Church*, 144; Jellicoe, "Prolegomenon," xiv.

61. Dines, *Septuagint*, 4, notes that DSS texts containing fragments of Deuteronomy (4Q122), Leviticus (4Q119) and Exodus (7Q1) have been dated to the second century BCE.

62. McLay, *Septuagint*, 102–3; Tov, *Greek and Hebrew Bible*, 9.

63. Deuteronomy (963, 957, 847, 848), Job (P.Oxyrh 3522) and Genesis (942). The numbers assigned to the papyri are based on the list published by Rahlfs, *Altens Testaments*.

brew text at Qumran meant that some Greek translations were attempts to conform to a *changing* Hebrew textual tradition.[64] The result of this scribal activity was the creation of a plethora of variants prior to the common era. Some of these variant texts would have been the source for Paul's, and other NT authors's, Scripture citations and allusions made in the Greek language.

Any modern investigation of Paul's use of the LXX is complicated further because the texts of the LXX underwent further revision after Paul wrote his letters. The rift between Judaism and Christianity resulted in further modifications of already-revised Greek texts of Jewish Scripture. Sundberg notes that Judaism rejected the Septuagint following its adoption by Christians and a closer attention to the Hebrew text after closure of the Jewish canon at the end of the first century CE. This led to more Jewish attempts to correct the LXX to the Hebrew as demonstrated by the second-century Greek translations of Aquila, Theodotion, and Symmachus, which were thus built on previous revisions.[65] Furthermore, additional witnesses to the LXX are preserved in the Christian revisions which ranged from the late first century to third century CE and beyond. Although his text is no longer extant, Origin sought to "heal" the Septuagint through the Hexapla, but assumed that the OG was based on the Hebrew text that existed during his lifetime (*circa*. 185–253/4 CE). He thus produced a mixed text that could not possibly restore the OG.[66] In addition to the fourth and fifth-centuries manuscript codices (Vaticanus, Sinaiticus, and Alexandrinus) witnesses to the LXX are also preserved in a great number of other uncials and minuscules from the ninth century CE onwards. We are therefore alerted to the fact that the LXX we have today is a vast, diverse corpus of religious texts in Greek and discerning the authentic features of the first translations is a difficult task.[67] Yet this is one of the goals of modern Septuagintal study, as Pietersma notes: "The primary focus in LXX text-criticism must always remain on the reconstruction of the original text."[68]

The LXX—Original Text of Individual Books

Not only was there a plurality of texts in Paul's day (perhaps more so in our own), but there is increasing recognition that the LXX must be approached on a book-by-book basis. The issue of whether we can determine the LXX

64. Cross, "History of the Biblical Text," 283.
65. Sundberg, *Old Testament of the Early Church*, 88.
66. McLay, *Septuagint*, 127.
67. Dines, *Septuagint*, 24.
68. Pietersma, "Septuagint Research," 297.

texts that Paul used as sources for his citations and allusions is linked with the long-running debate between two competing views of the origin of the LXX. On the one hand, Paul de Lagarde proposed the existence of an *Ur-Septuagint* or single original Greek text of the Pentateuch translated in the third century BCE.[69] The task of the scholar is, then, to "reconstruct" this original text. On the other hand, Paul Kahle proposed that there was no single original text but several translations. The task is then to collect and compare these translations which differed from the Christian standard text.[70] De Lagarde's position has been almost universally accepted, especially in light of the discovery of the DSS.[71] According to Dines, available manuscript evidence points to an *Ur-text* for most, if not all, books.[72] Differences between versions of the same book are thus accounted for as revisions of the Greek.[73] As we shall see, the textual history of the Septuagint, considered on a book-by-book basis,[74] has important implications for our investigation of the OT in Philippians.

Standard Editions of the LXX as Witness to Paul's Source

As we have shown above, the NT community did not know the Greek Jewish Scriptures in the exact form as that transmitted by the great uncials of the fourth and fifth centuries and preserved in our diplomatic editions of the LXX. Thus, to "impart our notion of the HB or the LXX on the Early Church is an anachronism."[75] Yet this tendency has prevailed. For example, Hübner's suggestion of an allusion to Dan 12:3 in Phil 2:15 cannot be borne out by an appeal to Brenton's *Septuagint*[76] because the alleged textual marker, φανοῦσιν ὡς φωστῆρες, does not appear in this version. This is because a second-century CE revision associated with Theodotion (LXXTH)[77] supplanted the LXX^OG of Daniel and appeared in Codex Vaticanus by the late

---

69. Jobes and Silva, *Invitation to the Septuagint*, 35–36.

70. Kahle, *Cairo Geniza*, 264.

71. Dines, *Septuagint*, 59. Although see Tov, *Text-Critical Use of the Septuagint*, 35, who suggests that de Lagarde's and Kahle's theories are not mutually exclusive.

72. Dines, *Septuagint*, 59.

73. Jobes and Silva, *Invitation to the Septuagint*, 45–46.

74. Marcos, *Septuagint in Context*, 247; Dines, *Septuagint*, 13.

75. McLay, *Septuagint*, 8–9.

76. Brenton, *Septuagint with Apocrypha*. Reprinted by Hendrickson 1986–2001. Still used by scholars today (See Jobes and Silva, *Invitation to the Septuagint*, 72).

77. It probably originates from a time later than OG but the label BCE Proto-Theodotion is sometimes used of a pre-Christian version.

fourth century CE.⁷⁸ It seems that both versions circulated at the time of Origin and Jerome, the latter recognizing wide differences between the texts and rejecting LXXTH.⁷⁹ As we argue below, noting the occurrence of the rare and unusual phrase φανοῦσιν ὡς φωστῆρες (with slight variation) in both Dan 12:3 LXX^OG and Phil 2:15, we should be open to the possibility that Paul is witnessing to a genuine OG reading different to that in the standard editions of the LXX.

In like manner, Kreitzer relies on a witness to the LXX based on Codex Vaticanus to claim that the verb used in Isa 45:23 is ὀμεῖται (swear) while the verb root in the reference to Isa 45:23 in Phil 2:10 is ἐξομολογέω (confess). He concludes that the change in verb indicates the liturgical nature of a hymn that serves as a confession of faith.⁸⁰ However, it is problematic to argue for Phil 2:6–11 as a hymn on this textual evidence since an earlier Greek witness supports the verb root ἐξομολογέω and is likely to be the source of a more precise reference to Isa 45:23 in Phil 2:10; in which case a textual variant, not authorial adaptation, explains the NT wording. Indeed the OT in the NT represents a witness to the original LXX three centuries earlier than the principal uncials.⁸¹ This means that exegesis of Philippians can no longer rely only on the witness to the LXX preserved in the major uncials of the fourth and fifth centuries CE.

Reconstructed LXX^OG as Witness to Paul's Source

The view that a single original text underlies a multiplicity of variants is reflected in the Göttingen Septuagint Series which aims to reconstruct the best available text of each book from various sources. Admitting that we may not (yet) have recovered the texts that Paul had at his disposal, these critical editions are concerned with the restoring of texts earlier than the Jewish and Christian recensions and earliest revisions of the Greek Bible, and which are more likely to be the ones used by Paul. A special case in point is the book of Daniel which has been identified as the source of the fourth allusion in our cluster of five. The problems of LXX textual plurality and its impact on exegesis of Philippians are particularly evident in Daniel as one of the "double texts" that circulated in two distinct forms.⁸² The work

78. Jellicoe, *Septuagint and Modern Study*, 86.
79. See the discussion in Jellicoe, *Septuagint and Modern Study*, 83–94.
80. Kreitzer, "When He at Last Is First," 120.
81. Marcos, *Septuagint in Context*, 323.
82. Others are Judges, Esther, Tobit and 1 and 2 Esdras. See Dines, *Septuagint*, 23.

of Timothy McLay has been especially helpful in our effort to establish the Septuagintal sources underlying the alleged scriptural allusion to Dan 12:3 in Phil 2:15.

Greek Versions of Daniel: LXXTH and LXX^{OG}

McLay rightly observes that we must establish a solid textual basis from which to investigate citations, allusions, and the use of the Jewish Scriptures in the NT.[83] As mentioned above, in the case of Daniel, we have two extant Greek textual traditions, LXXTH and LXX^{OG}. The LXXTH, a second-century CE revision associated with Theodotion, replaced the LXX^{OG} and found its way into the standard editions of the LXX such as Brenton's *Septuagint with Apocrypha: Greek and English*. However, McLay has noted 29 occurrences of possible corruption of the LXX^{OG} by LXXTH, confirming that the standard editions of the LXX are not the oldest Greek version that was likely available to Paul. While we argue for the functioning of a literary allusion in chapter 4, it is appropriate to our examination of the LXX that we corroborate the idea that Phil 2:15c might contain a witness to a text earlier than Dan 12:3a LXXTH:

Dan 12:3a LXXTH	καὶ οἱ συνιέντες <u>ἐκλάμψουσιν ὡς ἡ λαμπρότης</u> τοῦ στερεώματος[A]
Dan 12:3a LXX^{OG}	καὶ οἱ συνιέντες <u>φανοῦσιν ὡς φωστῆρες</u> τοῦ οὐρανοῦ
Phil 2:15c	ἐν οἷς <u>φαίνεσθε ὡς φωστῆρες</u> ἐν κόσμῳ

A. See McLay, *The OG and Th Versions of Daniel*, 199, who puts the difference down to phonological motivation: the LXXTH favors the like-sounding λάμπω.

This strongly suggests that the LXX^{OG} was the operative text for Paul, and explains why the allusion would be missed by exegetes using diplomatic editions of the LXX that print the text of one particular manuscript (usually Vaticanus).[84] In Dan 12:1–4, there are three other instances of textual differences, involving significant differences in meaning, between the extant Greek texts of Daniel that require investigation before we can establish the reliability of the textual tradition of Daniel that Paul allegedly alludes to in Phil 2:15.[85] The theory of allusion used in this investigation facilitates activation of parts of the texts not directly addressed through the allusion

---

83. McLay, *Septuagint*, 14.
84. Dines, *Septuagint*, 8.
85. Barr, "Paul and the LXX," 593–601.

marker, therefore adjacent passages and their referents should be clearly established as far as is possible. The relevant differences in the two texts are outlined in the table:

	LXX^OG	LXXTH
Dan 12:1	ὑψωθήσεται exaltation	σωθήσεται rescue/deliverance
Dan 12:3b	καὶ οἱ κατισχύοντες τοὺς λόγους μου and hold fast my words	καὶ ἀπὸ τῶν δικαίωντῶν πολλῶν and some of the many righteous
Dan 12:4	ἕως ἂν ἀπομανῶσιν οἱ πολλοὶ καὶ πλησθῇ ἡ γῆ ἀδικίας. until the many go mad and the earth is filled with injustice	ἕως διδαχθῶσιν πολλοὶ καὶ πληθυνθῇ ἡ γνῶσις. until many are taught and knowledge increases

It can be noted that the LXX^OG lacks the "evangelistic" or "wisdom teaching" emphasis of the LXXTH (and the MT, where Dan 12:3b states, "and those who lead the many to righteousness"), and conversely the LXXTH lacks the apostasy and suffering emphasis[86] of the LXX^OG. The possible connotations evoked by a literary allusion to surrounding verses in each text are significantly different—as we shall see in our exegesis of Phil 2:15c–16a. This important aspect of literary allusion theory has led us to an examination of the textual traditions of Daniel to determine if we can identify the LXX^OG as a reliable intertext for Paul's letter to the Philippians. The three verses noted above are of particular significance.

Dan 12:1

Despite Ziegler's text preferring σωθήσεται, the unparalleled emphasis on resurrection, leads McLay to consider that 88-Syh has correctly translated the Hebrew as ψωθήσεται (will be raised/exalted). Thus, ψωθήσεται should be accepted as the original Greek.[87] The LXX^OG can be considered reliable in this instance.

---

86. See the exegesis below.
87. McLay, *OG and Th Versions of Daniel*, 186.

Dan 12:3

The LXXTH translates the Hebrew as a preposition resulting in ἀπὸ τῶν δικαίων τῶν πολλῶν, which renders a meaning, "some of the many righteous." On the other hand, the LXX^OG translates the Hebrew as a hiphil participle resulting in οἱ κατισχύοντες τοὺς λόγους μου, which renders a meaning, "those who overpower my words."[88] Ziegler prefers the interpretation, "those who keep my words" as opposed to "those who overpower my words." Initially, this makes better sense, but Charles suggests the latter should be rendered, "they who hold fast my words," thus preserving the nuance of power or prevailing conveyed by κατισχύοντες.[89] The sense would be "those who powerfully hold to my words" or "those who prevail by holding to my words." According to McLay, the original Greek could be a dynamic equivalent translation of a text that read, "the righteous of the many." There is no reason to suggest that the LXX^OG offers an unreliable rendering.

Dan 12:4

We begin with a description of the *rabbim* (the many who go back and forth) in Dan 12:4:

Dan 12:4 MT	וְאַתָּה דָנִיֵּאל סְתֹם הַדְּבָרִים וַחֲתֹם הַסֵּפֶר עַד־עֵת קֵץ יְשֹׁטְטוּ רַבִּים וְתִרְבֶּה הַדָּעַת: many will *go back and forth* and knowledge will increase
Dan 12:4c LXXTH	ἕως <u>διδαχθῶσιν</u> πολλοὶ καὶ πληθυνθῇ ἡ γνῶσις. until many *are taught* and knowledge increases
Dan 12:4c LXX^OG	ἕως ἂν <u>ἀπομανῶσιν</u> οἱ πολλοὶ καὶ πλησθῇ ἡ γῆ ἀδικίας. until the many *go mad (rage violently)*^A and the earth is filled with injustice^B

A. LEH, Part I, 53: ἀπομαίνομαι—"to go mad." See also McLay, *OG and Th Versions of Daniel*, 201—"to rage violently."

B. See Bruce, "Oldest Greek Version of Daniel," 26.

In the LXX^OG, שׁוּט[90] has been translated as ἀπομαίομαι, meaning "to go mad / to rage violently," whereas in the LXXTH it has been translated as διδάσκω,

---

88. McLay, "Daniel," 1022: "those who strengthen my words."

89. Charles, *Daniel*, 331; McLay, *OG and Th Versions of Daniel*, 189.

90. BDB 1001–2: שׁוּט: to go, rove about. See Amos 8:12 MT, where it refers to "aimless seeking" of the word of the Lord—a clearly pejorative term describing an act of futility.

to teach. Both versions alter the meaning of the MT significantly, where it is translated "go to and fro / back and forth." McLay considers the LXXTH use of διδάσκω a guess based on the following clause: "and knowledge increases."[91] Charles proposes that in the context of the book, it is wickedness rather than knowledge which will multiply—evils will increase and the earth will be filled with iniquity.[92] The stark contrast between an increase in knowledge (MT and LXXTH) and an increase in injustice (LXX^OG) depends on translation technique. Day has convincingly argued that Dan 12:4 MT is better rendered "many shall run to and fro and *humiliation* will increase."[93] According to Day, this interpretation fits better in the suffering servant passages in Isa 53:3, 11 on which Dan 12:4 is probably dependent: Dan 12:3 and Isa 53:11 are the only two occasions in the HB of the expression, "those who make / he will make many righteous." Both contexts refer to the death and vindication of the righteous, with Day and others suggesting that it is by the humiliation of the suffering servant, not his knowledge, that many will be made righteous. To summarize, the referent of the "increase" in Dan 12:4 is probably "humiliation" or "wickedness," rather than "knowledge" (contra MT and LXXTH). This translation fits the context of Dan 12:3 as it emphasizes a time of great tribulation.[94] There is therefore good reason to take the LXX^OG reading, referring to panic and fleeing in the face of persecution, as a reliable translation and interpretation. Those who flee (run to and fro) are the רַבִּים (*rabbim*), those who remain and face persecution are the מַשְׂכִּלִים (*maskalim*—the wise ones of Dan 12:3):

> And you, Daniel, conceal the command/ordinance and seal the book until the time of the end, *until many shall fall away (become apostates)* and the earth *is filled with injustice* (Dan 12:4).[95]

We conclude that Paul alludes to a text close to Daniel LXX^OG and that this textual tradition can be of assistance in understanding why Paul's use of φαίνεσθε ὡς φωστῆρες in Phil 2:15 is influenced by φανοῦσιν ὡς φωστῆρες in Dan 12:3 LXX^OG. Consequently, we will use the individual critical editions

---

91. McLay, *OG and Th Versions of Daniel*, 201.

92. Charles, *Daniel*, 333.

93. Day, "DA'AT 'Humiliation' in Isaiah LIII 11," 99; Driver, "Linguistics and Textual Problems," 49; Allen, "Isaiah Liii.11 and its Echoes," 24–28.

94. See McLay, *OG and Th Versions of Daniel*, 208; Charles, *Daniel*, 333; Collins, *Daniel*, 369; Hartman & Di Lella, *Daniel*, 274.

95. Cf. Charles, *Daniel*, 392.

of the Göttingen Septuagint Series[96] because, at least for the time being, they are the best approximations to the presumed original translations.[97]

The Authority of the LXX, Textual Variants and Author Adaptations

We have already shown that when the wording of the NT allusion differs from known LXX witnesses the tendency might be to treat the deviation as a deliberate adaptation by the NT author. However, textual plurality and the complexity (if not impossibility) of reconstructing the LXX^{OG} mean that not all divergent texts are necessarily deliberate adaptations. While we deal with this matter in our analysis of Christopher Stanley's work in the next section, it is appropriate to introduce briefly a discussion of the relationship between the authority of the LXX, the fluidity of text forms available to Paul and his citation technique.

It seems certain that individual books of the Greek Jewish Scriptures were available to NT writers, and they were considered "authoritative."[98] Any notion of what books were authoritative must take onto account the content of the NT itself. The fact that a LXX text was cited rather than the Hebrew Jewish Scripture demonstrates that the Greek Jewish Scripture as witnessed to by the LXX were deemed to be Scripture by the NT authors.[99] It is noteworthy that the letter of Aristeas is generally accepted as a propaganda document written to defend the authority of the LXX for the Alexandrian Jewish community.[100] Furthermore, the fact that the LXX is preserved in the first Christian Bibles (the major uncials) is a simple testimony to the authority that the Greek Scriptures exercised in the life of the early Church.[101]

---

96. Wevers, *Genesis, Septuaginta*; Wevers, *Deuteronomium, Septuaginta*; Ziegler, *Isaias, Septuaginta*; Ziegler, *Susanna, Daniel, Bel et Draco, Septuaginta*; Rahlfs, *Psalmi cum Odis, Septuaginta*.

97. Dines, *Septuagint*, 9; Marcos, *Septuagint in Context*, 329. However, several scholars have recognized flaws in the Göttingen Septuagint Series. In particular, Rahlfs comes under criticism for omitting manuscript evidence in his reconstruction of the Psalms and underestimating the importance of the Lucianic recension. See Tov, *Greek and Hebrew Bible*, 477 and the discussion in Docherty, *Use of the Old Testament in Hebrews*, 127–32.

98. Charlesworth, *Old Testament Pseudepigrapha, Vol. 1*, xxiii. He claims that the "Law" and "Prophets" were defined as authoritative by the second century BCE.

99. McLay, *Septuagint*, 144.

100. Marcos, *Septuagint in Context*, 53; Brock, "Phenomenon of the Septuagint," 21–27.

101. McLay, *Septuagint*, 144.

This leads us to consider what conclusions can be drawn about the exegetical method and attitude to Scripture of an NT author who might have intentionally altered a sacred text in a citation or allusion. For example, Docherty has shown that the author of Hebrews took great care to reproduce his scriptural citations accurately, in line with post-biblical Jewish exegesis. Hence, his respect for Scripture is evident in remaining as faithful as possible to its original wording. She challenges the assumption that the *pesharim* take great liberties with the scriptural text in applying it to the life of the community.[102] In his evaluation of OT quotations in the NT, Marcos notes that Paul's application of the OT uses common interpretations, oral or targumic traditions, and the Targum method of exegesis. For example, using the method of *midraš pešer*, Paul's explanation of the text determines the text form of the quotation.[103] Fitzmyer has noted similar quotation techniques and exegetical practices between the OT in Qumran literature and the OT in the NT.[104] Marcos concludes that fluctuation and textual pluralism of the proto-Masoretic Hebrew text and the revisions that the LXX underwent *must be considered alongside* the frequent recourse to rabbinic exegesis by the authors of the NT.[105] Notwithstanding the difficulty of comparing Paul with the later rabbinic sources,[106] we concur with Marcos that both textual fluidity and authorial adaptation should be considered when analyzing the NT's use of the OT. In this investigation, we draw on the findings of both modern Septuagintal study (above) and Stanley's analysis of Paul's citation technique (below). In anticipation of our detailed analysis we note that for each of the suggested allusions under investigation Paul reproduces the words of the OT text precisely, leaving us to consider the significance of purposeful grammatical adaptations, word order reversals, insertions, and omissions:

Phil 2:10-11 NT   πᾶν γόνυ κάμψῃ . . . καὶ πᾶσα γλῶσσα ἐξομολογήσηται
Isa 45:23 LXX^OG   κάμψει πᾶν γόνυ καὶ ἐξομολογήσεται πᾶσα γλῶσσα

Phil 2:12 NT   φόβου καὶ τρόμου
Ps 2:11 LXX^OG   φόβῳ καὶ . . . τρόμῳ

---

102. Docherty, *Use of the Old Testament in Hebrews*, 140-42.
103. Marcos, *Septuagint in Context*, 329.
104. Fitzmyer, "Use of Explicit Old Testament Quotations," 297-333.
105. Marcos, *Septuagint in Context*, 332.
106. See Hays, *Echoes*, 10-14.

Phil 2:15 NT	γενεᾶς σκολιᾶς καὶ διεστραμμένης
Deut 32:5 LXX^{OG}	γενεὰ σκολιὰ καὶ διεστραμμένη

Phil 2:15 NT	φαίνεσθε ὡς φωστῆρες
Dan 12:3 LXX^{OG}	φανοῦσιν ὡς φωστῆρες

Phil 2:16 NT	κενὸν ἐκοπίασα
Isa 49:4 LXX^{OG}	Κενῶς ἐκοπίασα

Noting Paul's verbatim reproduction of the LXX^{OG} texts, the notion that he also adapted the texts in the manner described above should not be ruled out for two reasons. Firstly, as Stanley notes, purposeful adaptations do not necessarily reflect an author's disrespect for Scripture. His quote of Carpzov's forward-looking views from 1729 is helpful in this respect: "Sometimes the strength of the argument, as taken rather from the sense than from the words, obliged them [the New Testament authors] to recede from the strict tenor of the words in the original."[107] Although we might argue that Paul has not receded from the strict tenor of the words in the original, Carpzov's observation that (epistolary) argument determines the form of the citation/allusion is well taken and is the explicit conclusion of two major studies on Paul.[108] Secondly, the burden of reproducing the text exactly, if inherent in the introductory formulae (for example, "as it is written"), is somewhat attenuated for allusions.

SURVEY OF PREVIOUS APPROACHES

The key issues to be addressed in our investigation have been anticipated and itemized in the six questions above. We compiled this list of questions from an examination of the characteristics of the text of Philippians itself and a preview of our literature survey. We will now take a closer look at how several scholars have analyzed the use of Scripture in the NT, paying particular attention to the categories (such as terminology and how theoretical issues have been adopted as the framework for practical investigation) that are significant for our study.

---

107. Stanley, *Paul and the Language of Scripture*, 6–7; Carpzov, *Defence of the Hebrew Bible*, 111–12.

108. Stanley, *Paul and the Language of Scripture*; Koch, *Schrift*. Although, see Lim, *Holy Scriptures*, 143, who criticizes Koch for not adequately accounting for the possibility that Paul used an alternative source in some of his citations.

Richard Hays

In addition to providing the initial impetus for our study of Paul's use of Scripture in Phil 2:10-16, the work of Richard Hays has prompted four of the six questions we seek to address. It is therefore necessary for us to critique his work in some detail. Prior to Hays's book *Echoes of Scripture in the Letters of Paul*, studies of Paul's use of Scripture mainly focused on OT quotations.[109] Hays, however, breaks with tradition and examines Paul's use of "echo" in his letters. Hays's work has been highly influential resulting in a blossoming of interest in Paul's use of the OT,[110] although he is not without his critics.[111] From the perspective of this investigation, his primary contribution is to be found in how he defines tacit references using the categories of "allusion" and "echo," his criteria for detecting them, the method he uses to interpret them and the way he constrains their interpretation.

Interpretation of Tacit References—Intertextuality, Metalepsis, and Metaphor

Hays surveys the treatment of Paul's verbal divergence of quotations from their OT source, noting the reluctance of previous scholars to recognize that they are hermeneutically motivated.[112] Identifying occasions in which there are undeniable gaps between the "original sense" of the OT texts and Paul's interpretation, even in cases where the citations are in verbatim agreement with the LXX, he proposes that Paul reinterprets Scripture to address the concerns of his communities.[113] Recognizing Paul's letters as "hermeneutical events," Hays seeks to find the method or hermeneutic that accounts for Paul's exegesis: "How are we to understand the literary and theological transformations that occur when Paul cites and alludes to Scripture?"[114] Following a brief review of several theorists of the literary method of intertextuality (Kristeva, Barthes, Culler, Bloom), Hays settles on a method of

---

109. For example, Ellis, *Paul's Use of the Old Testament*.

110. Wagner, *Heralds of the Good News*; Keesmaat, *Paul and his Story*; Ciampa, *Presence and Function of Scripture*; Abasciano, *Paul's Use of the Old Testament in Romans 9.1-9*; Wakefield, *Where to Live*; Jobes, "Jerusalem, Our Mother," 299-320; Rosner, *Paul, Scripture, and Ethics*; Williams, *Wisdom of the Wise*; O' Day, "Jeremiah 9:22-23 And 1 Corinthians 1:26-31," 259-67.

111. See Evans and Sanders, 1993. In his critique of Hays, Hübner, "Intertextualität," 891, writes, "Intertextualität wird nun geradezu als *theologische Kategorie* verwendet."

112. For example, Kaiser Jr., *Uses of the Old Testament in the New*.

113. Hays, *Echoes*, 6.

114. Ibid., 9-10.

interpretation advanced by John Hollander: allusive echo is that which suggests to the reader (Hollander's contemporary reader) that text B should be understood in light of a broad interplay with text A, encompassing aspects of A beyond those explicitly echoed. Hollander names this interpretive function of allusive echo, *transumption* or *metalepsis*: it involves the recovery of unstated or suppressed material in the echoed text. Additionally, an important point of Hollander's theory is the revisionary property of allusive echo: "the revisionary power of allusive echo generates new figuration."[115] In the course of generating new figuration, the original voice is distorted in order to interpret it.[116] Hays, following Hollander, argues that Paul reappropriates Scripture and reinterprets it so that it takes on a meaning different from its original. This leads Hays to interpret the echoes of Scripture in Paul's letters *metaphorically*, as prefiguring the formation of an eschatological community.[117] He concludes that Paul interprets Scripture in an ecclesiocentric way, arguing for a particular vision of the church.

Although Hays concentrates on the effects of metalepsis, or intertextual echo, in Paul's letters to the Romans, Corinthians, and Galatians, he initially demonstrates the concept using an example from Philippians. He argues that Paul "echoes" Job 13:16 in Phil 1:19 by using a verbatim "citation" of five-words reproduced from the LXX: τοῦτό μοι ἀποβήσεται εἰσ σωτηρίαν. Hays claims that by echoing Job's words, "Paul the prisoner tacitly assumes the role of righteous sufferer, as paradigmatically figured by Job . . . and implicitly transfers to himself some of the significations that traditionally cluster about the figure of Job."[118] Hays proceeds to list several of these significations noting that some are correspondences between Paul and Job (Paul's rival preachers in Phil 1:15–17 correspond to Job's hollow comforters) while others are contrasts (God as Job's adversary contrasts God as Paul's defender). According to Hays, this example illustrates Hollander's principle that "the interpretation of a metalepsis entails the recovery of the transumed material."[119] The connection between Job's comforters and Paul's rival preachers results from an intertextual reading that recovers unstated material in Job that Hays believes corresponds to Paul's situation in Philippians. When Job is read in counterpoint with Philippians, "a range of resonant harmonics becomes audible."[120] This range of resonant harmonics

115. Hollander, *Figure of Echo*, ix.
116. Ibid., 111.
117. Hays, *Echoes*, 162.
118. Ibid., 22.
119. Ibid., 23.
120. Ibid.

results from the reader's reception of the text, which s/he then offers as a "satisfactory" interpretation.

We agree with Hays that certain approaches to intertextuality have developed within literary criticism that might prove illuminating when applied to Paul's letters; in particular, Hollander's theory of metalepsis, which involves recovery of unstated or suppressed material in the source or evoked text, we will develop along more theoretical lines with the help of Ben-Porat. There are, however, several aspects of Hays's findings that invite critique. According to Hays, Paul's intertextual readings are *metaphorical*; they generate new meanings that distort the original sense of the source text, that far exceed the conscious design of the author, and that produce unexpected correspondences.[121] For example, Hays describes Paul's use of Job 13:16 in Phil 1:19 as *a(nother) revisionary distortion* of Job's words.[122] Hays understands Job's and Paul's attitude to God as antithetical. For Job, God appears to be the adversary in the litigation who is inflicting injustice, whereas for Paul, God is his defender and vindicator.[123] Although both expect vindication, there is a contrast in their attitude to God's role in their suffering—whereas Paul expresses self-confidence in God, Job expresses defiance.[124] Despite the similarities between Job's and Paul's circumstances, this latter difference seems to prompt Hays to suggest that Paul's reading is "revisionary." In other words, the phrase meant something different for Paul than it meant for Job, so is used metaphorically. However, there is another explanation that recognizes all of the themes and motifs that Hays correctly identifies. If there are any *Philippians* who share Job's attitude to God, then Paul might not be metaphorically distorting Job's context as it applies to himself, but metonymically extending it to apply to some Philippians. In this case, the purpose of the echo is not for Paul to liken himself, tacitly, to Job, but the Philippians to Job. Although Hays has proposed, *prima facie*, a credible interpretation based on the thematic coherence between Job and Paul, the conclusion that Paul had misread or distorted the original sense of Scripture clearly depends on which part of the pretext (the book of Job) is actualized by the reader[125] and how it connects with Paul's argument. In proposing Hollander's model of interpreting echoes metaphorically, Hays

---

121. Ibid., 24, 156.
122. Ibid., 24.
123. Ibid., 22.
124. Ibid., 24.
125. God's sanctioning of suffering following Satan's protest (Job 1:12; 2:6), Job's complaint (chapter 13) or God's rebuke of Job (chapters 38–41).

writes: "it is less a matter of method than of sensibility."[126] Such an approach has stimulated a major criticism that Hays has devalued method in favor of sensibility. As Hübner points out, Hays has not used the full extent of the methodological toolbox provided by the literary scholars who deal with intertextuality.[127] In contrast to Hays, these theorists have not made metaphor the centre of their reflections.[128] Our investigation will test Hays's proposals that Paul's intertextual readings are metaphorical, distorting the original sense of Scripture and not consciously intended.

Definition of Tacit References and Relationship to Author and Audience

According to Hays, "Quotation, allusion, and echo may be seen as points along a spectrum of intertextual reference, moving from the explicit to the subliminal."[129] He claims that as we move further away from overt citation, intertextual relations become less determinate, placing greater demands on the reader's listening powers. Hays's definitions of quotation, allusion, and echo reveal his reader-oriented approach to interpretation. He seems to be considering the capabilities of his contemporary reader using a heuristic understanding of quotation, allusion, and echo as these categories of *reference* relate to the terms *explicit* and *subliminal*.[130] For example, Hays seems to rule out the possibility of an author intentionally placing a greater demand on a reader's listening powers by creating tacit references.[131] Should an author intentionally reference another text tacitly, the intertextual relations would be more determinate than Hays claims—even if they were difficult to discern by the reader. Along similar lines, Hays makes no systematic distinction between allusion and echo, but concludes that allusion is used

---

126. Hays, *Echoes*, 21.

127. Hübner, "Intertextualität," 892: "Hier rächt sich nun wieder, dass H[ays] zugunsten der von ihm beschworenen Sensibilität das von den Literaturwissenschaftlern zur Verfügung gestellte methodische Instrumentarium zur Untersuchung intertextueller Beziehungen nicht genügend nutzt."

128. Ibid., 895: "Zugleich muss jedoch gesagt werden, dass die Theoretiker der Intertextualität das Problem der Metapher so gut wie nicht in den Mittelpunkt ihrer Überlegungen gestellt haben."

129. Hays, *Echoes*, 23.

130. By this I mean that the terms "quotation," "allusion" and "echo" are effectively used to define the reader's ability to discover the reference.

131. Yet, if the author has a good understanding of the reader's capabilities, and expects him/her to detect those references, then what appears subliminal to the contemporary reader was not subliminal to the original reader.

of obvious intertextual references, echo of subtler ones.[132] He also observes that knowledge of an audience gleaned from Paul's letters complicates distinguishing between allusion and echo:

> The concept of allusion depends both on the notion of authorial intention and on the assumption that the reader will share with the author the requisite "portable library" to recognise the source of the allusion; the notion of echo, however, finesses such questions: "echo is a metaphor of, and for, alluding, and does not depend on conscious intention."[133]

Since he defines allusion as intentional and echo as not necessarily depending on conscious intention, two important consequences result. Firstly, the *mere definition* of allusion and echo can be used to support a particular reconstruction of the original audience (able to detect and understand allusion but not necessarily echo).[134] Secondly, the *mere definition* of allusion and echo facilitates the revisionary readings that Hays proposes—a metaphoric figuration of echo by a contemporary reader (Hays himself) can be proposed without recourse to authorial intention or whether the figuration was possible for the original readers/hearers: "Consequently, later readers will rightly grasp meanings of the figures that may have been veiled from Paul himself." In our opinion this places too much hermeneutical weight on a simplistic definition of allusion and echo.[135] As we shall see, there is an alternative case for treating all marked, unmarked, overt, and covert references to Scripture as intentional allusion. In light of this, some of Hays's assumptions should be re-evaluated, not least those regarding the determination of intentionality from degrees of subtlety.[136] This latter point takes us to an examination of Hays's view on intentionality. He writes, "To limit our interpretation of Paul's scriptural echoes to what he intended by them is to impose a severe and arbitrary hermeneutical restriction."[137] However, understanding Paul as intending to allude (echo) is not severe if we accept

---

132. Hays, *Echoes*, 29.
133. Hollander, *Figure of Echo*, 64.
134. Hays, *Echoes*, 32.
135. Porter, "Use of the Old Testament in the New," 92, writes, "The labels (quotation, allusion, echo) have a heuristic value, and end up shaping the interpretation of the evidence at hand . . . "
136. Although Hays claims that allusion is obvious, it is normally taken to mean an indirect, tacit or subtle reference—just as echo. He also uses the terms "faint echoes," "higher-volume echoes," "obvious echoes," "subtler echoes" and "overt allusions" (*Echoes*, 24). See also Williams, *Wisdom of the Wise*, 4, who writes, "the issue of intentionality will be the dividing line between a(n) allusion and echo."
137. Hays, *Echoes*, 33.

that he and some of his audience might have shared the same experience connoted by the echoes/allusions and not arbitrary if that shared experience can be identified from the rhetoric of the letter and other echoes/allusions. As we shall see, we have identified a more analytical and comprehensive definition of allusion—one that accommodates the notion that Paul intended to allude and was the first to experience the intertextual fusion, which is subsequently shared by the reader whose imagination is also curtailed by it. In other words, Paul's intentional rhetoric might constrain the reader's hermeneutical freedom.

Detection of Tacit References

Hays offers a "7-point criteria" for testing claims about the presence and meaning of scriptural echoes in Paul. *Availability:* was the proposed source of the echo available to the author and/or original readers? *Volume:* to what extent are words or syntactical patterns repeated and/or how distinctive and memorable are the words in the source text? *Recurrence:* how often does Paul elsewhere cite or allude to the same scriptural passage? *Thematic coherence:* how well does the alleged echo fit into Paul's argument? *Historical plausibility:* could Paul have intended the alleged meaning effect and could his readers have understood it? *History of interpretation:* have other readers heard the same echoes? *Satisfaction:* does the proposed reading make sense and offer a satisfactory account of the intertextual relation?[138] His criteria for detecting and interpreting echoes have been adopted by several writers,[139] with some claiming that they provide an objective guide for the task, especially as a counter to the pitfalls of "parallelomania."[140] However, Porter notes that Hays's first three criteria are problematic and the remainder are more concerned with the interpretation of echo than its detection.[141]

---

138. Ibid., 29–32.

139. Some seem to retain Hays's criteria *in toto* (Ciampa, *Presence and Function of Scripture*, 24–25; Abasciano, *Paul's Use of the Old Testament in Romans 9.1-9*, 22–24; Wagner, *Heralds of the Good News*, 11, 13, who emphasizes some criterion). Others propose adaptations (Williams, *Wisdom of the Wise*, 3, 4; Rosner, *Paul, Scripture, & Ethics*, 18–19; Keesmaat, *Paul and His Story*, 52. See Thomson, *Clothed with Christ*, 30–36, for the most thorough modification in his investigation of Jesus traditions in Paul's writings).

140. Rosner, *Paul, Scripture, and Ethics*, 18–19; Abasciano, *Paul's Use of the Old Testament in Romans 9.1-9*, 22; cf. Jauhiainen, *Use of Zechariah in Revelation*, 33–35.

141. Porter, "Use of the Old Testament in the New," 83, mentions the problems of using audience awareness (through "availability" of source text) to define the presence of an echo, how to determine "volume" from verbal coherence, and that "recurrence" can measure frequent echoes but cannot determine a singular echo.

Indeed, Hays ultimately falls back on "satisfaction" as the most important test for identifying and interpreting echoes based on "thematic coherence." Hays's criteria might be useful for judging the probability of allusion, but ultimately, the proof of the allusion lies mainly in its interpretation (see Jauhiainen below). Yet, it must be conceded that such an approach involves varying degrees of certainty since the allusion is verified or falsified based on levels of congruence advanced by the interpretation.

Constraining the Interpretation of Tacit References

A major hermeneutical issue is identified by two responses to Hays's findings. On the one hand, Evans accepts Hays's interpretation of the Job allusion in Philippians because of the verbal correspondences and the suggestive thematic parallels which provide the significant link between the texts necessary for an allusion to be present.[142] On the other hand, Beker, wanting to know what constraints curtail both Paul's imaginative freedom and that of Hays, when interpreting an echo, considers Hays's interpretation fanciful.[143] Beker's critique of Hays is well noted—he is concerned about how an intertextual method is able to maintain one of the most important features of Paul's letters, the confluence of coherence and contingency which requires paying attention to the social situation of the churches Paul writes to.[144] According to Beker, Paul uses Scripture only "when the contingent situation forces him to do so."[145] Beker is not satisfied with "thematic coherence" between texts as a proof of the presence of intertextuality. Particularly, Hays has failed to convince him of the "historical and social coherence" between Job and Philippians that might better justify an echo of the former in the latter. The legitimacy of Beker's complaint is affirmed by recognizing the constraints that Hays uses to interpret intertextual echo beyond his test case of Philippians. We will now turn to this important aspect of Hays's analysis.

Hays argues that Scripture's latent sense is disclosed only to those who "turn to the Lord."[146] The gospel is hidden in Scripture, and Paul, after his conversion, has found novel interpretations of gospel prefigurement by

---

142. Evans, "Listening for Echoes," 45.
143. Beker, "Echoes and Intertextuality," 64–65.
144. Ibid., 66–67.
145. Ibid., 67. We believe Beker has advanced a crucial point that addresses his concern about how to constrain intertextual exegesis, although he considers the contingent situation to be Paul's engagement with Judaism and Judaizers.
146. Hays, *Echoes*, 154.

misreading Scripture, and extending its meaning in new directions.[147] Hays claims that Paul's innovative readings provide an hermeneutical model that is normative for the church today: "True interpretation depends neither on historical inquiry nor on erudite literary analysis but on attentiveness to the promptings of the Spirit, who reveals the gospel through Scripture in surprising ways."[148] Thus, Scripture's mode of revelation is indirect and allusive (rather than an overt communication) with its meaning being recovered only by reading the text aright. This requires reading it through the "correcting lens" of God's righteousness made known in Christ. According to Hays, God's act in Jesus Christ illuminates a previously uncomprehended narrative unity in Scripture.[149] Scripture is a story about God's righteousness which is the ground for unity between Torah and gospel. *Thus, Paul's echoes of Scripture should be understood as alluding to the wider narrative of God's righteousness.* This is why, according to Hays, Paul quotes most often from Isaiah, Psalms, Deuteronomy, and Genesis—because these texts, more than others, prefigure an ingathering of Gentiles along with Israel as evidence of God's righteousness.[150]

But God's righteousness is only one of several pretexts in Scripture. Along similar lines to Beker, Hübner correctly notes the problem with Hays's approach to defining his pretexts assuming this single-story view of Scripture. He describes it as a "contaminating relationship" which is "the acquisition of singular elements from different pretexts (or systems of genre), where the singular elements become separated from their original structural and functional context and combined into a new text."[151] In other words, Hays has not methodologically justified activating those particular elements of Isaiah, Psalms, Deuteronomy, and Genesis which refer to the ingathering of Gentiles with Israel as a demonstration of God's righteousness. *The controlling mechanism for interpreting the echo depends upon the presupposition that the righteousness of God is the pretext Paul uses.*

Thus we see how Hays constrains his interpretation of tacit references using metalepsis. He evokes elements in the echoed text that cohere with the pretext, or intertext, of God's righteousness particularly evidenced by the theme of Jew and Gentile ingathering—the formation of the covenant community (ecclesiology) is the controlling mechanism which governs the recovery of unstated material in the echoed text. Hays uses a theological, or

---

147. Ibid., 5.
148. Ibid., 156.
149. Ibid., 157.
150. Ibid., 162.
151. Hübner, "Intertextualität," 893, quoting Monika Lindner.

perhaps more accurately, ecclesiological constraint to control interpretation of echoes.

Beker and Hübner have highlighted an important issue in the interpretation of tacit OT references. The crucial question is: What constrains the activation of unstated elements in another text when an allusion is interpreted? In answering this question, we suggest an alternative answer to Hays, and one that offers a way around Beker's objection to intertextuality and its relationship with the historical, social situation of Paul's churches. Our unique approach is to propose social (rhetorical-contingent) situation as the means of constraining intertextual interpretation. The elements to be activated in the interpretation of a tacit reference should be those congruent with the rhetorical situation of the alluding/echoing text, if indeed they can be identified. By using rhetorical situation, garnered from a rhetorical-exegesis of Phil 1:27—3:21, we will argue that this constraint is exegetically derived from the text of Philippians itself and not from theological presuppositions abstracted from many source texts. Our new, novel question is: How can the text of Philippians constrain the interpretation of allusion in Phil 2:10–16?

Christopher Stanley

Christopher Stanley's work is relevant to this investigation because of his contribution in two areas: firstly, how Paul handles the wording of his Scripture citations, which includes definitions of citation/quotation; secondly, the capability of Paul's readership to detect Scriptural citations/allusions and understand their broader context in the source text(s).[152] These two important areas of Stanley's work relate to questions one, two, and especially, five above and will now be critiqued in turn.

The Rhetorical Purpose of Adapting the Words of a Cited Text

How do we account for the discrepancies between the wording of Paul's quotations and the language of his presumed *Vorlage*? Stanley answers by first charting the development of traditional views that Paul's deviant wording can be put down to irregularities of sources. For example, when Paul's quotations of Scripture differed from both the MT and LXX, he was either quoting loosely from memory,[153] correcting a corrupted Greek *Vor-*

---

152. Stanley, *Arguing With Scripture*.
153. He cites Ellis, *Paul's Use of the Old Testament*, 14–15; Lindars, *New Testament*

lage using a Hebrew original, or quoting from a non-extant copy.[154] Stanley highlights the apologetic background of these views which sought to protect the verbal accuracy of NT quotations and defend their authors's adherence to the wording and context of their biblical sources.[155] More recent scholars entertained the idea that Paul had adapted a text, for which we have an extant copy, for his own theological, sociological or literary purposes. Given that purposeful adaptation need not be taken as unfaithful or dishonest,[156] Stanley investigates whether Paul adapted a text to advance his rhetorical purposes, and whether explanations can be found for how he handled the wording of his citations.

Firstly, the citations must be identified. Stanley does this by limiting his study to those citations considered explicit. Explicit citations have three characteristics: passages that are introduced by an explicit citation formula (most commonly, "as it is written"), are accompanied by a clear interpretive gloss[157] or stand in clear syntactical tension with their present linguistic environment.[158] He is thus interested in what markers the author uses to signal the presence of a citation. Stanley describes this approach to defining citation as reader-centered, suggesting that uninformed readers might mistake unmarked citations for Paul's own work, whereas the presence of explicitly marked citations is obvious to any attentive reader.[159] Having decided on what texts qualify as citations, and should be included in the investigation, Stanley then sets out to establish the text that Paul cites from; this is required before a decision can be made on whether Paul retains or adapts the original wording. For this task, Stanley uses the printed editions of the MT, Qumran biblical manuscripts, the Samaritan Pentateuch, and the full range of Septuagintal traditions in his investigations.[160] Only when all of these possible sources have been analyzed will divergent wording be considered to be a possible authorial adaptation. Unsympathetic to the notion that Paul cited from memory, Stanley suggests that Paul had a written source from

---

Apologetic, 26; Hanson, *Studies in Paul's Technique*, 148.

154. Stanley, *Paul and the Language of Scripture*, 6.

155. Ibid., 10–11. For this group of scholars the wording of the citation was incidental since Paul was using the quoted texts as proofs, the focus being on his method of interpretation.

156. Ibid., 6–7.

157. Ibid., 37. For example, in 1 Cor 15:27, "But when he says" is Paul's interpretive signal that the preceding text was quoted.

158. Ibid., 37. For example, in Rom 9:7 where there is a shift to second person singular.

159. Stanley, *Arguing With Scripture*, 66.

160. Stanley, *Paul and the Language of Scripture*, 67.

which he drew his citations.[161] This anthology of Scripture was in a format (wax tablets or parchment) that Paul created during the course of his own personal study, he carried with him, and that accounted for the diversity of text-types that appear in his quotations.[162]

Where the wording of Paul's citations resist manuscript-based explanation, Stanley develops a standard using contextual and linguistic criteria to establish the presence of an adapted citation more reliably. He concludes that Paul adapts Scripture in roughly half of the incidents where he deviates from the primary LXX tradition.[163] In doing so, he uses a "normal citation technique" that prevailed among Greco-Roman authors in the late Hellenistic and early Roman eras.[164] Stanley, following Koch, catalogues the type of adaptations Paul makes in the cases where he digresses from his presumed *Vorlage*. His citation techniques include the following:

1. Reversing the order of words[165]
2. Grammatical changes
3. Omitting words from the text
4. Adding words to the text
5. Replacing words or phrases
6. Conflating texts
7. Combining texts back-to-back.[166]

These adaptations are designed to fit the quoted text into the structure of Paul's own argument and thus advance the pastoral and rhetorical interests

---

161. Ibid., 69.

162. Ibid., 74–79. Other views accounting for Paul's quotations from written sources propose that he carried biblical scrolls with him during his travels (Ellis, *Paul's Use of the Old Testament*, 19). Hickling, "Paul's Reading of Isaiah," 215, 219, suggests that Paul carried biblical scrolls during his travels, like the Ethiopian eunuch (Acts 8:28). A standard biblical scroll in Greek was easily portable, rolling up into a cylinder of about 1/1.5 inches in diameter. Paul might also have had access to biblical scrolls owned by local church leaders (Theissen, *Social Setting of Pauline Christianity*; Meeks, *First Urban Christians*; Malherbe, *Social Aspects of Early Christianity*) or drew his quotations from a pre-existing Christian "testimony book" (Harris, *Testimonies*).

163. Stanley, *Paul and the Language of Scripture*, 259–60. Cf. Koch, *Schrift*, 186–90, who calculated that 56 percent of Paul's quotations were adaptations.

164. Stanley, *Paul and the Language of Scripture*, 61, 348.

165. Ibid., 349. Shifts in word order occur far more often in Paul's quotations than in those of contemporary Jewish and Greco-Roman writers.

166. Ibid., 349–50.

of the letter.¹⁶⁷ Thus according to Stanley, Paul actively adapted the source text in his quotations to communicate his own understanding of the passage and obviate others, and he did so consciously but *unreflectively* in the manner of the conventions of his day.¹⁶⁸

Stanley has made a significant contribution to the evaluation of Paul's use of Scripture and several aspects of his findings are relevant to our own investigation. Firstly, as we will argue below, he is correct in noting that Paul reshapes Scripture to fit his rhetorical purpose.¹⁶⁹ Secondly, he has discovered a major factor in determining authorship of texts that reproduce earlier texts—citation technique. Stanley's analysis is also helpful because of his attention to establishing the presumed *Vorlage* of Paul's citations. Following Koch, he recognizes that Paul uses non-standard versions of the LXX, sometimes using one strand over another.¹⁷⁰ However, several aspects of Stanley's analysis invite critique.

He excludes "unmarked" references to Scripture on the grounds that the *uninformed* reader would not be able to tell if a (an unmarked Scripture quotation) passage is Pauline or not.¹⁷¹ He therefore seems to assume a homogeneous readership (excluding informed readers) whose competence can be determined from the form of the citation marker—reader competence is inferred from the presence or absence of textual elements embedded along with the quoted text. It is questionable whether audience competence should be determined in this way, since Paul might have intended either an overt reference without a textual element that introduces the citation,¹⁷² or a covert reference directed to a more informed section of the readership/audience. As we shall see, the marking element of a quotation (for example, "as it is written") should be distinguished from the reproduced text itself. The latter might be so distinctive that an author chooses not to include a marker. For example, Koch identified a condition that would have allowed the reproduction of Isa 45:23 in Phil 2:10, 11 to qualify as a citation. According to Koch, when the same words appear in another context where they are marked clearly as a citation (for example, in Rom 1:17 and Gal 3:11, where Hab 2:4 is marked in the former and unmarked in the latter), then the second occurrence (or, "unmarked" occurrence) can also be considered

---

167. Ibid., 264.
168. Ibid., 29. Italics mine.
169. Ibid., 347.
170. Ibid., 51.
171. Ibid., 66.
172. As with Isa 45:23 in Phil 2:10–11.

a citation.¹⁷³ Since Isa 45:23 occurs in Rom 14:11 and is explicitly marked, Phil 2:10–11 qualifies as a citation using Koch's criteria but not Stanley's. Finally, one of Stanley's fundamental theses is that Paul adapted his citations of Scripture consciously but *unreflectively*. It remains to be seen whether this view can be borne out by our investigation or whether Paul carefully chose his citations/allusions having reflected on the correspondences between their original contexts and his audience's circumstances. This forms the nub of another key issue which Stanley has championed—the competency of Paul's audience to recognize tacit Scripture references and recover their original context.

Audience Scripture Literacy and Recovery of Context

Stanley has written extensively on Scripture literacy in Paul's congregations.¹⁷⁴ In *Arguing With Scripture* he seeks to explain how Paul used Scripture quotations to further his arguments and how effective his use of quotation would be when addressing his first-century audience. He therefore examines Paul's quotations from both an author and audience perspective. He bases his study of Paul's use of Scripture on the "New Rhetoric" of Eugene White and Chaim Perelman, and correctly identifies Paul's letters as responses to "rhetorical urgencies." Rhetorical speech is audience-centered, designed to promote action on the part of the audience to correct or alter an emergency situation.¹⁷⁵ Thus, primary attention is given to the way Paul's quotations of Scripture advance (or fail to advance) his rhetorical strategies in a given passage.¹⁷⁶ With this rhetorical framework, Stanley draws on contemporary literary studies about the art of quotation to support his claim that the "original sense" of the quoted passage is not important in determining the meaning of the quotation, but rather the literary and rhetorical context of the quoting text.¹⁷⁷ This opens the door to a view of Paul's use of quotation

173. Koch, *Schrift*, 11–24.

174. Stanley, "'Pearls Before Swine,'" 124–44; Stanley, *Arguing With Scripture*; Stanley, "Paul's 'Use' of Scripture." See the critique of Stanley in Abasciano, "Diamonds in the Rough," 153–83.

175. Stanley, *Arguing With Scripture*, 15–16.

176. Ibid., 20.

177. Ibid., 22–37. He rejects Wierzbicka's view that, in a quotation from Scripture, the audience can make the same associations that the author made (Wierzbicka, "Semantics," 267–307). Stanley suggests that direct quotation empowers the audience to make associations different from those that the author intended. To guard against these "mistaken" interpretations the author includes interpretative comments around the quotation—but only in argumentative texts (*Arguing With Scripture*, 26.) In assessing,

that does not require his audience to understand the original context, and thus explains Paul's use of Scripture to an audience unfamiliar with the OT.

For Stanley, rhetorical analysis also investigates the author's perception of the intended audience and how well that perception corresponds to what we know about the audience from other sources.[178] He believes the best way to determine Paul's understanding of his audience is by historical reconstruction. This is crucial to Stanley's approach especially since he observes a discrepancy between the level of biblical knowledge that Paul assumes in his letters and external data that suggest a much lower level of biblical literacy among Paul's addressees. He suggests that "external evidence regarding literacy levels in antiquity should take precedence over evidence derived from a 'mirror-reading' of Paul's quotations because the letters give only a partial and one-sided picture of the intended audience." He justifies this because "Paul's letters are rhetorical works, not objective depictions of reality."[179] Stanley draws on the social models of literacy advanced by Harris and Gamble[180] to argue that Paul's audiences are illiterate Gentiles incapable of understanding the meaning and significance of his quotations from Scripture. This view is supported by claims that the high cost and low availability of biblical scrolls would have inhibited Scripture literacy in the community.[181] This coheres with Stanley's earlier conclusion that in Paul's use of quotation, the "original sense" of the quoted passage is not important in determining the meaning of the quotation. Thus Stanley understands Paul's audience as illiterate and his use of quotations should be understood according to this presumption. He concludes that Paul quotes

---

and agreeing with, Sternberg, "Proteus," 107–56, Stanley notes the concept that the quotation acts like an inset where the original context is not important. The new context reshapes the original context as the quotee becomes subordinate to the quoter. The audience must be able to interpret without access to the original context (*Arguing With Scripture*, 28–29). Stanley rejects the proposal of Clark and Gerrig, "Quotations," 786–88, that quotation demonstrates a shared background and interpretation between author and audience. He views the chief weakness of their theory as the function of the quotation marker to depict primary and secondary aspects of the quoted text (*Arguing With Scripture*, 32). As we shall see, this concern can be addressed by examining the approach to allusion of other literary theorists. The fourth and final theory Stanley reviews is that of Lane-Mercier, "Quotation," 199–214, whose "parodic" use of quotations is a rhetorical strategy for bringing about "the metaphorical death of the quotee, whose utterance, apparently intact, has nonetheless been decontextualised, severed from its 'origin,' and subsumed by the utterance of the quoter" (*Arguing With Scripture*, 35, citing Lane-Mercier, "Quotation," 206).

178. Stanley, *Arguing With Scripture*, 20–21.
179. Ibid., 63.
180. Gamble, *Books and Readers in the Early Church*; Harris, *Ancient Literacy*.
181. Stanley, *Arguing With Scripture*, 41–42.

either because he has misjudged their competency or because his quotations are part of a rhetorical strategy that does not evoke Scripture context.

Stanley has provided valuable insights into the impact that Paul's quotations, as rhetorical element in his letters, have on an audience with diverse literacy. With Stanley, we will approach Paul's quotations (and allusions) as rhetorical devices designed to influence thoughts, feelings, and actions of an audience. Stanley is correct to note that Paul's letters are rhetorical discourse prompted by exigencies which his writing is designed to address. As such it is more fruitful to approach Paul's use of Scripture with a view to understanding its place in his overall argument and not as a window into his exegetical technique: "The decision to include direct quotations in a written work depends entirely on the rhetorical aims of the quoting author."[182] However, we believe there are several weaknesses in Stanley's view of Paul's rhetorical strategy and his audience's capabilities.

Firstly, Stanley's rejection of literary theorists who advocate a shared knowledge of quoted-text context between author and audience may be premature. By confining his investigation to Paul's use of quotation, the works of other literary theorists such as Ben-Porat, Perri, Combs, and Irwin have not been considered. As we shall see, their investigations shed light on how quotations and allusions work from the perspective of what happens when authors and readers actualize evoked texts in the acts of writing and reading respectively. These theories would have benefited Stanley's reading in his case studies on Paul's letters. For example, to make an informed judgment about the literacy of Paul's audience and the effectiveness of using quotations as part of his rhetorical strategy, Stanley proceeds to define three hypothetical audiences: the "informed audience," "competent audience," and "minimal audience."[183] Since each of these would respond differently to Paul's quotations, the effectiveness of Paul's strategy can be assessed. He then proceeds to test each of these audiences using quotations from Romans, 1 and 2 Corinthians, and Galatians. In his case study of how an "informed audience" would interpret Isa 29:14 in 1 Cor 1:19, Stanley concludes they would have been confused because of the lack of coherence between the contexts of Isa 29:14 and 1 Cor 1:19. In fact, Stanley claims that none of the three proposed hypothetical audiences would have been capable of understanding the meaning and significance of the quotations as Paul seems to have understood them.[184] Yet, the context of Isa 29:14 and its associated themes within Jewish literature are related to the disobedi-

---

182. Ibid., 31.
183. Ibid., 68–69.
184. Ibid., 81–82.

ence and divided status of the church in Corinth.[185] In his reading, Stanley has not actualized the wider elements of Isa 29 and early Jewish literature that connect the absence of wisdom with division and strife. An audience familiar with the context of Isa 29 could easily have made these associations which are already present in Paul's non-quotation rhetoric. We therefore suggest that Stanley has misjudged the "informed audience" of first-century Corinth because of a flawed assumption about how the quotations function rhetorically—that is, quotations do not evoke elements of context.

Secondly, Stanley's argument that Paul either misjudged his audience or that he used quotation not expecting his audience to have recourse to the source text or its context, is weakened when he admits that some members in Paul's audience might have been Scripture literate.[186] As such, there is no reason why they should not be considered the "implied" audience since they would be the agents whom Paul targeted to address the rhetorical urgency, at least in the first instance.[187] As Stanley rightly points out, a single congregation probably included all three types of members (informed, competent, minimal) but it is not necessary that the *whole* congregation constitutes the implied audience. For example, it cannot be shown that at least one person in the Philippian Church did not have access to, or knowledge of, a Greek version of the parts of Scripture that we suggest Paul alludes to in his letter (Isaiah, Psalm 2, Deuteronomy, Daniel).[188]

Thirdly, Stanley seems inconsistent in his use of literary evidence. Given that the "implied" audience in Paul's letters where Scripture is reproduced suggests Scripture literacy, Stanley speculates that Paul might have been mistaken in constructing this audience. Paul's lack of knowledge of their abilities, and their inability to recall his teaching are offered as reasons:[189] "We should not assume that Paul had either the knowledge or the intention to depict his audience accurately in every case." As evidence for this point, he notes that Paul did not know the congregation he wrote to in Romans and consequently what verses they knew. Therefore, "Paul's quotations cannot be taken as reliable indicators of the level of biblical literacy in his

---

185. Williams, *Wisdom of the Wise*, 92.

186. Stanley, *Arguing With Scripture*, 47–51, 68.

187. Paul's instructions would most likely have been relayed to even the most illiterate members of the congregation. See Hezser, *Jewish Literacy in Roman Palestine*, 24, citing Bowman: "illiterates could participate in it [a profoundly literate society] through intermediaries who wrote and read for them."

188. According to Gamble, *Books and Readers in the Early Church*, 9, "it is difficult to imagine any Christian community where either no one could read or no authority accrued to those who could."

189. Stanley, *Arguing With Scripture*, 63–64.

congregations."[190] Stanley rightly raises the issue of the author's perception and the depiction of "objective reality" in his/her text (we will address this matter in the section on situational rhetoric). However, it is questionable to imply that because the data presented by Paul in his letters are (merely) his perceptions, they are not reliable. There seems to be no good reason why we should not accept Paul's perceptions as "corresponding" to a real situation which included his audiences's awareness of Scripture.[191] Indeed, Stanley has confidence in Paul's perceptions of objective reality in other respects. For example, he accepts the reality of a Paul who had never been to Rome before writing the epistle.[192] But this "reality" is gleaned from the data presented by Paul in the letter (Rom 1:13, 15). Similarly, Stanley accepts the reality of a Paul who had a long-standing relationship with the Philippians. Again, we know this from data presented by Paul in his letter, in which he depicts the Philippians as those whom he knew well, visited several times, and with whom he had a uniquely personal relationship and financial arrangement. In similar vein, Stanley uses the literary evidence of explicitly marked quotations in a determination of audience understanding: "The only quotations that Paul's first-century audience definitely would have recognized are *those marked as such within the text* . . . we should not assume that the original recipients of his letter would have recognized even a verbatim quotation from Scripture unless *it was marked as such within the text*."[193] Here, the presence of textual elements created by Paul is being used to argue for quotation as received by a "type of audience." Finally, in our opinion, Stanley's prioritizing of historical reconstruction over literary evidence seems unbalanced. He subordinates the literary evidence of Paul's perceptions of audience literacy gleaned from data he presents in the text to speculative historical reconstructions of literacy. But these reconstructions of the historical audience might not be an objective depiction of reality either.[194] There is no way of knowing for certain the literacy levels of a first-

190. Ibid., 64.

191. Gamble, *Books and Readers in the Early Church*, 212-13, concludes that Paul's expectations of audience familiarity of Scripture imply that the Jewish Scriptures were regularly read and taught in the Pauline congregations. See also Stenschke, *Luke's Portrait of Gentiles Prior to Their Coming to Faith*, 340, who describes the content of Paul's teaching to Gentile converts in Corinth (Acts 18:1-11) as that taught in the synagogue, namely the "word of God." Stanley also concedes that Paul might have directed his unmarked references to Scripture to the Jewish members of his audience (*Arguing With Scripture*, 48).

192. Stanley, *Arguing With Scripture*, 138.

193. Ibid., 47. Italics mine.

194. Much of Stanley's analysis appears to assume that the findings of literacy levels in Greco-Roman society can be uniformly applied to the Christian community, as if

century Christian community from conjecture about the cost or availability of biblical scrolls, or generalizations about Greco-Roman education.[195] As Stamps correctly observes: "Assessing the level of audience understanding and perception is virtually impossible. Scholars may feel confident in providing a profile of the original historical recipients, but this is as subjective, or even more so, than reconstructing the historical author."[196]

We therefore do not think that Stanley has made the case against Paul's audiences being sympathetic to his message and capable of recovering the context of his Scripture references. Paul's implied audiences were not fixed, but varied across his congregations. As we shall see, a reconstruction of the implied audience in Philippians does not support Stanley's theory. Neither does an investigation into the rhetorical exigency at Philippi. We shall investigate the possibility that Paul and the Philippians were aware of the context of his Scriptural references and whether specific Scripture texts were chosen by Paul because their situations were similar to his and the Philippians, and were uppermost in his mind when writing.

Marko Jauhiainen

In *The Use of Zechariah in Revelation*, Jauhiainen defines and identifies allusions and proposes how they function in their context.[197] His evaluation of the quest for scientific and objective criteria for detecting allusions is especially enlightening. He does not focus on the probability of allusion, rather, after surveying several scholars (including Hays), he concludes that, with the arrival of Postmodernism, the quest for objective, scientific criteria for determining OT allusions is (at least partially) misguided.[198] There is no consensus regarding objective criteria for detecting allusions with most proposals identifying two critical measures—verbal similarities, and thematic parallels between texts. According to Jauhiainen, regardless of how an interpreter discovers an allusion, his/her main task is to give a satisfying account of the passage containing the allusion, which includes an account of the rhetorical purpose of the allusion. Consequently, his assessment of the

---

such a faith community would not be more inclined towards literacy.

195. See Gamble, *Books and Readers in the Early Church*, 9–10, who recognized that the church was a community in which texts had constitutive importance—those who could read and interpret became leaders.

196. Stamps, "Use of the Old Testament in the New Testament," 17. See also Porter, "Paul and His Bible."

197. Revelation and Philippians are two texts in which all proposed Scripture references are tacit.

198. Jauhiainen, *Use of Zechariah in Revelation*, 33.

presence of an allusion depends upon identifying motifs shared between the texts—the proposed interpretation must appeal to perceived verbal or thematic parallels.[199] For example, John's use of horsemen instead of chariots in Rev 6:1–8 is one aspect that distinguishes Zech 1:8–17 from Zech 6:1–8 as the likely alluded-to text (despite both texts describing a number of horses of different colors). Furthermore, both Rev 6 and Zech 1 reflect a situation where the nations have the upper hand over God's people with the prospect of a future reversal. He concludes that the context of Zech 1:8–17 enhances the interpretation of Rev 6:1–8 because the horsemen in the former signal the imminent restoration of the people of God.[200] Jauhiainen thus appeals to shared motifs and thematic coherence or contextual affinity between texts to determine the presence and interpretation of an allusion (and to distinguish the correct text where there is more than one candidate).

Jauhiainen uses Ben-Porat's model, considering it to offer advantages such as distinguishing between allusions and echoes, and between two types of allusion based on reader competence. However, he stops short of exploiting the fullness of Ben-Porat's method choosing to concentrate on how it can help to define and categorize allusions such as "simple allusion," or "echo." Yet Ben-Porat proposes a detailed step-by-step process for the actualization of an allusion that describes "evoking the marked text as a whole in order to form maximum intertextual patterns." Although Jauhiainen accepts that this latter step is the main aim for which the literary allusion is employed, he does not apply the concept. This is not surprising since forming intertextual patterns embraces a semiotic hermeneutic which he seems to eschew.[201] Unlike Jauhiainen, and with Hays, we consider the best way to analyze alleged allusions is through an in-depth, intertextual, investigation. Consequently, we limit our research to an extensive use of Ben-Porat's method on the cluster of five allusions in Phil 2:10–16 (compared with Jauhiainen who analyzes 81 proposed allusions to Zechariah in Revelation but does not have time or space to explore the wider intertextual patterns made possible through Ben-Porat's model).[202]

However, notwithstanding his observations on Postmodernism, we concur with Jauhiainen that the plausibility of the presence and interpretation of an allusion cannot be argued from a set of criteria—analyzing allusion is, and remains, a subjective enterprise. After all, allusions are "allusive"

199. Ibid., 33.

200. Ibid., 63–65.

201. Ibid., 18. "From the perspective of the present study, there is nothing to be gained by the use of 'intertextuality' or its cognates." However, Ben-Porat's method is structuralist and she defines her stage 4 as "forming maximum intertextual patterns."

202. Ibid., 62, 102.

and, unlike quotations, there can be no certainty that an author intentionally incorporated the proposed allusion into his/her text; detecting allusions is a matter of intuition, guesswork, and our own and others's insights.[203] Consequently, as we saw above, published compendia of Scripture allusions tend to differ.[204] Essentially, Jauhiainen tests the proposal of an allusion (from published compendia) by offering a satisfactory interpretation which is left to the scholarly community to assess. He rightly notes that the issue is not how we identify allusions but are we able to argue that our reading of the text makes the most sense.[205] We will take a similar approach in our investigation by using a list of allusions already compiled from various sources. In analyzing each alleged allusion we will construe the evidence to support a certain interpretation which we believe coheres with Paul's argument as we have constructed it. We are not claiming that this is the correct interpretation, but that it is a possible interpretation that recognizes the presence and functioning of allusion and, importantly, one that considers epistolary argument as the constraining influence on the interpretation of allusion. We are essentially testing the suggestion of allusion within a new framework of constraint—epistolary argument as constructed from the rhetorical situation.

Andrew Wakefield

Wakefield investigates how the OT citations in Gal 3:1–14 function as intrinsic components of Paul's argument.[206] His investigation is driven by the tensions in six densely-packed citations of the OT in eight verses of Gal 3:6–13 and the search for a method to resolve them.[207] These tensions relate to apparent contradiction between citations, especially Deut 27:26 in Gal 3:10, Lev 18:5 in 3:12, and Hab 2:4 in 3:11 and their use in Paul's argument. According to Wakefield, the tensions only exist in a heuristic, or surface-level, reading of the passage and can be resolved in a deeper, intertextual reading. To achieve this intertextual reading Wakefield uses Riffaterre's model to treat Paul's use of citations in Gal 3:1–14 like "ungrammaticalities," or

---

203. Ibid., 27. See also McLean, *Citations and Allusions to Jewish Scriptures*, 2: "The identification of allusions and verbal parallels is, to a great extent, a matter of interpretation."

204. McLean, *Citations and Allusions to Jewish Scripture*, 2, identifies an allusion only if it is listed by both NA and UBS editions.

205. Jauhiainen, *Use of Zechariah in Revelation*, 34.

206. Wakefield, *Where to Live*, 6.

207. Gen 15:6 in Gal 3:6; Gen 12:3 in 3:8; Deut 27:26 in 3:10; Hab 2:4 in 3:11; Lev 18:5 in 3:12; Deut 21:23 in 3:13.

inconsistencies within the text, as the key to discovering its true unity and significance. In Riffaterre's model, the ungrammaticalities are equivalent and a variation or modulation of the same structural matrix. This matrix, from which the entire text is derived and its unity and significance found, is based on a commonplace or cliché—a phrase or sentence or even a single word. According to Wakefield, Paul carefully builds the citations into a chiastic structure that creates an intertextual connection, the crux of which is the innermost pair of citations (Hab 2:4 and Lev 18:5) in which the issue revolves around *carrying out life*, as opposed to *gaining life*.[208] He concludes that "where to live" (in the new creation instead of in the old age of which both the law and its curse are a part) is the matrix statement that best accounts for why Paul used the citations in Gal 3:1–14. This matrix resolves tensions between the citations by uniting them through a common theme and gives significance to the passage as a whole.[209] Wakefield concludes that the citations not only play a major role in Paul's thought and argument, but they may well act as the framework of his argument in this section of the letter.[210]

Wakefield also recognizes the importance of treating the citations in Gal 3:1–14 as a *group*, in order to see if any anomalies or intertextual clues may lurk in the overall structure and arrangement of the citations within Paul's argument.[211] Noting that previous approaches did not take seriously the unusual compactness of the citations and the possibility that they function *all together*, he adds that only in Galatians and Romans do we see such a concentration of OT references.[212] He contrasts his approach to those that perform a heuristic or mimetic reading of the text, analyzing the citations individually and focusing mostly on identifying source texts and Paul's modification of them.[213]

In using Riffaterre's model to find the matrix by which the OT citations in Gal 3:1–14 are brought into unity and significance,[214] Wakefield highlights three characteristics of Gal 3:1–14 that it shares with Phil 2:10–16. Firstly, both passages contain an unusual, tightly-packed grouping of OT

208. Wakefield, *Where to Live*, 138–9, 170.

209. Ibid., 134–36. These two citations are at the centre of the chiastic structure that conveys the blessing-curse-life motif in Gal 3:1–14.

210. Ibid., 137–38.

211. Ibid., 132. Italics his.

212. If we had to invent a "Scripture density index" for OT references in a NT passage, Gal 3:8–13 would have an "index" of 75 percent (6 citations in 8 verses). Phil 2:10–16 would have an "index" of 71 percent (5 allusions in 7 verses).

213. Wakefield, *Where to Live*, 132.

214. Ibid., 132.

references; secondly, both passages invite the possibility of determining a single theme that unites these references; thirdly, both passages offer the possibility that Paul's argument might become clearer through an intertextual reading that goes beyond the mimetic or surface-level reading. We will therefore take a similar approach to Wakefield by attempting to determine if an unwritten intertext can unite the suggested allusions. Any perceived unity might shed light on the question of whether or not the allusions play a major role in Paul's thought or even act as the framework of his argument in Phil 2:10–16. However, there are three key differences between Wakefield's use of Riffaterre and our own. Firstly, Wakefield can be more certain of identifying a cited text than we can of identifying an alluded-to text. Despite this, it might be argued that Riffaterre's model is more appropriate to a study of Philippians since most poetic texts do not overtly announce the presence of other texts by using introductory formulae—in other words, Riffaterre's poems do not cite, they allude. Secondly, and consequently, Wakefield does not evoke wider elements of the cited texts to interpret the citation-group;[215] although "where to live" defines the crucial intertext through which Gal 3:1–14 is interpreted, the contexts of the OT cited texts do not seem to play a major role in the interpretation.[216] However, unlike citation, the identification and interpretation of allusion are inextricably linked,[217] and require evocation of wider elements of the alluded-to text (Ben-Porat).[218] Thus, testing our hypothesis mandates a different and more expansive approach to the relationship between the epistolary argument and OT contexts—one that seeks to present different levels of plausibility as density and quality of interconnections between OT and NT contexts increase. Thirdly, Wakefield limits his choice of intertexts to those that are presupposed by the citations in Gal 3:1–14[219] and consequently does not offer a substantive analysis of the argument of Galatians as a whole. More particularly, "where to live" is the crucial intertext for Gal 3:1–14, but is it the crucial intertext for all of Galatians? In our case the crucial intertext is the epistolary argument or the rhetorical situation constructed from the body of the epistle.[220] Like

---

215. This is simply to recognize that citations and allusion might function differently.

216. See Wakefield, *Where to Live*, 140, 145–84, where he uses a "structural parallelism at a deeper level" and the idea of presupposed intertexts.

217. See our discussion of Hays and Jauhiainen above.

218. Contra Jauhiainen, we seek to arrive at stage four (the main aim of literary allusion) of Ben-Porat's process and form maximum intertextual patterns. This, we believe, will provide the most comprehensive and rigorous test of congruence between the alluding and alluded-to texts.

219. Wakefield, *Where to Live*, 145–46.

220. We treat the terms "crucial intertext," "epistolary argument" and "rhetorical

Wakefield, our proposal is that the crucial intertext (epistolary argument) is found at a deeper level and cannot be determined from a purely surface-level reading of the text. This crucial intertext gives significance, not only to the alleged allusions, but indeed the whole letter. It must also be pointed out that our intertext is constructed using an historical exegesis of Paul's text: we seek to find the epistolary argument from a rhetorical-exegesis of Phil 1:27—3:21. Such an intertextual approach to the text as a whole, and the allusions in particular, seem justified when we consider the lack of consensus regarding the meaning and unifying theme of Philippians and the current stalemate surrounding the role of the OT language in Phil 2:10–16.

PROCEDURE

The issue of how to deal with tacit references to the OT in Philippians would seem to have reached an impasse. In his paper presented at the SBL in 2009, Stephen Fowl concluded: "From the perspective of those contemporary scholars interested in the use of Scripture in Paul's letters, the example of Philippians is not particularly rich in material for examination."[221] Yet, even Fowl concedes the presence of OT language in the letter. Clearly a different approach is needed for how we should treat this language. In particular, is there an exegetical framework through which different conclusions can be reached regarding the OT in Philippians? One way forward would be a fresh approach to exegesis that advances a theoretical/exegetical framework through which tacit references to the OT in Phil 2:10–16 might be interpreted as functioning *argumentatively*. We have suggested that this framework involves proposing the epistolary argument of Philippians using a rhetorical-exegetical analysis and using it to control (constrain) the interpretation of the alleged allusions. If alluded-to texts are somehow variants of the rhetorical situation, then it can act as a constraint in the interpretation of allusions—in the sense that it limits activation of elements in the alluded-to text. Thus the epistolary argument must be established first in order to determine in what way the alluded-to texts might be variants of it. Or more precisely, can congruence between OT and NT contexts be established if certain elements in the alluded-to texts are evoked (instead of others) and compared with our construction of the epistolary argument? If so, possible allusions to the OT can be tested and interpreted. There are obvious complications with this approach.[222] The epistolary argument is our construction

situation" as synonymous.

221. Fowl, "Use of Scripture in Philippians," 14.

222. See Eriksson, *Traditions as Rhetorical Proof*, 65–67. He describes an

of what we believe to be Paul's perception of the situation gleaned from data presented in the text of Philippians. Moreover, we decide which elements to activate in the alluded-to texts in an attempt to establish degrees of congruence with this construction. However, a few points are worth noting. Firstly, although the epistolary argument is our opinion of why Paul wrote Philippians, it is not *merely* subjective nor been constructed without exegetical rigor. We might never know why Paul wrote to the Philippians, but we can suggest situations for which his letter seems a fitting response. This is simply to analyze those elements of Paul's text that can be described as his "communicative intentions." Fowl distinguishes between "motives" and "communicative intentions" the latter being a matter of attending to semantics, linguistic conventions, implication, and inference—a decidedly historical endeavor.[223] If the situation proposed most economically accounts for the greatest number of formal and semantic features in the passages exegeted, it has increased probability of being correct. We therefore seek to construct an epistolary argument that is within the range of textual plausibility. Secondly, we are setting out to test if intertextual linkages exist in Phil 2:10–16 and in particular if any circumstances can be proposed under which the alleged allusions can be viewed as functioning argumentatively. We aim for a demonstration of intertextuality that is within the bounds of imaginative possibility by establishing the existence of plausible elements of congruence among several passages and disparate texts. We should also remember that it is the lack of congruence between OT and NT contexts that leads contemporary scholars to refute the OT's influence in Philippians[224]—so, the congruence argument works both ways. The issue becomes one of whether to compare surface-level textual elements or deeper rhetorical-intertextual elements (argument) with OT context. Like Wakefield, we are not suggesting we are free to propose arbitrary intertexts, but one(s) that can be derived from Paul's text—specifically, from rhetorical exigencies and constraints incorporated in the text. As part of our exegesis, we will ask a key question of each textual unit examined: for what problem could this text be a fitting response? This requires us to expand our traditional historical-grammatical exegesis, which analyzes what Paul wrote, to ask why he wrote it and is

---

"unavoidable hermeneutical circle" facing both historical and rhetorical critics—"the reconstruction of the situation behind the text influences the interpretation of the text, at the same time as the interpretation of the text influences the reconstruction of the situation behind the text."

223. Fowl, "Use of Scripture in Philippians," 3; See also Brett, "Motives and Intentions in Genesis 1," 1–16.

224. See our comments on Reumann and Bormann above.

essentially the task of rhetorical criticism. Our interest is whether or not this approach will yield a plausible consideration of allusion as argumentative.

Consequently, the procedure followed in this investigation will be as follows. In chapter 2, section one we will survey several theories of the "rhetorical situation" and how the concept has been used in analyses of Philippians. In sections two and three we will critically evaluate various theories of intertextuality and allusion respectively, surveying several literary theorists who have made important contributions in these areas. Our purpose is to determine whether we can identify a suitable theoretical foundation for our critical investigation into Philippians—one that addresses the issues identified by our six questions above. In chapter 3, we lay the rhetorical-exegetical foundation for our investigation of Paul's use of Scripture in Phil 2:10–16. We analyze five key passages in an effort to determine Paul's argument in the letter: Phil 1:27–30; 2:1–4, 5–11, 14; 3:1–21. Our aim is to engage with the dominant interpretations of these passages and propose alternative interpretations which reflect the rhetorical situation for which the passages seem to be a fitting response. We are particularly interested in the possibility of an underlying unity that binds these passages together. In chapter 4, we will follow the process that defines the operation of actualizing a literary allusion for each of the five alleged literary allusions in Phil 2:10–16. Using the findings from this analysis, along with insights from situational rhetoric and intertextuality, we will propose how the allusions function and contribute to the meaning of Philippians.

CHAPTER 2

Theories and Methodologies

IN THIS CHAPTER WE will present and appraise the theories and methods that are particularly appropriate for testing the proposal that Paul intentionally authored a cluster of literary allusions to Scripture in Phil 2:10–16. To recapitulate, the six key questions foundational to our exegesis of Phil 2:10–16 are:

1. How are allusions detected?
2. How are allusions defined and interpreted?
3. What special consideration, if any, should be given to the interpretation of a cluster of successive allusions, most of which occur in a single sentence?
4. Given that allusion is a form of tacit reference, how can its interpretation be reasonably (exegetically) constrained?
5. What role should audience recognition and authorial intention play in our analysis of Paul's use of allusion?
6. What role does epistolary argument play in the interpretation of allusions?

The first step is to evaluate a method to determine the epistolary argument of Philippians because our test for allusion is essentially a test of congruence between epistolary argument and Scripture context.

SITUATIONAL RHETORIC

The task of finding the historical situation has traditionally been one of the key factors in interpreting New Testament texts. It describes the circumstances that lead to the text being produced and is often referred to as the "epistolary occasion." Recently, rhetorical criticism has grown in popularity as a method of analyzing New Testament texts.[1] This criticism has used both classical and modern theories to develop the concept of the "rhetorical situation."[2] These two approaches to rhetorical criticism of the NT can be broadly categorized as an historical-critical approach using classical Greco-Roman rhetoric, and a literary-critical approach that uses modern theories of rhetoric called "the new rhetoric." Both methods have offered insights into the interpretation of Philippians. The focus of scholars using the classical method tended to be on the arrangement of the texts, or the *dispositio*. Although providing useful insights into the fundamental characteristics of oral and written arguments, this approach tended to concentrate on the form and function of the text when compared with other ancient examples of rhetoric.[3] During the last two decades, however, scholarly attention has been drawn to the rhetorical argumentation in the text through its distinctive features and means of proof. Some writers are seeking to understand how various biblical authors present their arguments, support their claims, and attempt to persuade their readers. In this investigation, we will appeal more to the modern theories of rhetoric, in which rhetoric is essentially related to situation, with an emphasis on the author's perspective as a factor in determining the historical audience and problem. We therefore propose that Bitzer's theory of situational rhetoric can assist our exegesis of Philippians through a construction of the epistolary argument and hypothetical historical situation of the epistle.

---

1. See Porter and Olbricht, *Rhetoric and the New Testament*; Porter and Olbricht, *Rhetoric, Scripture and Theology*; Porter and Olbricht, *Rhetorical Analysis of Scripture*; Porter and Stamps, *Rhetorical Interpretation of Scripture*; Porter and Stamps, *Rhetorical Criticism and the Bible*; Eriksson et al., *Rhetorical Argumentation in Biblical Texts*; Olbricht and Sumney, *Paul and Pathos*; Watson, "New Testament and Greco-Roman Rhetoric," 465–72.

2. See Thurén, *Rhetorical Strategy of 1 Peter*, 70–75.

3. There is no consensus on the rhetorical genre of Philippians, although the majority opt for *deliberative* (for example, Watson, "Rhetorical Analysis of Philippians," 59) while others prefer *epideictic* (Kennedy, *Rhetorical Criticism*, 77). Neither is there agreement on the rhetorical arrangement. Compare, for example, Bloomquist, *Suffering*, 121 and Witherington III, *Friendship*, 18–19.

Lloyd Bitzer—The Rhetorical Situation

Lloyd Bitzer was the first to treat the "rhetorical situation" as a distinct subject in rhetorical theory. In his 1968 article, he suggested that "the rhetorical situation" is the context in which speakers or writers create rhetorical discourse. The situation controls the rhetorical response in the same sense that the question controls the answer.[4] Yet he wants to avoid the idea that rhetorical discourse is a response to general circumstances: "We need to understand that a particular discourse comes into existence because of some specific condition or situation which invites utterance."[5] For Bitzer, the *particularity* of the discourse is the result of the *specificity* of the situation. Bitzer defines the rhetorical situation as "a complex of persons, events, objects, and relations presenting an actual or potential exigency which can be completely or partially removed if discourse, introduced into the situation, can so constrain human decision or action as to bring about the significant modification of the exigency."[6] Prior to the discourse being composed there are three constituents of any rhetorical situation: *the exigency, the audience* to be constrained in decision and action, and *the constraints* which influence the author and can be brought to bear upon the audience. First, the exigency is an imperfection marked by urgency, a defect, or obstacle waiting to be overcome. Bitzer claims that any context results in numerous exigencies. However, those which come about of necessity, for example, death or winter, cannot be changed by discourse and are therefore not rhetorical. "In any rhetorical situation there will be at least one controlling exigency which functions as the organizing principle: it specifies the audience to be addressed and the change to be effected."[7] According to Bitzer, when the controlling exigency is perceived as strong and important by the rhetor, then it constrains his thought and action. Second, Bitzer suggests that the rhetorical audience must be distinguished from a body of mere hearers, and include only those persons capable of being influenced by the discourse and of being mediators of change. Rhetoric functions ultimately to produce action or change in the world by altering reality through the mediation of thought and action—the rhetor creates the discourse, his/her audience being the mediator of change.[8] Third, Bitzer conceives of rhetorical situations that contain constraints made up of persons, events, objects, and relations

---

4. Bitzer, "Situation," 251.
5. Ibid., 250.
6. Ibid., 252.
7. Ibid., 253.
8. Ibid., 250.

which have power to constrain decision and action needed to modify the exigency. Among these are beliefs, attitudes, documents, facts, traditions, and images. Additionally, the rhetor introduces his/her own constraints into the situation when the discourse is created; the rhetor's personal character, logical proofs, and style become constraints.[9]

Bitzer also chronicles key characteristics and features of a rhetorical situation. Firstly, the situation prompts the writing of the rhetoric, for which it is a fitting response: in other words, the rhetoric must address the pressing issues of the situation. As such, the situation must somehow prescribe and constrain the response. The situation is not determined by the rhetor's intentions nor the audience's demands or expectations; the former is determined by the situation and the latter is keyed to the situation.[10] Secondly, the rhetorical situation which generates rhetorical discourse is located in reality, and is not the product of a rhetor's imaginary mind at play. Thus the complex of persons, objects, events, and relations which generate the rhetorical situation are objective and publicly observable facts in the world we experience.[11]

Responses to Bitzer

Bitzer's theory has prompted various responses, especially in the debate concerning the depiction of "reality" in rhetorical situations.[12] For example, Miller cautions that the rhetorical response is a perception of the rhetor—the ultimate or perceived nature of the exigence is a conclusion in the mind of its perceiver.[13] Vatz, arguing along similar lines, claims that rhetorical response (discourse) is not determined nor called into existence by the situation, but that the rhetorical response controls the situation as the author (rhetor) creates meaning from certain facts.[14] In contrast to Vatz, Brinton argues that the exigency is a property of a set of facts. Thus, the rhetor finds or discovers the situation and reacts to it evaluatively. The rhetor's rhetorical acts are his response to a set of given facts and are thus grounded in the rhe-

---

9. Ibid., 254.
10. Ibid., 255–56.
11. Ibid., 256–57.
12. Bitzer, "Functional Communication," 25. According to Bitzer, the rhetorical situation includes thoughts (of the rhetor and audience,) as well as 'things,' as part of historic reality. This calls attention to the close relationship of pragmatic communications to actual historic conditions.
13. Miller, "Rhetorical Exigence," 111–12.
14. Vatz, "Myth," 154–61.

torical situation.[15] Similarly, Consigny notes that the rhetorical situation is not one created solely through the imagination and discourse of the rhetor. It involves particularities of persons, actions, and agencies in a certain place and time; and the rhetor cannot ignore these constraints if he is to function effectively."[16] Thus, even though rhetorical discourse contains the author's perceptions, these cannot be merely personal preference or speculation. Instead, the discourse is shaped by rhetorical realities shared between author and audience.[17] The communal nature (that is, shared by author and audience) of rhetorical realities is described by Hunsaker and Smith who suggest that the rhetorical situation allows certain issues and prevents others. The issues are mental constructs whose actualization requires the commonality of perception of rhetor and audience. The issues created by the rhetor are entextualized and are consistent with and complementary to those already perceived by the actual audience.[18] Such an approach to situational rhetoric allows us to consider that Paul's reading of the situation in Philippi overlaps with that of the Philippians themselves—Paul is not addressing an unreal situation in Philippi.[19]

Such a conclusion drawn from the use of situational rhetoric leads us to survey the reception of Bitzer's ideas among biblical scholars. The need for a method of reconstructing the historical setting of a biblical text using rhetorical criticism is highlighted by Mack: "The move from rhetorical analysis to the social setting of a text is not yet a dominant feature of this scholarship [rhetorical criticism]. It is no doubt too soon to expect elaborate reconstructions of the social implications uncovered in the investigation of a rhetorical situation."[20] Although the proposals of using rhetorical criticism to reconstruct historical occasion have not met with widespread favor,[21] important ideas have been developed by several scholars.

---

15. Brinton, "Situation," 246–47.

16. Consigny, "Rhetoric," 178.

17. Patton, "Causation," 49. See also Fiorenza, *Revelation*, 188.

18. Hunsaker and Smith, "Nature of Issues," 155–56.

19. Cf. Schmithals, *Paul and the Gnostics*, 70: "Paul himself is probably too little informed to be able to give more concrete admonitions [to the Philippians]."

20. Mack, *Rhetoric and the New Testament*, 24.

21. For a brief survey on the use of rhetorical criticism to reconstruct historical situation see Olbricht, "Classical Rhetorical Criticism," 108–24. He concludes that rhetorical genres are unlikely to prove beneficial in determining an audience's profile.

George Kennedy

Kennedy recognizes that rhetoric is that quality in discourse by which a speaker or writer seeks to accomplish his purposes.[22] Rhetorical criticism "takes the text as we have it and looks at it from the point of view of the author's intent, the unified results and how it would be perceived by an audience of near contemporaries."[23] Kennedy considers rhetoric to be a universal phenomenon, a universal facet of human communication conceptualized by the Greeks.[24] He deviates from Bitzer's theory by suggesting that the rhetorical situation corresponds to the *Sitz im Leben* of form criticism.[25] He also suggests that in many rhetorical situations the speaker will be faced with one overriding rhetorical problem which exists as a difficulty the audience might have in accepting the rhetor's argument. According to Kennedy, the rhetor anticipates this problem and addresses it in the beginning of the discourse before engaging with the central problem.[26]

Two important aspects of Kennedy's theory are worthy of comment. Firstly, Kennedy incorrectly assumes that the historical and rhetorical situations are identical.[27] This leads to reconstructions of the rhetorical situation from "facticities" recorded in the text, rather than the argument of the letter. Secondly, Kennedy seems to confuse the function of Bitzer's "exigency" with his own "rhetorical problem." Bitzer defines the controlling exigency as that dominating imperfection that must be overcome by the introduction of rhetorical discourse. Kennedy, on the other hand, describes an overriding *rhetorical problem* that seems to be a further barrier to the success of the rhetoric. He describes *the* problem that must be addressed before bringing up *the central problem*.[28] Two notable studies of the rhetorical situation of Philippians that follow Kennedy are, P. Holloway, *Consolation in Philippians: Philosophical Sources and Rhetorical Strategy* (Cambridge: CUP, 2001) and D.K. Williams, *Enemies of the Cross of Christ: The Terminology of the Cross and Conflict in Philippians* (London: Sheffield Academic, 2002). In our opinion, they both fail to identify the controlling exigency that divides the

---

22. Kennedy, *Rhetorical Criticism*, 3.

23. Ibid., 4–5. Kennedy argues that the intention of the biblical writers is what distinguishes rhetorical criticism from literary criticism of the Bible.

24. Ibid., 10–11.

25. Ibid., 34.

26. Ibid., 36.

27. See also Stamps, "Rethinking," 194–98; Watson, "Contributions," 129–30.

28. Kennedy, *Rhetorical Criticism*, 36.

Philippian community because they adopt Kennedy's notion of the "rhetorical problem" rather than Bitzer's "exigency."[29]

Wilhelm Wuellner

Wuellner proposes that Paul's letters are neither propositional theology nor literature, but argumentation.[30] Argumentation is the use of discourse "to influence the intensity of an audience's adherence to certain theses," and is basically a rhetorical process.[31] He suggests that Paul's method of arguing was self-consciously Greek and that he had skill in rhetoric.[32] Wuellner utilizes both ancient and modern rhetorical theories, drawing on the framework of argumentation advanced by Perelman, but also proposing a case for the epideictic genre. Wuellner proposes that the framework of argumentation is determined by three factors; the argumentative situation, the need for Paul to interpret his audience, and the relationship between argumentation and praxis: "The choice of the actual argument in 1 Cor. is mainly made in the light of the action or commitment desired by Paul, and only secondarily so by the attitude of opponents."[33] In contrast to Kennedy, Wuellner affirms that the argumentative (rhetorical) situation is not the same as the historical situation or the *Sitz im Leben* of form criticism. "The rhetorical situation differs both from the historical situation of a given author and reader and from the generic situation or conventions of the *Sitz im Leben* of forms or genres in one point: the rhetorical critic looks foremost for the premises of a text as appeal or argument."[34] For Wuellner, discussion of the rhetorical situation is the necessary precursor to analysis of invention, or argumentation.[35]

Elizabeth Schüssler Fiorenza

Fiorenza is interested in whether a critical rhetorical interpretation of Paul's letter (to the Corinthians) is able to shed light on the actual historical

---

29. Holloway suggests that the controlling exigency in Philippians is the distress the Philippians felt over Paul's imprisonment (*Consolation*, 55). Williams proposes two controlling exigencies—unity (or disunity) and opponents and suffering (*Enemies*, 98).

30. Wuellner, "Paul's Rhetoric," 334.

31. Ibid., 330. He draws on the work of Perelman and Olbrechts-Tyteca, *New Rhetoric*, 14.

32. Wuellner, "Greek Rhetoric," 177.

33. Ibid., 183.

34. Wuellner, "Rhetorical Criticism," 456.

35. Ibid., 455.

communicative situation to which the letter is addressed.[36] She proposes a way of moving from the "world of the text" of Paul to the actual world of the Corinthian community.[37] Following Wayne Booth, she distinguishes between the actual author/audience and implied author/audience.[38] The actual author and audience are the real, historical persons of Paul and the Corinthians. The implied author is not the real author, but the picture, shadow or image of the real author constructed by the reader of the text. For example, the Paul constructed from Philippians is a Hebrew of Hebrews and a persecutor of the church. Yet the Paul constructed from 1 Corinthians is not the same "shadow." The implied audience, or implied intended audience, is the more idealized audience Paul has in mind and creates in the text. Paul assumes that this idealized audience possesses the knowledge necessary to actualize the text's meaning and respond to it. The implied audience is called upon to agree with the values of the implied author.[39] Fiorenza reconstructs the rhetorical situation from an analysis of 1 Cor 1:11—4:21; 9; 15:1–12 and 16:5–11 and concludes that Paul argues for his authority as *sole* founder and father of the Corinthian Church.[40] Then, she reconstructs the historical situation as one where the Corinthians had competing interpretations and practices about what it meant to realize the "new life" in Christ. The value of Fiorenza's work is her proposal that situational rhetorical criticism offers a mediating position between historical and literary criticism. She proposes that the concept of the rhetorical situation might help to gain access to the historical communicative situation of New Testament writings.[41] Our investigation will follow Fiorenza's pattern insofar as we view Philippians as following this communicative model in which the ethical and ideological content of the message is the produce of the "implied author" (the Paul who wrote Philippians)[42] and derives from his values and beliefs. The implied author is the author whom we (as the actual, contemporary reader) reconstruct from the text. The counterpart to the "implied author" is the "implied audience" or original intended audience (the Philippians). The "implied audience" is the product of the author's perception. Fiorenza has also demonstrated that a reconstruction of the historical situation from

---

36. Fiorenza, "Rhetorical Situation," 387. Although she deals with 1 Corinthians, her methodology can be used with any of Paul's letters.

37. Ibid., 388.

38. Booth, *Rhetoric*, 70–71.

39. Ibid., 138. See also Suleiman, "Introduction," 14.

40. Fiorenza, "Rhetorical Situation," 397. Italics hers.

41. Ibid., 387.

42. Booth, *Rhetoric*, 71. "[an author's] different works will imply different versions [of himself]."

the rhetorical situation is possible. This is perhaps the most difficult task, yet considering Paul's letter as a fitting response to both rhetorical and historical situations aids in the endeavor.

Other scholars such as Duane Watson and Dennis Stamps have critiqued Bitzer on the key issue of the reality of the rhetorical situation and its relationship to argumentation. Watson credits Bitzer with the seminal contribution on rhetorical situation and recognizes that such an approach to rhetoric moves beyond form to functional analysis as questions arise about why Paul used certain rhetorical features. He acknowledges the distinction between the rhetorical and historical situation and their relatedness and is the only writer we have encountered who suggests that Paul's use of the OT is an inartificial proof of argument.[43] Dennis Stamps argues that the story embedded in an epistle is the literary-rhetorical situation and, although references to it are "randomly" interspersed throughout the letter, it can be extracted from the letter message by identifying the deictic references to the situation or the situation specificity between letter parties.[44] We agree with Stamps that the clue to recovering the rhetorical situation from the text lies in the specificity of the references Paul uses. We suggest that the "narrative specifics" are to be found in the admonitions and imperatives Paul uses and not merely deictic references. We will argue that certain parts of Paul's discourse reveal the prominent theme in the narrative behind the letter to the Philippians—this narrative must make sense of the particular concerns addressed by Paul in his letter. For the remainder of this study, we will use "central theme," "epistolary argument" and "rhetorical situation" as synonymous terms.

Conclusions

Bitzer's theory provides a key methodological impetus for our investigation for two reasons. Firstly, his idea that rhetoric is *functional communication* is helpful since it can be used to interpret Paul's letter as a text arising out of a human context—the context of Paul and the Philippians. Paul and the Philippians belong to social and political history, and as a writer of rhetorical discourse, Paul desires to instigate change through persuasion. It is because the environment and persons involved in Philippians invite change that a

---

43. Watson, "Contributions," 135.

44. Stamps, "Rethinking," 201, 209. Deictic references are those referring to the relationship between the letter parties and the circumstances about how the letter came to be. Deictic grammar includes words like "this," "here," "now," "you," etc.

rhetorical approach to Paul's letter is appropriate.[45] This rhetorical approach views the literary text as a form of communication through which author and audience share perceptions of factual conditions, with the controlling exigency as one possible interpretation of those factual conditions.[46] Yet, what makes rhetoric functional is that it alters the situation, through the mediating thoughts and actions of the audience. This helps our understanding of the audience as those who are capable of facilitating the change desired by Paul, and not merely the whole congregation, or everybody who reads or hears his message: "*Listeners/readers of rhetorical discourse who are incapable of positively modifying the exigence are not a rhetorical or functional audience.*"[47] Moreover, Bitzer's idea that the controlling exigency, when perceived as strong and important by the rhetor, constrains his thought and action is an important consideration when attempting to construct the rhetorical situation of Philippians. The rhetorical situation is constructed from Paul's conclusions about the Philippians presented in the letter. Therefore the exigency of the rhetorical situation determines the language he uses, implicitly and explicitly, in the production of his text. As we argued in chapter 1, this is no more than to acknowledge that Paul writes a pastoral response to a particular situation, and his language will be constrained by that situation. Yet Bitzer's theory proposes that the pastoral response (that is, the rhetorical discourse) must be both a *specific* and *fitting* response that addresses the pressing issues of the situation. In our exegesis of Philippians in chapter 3 we will consider the specificity of Paul's language and how it can be a fitting response to the problem in Philippi.

Secondly, Bitzer's theory of situational rhetoric can assist our exegesis of Philippians through the construction of the epistolary argument and hypothetical historical situation of the epistle. This is because our study uniquely proposes that epistolary argument should be used in the test of congruence when deliberating the presence and function of tacit Scripture references in Philippians. As we shall see, the epistolary argument (rhetorical situation) can be used (by us) to control the intertextual patterning produced in the processing of literary allusions (as our test for allusions). Although there have been several useful analyses of Philippians using

---

45. Bitzer, "Functional Communication," 26.

46. Cf. Marshall, "Ethical Appeal," 361, who suggests that Paul did not know what he was writing against, given the lack of consensus in NT scholarship; Räisänen, *Paul and the Law*, 228. See van Spanje, *Inconsistency in Paul?*, 197–99, who notes that the presence of rhetoric in Paul's texts renders as incorrect Räisänen's assessment of certain of Paul's texts being interpreted only in terms of logic.

47. Bitzer, "Functional Communication," 23. Italics mine. See also Wichelns, "Differences," 221.

rhetorical criticism,[48] and four that have referenced Bitzer's theoretical framework in their interpretations of the letter,[49] we are not aware of any monograph that substantively treats situational rhetoric and intertextuality as complementary methodologies in an interpretation of a NT letter.

INTERTEXTUALITY

Intertextuality as a concept or theory[50] grew out of the revolutionary atmosphere of French poststructuralist ideology in the 1960s.[51] The term "intertextuality" was first used by Julia Kristeva in her presentation of texts, plurality in their meaning, and indeterminacy of their origins. The concept was developed by Roland Barthes in his theory of text, and his mode of interpretation that displaces the author with the reader in the production of meaning.[52] The ideological motivations that lie behind Kristeva's and Barthes's theory of intertextuality explain much of its complexity, and, for some, call into question its validity for use with biblical texts.[53] Neverthe-

48. Notably, Bloomquist, *Suffering*; Witherington III, *Friendship*; Geoffrion, *Rhetorical Purpose*; Watson, "Rhetorical Analysis of Philippians"; Davis, *Oral Biblical Criticism*; Marchal, *Hierarchy*. See also the collection in Porter and Olbricht (eds.), 1993.

49. Holloway, *Consolation*; Williams, *Enemies*; Robuck, *Christ-Hymn*, 155, has a section on "rhetorical situation," but does not develop the idea as advanced by Bitzer. He settles on correct mental attitude as the overarching theme, with no single rhetorical problem. Fields, *Paul as Model*, 101, 161, argues that Paul is influenced by the OT tradition that Israel was a model of a nation in relationship with God. However, he does not use "situational rhetoric" as defined.

50. Intertextuality is a theoretical rather than methodological term according to Beale, "Ideology," 27. See also Moyise, "Intertextuality and Historical Approaches," 447; Orr, *Intertextuality*; Allen, *Intertextuality*; Worton and Still, "Introduction"; Clayton and Rothstein, "Figures"; Friedman, "Weavings"; Keefer, "Reports."

51. Irwin, "Intertextuality," 231, identifies four major motivating factors for Kristeva's and Barthes's intertextuality—the oppression of the French Academy, post holocaust pessimism, mistrust of communications, and Marxist principles. It is beyond the scope of this study to engage with these issues, but we take note of Irwin's analysis and the association of intertextuality with poststructuralist ideology which opposes the notion of author-influence. We do not believe it necessary to reject a theory nor a practice of intertextuality because of this association, as we shall see. See also Mai, "Bypassing Intertextuality," 41: "Kristeva's intertextuality is a politically transformative practice, aimed at empowering the reader/critic to oppose the literary and social traditions at large."

52. See Kristeva, "Word"; Kristeva, "Revolution"; Kristeva, *Desire in Language*; Barthes, "Death"; Barthes, "Work to Text"; Barthes, "Theory"; Barthes, *S/Z*.

53. Hatina, "Intertextuality," 32. He claims that intertextuality replaces the rules of reason and identity by the notion of "contradiction"; Irwin, "Intertextuality," 235; Elam, "Intertextuality," 621.

less, our interest is in the appropriateness of intertextuality as a means of investigating Paul's use of Scripture in Philippians. Consequently, the kind of intertextuality proposed by Kristeva and Barthes does not provide an effective tool for analyzing literary texts. This is due to a central tenet of the concept—it designates a vast and undefined discursive space; the texts which provide meaning to any text are untraceable and anonymous, and any attempt to identify them results in a violation of the theory itself. Without reference to some particular pretext, or even a particular edition of a text, it is difficult to begin an intertextual inquiry. A critical intertextual investigation on specific biblical texts cannot proceed from this theoretical foundation. However, two aspects of the theory offer intriguing challenges for a study of Philippians. Firstly, the idea that intertextual or discursive space can be used to explain the writing and reading dynamics when two or more texts interact. Secondly, the idea that a "volume of secondary or derived, associated senses, the semantic 'vibrations' can be grafted on to a denoted message";[54] although we might prefer to consider the plurality of 'significant associations' connoted rather than polysemy. As we shall now see, Michael Riffaterre has developed a theory of intertextuality different from those of Kristeva and Barthes and one which has been used in the interpretation of a cluster of Scripture citations in Paul's letter to the Galatians.

Michael Riffaterre

In the *Semiotics of Poetry* (1978), Michael Riffaterre advances a theory of reading based on the structure of meaning in poems. In contrast to the poststructuralism of Kristeva's and Barthes's open text, Riffaterre theorizes about how readers perceive meaning in a closed text, with intertexuality as the means of achieving this. He is interested in what the reader must know and do to understand the significance of a text: "An intertext is one or more texts which the reader must know in order to understand a work of literature in terms of its overall significance (as opposed to the discrete meanings of its successive words, phrases, and sentences)."[55]

Riffaterre's intertextuality is therefore pragmatic, describing a comprehensive convention for reading literary texts.[56] However, he claims that the text itself guides the reader towards the intertexts required to complete meaning: "the intertext leaves an indelible trace in the text, a formal con-

---

54. Barthes, "Theory," 37.

55. Riffaterre, "Compulsory," 56. Although focusing on reader-perception in poetry, he considers intertextuality as the reading method for all literature.

56. Mai, "Bypassing Intertextuality," 46.

stant which plays the role of an imperative for reading, and which governs the decoding of the message."[57] The trace of the intertext is left by what Riffaterre calls "ungrammaticalities" on the surface of the text; these appear as deviations in syntax or vocabulary which do not make sense in the framework of ordinary language.[58] They are usually contradictions in the text, but spurious syntax, or quotations can also be ungrammaticalities.[59] Riffaterre argues that the act of reading involves two stages.

The first stage, "linguistic competence," involves the reader in detecting the ungrammaticalities on the surface of the text; this is a mimetic[60] reading which fails to resolve the difficulties posed by the ungrammaticalities. The reader then enters stage two, "literary competence." Here, rereading of the text is required along with the reader bringing together his/her familiarity with descriptive systems, clichés, themes, society's mythologies, and other texts.[61] This second reading results in a semiotic process which takes place in the reader's mind wherein the difficulties posed by the ungrammaticalities are resolved[62]—the significance of the poem is never located in the first "heuristic" phase of reading, but only appears during the "retroactive" or "hermeneutic" phase. According to Riffaterre, meaning is conveyed at the mimetic level, significance at the semiotic level of reading.

In Riffaterre's model, the descriptive systems or clichés which contribute to the reader's literary competence are *hypograms*, or pre-existent word groups. These hypograms serve as "thematic complexes" which are already set in the reader's mind allowing him/her to fill the gaps in the mimetic reading. They are recognized by words embedded in a sentence and are components and variants of a matrix which is determinate for the text to be interpreted.[63] This matrix is hypothetical, being only the grammatical and lexical actualization of an abstract structure made known to the reader by the presence of its variants, the ungrammaticalities.[64] The matrix can be reduced to a word, phrase, or idea and the whole poem is derived from it (an expansion of it, or a transformation of it).[65] For example, *In Deserto* by

57. Riffaterre, "La Trace de l'intertexte," 5.
58. Riffaterre, *Semiotics*, 2; Morgan, "Intertext," 25.
59. Riffaterre, *Semiotics*, 4–5. See also Worton and Still, "Introduction," 27. Riffaterre offers an example of an ungrammaticality from the poem, "Comme deux gouttes d'eau" by Paul Eluard: " . . . I have been keeping false treasures in empty wardrobes."
60. The literary representation of reality.
61. Riffaterre, *Semiotics*, 5.
62. Ibid., 4.
63. We understand the hypogram to be referenced by the ungrammaticality.
64. Ibid., 19.
65. See Allen's glossary in *Intertextuality*, 215.

Theophile Gautier is derived from, "the despair of one crying out in the desert."[66] The concept of intertextuality enters through the structural matrix, or the semiotic grid which is the site of textual interaction. Central to Riffaterre's model is the idea that a text and its intertexts are variants of the same structural matrix (the crucial intertext). The reader recognizes that successive ungrammaticalities are equivalents and variants of the same structural matrix.[67] The text itself is a variation or modulation of one structure (thematic, symbolic, or other).

Although Riffaterre is primarily interested in reading convention, in his model of intertextuality it is the text that controls the reader's interpretation.[68] The idiolect is the text produced by an individual using the sociolect (the language of the group). The sociolect is already actualized within the reader's mind, enabling him/her to arrive at the one, correct interpretation of the text. Indeed, Riffaterre argues that the text is a hierarchy of representations imposed upon the reader despite his personal preference.[69] He argues against Barthes's *aleatory*[70] intertextuality in favor of *obligatory* intertextuality, where the reader is constrained by, and obliged to recover, the intertexts that result in the one, correct interpretation of the text. The intertexts constrain the reader's freedom—without this constraint, the reader can freely associate whatever texts s/he has read at the moment of reading—these might be accidental associations due to similarities in lexicon or situation.[71] The literary intertexts the reader is obliged to discover are restricted to those pointed to by the ungrammaticalities. Paradoxically, what the reader is obliged to discover, s/he might never discover. Here Riffaterre proposes the concept of "minimal reader response"[72] wherein the reader is aware of the intertext's existence, yet is unable to recover it. For Riffaterre this is nonetheless an intertextual reading of the text, since an unknown intertext has been presupposed by the reader. The lack of distinction between ordinary and sophisticated readers would seem to constitute a weakness in Riffaterre's theory.[73]

66. Riffaterre, *Semiotics*, 6–12.
67. Ibid., 6.
68. Ibid., 81.
69. Ibid., 12.
70. Highly improvised readings that seek to obtain freedom from the past and academic strictures.
71. Cf. Sandmel, "Parallelomania," 1–13 and, below, the notion of Irwin's "unsuccessful allusion."
72. Riffaterre, "Compulsory," 57.
73. Riffaterre, *Semiotics*, 16–19. However, his theory does allow for the reader to learn. See also Riffaterre, "Interview," 14; Riffaterre, "Interpretation and Undecidability,"

Riffaterre argues that the poet creates the poem by taking a word or sentence and expanding it into a text using a series of hypograms (descriptive systems or clichés common to the sociolect) which are modified to make them variants of the structural matrix. The reader recognizes the reference to the hypograms when language fails at the mimetic level. The incompatibilities in the text vanish once the text is read the way the text was built to be read.[74] To discover the true meaning of a poem, one must interpret it in accordance with the principles by which it was constructed.[75] Although he is concerned with reader perception, Riffaterre opens the door to a consideration of poem (text) construction since his reader must take account of some originating pre-existent word group (the hypogram) of which each segment in the poem is a variant;[76] the reader must work his/her way back to the structures that generated the text.[77] As Worton and Still point out, Riffaterre is aware of the author's choice of pretext,[78] but focuses on the effect on the reader of intertextual presupposition.[79]

Evaluation: Clusters and Constraints

According to Riffaterre, the intertextual method of reading guides the reader to the one, correct interpretation of the text.[80] Thus, with a limited set of intertexts (those pointed to by the ungrammaticalities), and the eschewing of open-ended meaning for the text (each text is derived from a *determinate*, structural matrix) Riffaterre demonstrates an intertextual theory and praxis distanced from the poststructuralist intertextuality of Kristeva and Barthes with its infinitude of intertextual relations.[81] There are several aspects of Riffaterre's model that are of particular interest to an investigation of Paul's alleged use of a successive cluster of pretexts (Scripture) in his letter to the Philippians.

227–42.

74. Riffaterre, *Semiotics*, 85.

75. Culler, *Pursuit*, 98–99, says that Riffaterre thus operates with a method of interpretation based on a theory of origins.

76. Worton and Still, "Introduction," 25.

77. Riffaterre, *Semiotics*, 168.

78. An anterior literary text.

79. Worton and Still, "Introduction," 27.

80. Clayton and Rothstein, "Figures," 24.

81. See also Genette, *Palimpsests*. See Pfister's evaluation of Genette in "Intertextuality," 210–11.

Firstly, Riffaterre limits the intertexts to those determined from the text itself through the identification of ungrammaticalities. The ungrammaticalities point to previous word groups or hypograms that are diachronically related to the text—the text has literary pretexts. The ungrammaticalities are formal constants which leave a trace of an intertext, the retrieval of which is within the grasp of the reader on subsequent readings. This idea is similar to the concepts of quotation and allusion which rely on textual elements (fragments of other texts) to alert readers to the presence of other texts and traditions.

Secondly, Riffaterre's method is text-centered, yet the only significant structure in interpretation is that which the reader can perceive.[82] Surprisingly however, the reader cannot fail to perceive it. Riffaterre's claim that even the most ordinary reader has the linguistic and literary competence to detect the ungrammaticalities and resolve them in a second, retroactive reading, is doubtful. However, his idea about two-stages of reading and its impact on the competency of the reader raises the nub of a problem in intertextual research, namely, prior knowledge of the reader/text.[83] On a related point, Riffaterre does not give much attention to the possibility of something of the author's intentions being recovered from the text. Yet the reader discovers the poet's ungrammaticalities which lead him/her to the recovery of the poet's original structural matrix from the semiotic grid. It seems that the poet and reader must, at least, share something in common for the recovery of meaning through textual semiotics. What Riffaterre seems to achieve in his theory is a synergy between poet and reader mediated through the semiotic matrix—the text is read in the way the text was built to be read. How far this claim can be taken in terms of Paul's letter to the Philippians will be addressed in this study. Riffaterre's position on the readers's literary competence raises issues as to what other texts, descriptive systems, and social mythologies constitute the customary knowledge of a community of readers,[84] but he also implies intentional, authorial activity in the origins of a text's structures.[85]

Thirdly, and most pertinently, Riffaterre demonstrates a non-poststructuralist theory of intertextuality that seems compatible with the

---

82. Clayton and Rothstein, "Figures," 23.

83. Orr, *Intertextuality*, 39.

84. Clayton and Rothstein, "Figures," 26, rightly note that literary, not linguistic, competence is in view.

85. Riffaterre, *Semiotics*, 150. Riffaterre maintains that the relevance of poetics is to the text itself, not to the author's intention (ibid., 169–70). Cf. Chandler, "Romantic Allusiveness," 464–65.

historical-critical exegesis in this study.[86] The idea of a poem containing a succession of ungrammaticalities which all point to precursor hypograms corresponds to the notion of a cluster of allusions in Philippians referring to a group of Scripture pretexts. Furthermore, the concept of a structural matrix from which the whole poem is derived, can be thought of in terms of the central or main theme of the epistle occasioned by some controlling exigency—the rhetorical situation. Additionally, the summarizing of the structural matrix by a single word or phrase is compatible with the tradition of NT exegetes who have done likewise with the central unifying theme of Paul's letters (we saw examples of this in chapter one). Yet Riffaterre's ungrammaticalities are equivalent and the hypograms are variants of the structural matrix. Thus, his model allows for an explanation of the presence of the cluster of ungrammaticalities based on the relatedness of the variants (to which the ungrammaticalities point) to the structural matrix. From the poet's or analyst's perspective, the ungrammaticalities have been chosen and embedded in the poem *because* the hypograms are variants of the poem's originating structure. Riffaterre's model provides a schema for testing: can the presence of an unusual cluster of Scripture references in Phil 2:10-16 be explained in terms of the relatedness of the broader context of those Scripture texts to the central or main theme of Philippians? In other words, if plausible (yet variable) degrees of congruence can be established between the rhetorical situation of Philippians and the contexts of Isa 45:23, Ps 2:11, Deut 32:5, Dan 12:5, and Isa 49:4, can we propose the presence and functioning of Scripture in Philippians? If so, Riffaterre's method is useful in addressing question three above.

Riffaterre's theory serves our study in another important way. From the stance of the analyst testing for intertextual connections, we have to include and exclude elements, themes, motifs, and such like from the intertexts under consideration—we must constrain our interpretation of allusions.[87] For example, we have shown how Hays constrains his interpretation of echoes by limiting evocation of the intertexts's themes to those considered consonant with the presupposed, crucial intertext, "God's righteousness." Hays, the analyst, might then propose that Paul read the echoes in the

---

86. For example, that every text has a discoverable, fully explicable meaning, notwithstanding opinions about the locus of that meaning.

87. For the necessity of limiting the scope of intertextual potential in any analysis refer to the following: Plett, "Intertextualities," 7; Culler, *Pursuit*, 100–118; Kristeva, *La Révolution Du Langage Poétique*, 343; Lack, "Intertextuality or Influence," 130–42; Beale, "Ideology," 31, who writes: "Interpretation is the production of meaning from a surplus of meaningful possibilities."; Jenny, "Strategy of Form," 40; Morgan, "Intertext," 19; Voelz, "Multiple Signs and Double Texts," 30.

same way. However, within a single poem or epistle containing clusters of successive allusions, Riffaterre allows us to contemplate commonality between clustered intertexts and the unique, determinate structural matrix for that individual poem or epistle. Therefore, from the analyst's perspective, what should constrain the activation of themes in the evoked text is not a canon-wide, crucial intertext presupposed from theology or ecclesiology (Hays) but one recovered from the alluding text itself. A corollary of this, and indeed the original contribution made by our study, is that the rhetorical situation should act as the constraining intertext in the interpretation of literary allusions in Phil 2:10–16. Thus, Riffaterre's semiotic framework enables us to address question four above.

As a result of our analysis of Riffaterre, a practical intertextual investigation can be carried out into the role that Scripture plays in Paul's argument in Philippians. However, before proceeding on this basis, the issue of influence and allusion and their relationship to intertextuality should be addressed. This issue is a long-standing one and has resulted, in our opinion, in an unnecessary polarization of the concepts as postulated by Sommer: "influence and allusion belong together in opposition to intertextuality."[88] Such a sentiment is commonplace, but as we shall see, intertextuality and allusion have more in common than many critics concede.

Intertextuality, Influence, and the Author

Thomas Hatina's assessment of the use of intertextuality in historical-critical exegesis merits comment.[89] He argues that intertextuality is inimical to current historical-critical enquiry due to the former's poststructural framework.[90] Hatina's view is based on three observations about intertextuality—its ideological context, its concept of text, and its relationship to influence. He doubts that intertextuality can contribute new content and insights to traditional approaches of studying the use of Scripture in the NT. This view he shares with reader-oriented critics who claim that in the hands of historically oriented biblical scholars, intertextuality becomes a fashionable label for source-influence studies.[91] Influence and its association with

---

88. Sommer, *A Prophet Reads Scripture*, 206.

89. Hatina, "Intertextuality," 28–43.

90. Ibid., 29. See also Elam, "Intertextuality," 620–21, for an excellent explanation of the major premises of traditional criticism which advance the notion of determinacy between texts and influence of the author, and that of Structuralism and Poststructuralism which discard the notion of influence in textual relations.

91. Hatina, "Intertextuality," 36.

authorial intention were that which intertextuality sought to displace.[92] Hatina observes that the relationship between influence and intertextuality has been neglected by historical critics desiring to employ intertextuality—even Hays does not depart from traditional source-influence theory, and uses the term intertextuality to broaden the boundaries of influence.[93] He sums up the practical implementation of intertextuality by the historical critic: "[Intertextuality] is used as a substitute category for uncovering and investigating conscious or unconscious allusions to scripture in the New Testament."[94] According to Hatina, allusion (whether conscious or unconscious), presupposes influence and has been tacitly incorporated as a major component of intertextuality by historical critics.[95] He concludes his evaluation of influence and intertextuality by claiming that they are mutually antagonistic to a large degree.[96]

As an initial counter to Hatina's views we have seen that Riffaterre (and others such as Genette) have devised and implemented intertextuality in "post-poststructuralist" terms.[97] We would therefore modify Hatina's observation by suggesting that the Kristevan and Barthesian variety of intertextuality might be inimical to historical-critical enquiry. As to his second concern, as we have seen, the concept of text can be limited to literary texts in diachronic relationship—a notion compatible with historical-critical enquiry.[98] Related to this second concern is the third; intertextuality's relationship to influence.[99] Although we disagree with Hatina that influence and intertextuality are mutually antagonistic, we agree that there has been a

---

92. Clayton and Rothstein, "Figures," 3: "One may see intertextuality either as the enlargement of a familiar idea or as an entirely new concept to replace the outmoded notion of influence." A particular target for ousting would be the central concern with the author and conscious authorial intentions and skills.

93. Hatina, "Intertextuality," 36–37.

94. Ibid., 28.

95. Ibid., 37.

96. Ibid., 32.

97. See also Pfister, "Intertextuality," 210.

98. Contra Van Wolde, "Trendy Intertextuality?" 45–46, who advocates the replacement of the diachronic approach of comparative exegesis with the synchronic approach of intertextual exegesis."

99. Several critics of historical-critical exegesis view the method as concerned with influence and the author's intentions. They believe intertextuality replaces influence with its focus on genesis of text. See Aichele and Phillips, "Introduction," 7; Orr, *Intertextuality*, 61. Cf. Clayton and Rothstein, "Figures," 4, recognize that distinctive and thoughtful attitudes towards intertextuality have been developed by practicing critics outside full-dress theories.

lack of commitment to, or consideration for, theoretical issues.[100] Theoretical issues arising from a non-poststructuralist perspective on intertextuality have been examined above, now we will proceed to a theoretical treatment of allusion. This, we feel, is required because we propose that Paul alludes to Scripture in his letter to the Philippians, and also because intertextuality had become synonymous with allusion by the end of the 1970s. We will use theories of allusion developed by Ziva Ben-Porat and William Irwin as the point of departure. As we shall see, hermeneutically, author influence through allusion and intertextuality share *the same key concept*.

ALLUSION

There are many critical studies on the use of allusion, but few on the theory of allusion.[101] A consequence of this is the general acceptance of an intuitive understanding and rudimentary definition of allusion as a covert, implied, or indirect reference.[102] This assumed covertness of allusion is often contrasted with the overt category of quotation; whereas the hiddenness implicit in allusion invites doubts about the presence of allusion and difficulties of discovery for the reader, quotation provides an overt, unmissable signal to the reader which is often labeled by an introductory formula or textual element such as quotation marks.[103] These definitions of allusion and quotation are not incidental and have exerted an influence on broader aspects of exegesis.[104] Not only does this highlight a problem with terminology, it demonstrates the hermeneutical effects of understanding allusion intuitively rather than theoretically. Ben-Porat's analysis provides a welcome corrective which explicates the allusion process. An analysis of her theory and its relationship to theories and practices of intertextuality might help our understanding of Paul's use of Scripture in Philippians.

---

100. See Hübner's criticism of Hays in "Intertextualität," 881–98.

101. Ben-Porat, "Allusion," 105–28; Perri, "Alluding," 289–307; Combs, "Allusion Defined and Explained," 475–88; Irwin, "What Is an Allusion?" 287–97; Irwin, "Aesthetics," 521–32; Alter, *Pleasures*; Hermerén, "Allusions"; Ross, "Art," 59–70; Leddy, "Limits," 110–22; Conte, *Imitation*.

102. Miner, "Allusion," 18, defines allusion as "Tacit reference to another literary work, to another art, to history, to contemporary figures, or the like." Bloom, *Map*, 126, considers allusion to be "any implied, indirect or hidden reference."

103. Orr, *Intertextuality*, 130.

104. For example, the composition of the Philippian Church has been described as having no (negligible) Jewish members or influence because the text is devoid of OT quotations (Portefaix, *Sisters*, 137).

Ziva Ben-Porat

Ben-Porat offers a theoretical analysis that leads to a more dynamic conception of the allusion process. She notes that literary critics had based their usage of the term on their linguistic intuition rather than on a clear notion of what "allusion" signifies as a technical term in literary study. This intuitive approach (followed by most biblical scholars) understands "allusion" as an indirect reference to a known fact (synonymous with "hint"), saying one thing and meaning another, or an indirect, casual, or brief reference. From this intuitive understanding of allusion the definition of a "literary allusion" followed: an indirect reference to a known fact to be found in a work of literature.[105] Ben-Porat, however, points out a difference between allusion in general and literary allusion, suggesting that when the latter is thought of as a "device" it need not be limited to literature—not all "literary allusions" occur in literature[106] and not all allusions operating in a literary text belong to the class of "literary allusion" (since indirect or casual references abound in literature and other forms of linguistic communication).[107] According to Ben-Porat there are four constant features always present when the device (that is, literary allusion) is employed: the independent existence of two texts (the alluding and evoked texts); the presence of a signal in the alluding text; the presence of elements in both texts which can be linked together in unfixed, unpredictable intertextual patterns; the process of actualization which reflects in all its stages the effort to reconstruct a fuller text.[108] It is essentially this treatment of literary allusion as a device that underlies Ben-Porat's theoretical approach—an approach designed to eliminate the gap between definition and intuition and one which we will now look at in more detail.

Ben-Porat defines a literary allusion as a device for the simultaneous activation of two texts.[109] The activation is achieved through the manipulation of a sign or marker in the alluding text to a referent which is always an independent text. The simultaneous activation of the two texts results in the formation of intertextual patterns that cannot be predetermined.

---

105. Ben-Porat, "Allusion," 105, 107.

106. See our example below, in which Jesus' cry from the cross (a verbal text: Ibid., 107) and Matthew's record of it (Matt 27:46) can both be considered as literary allusion or literary device.

107. Ben-Porat, "Allusion," 107.

108. Ibid., 127.

109. Ibid., 107. Text refers to the closed recorded system which is activated by a literary allusion. The focus is on literary texts activated from within other texts, although she notes the analogy between literary text and music or painting.

This is because the same sign or marker in the referent or evoked text (alluded-to text) might acquire different denotations. The denotations are the referents belonging to the reconstructed world of the evoked text and are independent of, and may be incompatible with, the reconstructed world of the alluding text. The marker is used to activate independent elements from the evoked text which are never referred to directly.[110] For example, a text that refers to Shakespeare's *Hamlet* by name, might be referring to the play or the hero directly, but may also be indirectly referring to ideas of indecision, cowardice versus heroism, or the contemplation of suicide.[111] Ben-Porat thus connects the indirect feature of allusion to those elements in the evoked text not mentioned in the alluding text—this is the common base for all allusions.[112] Ben-Porat uses the language of semiotics, describing how the allusion marker maintains the metonymical structure of the relationship, sign-referent: an object is represented by one of its components.[113] She argues that the signifier in a literary text is never substituted by other signifiers—she refers to this as the identification and substitution of a veiled referent for the signifier in the alluding text. Such substitution would be tantamount to the text saying one thing and meaning another. Rather, there is a single signifier which triggers multiple elements in a literary signified.[114]

An important aspect of Ben-Porat's theory is the way it allows for the distinction between the allusion marker and the allusion device: "immediate identification of the source-text does not substitute for the activation of elements which remain to be identified."[115] The "allusion marker" is the textual element (word or string of words) in the alluding text and the "allusion device" is the process of activating another text (the alluded-to text). The marker performs a denotative function as the reader recognizes the alluded-to text, and the device a connotative function as the reader calls to mind unstated associations in the alluded-to text. The allusion process is "a movement starting with the recognition of the marker and ending with intertextual patterning."[116]

---

110. Ibid., 108–9.

111. Ibid., 109. This is how T. S. Eliot seems to use the allusion to *Hamlet* in "The Love Song of J. Alfred Prufrock."

112. This challenges the view that allusion is indirect in the sense of being accidental or casual, and lesser in significance or importance than, for example, "explicit citation/quotation."

113. Ben-Porat, "Allusion," 108.

114. This semiosis is clearly inimical to that advanced by Kristeva and Barthes.

115. Ibid., 109.

116. Ibid.

The four stages of the allusion process are as follows:[117] First: *Recognition of a marker in a given sign*. Recognition entails the identification of the marking element(s) as belonging to or closely related to another independent text. The identification does not depend on formal identity—it can happen when the textual elements which make up the marker are arranged differently in the alluded-to text. An example might be a distorted quotation, or grammatical changes such as noun declension or verb tenses.[118] This theory is consistent with what scholars have observed in studies of the NT in the OT, where the author "misquotes" usually as a result of faulty recollection.[119] Second: *Identification of the evoked text*. It is self-evident that before elements in the evoked text can be activated, the text itself has to be identified. However, Ben-Porat distinguishes between identification of the alluded-to text containing the marker, and recollection of the marker in its setting in that text:

> The recollection of the marker's original form may suffice for a modified and fuller interpretation of the sign as it appears in the alluding text [see below]. Identification of the marker's larger "referent," the evoked text, is mandatory for intertextual patterning beyond the modified interpretation of the marker itself.[120]

Third: *Modification of the Initial Local Interpretation of the Signal*. This modification is the result of the interaction of the two texts and reveals the formation of at least one intertextual pattern. This happens when the context of the marker in the alluded-to text is recognized and its interpretation "impinges upon" the alluding text. This patterning of the two independent interpretations yields a modified interpretation of the alluding text. The completion of this stage is enough to determine the existence of a literary allusion. Fourth: *Activation of the evoked text as a whole in an attempt to form maximum intertextual patterns*.[121] This stage achieves the aim of the allusion—activation of the whole alluding text with the evoked text as a whole. Intertextual patterns are formed from the activation of the elements in the alluded-to text that might not have the marker as their components.

In addition to the mechanics of allusion spelled out in the above process, Ben-Porat offers a typology, identifying two types of allusion;

---

117. Cf. Plett, "Intertextualities," 16, where he describes the stages of perception of quotation.

118. For example, in the alleged allusion to Ps 2:11 in Phil 2:12, the words "fear" and "trembling" are separated in the "marked" text of Ps 2.

119. See the discussion in Stanley, *Paul and the Language of Scripture*, 3–30.

120. Ben-Porat, "Allusion," 110.

121. Ibid., 110–11.

"metaphorical" and "metonymical."[122] In the former, the literary allusion is a device for linking texts that can initially appear totally unrelated, whereas in the latter the texts can appear as closely related.[123] In metaphorical allusion, only the marker is common to both alluding and alluded-to texts, and the reason for its existence in both texts is the potential analogies between reconstructed patterns.[124] In metonymical allusion, the existence of the allusion marker is a product of the link between the texts. Initially-related texts share world components so that the reason for linking such texts is their explicit relatedness. The alluding text is, in some form or another, a continuation of the alluded-to text.[125]

Ben-Porat has advanced a theory of allusion that offers an insightful and comprehensive model of how literary allusion operates in poetic literature. Just as Riffaterre provides a potential theoretical framework for an intertextual investigation of Philippians, Ben-Porat's methods can now be considered in this light also.

Terminology: Allusion or Quotation?

A significant consequence of Ben-Porat's theory is that it challenges the validity of the distinction often made, intuitively, between allusion and quotation. She achieves this by differentiating between "allusion marker" and "allusion device"; the former is the textual element (word or string of words) in the alluding text and the latter is the process of activating another text (the alluded-to text). The marker performs a denotative function as the reader recognizes the alluded-to text, and the device a connotative function as the reader calls to mind unstated associations in the alluded-to text. Quotation and allusion are therefore similar in the connotative sense, only differing in the denotative sense. In fact, the only difference between quotation and allusion is that a quotation always contains an addition to the allusion marker that makes the presence of the allusion overt. As Hebel notes:

> The question whether allusion or quotation is the superior concept becomes insignificant as soon as any textual element

---

122. Ibid., 117.

123. Ibid., 118–25. She uses T. S. Eliot's metaphorical allusion in "The Love Song of J. Alfred Prufrock" to "The Relic" by John Donne and Natan Zach's metonymical allusion in "Dantes, No" to Dumas's *Le Comte de Monte-Cristo*.

124. Here, "analogy" refers to associations between dissimilar things.

125. Ben-Porat, "Allusion," 117.

relating one text with another outside itself is granted the status and quality of an allusional marker.[126]

An example from Paul's use of Scripture can demonstrate the need to distinguish between *allusion marker* and *allusion device* in an effort to develop a more meaningful terminology. In Rom 14:11, Paul reproduces the text of Isa 45:23 following an explicit textual element (or introductory formula) that informs the reader that Isa 45:23 exists as another text; namely, "For it is written." In Phil 2:10, 11, no such explicit textual element is present, yet the same string of words from Isa 45:23 is reproduced there. When we recognize that this rarely-occurring string of words only appears in three extant Greek texts, it is obvious that Romans and Philippians, both written by Paul, contain an overt "reference" to Isa 45:23. The textual element which *denotes* Isa 45:23 (πᾶν γόνυ κάμψῃ ... πᾶσα γλῶσσα ἐξομολογήσηται in Phil 2:10, 11 and κάμψει πᾶν γόνυ ... πᾶσα γλῶσσα ἐξομολογήσεται in Rom 14:11) does not require to be preceded by a formal citation or quotation formula to be granted the status of an allusion marker or to be considered overt. Since it is possible for a reader to recover the association(s) *connoted* (in our case by Isa 45:23 in Rom 14:11 and Phil 2:10, 11) independently of the form of the marker, we propose that some quotations are particular types of allusion[127]—that is, a type of allusion where the allusion marker always follows a citation formula, or is enclosed in quotation marks. By recognizing that some quotations are allusions, and that all allusions are either overt or covert, we are able to advance the first working hypothesis concerning our approach in this investigation: *the presence of Scripture in Paul's letter to the Philippians cannot be determined from a consideration of explicitly-marked, overt allusions (quotations) alone.*

Audience Competency and the Allusion Marker

A corollary of this theory of allusion is that, given the distinction of marker and device proposed by the above analysis, a poorly crafted denotative marker (rendering detection of the allusion difficult) does not mean there is not a valid connotative association between the texts; a badly denoted allusion, is still an allusion. Along similar lines, a well crafted denotative

---

126. Hebel, *Intertextuality*, 7.

127. For allusion as the generic term under which quotation should be subsumed, see Oppenheimer, *Literary Allusion*; Plett, *Die Kunst der Allusion*; Wheeler, *The Art of Allusion*. For the opposite view, see Laub, *The Poetics of Literary Allusion*; Neumann, "Das Eigene und das Fremde," 292–305; Stierle, "Werk und Intertextualitaet"; Tetzeli von Rosador, *Kunst im Werke George Eliots*.

THEORIES AND METHODOLOGIES   75

marker might not be recognized by a particular reader or class of reader; nonetheless, an allusion might still be present. In other words, the detection of the allusion (denotative function of the marker) should be distinguished from determination of the presence of the allusion (whether the connotative function of the device triggers unstated associations with the alluded-to text). This latter point highlights an inherent quality of allusion, namely that "allusion is predicated upon the possibility that some will catch the point while others will miss it."[128] This helpful reminder from Leddy introduces the idea of a *successful* and *unsuccessful* allusion. An allusion that is unsuccessful is one that was not detected by its audience, nonetheless it is still present as an allusion. To demonstrate this point, an example of an obviously misinterpreted verbal allusion is offered. We begin our example by suggesting that Jesus' allusion to Psalm 22 recorded in Matt 27:46-49 ("My God my God, why have you forsaken me")[129] was (intentionally) well crafted and aesthetically valuable both as an expression of his abandonment and a reminder of the Davidic king's anguish.[130] But this allusion was not recognized by some of the original audience who misinterpreted it for an appeal to, or for, Elijah.[131] Jesus' allusion to Ps 22 was unsuccessful since his antagonists failed to connect him with the anguish of Israel's great king—but the allusion is present nonetheless.[132] What can be proposed is, as Matthew

---

128. Leddy, "Limits," 111.

129. An allusion to Ps 22:1. See also the allusion (citation) to Ps 22:18 in John 19:24 in the context of Jesus as king of the Jews (John 18:36-37; 19:14-15, 19-21).

130. This is at least the meaning of the lament portion of Ps 22 (vv. 1-18). Snodgrass, "Use," 432, recognizes Ps 22 as a lament of a righteous sufferer.

131. It is possible that this was a case of mis-hearing (the volume of the cry notwithstanding and Jesus' physical condition impairing the clarity of verbal communication). The mis-hearing might result because of the similarity in sound between the transliterated ἠλι (my God) and Ἠλία (Elijah). Matthew's gospel contains a translation from the Hebrew, whereas Mark's gospel translates from the Aramaic to provide ἐλωι (Hagner, *Matthew 14-28*). Lane suggests that Jesus' antagonists were taunting him concerning his alleged appeal for divine help in the form of Elijah, although that could not have been David's meaning in Ps 22 (Lane, *Mark*, 573.) Perhaps the allusion marker (verbal) to Ps 22 was recognized, yet the connotative aspect of the Davidic king's anguish was not "picked up." Instead, the wrong association was made, in this case, to an Elijah tradition concerning delivery of the suffering (see Jeremias, "Ἠλ(ε)ίας," 928-41). We would say that the correct Ps 22-association to make was to the anguish and rejection of the divinely anointed king of the Jews. This is congruent with Jesus' claim to kingship (Matt 27:11; John 18:37) and the indignation of some Jews to Pilate's inscription "Jesus the Nazarene, the king of the Jews" recorded in John's gospel (John 19:19-22). It is doubtful that Jesus was asking for Elijah's help through an allusion to Ps 22.

132. It is possible that Jesus did not intend his antagonists to understand, but that seems unlikely given the source of his allusion and the audience's competency. On the other hand, Jesus' parable-telling was part of a strategy of intentionally restricting

records it, that Jesus intended the allusion and, given the Scripture content of the verbal (textual) marker and the Scripture competence of some of the audience, it was in principle possible for them to recognize the allusion. This seems a justifiable position to adopt when we consider how the gospel writers, much later, connected Ps 22 with Jesus' treatment during his crucifixion.[133] In John's gospel, the writer successfully connects the treatment of the Davidic king in Ps 22:18 with Jesus' treatment at the hands of his executioners.[134] The point here is that the *presence* of the allusion cannot be determined from a consideration of original-audience comprehension; although the *success* or *failure* of the allusion should be considered in this way. Thus, audience recognition is not a necessary condition for allusion. By identifying the distinction between the presence of an allusion, and its successful recognition and activation of the correct associations, we are able to advance the second working hypothesis concerning our approach in this investigation: *the presence of Scripture in Paul's letter to the Philippians cannot be refuted by an appeal to the competency of the Philippians. Rather, the success of the allusion depends on the denotative quality of Paul's allusion marker and the connotative competency of the Philippians.*

What is significant to our study is correctly aligning allusion-success and not allusion-presence with audience competency. Allusion-presence is a task executed by the author, allusion-success is a task executed by the reader although affected by the denotative quality of the author. With this distinction in mind, we can examine ways in which audience competency might be related to the allusion process (see Irwin below).

Deviation in the Form of the Allusion Marker

Ben-Porat distinguishes between the allusion marker in the alluding text and the evoked text. In the alluding text it is called the *marker*, whereas in the evoked text it is called the *marked*. This taxonomy is useful if only in

---

information to a selected audience. Irwin notes the possibility for an allusion to be so obscure that no one but the author is aware of it, although in principle others could detect it (Irwin, "What Is an Allusion?" 290). But Leddy, "Limits," 121, rejects the idea of an allusion intended not to be recognized—this he calls unacknowledged borrowings, lies, obfuscations, sarcastic mutterings.

133. Matt 27:35, 39, 42–43, 46; John 19:24.

134. John 19:24. He does this with an overt allusion preceded by a citation formula ("this was to fulfill the Scripture"). Although John does not include the same textual marker to Ps 22, that is, "My God my God, why have you forsaken me," he makes the connection between Jesus and the Davidic king's anguish through the textual marker, "They divided my garments among them and cast lots for my clothing" (Ps 22:18).

recognizing the possible deviations in form between the two. Deviation in form of the marked and marker has prompted many proposals about Paul's citation technique and his presumed *Vorlage* (MT, LXX, other).[135] Valuable as they are, these studies have a tendency to overlook the question of how successful any deviation is in activating elements in the evoked text. Notwithstanding how these deviations are accounted for,[136] the role of the marker/marked is to activate elements in the evoked text. In this investigation of Philippians, the results of citation studies will be used as they contribute towards this central tenet of intertextuality and allusion theory.

Activation of Alluded-to Text—Constraining Intertextual Patterning

Ben-Porat's choice of terminology in describing the result of the simultaneous activation of two texts as intertextual patterning seems apt. Since activated elements in the evoked text might be independent of, and even incompatible with, the allusion marker, it is theoretically possible to produce unlimited associations between the texts.[137] Ben-Porat's theory would therefore seem to be in need of some kind of containment strategy as discussed above for intertextuality; the question posed is: How much of the evoked text(s) is activated by the allusion? The formal indications of the allusion marker may not provide guidelines/clues to what elements of the evoked text are consonant with the alluding text.[138] Not every (or any) allusion marker will act metonymically, wherein the connoted association is brought to mind from an associated notion conveyed in the marker.[139] According to Alter, the relationship of the alluding text to the evoked text can be, logically, "whole to part"; "part to whole"; "part to part";[140] the latter being the most common occurrence of allusion. Although the part(s) in

---

135. See our discussions on Septuagintal studies and citation technique in ch. 1.

136. Stanley, *Paul and the Language of Scripture*, 3–30.

137. Ben-Porat, "Allusion," 108. The theory seems to allow for this even though both texts are "closed." Ben-Porat also suggests that it is possible to read and understand the alluding text without actualizing the allusion. Actualization of the allusion is a step towards a richer interpretation ("Allusion," 115). See also Hebel, "Towards," 138: "A successful allusion always evokes theoretically unlimited and unpredictable associations and connotations."

138. Alter, *Pleasures*, 129.

139. See Perri, "Alluding," 291, She argues that allusion-markers tacitly specify the property(ies) belonging to the source text's connotation relevant to the allusion's meaning.

140. Alter, *Pleasures*, 129–31.

question could be motif, theme, character, isolated phrase, or image, every conceivable relation to the evoked text consonant with value, purpose, viewpoint, tone, feeling and predicament can be evoked.[141] Thus the allusion process is akin to the intertextual process in that there is, theoretically, the potential for an indeterminate number of associations to be made, even if these are between determinate pretexts. However, as we have shown above, Riffaterre's idea of an intertextual matrix, of which a cluster of hypograms are all variants, helps the analyst to define limits on activation of elements within those hypograms—namely, those elements which the hypograms have in common with the intertextual matrix. In our case, each alluded-to text might contain "hypogrammic data" that is congruent with the rhetorical situation, and this is what should be activated in the test of congruence. This synergy does not exist in Ben-Porat's model since she concentrates on the mechanics of an individual allusion. Her theory does not define a method for relating clusters of allusions that might be variants of one overarching theme in some way.[142] Riffaterre's is a theory of the poem, not its individual ungrammaticalities. This is an important theoretical consideration if a text being analyzed contains clusters of ungrammaticalities or allusions.

William Irwin

Whereas Ben-Porat's theory focuses on the reader's actualization of an alluded-to text by describing the four-stages of the allusion process, several scholars have considered allusion from the perspective of artistic intention: "allusions are particular intentional elements within the text's artistic structure."[143] Among them, William Irwin adds a further dimension to the theory of allusion described above. Like Ben-Porat, he recognizes both overt and covert allusions, and the necessity of indirectness of allusion, but he introduces a new dimension by emphasizing author intent and the

141. Ibid., 131.

142. Ben-Porat, "Allusion," 119, describes a thematic link between two discrete allusions in T. S. Eliot's poem "The Love Song of J. Alfred Prufrock" to John Donne's "The Relic," and Andrew Marvell's "To My Coy Mistress." But she does not elaborate on how the time-death pattern in Eliot's poem links Donne's and Marvel's poems in terms of their activation as allusions. Ben-Porat argues that activation of the evoked text produces intertextual patterns whose nature cannot be determined, yet offers an example where activation produces intertextual patterns spiraling around the poem's time-death theme. See Perri, "Alluding," 293, who rightly claims that the context of the alluding text provides a tacit aid in determining what aspects of the evoked text should be activated by the allusion.

143. Hebel, *Intertextuality*, 7. So too, Chandler, "Romantic Allusiveness"; Schaar, *The Full Voic'd Quire Below*; Schaar, "Vertical Context Systems," 146–57.

interaction between author and reader in the actualization of allusion. He critiques three views of allusion—intentionalist, internalist, and hybrid. The intentionalist view is when an author includes a reference to another text which he intends as an allusion; the internalist view is when one text alludes to another when internal properties of one resemble and call to mind another; the hybrid view is a combination of intentionalist and internalist views.[144] The internalist view, Irwin argues, is not sufficient since two texts may have internal properties in common on the basis of something other than allusion.[145] The hybrid view is defined by Göran Hermerén who suggests that the allusion is intended by the author, as a matter of fact detected by the reader who also recognizes the author's intention.[146] Stephanie Ross also supports a hybrid view of allusion by arguing that the artist of artwork A intends to refer to artwork B and incorporates into A an indirect reference to B.[147] Irwin notes that Hermerén's definition does not allow for the reader to fail to detect the allusion which can draw on information not readily available to every member of a culture and linguistic community.[148] He also argues that Ross's use of the author's intention to "refer" is too weak; the author intends to "allude," that is to activate specific elements in artwork B. According to Irwin, Ross does not adequately describe the allusion marker; incorporation of an indirect reference does not convey the sense that the author intends to allude by embedding words or structures that communicate his/her intentions.[149] Irwin concludes that the hybrid view "collapses" into the intentionalist view and offers his definition of the conditions for allusion: "a reference that is indirect in the sense that it calls for associations that go beyond mere substitution of a referent. An author must intend this indirect reference, and it must be in principle possible that the intended audience could detect it."[150] All three aspects provide the necessary and sufficient conditions for allusion.

Notwithstanding his emphasis on authorial intention, Irwin recognizes that the reader must play a vital role in understanding an allusion. But reader understanding of an allusion must be in accord with the author's intent since the author created the allusion in the first place by embedding

---

144. Irwin, "What Is an Allusion?" 289.

145. Ibid., 289; Also Sandmel, "Parallelomania," 1–13.

146. Hermerén, "Allusions," 211.

147. Ross, "Art," 63.

148. Irwin, "What Is an Allusion?" 289. See also Alter, *Pleasures*, 121: "one can hardly expect that all readers will take away all encoded messages and implications from all texts."

149. Irwin, "What Is an Allusion?" 290.

150. Ibid., 293.

the marker in his/her text following the connotations s/he has made with the anterior text.[151] For an allusion to be successful the reader must call to mind something not explicitly in the text—*but that something must be what the author intended him/her to call to mind*.[152] What the author leaves unexpressed, yet tacitly intended, in the allusion are the connotative aspects [that s/he recalled when writing] that can be recovered from the alluded-to text. Without limiting reading to recognizing authorial intent, if these connotative aspects can be shown to be in accord with the author's intentions then we can propose an interpretation of the alleged allusion—one that distinguishes it from an interpretation that does not accord with authorial intent.[153] For Irwin, authorial intent is a necessary condition of allusion.[154]

Author and Reader Relationship in the Allusion Process

Irwin makes a key contribution in two areas: firstly, his definition of allusion is most helpful and comprehensive as it is grounded in theory, and defines roles for both author and reader; secondly, he includes both author and reader in his insights into the allusion process and aesthetics.[155] Irwin

---

151. Brand and Brand, "Surface Interpretation," 464. In creating the text, the author had intentions—this is true whether someone other than the author can know anything of those intentions. See Pucci, *Full-Knowing Reader*, 40. He argues persuasively that the connection of two discrete systems of reference in an allusion can only occur in the mind of the reader—thus the reader creates the allusion, the author only intending the language of the allusion not its meaning. We agree with Pucci that the allusion *functions* at the point of reading or that *actualization* of the allusion is an action of the reader, but we maintain that the allusion is created by the author who intends the associations s/he has already made and which produces the allusion in the first place. Thus the author does not simply make possible the interpretation of the allusion (*Full-Knowing*, 36).

152. Irwin, "What Is an Allusion?" 293–95. Irwin does not rule out the reader using his/her imagination to fill the gaps created by the allusion in order for the author to communicate his intention successfully. If the reader's creative associations are in accord with authorial intent, the allusion will be successful—otherwise "accidental associations" result in misinterpretation. See also Campbell, "Allusions and Illusions," 19: "Allusions invite us to elect from our mental library, knowledge which is not in the text itself and without which the writer's intention will not be fully communicated." Here, Campbell describes what correlates to Riffaterre's descriptive systems and clichés of the sociolect.

153. Irwin, "What Is an Allusion?" 295.

154. Ibid., 291. Cf. Jauhiainen, *Use of Zechariah in Revelation*, 33. For more detail on "intentionalist interpretation" see Irwin, *Intentionalist Interpretation*.

155. Even though he argues from an intentionalist perspective, Irwin also recognizes that allusions are attempts to communicate, and so audience comprehension is important: Irwin, "Aesthetics," 521. See also Conte, *Imitation*, 56–57. Cf. Pucci,

argues for the activation of elements in the evoked text by the reader as the counterpoint to the activation performed by the author in producing the text. The author is first to experience the intertextual patterning as s/he *creates* the allusion in the production of the text—thus intertextual connections are the product of authorial design.[156] As Alter suggests, the text(s) alluded to have presented themselves to the author as a model of achievement in a particular genre or literary mode.[157] Or, according to Genette, the poet is aware of appropriate materials to imitate; "worthy material is arranged anew, yet in accordance with predisposed parameters."[158] The author alludes, not in an arbitrary way, but because, in his/her mind, his/her writing *requires* the allusion.

The reader, on the other hand, engages in intergesis, recovering meaning in the space between texts,[159] and decides what to include as an activated element and what to exclude. Connecting the text with his/her own experience and knowledge s/he produces intertextual patterning, either shared with the author at the text production stage (successful allusion), or not (unsuccessful allusion).[160] In a successful allusion, the intertextual patterning is the produce of the author prepared in advance for the reader, for whom it is "already read" because of the shared experience and knowledge with the author.[161] The activation of textual elements across texts is, theoretically, controlled by the author through his choice and position of the allusion marker. However, although the allusion marker's presence and position exert a controlling function, they might not prevent accidental readings. Compare this notion with that of Riffaterre's criticism of Barthes:

> This concept of an aleatory process exposes Barthes to a confusion between the intertext and accidental connections due to

---

Full-Knowing, 28.

156. See Conte, *Imitation*, 35: "Before the allusion can have the desired effect on the reader, it must first exert *that* effect on the poet." Italics mine. Pfister, "Intertextuality," 210, notes a form of European structuralist intertextuality: "Only those references count as intertextual that are clearly intended by the author, distinctly marked in the text and recognised by the reader."

157. Alter, *Pleasures*, 132.

158. Quoted in Orr, *Intertextuality*, 108.

159. Aichele and Phillips, "Introduction," 14.

160. The reader's textual space includes accidental associations not in accord with the author's intentions. The reader can make these accidental associations and claim them as his/her "reading," but s/he should not attribute them to the author.

161. See Conte, *Imitation*, 35. He proposes that the author and reader have the source of the allusion stored in both their memories.

similarities in lexicon, in situation, or to resemblances on the level of apparent or real reference to the non-verbal world.[162]

The reader is not free to make any associations that s/he desires at the point of reading. Any associations made that are not in accord with the author's intended associations are accidental and result in an unsuccessful allusion. In Riffaterre's model of intertextuality the *text* imposes limitations on the reader so as to prevent accidental readings: "It [the text] is a hierarchy of representations imposed upon the reader, despite his personal preferences."[163] In Irwin's model of allusion, the *author* imposes limitations on the reader: "... the reader must call to mind what the author intended for him or her to call to mind."[164]

Communication Structure: Author and Audience Intimacy

Irwin's observations on the aesthetics of allusion might help in understanding why Paul uses such a literary device since it might be doubted that an author would communicate indirectly what he could state explicitly in support of his argument. However, when they are understood, allusions are potent strategies of communications.[165] Irwin considers audience comprehension of an allusion to be related to the aesthetic value of an allusion. What makes an allusion successful is that a reasonable part of the intended audience must correctly understand the allusion.[166] But Irwin probes deeper into what happens when an audience understands an allusion, and the role that aesthetic value plays in the author's production and the audience's appreciation of an allusion.[167] Key to this is the way allusion works in communicating information. The author is communicating something but not in a straightforward way, requiring some effort for the reader to discover what s/he has intended. The process of allusion actively involves the audience in a way that straightforward statements do not, resulting in a common bond being forged between a reader and an author.[168] Allusion therefore calls for

---

162. Riffaterre, "Sémiotique intertextuelle," 132.

163. Riffaterre, *Semiotics*, 12.

164. Irwin, "What Is an Allusion?" 293.

165. Hays, "On The Rebound," 86.

166. Irwin, "Aesthetics," 525–27. In suggesting that allusion can produce a sense of belonging, he notes that the intimate community created by the understanding of an allusion may be as small as two, and in some cases intimacy may increase as the size of the community decreases.

167. Ibid., 521.

168. Ibid., 522.

audience creativity and cultivates an intimacy between author and reader. It is through the association(s) connotatively identified that the intimacy is cultivated—the author makes an association at the point of writing and the reader discovers it (the same association) at the point of reading.[169] Ted Cohen describes the unique way that the maker and appreciator of a metaphor are drawn closer to one another; his findings can also be applied to allusion: "Three aspects are involved: (1) the speaker issues a kind of concealed invitation; (2) the hearer expends a special effort to accept the invitation; and (3) this transaction constitutes the acknowledgment of a community."[170]

According to Irwin, even when the subject matter alluded to is not pleasant, the readership can have some pride or pleasure in knowing it.[171] This coheres with Cohen's claim that intimacy can be used to deal a penetrating thrust.[172] In this way, allusion can be a means to reveal and conceal emotions and communicate difficult instructions to friends. This is consistent with the use of "connotation" in literary criticism. Here, "connotation" is recognized as a device used for emotive purposes: "denotation can name feelings, but it cannot express or evoke them with fullness and intensity."[173] Similarly, in rhetorically oriented discourse, "connotation" could be used to ornament, reinforce, or exemplify moral or other programmatic truths.[174] The recovery of tacit intentions in the allusion process seems problematic, yet in principle is possible, indeed more probable, if there is an intimate sharing between author and reader: "in the case of allusion, the intimacy is the realization through the association [connoted by the marker] that the reader shares something in common with the author."[175] This is what Cohen, speaking of a figurative use of language, calls the cultivation of intimacy claiming that it can only be inaccessible to all but those who share information about one another's knowledge, beliefs, intentions, and attitudes.[176]

---

169. Or at the point of understanding—the reader may have multiple opportunities to discover the association.

170. Cohen, "Metaphor," 8. Elsewhere, he applies the principle to Joke-telling; when a listener fails to "get the joke" what has failed is the effort to achieve an intimacy between teller and hearer. See Cohen, *Jokes*, 26. Perri, "Alluding," 289, also notes the comparison between alluding and joking, noting the etymological origin of 'allusion' as the Latin *alludere*, to joke, jest, mock, or play with ("Alluding," 301).

171. Irwin, "Aesthetics," 525.

172. Cohen, "Metaphor," 12.

173. Gudas, "Connotation and Denotation," 236; Conte, *Imitation*, 55.

174. Gudas, "Connotation and Denotation," 236.

175. Irwin, "What Is an Allusion?" 296.

176. Cohen, "Metaphor," 9.

Audience Competency: Learning the Allusion

In Ben-Porat's model, recognition of a textual element as a signifier is distinguished from, and chronologically prior to, the identification of the signified or object text. For example, the phrase "fear and trembling" in Phil 2:12 might seem an odd qualifier to the reader striving to understand "how to work out one's own salvation." At first glance the phrase might only be a signal pointing to another text. For Riffaterre, this is sufficient for an intertextual reading since the presupposition of a hypogram can be made. A second reader, in the same audience as the first but "nurtured on the LXX, without consciously marking the allusion, might sense a momentary ripple of elevated diction in the phrase, producing a heightened dramatic emphasis."[177] A third reader, from the same audience, might not only be able to discern the allusion marker (stage 1 of Ben-Porat), "but also locate the source of the original voice (stage 2) and discover a number of intriguing resonances (stage 3 and 4)."[178] According to Ben-Porat's model, a single intertextual pattern can be made, in stage three, from a basic understanding of the evoked text—discovering a number of intriguing resonances is not the necessary outcome of the allusion process. Essentially, Ben-Porat's model accommodates degrees of reader competence. The level of competence in fact might be quite rudimentary in a given reader/hearer requiring subsequent learning from/about both alluding and alluded-to texts for the "number of intriguing resonances" to be developed. Allusion must include the possibility of learning. Hebel describes the reader's learning as an "archaeological activity." If the reader does not possess the allusive competence to recreate the textual space s/he must compensate for this deficit by working towards becoming an "informed reader." The reader becomes an "informed critic," a text archaeologist who has moved on from a spontaneous act of reading.[179] Irwin's theory about the aesthetic value of allusion is useful in this regard. He describes aesthetic value as the pleasure derived from discovering the allusion. The ideal aesthetic value is achieved when the allusion is neither too easy nor too difficult to detect; the audience derives pleasure in the reasonable effort expended in discovery. If an audience has to do significant research before understanding an allusion, this might be said to detract from the aesthetic value of the allusion; in this case the aesthetic value of the allusion may be diminished or changed to that of puzzle pleasure or

---

177. Hays, *Echoes*, 21–22.
178. Ibid., 21–22.
179. Hebel, "Towards," 140–41.

investigation.[180] Clearly, for the uneducated reader, the allusion might be missed or have low aesthetic value while for the educated reader the allusion can have high aesthetic value. In either case, the allusion is present and awaiting discovery with potentially high aesthetic value for those who have ears to hear.[181] Allusions are therefore capable of being successful with (Hebel) or without (Irwin) exegesis.

CONCLUSIONS

No one theory lock, stock, and barrel, can serve as the model for investigating Paul's use of Scripture in Phil 2:10-16—the complexities of the passage with its puzzling cluster and the tacit nature of the references see to that. However, insights drawn from studies of intertextuality, allusion, and rhetorical situation address the six key issues identified as foundational to this investigation. We start by pointing out that intertextuality and allusion share a key concept that is necessary and common to both—the recovery of unstated material in the interpretive process. In Riffaterre's version of intertextuality, this is the discovery and recovery of hypograms, whereas in Ben-Porat's theory of allusion it is the recovery and activation of elements in the alluded-to text. In both cases, additional meaning or significance lies outside the written text being interpreted. Intertextuality and allusion (historical influence) therefore share the same interpretive principle—authors and readers make extra-textual associations in the production and reading of their texts. We suggest that this is *the defining characteristic of intertextuality and allusion*. Moreover, intertextuality and allusion are the same process for both text production (the author's activity) and text reception (the reader's activity). The choice comes down to what emphasis an intertextual investigation gives to one (author) or the other (reader), and subsequently which intertexts are to be included for analysis and whether they exist in synchronic or diachronic relationship to each other.

The examination of Riffaterre's theory has shown that hypograms can be literary pretexts which contribute to meaning and which have a fixed, historical origin. For Ben-Porat literary allusion involves the diachronic relationships between an alluding text and an anterior alluded-to text. In both of her examples of metaphorical and metonymical allusion, literary

---

180. Irwin, "Aesthetics," 528. Although he recognizes that aesthetic experience can be enriched by the difficulty of search required to understand the allusion.

181. If the form of the allusion marker is used to determine audience competency, then there is a case that covert allusion implies the higher readership skill.

pretexts provide the source for the allusion.[182] So we have common ground between theories of intertextuality and allusion with regard to diachronic pretexts with a fixed historical origin. Furthermore, an author-oriented text production approach is as intertextual as a reader-oriented text reception approach as a means of limiting the scope of the project.[183] Evidence of an author's preference to cite or allude to a precursor text suggests some level of importance be assigned to the precursor as it takes part in the discursive space—the author "flags up" these texts as important by quoting from or alluding to them. Hence, a practical intertextual investigation can be carried out on the role that Scripture plays in Paul's argument in Phil 2:10–16—one that gives attention to those intertexts we suggest Paul intended to have a meaningful impact on his audience. Thus the agency of the author can be acknowledged in an intertextual investigation of Philippians.[184]

Further to this point about the author's role in the creation of the intertextual and allusional dynamic, is the thorny issue of intentionality. Here, we note Irwin's contribution in arguing for an intentionalist, as opposed to internalist or hybrid, view of allusion. We take Irwin's definition of allusion as the most complete, especially as it encompasses both author and audience—an allusion is the product of the author, wherein his intended tacit specifications can, in principle, be recovered by some of the intended audience. We have seen that Irwin and Cohen use a theoretical approach to allusion and metaphor to explicate a balanced author-reader hermeneutic: "the aesthetic success of an allusion is judged in part on the basis of the exchange between author and audience, the intimacy and community forged."[185] Thus, they answer question five above, by addressing the role that audience recognition and authorial intention can play in analyses of allusion. The intimate relationship between Paul and the Philippians could account for his use of allusion. Philippians is broadly accepted as a personal and intimate correspondence because of the frequency of friendship, affection, sharing, and solidarity motifs.[186] Specifically, Paul and the Philippians were sharing in the common experience of conflict and suffering for the same cause. Philippians is therefore the type of letter (rhetorical discourse)[187]

---

182. Ben-Porat, "Allusion," 123.
183. See the excellent discussion on this in Wakefield, "Where to Live," 102–10.
184. Clayton and Rothstein, "Figures," 7; Bloom, *Map*, 60, 70.
185. Irwin, "Aesthetics," 530.
186. See, among others, Stowers, "Friends"; Fee, *Philippians*, 2–7.
187. Allusion can be the device used by Paul as a means of drawing attention to the imaginative centre which amplifies the text's rhetoric.

where allusion might be expected.[188] With such a background of intimacy and shared experience between author and reader, it should come as no surprise that tacit specifications in a correspondence would be capable of being recovered. *Our proposal is that the presence of allusion is a sign of intimacy and shared knowledge*[189] *which presupposes audience competency, rather than casts doubts upon it.* With this approach, it would seem justifiable that the alleged allusions in Paul's letter to the Philippians would be successful, with varying degrees of aesthetic value, for the deacons, overseers, Euodia, Syntyche, the "true companion," Clement, the rest of Paul's fellow workers, and the majority of the Philippian congregation.

---

188. This is not intended to imply that Paul does not allude in other types of letter.

189. Irwin, "Aesthetics," 526. He notes that allusions might depend on knowledge that the average educated person of the time possessed and which such a person in our time does not possess.

CHAPTER 3

The Rhetorical Situation in Philippians

> If the church of Philippi had particular problems, they are presented with too much subtlety for the modern reader.[1]

McKenzie's claim points to the need for a different approach to exegesis. The notion that subtlety can be characteristic of an intentional literary device (covert allusion) prompts exploration of literary allusion as a methodology for exegetical analysis of Philippians. Additionally, the availability of a methodology (situational rhetoric) that supports the recovery of particular problems (exigencies) and particular solutions (constraints) in rhetorical discourse merits consideration. In this chapter, we will conduct an exegesis of five key sections of Philippians, with a view to constructing the rhetorical situation using Bitzer's theory as the framework for analysis. The rhetorical situation corresponds to the epistolary argument or central theme of the epistle and can be thought of as the crucial, unwritten intertext that gives significance, not only to the alleged allusions, but the letter as a whole. According to Riffaterre, this crucial intertext, or structural matrix, is found at a deeper level and cannot be determined from a purely surface-level reading of the text. The matrix is not the result of reader-perception but the analyst's logical inferences from the text. "Analysis is obliged to find the matrix sentence that most economically accounts for the greatest number of formal and semantic features in the text."[2] Furthermore, and significantly,

---

1. McKenzie, *New Testament for Spiritual Reading*, vii.
2. Riffaterre, "Interview," 14. He distinguishes between the reading-act proper and

not only does this structural matrix account for the text's invariants (commonality among passages), its recognizable patterns and structures, but any alluded-to texts are variants of it. Therefore, Riffaterre and Bitzer provide a methodological platform for our unique approach in analyzing Paul's use of Scripture in Phil 2:10–16; namely, that rhetorical situation provides the new frame of reference for congruence in the testing of alleged allusions. Of course, there is always the possibility that our suggestion of a relationship between Paul's argument, its recovery using a situational-rhetoric oriented exegesis and its connection to tacit references to the OT is incorrect. Nevertheless, we offer our approach for evaluation because there is currently no interpretation of Philippians that satisfactorily explains the cluster of OT references in Phil 2:10–16 whilst giving an economical account of the range of formal, semantic and linguistic conventions in Phil 1:27—3:21—indeed we suggest this as the yardstick for judging our results.

In constructing the rhetorical situation of Philippians we will use a traditional, historical exegetical approach to try to determine Paul's 'communicative intentions' from data contained in his letter. We therefore follow a common exegetical trajectory before taking a "rhetorical turn" by asking *why* Paul might have composed the rhetoric. The main question which we will attempt to answer is: What does Paul present as the main problem in Philippi? The answer will flow from our argument that Philippians is a form of communication which is a fitting response to this problem. More specifically, the determination of the controlling exigency in Philippians will assist in proposing the matrix from which Philippians might have been composed. This can be summarized by a word, sentence or idea as demonstrated by Wakefield for Gal 3:1–14. As we argued in chapter 1, such an approach is consistent with the convention of traditional, historical exegetes who have sought to summarize the letter's central theme. Therefore, constructing the rhetorical situation of Philippians will precede an analysis of Paul's literary allusions to Scripture in order to establish in what way the latter are variants of the former.[3] We will focus our attention on those textual units in which Paul gives explicit instructions to the Philippians so that we can identify the main contours of his argument.

---

analysis. The analyst uses special knowledge and training when he sets out to prove the intertextual linkages in a text exist; the reader experiences the reading process without always being able to put his finger on just what is going on in his mind and locating the intertext.

3. As we shall see, to fully utilize Ben-Porat's method of interpreting an allusion, the control mechanism for evoking unstated elements in the alluded-to text must be available to us.

THE RHETORICAL SITUATION IN PHIL 1:27-30

F. F. Bruce writes, "The purpose of the letter [Philippians] can be inferred only from a consideration of its contents."[4] A good place to start in determining Paul's purpose in writing Philippians is Phil 1:27-30, which introduces the major proposition for the entire letter.[5] Following the introduction, Paul informs the Philippians of the circumstances of his imprisonment (Phil 1:12-26), then proceeds to focus on their own circumstances. Fee notes the transition from a predominately narrative (Phil 1:12-26) to imperative (Phil 1:27—2:18) section of the letter.[6] In Phil 1:27—2:18, Paul commands the Philippians to correct attitude and action, especially concerning suffering, selfishness and grumbling. Within this section of the epistle, Phil 1:27-30 states the main point that Paul argues, and in Phil 1:27a he issues his first imperative:[7] Μόνον ἀξίως τοῦ εὐαγγελίου τοῦ Χριστοῦ πολιτεύεσθε. The emphatic adverb μόνον (only) modifies πολιτεύεσθε and conveys the importance of the demand to "live worthily as citizens of the gospel of Christ." Its position at the beginning of this parenetical section of the epistle points to its importance in Paul's argument. This single word is paraphrased in some form by most commentators who recognize that it brings out the emphatic nature of the following imperative (for example, "Now the important thing is this").[8] The adverb, and its paraphrase, provide a deictic reference that Stamps argues can help to identify the rhetorical situation.[9] Furthermore, the imperative that follows highlights the passage as *volitional*;[10] Paul wants the Philippians to do something. The imperative, πολιτεύεσθε, defines how the Philippians are to live, and is a technical term which Paul uses in a distinctive way in reference to their earthly existence

---

4. Bruce, *Philippians*, 19.

5. Geoffrion, *Rhetorical Purpose*, 35, points out that Paul introduces "most of the key concepts for the entire letter in Phil 1:27-30: political identity, Gospel, ambiguity over future events, steadfastness, unity, faith, witness, fear(lessness), adversaries, salvation/destruction, concern for suffering, God's role in the believers's lives, and the values and experiences shared by Paul and the Philippians." See also Tellbe, *Synagogue*, 232; Watson, "Rhetorical Analysis of Philippians," 79; cf. Bloomquist, *Suffering*, 124, who proposes that the *narratio* of Phil 1:12-14 reveals the issue in Paul's discourse, namely, that the gospel has been preached in vain because Paul is in prison.

6. Fee, *Philippians*, 156: Phil 1:27—2:18 contains fourteen verbs, of which ten are imperatives, the remaining four being implied imperatives.

7. Ibid., 161, writes, "This imperative (πολιτεύεσθε) controls the argument from here to 2:18."

8. Loh and Nida, *Handbook*, 38.

9. See Stamps, "Rethinking," 201, 209.

10. Callow, "Patterns," 196.

in the Roman colony (cf. Phil 3:20a).[11] Paul's use of this term suggests he is not simply concerned with moral behavior (cf. περιπατέω, his usual word for this) but the pattern of conduct that flows from belonging to a particular commonwealth, and having allegiance to its ruler (Phil 3:20b, c). The adverb ἀξίως (worthily) also modifies the verb πολιτεύεσθε and provides the reference point to the genitive of personal interest, τοῦ εὐαγγελίου τοῦ Χριστοῦ. The qualifier "of Christ" refers to the content of the gospel, not its source.[12] Therefore the genitive of personal interest is best taken to refer to Christ's prior action which Paul goes on to describe in Phil 2:6–8. The Philippians are to live worthily of Christ and in consideration of what he has done, as described in the gospel. Christ is therefore the focus of the allegiance and behavior Paul is demanding. This is particularly significant in light of what unfolds in the following verses.

Following Phil 1:27a, the ἵνα clause continues the long complex sentence into verse 28, and describes *how* the Philippians are to live as citizens of the gospel—by standing firm. The verb στήκω[13] can mean "to stand firm" or "persevere" when used in a context of persecution—it is "part of a well-formed tradition of teaching in the context of persecution"[14] and is used by Paul in a similar context of opposition, distress and affliction in 1 Thess 3:8 (cf. Eph 6:11, 13–14). The verb στήκετε is modified by the prepositional phrase, ἐν ἑνὶ πνεύματι meaning that the Philippians are to stand firm "in one spirit." So, ἐν ἑνὶ πνεύματι functions adverbially and is grammatically subordinate to the verb στήκετε—the prepositional phrase further qualifies the manner of standing firm,[15] or the sphere in which they are to stand firm.[16] Either way, "unity in the spirit" is subordinate to "standing firm."

Paul provides specific content to στήκετε in the following participial phrases: the Philippians are to contend together (συναθλοῦντες) and not be frightened (μὴ πτυρόμενοι). Here, συναθλοῦντες and πτυρόμενοι are

---

11. Since Brewer, "Meaning of *Politeuesthe* in Philippians 1:27," 76–83 and Miller, "Πολιτεύεσθε in Philippians 1:27," 86–96, most scholars concur that πολιτεύεσθε is a technical (political) term denoting "living as a citizen" rather than a verb of ethical action; Lincoln, *Paradise Now*, 97–101.

12. So O'Brien, *Philippians*, 148.

13. BDAG, 944: "to be firmly established in conviction or belief"; Grundmann, "στήκω," 637–38.

14. Donfried, "Setting of 2 Thessalonians," 88; Selwyn, *First Epistle of St. Peter*, 454–58.

15. Taking ἐν ἑνὶ πνεύματι as a dative of manner.

16. Fee, *Philippians*, 165, interprets ἐν ἑνὶ πνεύματι as referring to the Holy Spirit with the prepositional phrase as locative. His argument is that there is no Pauline analogy for a dative of manner used with "spirit."

participles which amplify the indicative στήκετε.[17] συναθλοῦντες can mean to "contend, struggle along with"[18] or "to engage in competition or conflict."[19] In the NT writings, it only appears in Philippians (Phil 1:27 and 4:3) and both times alongside στήκω and in reference to contending for the gospel. In the LXX, the word is used in 4 Macc, where it denotes the conflict of martyrs, and is a "stock martyrological motif."[20] Krentz and Pfitzner, in particular, have argued that it can be a metaphor used to describe the athletic competition or the military response to conflict.[21] συναθλοῦντες is modified by the prepositional phrase μιᾷ ψυχῇ[22] which functions adverbially and describes the way in which the Philippians are to contend together for the faith of the gospel—namely, with one accord. Both prepositional phrases, then, elaborate the idea of perseverance with a sense of solidarity.[23] Additionally, the Philippians are to contend τῇ πίστει τοῦ εὐαγγελίου. Here, we understand τῇ πίστει as a dative of interest ("for the faith of the gospel") rather than a dative of instrument ("with the faith of the gospel") and τοῦ εὐαγγελίου as a genitive of origin ("the faith based on the gospel") as opposed to an appositional genitive ("the faith which is the gospel") or objective genitive ("faith in the gospel").[24] Loh and Nida's translation seems fitting: "the faith which is appropriate to the gospel."[25] The Philippians are to live as citizens worthy of, and to contend for a faith that is somehow characterized by, the gospel

---

17. De Witt Burton, *Syntax*, 54–55: "the verb and the participle of identical action, though denoting the same action, usually describe it from a different point of view"; Geoffrion, *Rhetorical Purpose*, 24; Tellbe, *Synagogue*, 232; cf. Fee, *Philippians*, 166, who proposes that συναθλοῦντες provides the reason the Philippians's need to stand firm in one spirit. But this does not seem to be the function of the participial modifier, and anticipates his view that unity is the issue, rather than perseverance; cf. Michael, *Philippians*, 66, who writes, "To fight is one of the conditions of *standing firm*. When we cease to fight we are bound to fall." Emphasis his.

18. BADG, 964.

19. Stauffer, "ἀθλέω," 167.

20. Pobee, *Persecution*, 109. The term occurs in 4 Macc 6:10; 9:23; 11:20; 13:15; 17:12ff; Wis 10:2; 2 Tim 2:5; 4:7; Ign.Pol. 6:1.

21. Krentz, "Military Language"; Pfitzner, *Paul and the Agon Motif*.

22. μιᾷ ψυχῇ does not modify στήκετε. So, Vincent, *Philippians*, 34; Meyer, *Philippians and Colossians*, 62, rightly notes that συναθλοῦντες needs a modifier in line with the context; cf. Fowl, *Story of Christ*, 86, who interprets " . . . stand firm in one spirit and in one mind, striving together . . . "

23. We prefer the term "solidarity" because the feeling or quality of fellowship inherent in the term arises from a union of *specific* interests, aspirations or sympathies among members of the Philippian community.

24. So O'Brien, *Philippians*, 152.

25. Loh and Nida, *Handbook*, 41.

message itself—the content of which is Christ, whose paradigm (described in Phil 2:6–11) is seemingly anticipated here.

In the second participial phrase, πτυρόμενοι which is almost always found in the passive voice, means "to be frightened" or "let oneself be intimidated."[26] The word does not occur in the LXX, but is found in classical Greek literature to describe the crippling timidity of horses before battle.[27] Whether or not it carries a similar meaning in Phil 1:28, Paul uses the word as a description of a negative response to adversaries, and as further amplification of what it means to stand firm. It is difficult to understand Paul's choice of the word if he did not perceive that the Philippians were experiencing fear of their adversaries.

When coupled with συναθλοῦντες and πτυρόμενοι, στήκετε may convey the sense of standing firm in the face of a formidable foe, and seems to be the expression of citizenship that Paul wants to single out in this passage.[28] Paul's use of these terms in this particular context suggests that the Philippians are involved in some kind of conflict. In Phil 1:27, 28a, he is therefore commanding the Philippians to be steadfast by contending for the gospel and by not allowing themselves to be intimidated by their opponents; συναθλοῦντες and πτυρόμενοι are descriptions of what it means to stand firm during conflict.

The explicit mention of opponents in Phil 1:28 confirms that the Philippians are experiencing conflict—ὑπὸ τῶν ἀντικειμένων (by your adversaries). In the NT, the verb ἀντίκειμαι can mean "to be opposed to" (Gal 5:17; 1 Tim 1:10), with the participial form meaning "the enemy."[29] In the LXX, it appears in Exod 23:22 in a context parallel to Phil 1:27; ἐχθρεύσω τοῖς ἐχθροῖς σου καὶ ἀντικείσομαι τοῖς ἀντικειμένοις σοι—"I will be an enemy to your enemies and an adversary to your adversaries."[30] Paul's choice of this word clearly reflects conflict. The notion of conflict is continued in the eschatological dualism of Phil 1:28 where the Philippians can expect salvation for themselves but destruction for their opponents—ἥτις ἐστὶν αὐτοῖς ἔνδειξις ἀπωλείας, ὑμῶν δὲ σωτηρίας, καὶ τοῦτο ἀπὸ θεοῦ. Here, the relative

---

26. BADG, 895.

27. Diod. Sic. 2.19.2; 17.34.6; Plut. Vit. 175.

28. Taking στήκετε, the main verb in the dependent clause, to specify the sense of πολιτεύεσθεν. So too Barth, *Philippians*, 46; Geoffrion, *Rhetorical Purpose*, 55, thinks στήκετε has imperatival force because of its close link to πολιτεύεσθεν; Kennedy, *Philippians*, 430, also notes that Paul's second reference to citizenship (Phil 3:20) is followed by the same two verbs (στήκειν and συναθλεῖν).

29. Büchsel, "ἀντίκειμαι," 655. The participial form is also found in Luke 13:17; 21:15; 1 Cor 16:9; 2 Thess 2:4; 1 Tim 5:14.

30. LEH, Part I, 40.

clause introduced by the indefinite relative pronoun ἥτις has as its antecedent the perseverance of the Philippians in the face of opposition.[31] O'Brien rightly sums up the referent of ἥτις as "which circumstance," that is, the steadfastness of the Philippians in the face of opposition.[32] The perseverance of the Philippians therefore acts as a twofold sign[33] with eschatological significance—it is a sign *for* the protagonists (the Philippians) *only*, but it signals the consequences for both protagonists (salvation) and antagonists (destruction) in the conflict.[34]

The conflict Paul introduces with military metaphors in Phil 1:27-29, he mentions specifically in Phil 1:30—τὸν αὐτὸν ἀγῶνα ἔχοντες, οἷον εἴδετε ἐν ἐμοὶ καὶ νῦν ἀκούετε ἐν ἐμοί. Paul reveals that the Philippians are experiencing the same conflict (the word ἀγών can mean conflict)[35] they had previously witnessed Paul experiencing, and which he is currently experiencing.[36] Although the exact nature of the conflict is not disclosed here, Paul had already recorded the suffering and mistreatment he received in Philippi in his letter to the Thessalonians (ἀλλὰ προπαθόντες καὶ ὑβρισθέντες, καθὼς οἴδατε, ἐν Φιλίπποις—1 Thess 2:2). In 2 Cor 7:5 he described his experience

---

31. Cf. Hawthorne, *Philippians*, 58-59, who has τῇ πίστει as the antecedent because it matches gender and number. Hawthorne's point is well taken but the context might demand a different treatment of the grammar. If faith is the antecedent, then it stands apart from its context as a sign, yet Paul seems to intend that faith expressed in some context is the sign. Additionally, the phrase οὐ μόνον ... ἀλλὰ καί in Phil 1:29 suggests Paul has a perception that "not only" faith "but also" suffering is important in the Philippians's situation (see below). Thus, the sign, and what the sign signifies suggest more than faith. More likely, the antecedent of ἥτις is defined loosely by the whole of Phil 1:27c-28a as it represents perseverance denoted by στήκετε ἐν ἑνὶ πνεύματι, μιᾷ ψυχῇ συναθλοῦντες τῇ πίστει τοῦ εὐαγγελίου καὶ μὴ πτυρόμενοι ἐν μηδενὶ ὑπὸ τῶν ἀντικειμένων. Thus, the feminine, singular form of the indefinite pronoun is attracted from ἔνδειξις, but has the "collective" qualities of perseverance as its antecedent (Hawthorn concedes this is grammatically possible).

32. O'Brien, *Philippians*, 154.

33. ἔνδειξις is modified by σωτηρίας and ἀπωλείας. Calvin, *Epistles*, 242, translates as "manifest proof."

34. Taking αὐτοῖς as a dative of reference, such that the sign would not be recognized by the opponents; cf. Beare, *Philippians*, 68, who thinks the sign is understood by the enemies who are somehow aware of their own destruction; Craddock, *Philippians*, 33, thinks the "omen is to the opponents, not the Christians."

35. Stauffer, "ἀγών," 135; Krentz, "Military Language," 126, who notes that ἀγών is frequently used of a military engagement.

36. The nominative participle ἔχοντες is best taken to modify the dative ὑμῖν in v. 29, thus it is an "irregular nominative" (Fee, *Philippians*, 172; O'Brien, *Philippians*, 161). This preserves the sense that the manifestation of God's gift of faith and suffering (to you) is the conflict the Philippians are currently experiencing. NASB "forces" this meaning by creating a new sentence at v. 29.

of "conflict and fear" in Macedonia (which might be a reference to Philippi), and the afflictions experienced by the Macedonian Churches (2 Cor 8:1, 2—again a possible reference to Philippi). In 2 Cor 11:25 he revealed that "three times I was beaten with rods," and Luke also describes Paul being beaten and imprisoned in Philippi (Acts 16:22, 23).[37] We are therefore justified in suggesting that Paul's conflict in Philippi probably involved physical suffering, which was witnessed by the Philippians (οἷον εἴδετε ἐν ἐμοί). But in what way is the conflict shared by Paul and the Philippians τὸν αὐτόν? The "sameness" might simply refer to the common struggle resulting from gospel partnership (Phil 1:5, 7), or to a common source of persecution,[38] or to be more specific to beating and imprisonment. It certainly involves suffering and mistreatment (cf. 1 Thess 2:2). It is therefore not necessary to postulate a strict correspondence between Paul's ἀγών and those of the Philippians (for example that some Philippians were imprisoned),[39] but that both struggles entailed suffering and mistreatment which required a correct response. This final clause characterizes v. 29[40] so that both Paul's and the Philippians's suffering is a gracious gift from God and therefore merits the same response.

Perseverance or Unity?

We have argued that the prominent theme in Phil 1:27–30 is perseverance, characterized by a determination not to be intimidated by adversaries who are inflicting suffering. However, there has been a tendency in scholarship to view unity (in an absolute sense) as the main theme of the passage,[41] if not the whole letter.[42] This is mainly due to overstressing the role of the prepositional phrases ἐν ἑνὶ πνεύματι, μιᾷ ψυχῇ and the use of the prefix συν- in

---

37. There seems little reason why Acts 16:22–23 cannot be taken as corroborating evidence given the consistency of the Pauline sources (2 Cor 7:5; 11:25; 1 Thess 2:2; Phil 1:30).

38. The Roman Empire. So, Fee, *Philippians*, 167, 172 and Vincent, *Philippians*, 36, 69.

39. See also Houlden, *Letters*, 65–66.

40. Meyer, *Philippians and Colossians*, 66.

41. Chrysostom, "Homilies," 199–200; Aquinas, *Philippians*, 73–74; Plummer, *Philippians*, 32; O'Brien, *Philippians*, 164; Houlden, *Letters*, 66.

42. Bruce, *Philippians*, 19; Garland, "Composition and Unity," 162, 172–73; Stagg, "Mind In Christ Jesus," 337; Fee, *Philippians*, 155, recognizes the important link with steadfastness and suffering; Pollard, "Integrity," 66; Peterlin, *Disunity*, 9; cf. Fortna, "Philippians," 221, who wrongly proposes that Paul's self-concern with his own imprisonment is the occasion of the letter.

συναθλοῦντες. For example, Fee subsumes his exegesis of στήκετε under ἐν ἑνὶ πνεύματι and anticipates "unity" as the main theme.[43] Peterlin labels his exegesis of Phil 1:28–30 as "transition: to the theme of unity."[44] Although he recognizes the military metaphors in the text, he might have overlooked the theme of perseverance that the verb and participles convey. Silva suggests a chiastic pattern that points out the need for unanimity:[45]

    A   στήκετε
       B   ἐν ἑνὶ πνεύματι
       B¹   μιᾷ ψυχῇ
    A¹   συναθλοῦντες

It is easy to see how such a scheme would lead to the view that μιᾷ ψυχῇ is synonymously parallel to ἐν ἑνὶ πνεύματι, thus forming the centre of the chiasm and containing the central thought of the text, namely, unity. This structure would then take συναθλοῦντες as being synonymously parallel with στήκετε. But we have shown that, rather than being parallel, συναθλοῦντες elaborates on στήκετε and develops the idea of perseverance to include "contending together." Standing firm (persevering) involves an active contending for the gospel *combined with* a refusal to be intimidated by adversaries. Therefore, as modifiers of στήκετε and συναθλοῦντες respectively, ἐν ἑνὶ πνεύματι and μιᾷ ψυχῇ do not stand in a synonymously parallel relationship.[46] Undoubtedly, ἐν ἑνὶ πνεύματι and μιᾷ ψυχῇ may be understood as reflecting unity, but they modify a main verb and participle which describe something more than a generic appeal to community harmony.

God's Role in Suffering

Paul does not stop at issuing a command to persevere, but also provides a reason for it. In the final clause of verse 28, Paul perceives God having the determinative role in the conflict, and being the source of the Philippians's perseverance—καὶ τοῦτο ἀπὸ θεοῦ. τοῦτο is neuter and refers back to the "circumstance," not simply to σωτηρίας or ἔνδειξις.[47] It seems that the

---

43. Fee, *Philippians*, 163.
44. Peterlin, *Disunity*, 55–59.
45. Silva, *Philippians*, 82.
46. There is no consensus about whether ἐν ἑνὶ πνεύματι refers to the Holy Spirit (Barth, *Philippians*, 47) or "human or community spirit" (Michael, *Philippians*, 65). If the former, then it cannot be synonymously parallel with μιᾷ ψυχῇ.
47. So too Silva, *Philippians*, 83, who describes the antecedent of τοῦτο as, "conflict, destruction, perseverance and salvation"; Hendricksen, *Philippians*, 90, doubts that

Philippians needed to be reminded that their salvation, and the sign (proof) of their salvation (their perseverance) in their acceptance of suffering on account of Christ, come from God, establishing God as an active agent in the conflict. This is corroborated in v. 29: ὅτι ὑμῖν ἐχαρίσθη τὸ ὑπὲρ Χριστοῦ, οὐ μόνον τὸ εἰς αὐτὸν πιστεύειν ἀλλὰ καὶ τὸ ὑπὲρ αὐτοῦ πάσχειν. The ὅτι-clause is linked to καὶ τοῦτο ἀπὸ θεοῦ and provides the reason (ὅτι as causal conjunction) why the Philippians are to stand firm: "*because* to you it has been graciously granted (by God) on behalf of Christ, not only to believe in him but also to suffer (πάσχειν)[48] on his behalf." Paul's use of the causal conjunction, ὅτι, is significant because it continues the thought of God's active involvement expressed by Paul in the previous clause—the Philippians's steadfastness is a sign of their salvation and their opponents's destruction, and is from God. Now, Paul explicitly links perseverance to suffering, and develops further God's role in it. χαρίζομαι means to give freely as a favor, or to give graciously.[49] ἐχαρίσθη is passive and is mainly used by Paul to refer to the gracious gift of God.[50] The same word is used in Phil 2:9 (ἐχαρίσατο) to describe God's action of graciously bestowing a name on Jesus following his suffering and death. Paul reveals that the suffering experienced by the Philippians is a gift from God. But this suffering has another referent—the prepositional phrase τὸ ὑπὲρ Χριστοῦ. ὑπέρ is probably best rendered "because of" or "on account of," meaning that Christ is the reason behind the suffering that the Philippians are experiencing[51]—*but also that their suffering is characterized by him.* This coheres with the command to "live worthily as citizens of the gospel of Christ," and "contending together for the faith of the gospel," both of which define perseverance as suffering for Christ. According to Müller, "On account of his connection with Christ, suffering, however, is also inflicted upon the believer, with the purpose of doing harm to the cause of Christ."[52] Phil 1:27–28 therefore anticipates the suffering motif in verse 29, Christ's suffering in Phil 2:6–11 and Paul's solidarity with Christ through suffering in Phil 3:10. Additionally, ὑπὲρ Χριστοῦ resonates with τοὺς δεσμούς μου ... ἐν Χριστῷ (Phil 1:13) where Paul describes his imprisonment in the cause of Christ, and with εἰς ἀπολογίαν τοῦ εὐαγγελίου

τοῦτο cannot refer to a feminine noun (ἔνδειξις); cf. Bruce, *Philippians*, 60, who takes the antecedent of τοῦτο as ἔνδειξις.

48. BDAG, 785; Krentz, "Military Language," 126, suggests that πάσχειν is used of suffering harm from a military opponent; cf. Michaelis, "πάσχω," 920.

49. BDAG, 1078.

50. e.g., Rom 8:32; 1 Cor 2:12; Gal 3:18; Phlm 22.

51. The preposition ὑπέρ, when used with verbs of suffering, gives the reason for it. See Riesenfeld, "ὑπέρ," 514. τὸ ὑπὲρ Χριστοῦ is best construed with πάσχειν.

52. Müller, *Philippians*, 71.

κεῖμαι (Phil 1:16) where his imprisonment is for the defense of the gospel. Finally, in Phil 1:30, Paul reveals that the Philippians share in the same conflict; clearly, Paul and the Philippians are suffering because they are proclaiming the message that Christ is Lord.[53]

The ὅτι-clause therefore provides more details of the conflict introduced in Phil 1:27–28, by describing its impact on the Philippians (suffering), the reason behind the suffering (Christ) and perhaps, most surprisingly, the ultimate source of suffering (God). This latter aspect is significant because with it Paul justifies his exhortation to continued perseverance, which is now clearly defined by acceptance of suffering—persevere *because* your suffering is divinely sanctioned and approved.[54] Why would Paul want to "implicate" God as an active agent in the Philippians's suffering? This question is rarely asked in the commentaries and the matter of God's role in suffering has gone largely undeveloped in Philippian scholarship. Some take a less contextual approach and end up commenting on "a theology of suffering." For example, Holloway suggests that Paul follows a consolation *topos* citing "the divine law of suffering for all (believers)." He considers the most significant feature of Phil 1:27–30 to be the remarkable concentration of consolatory *topoi* of which the divine law is one.[55] But the consolatory *topos* of the divine law does not offer an explanation as to why Paul introduces God's role in the Philippians's suffering. Others rightly note the important function of suffering, but do not develop God's role in it. Bloomquist defines God's role in Phil 1:29, 30 as his gracious enabling of Paul's and the Philippians's fruitful service.[56] Oakes takes τὸ ὑπὲρ Χριστοῦ . . . πάσχειν as the "centre-point" of Phil 1:27–30, but in the process seems to overlook ἐχαρίσθη and God's role in the Philippians's suffering.[57] Geoffrion suggests that Paul presents the Philippians's obligation to suffer as a "given or assumed fact without providing any basis for his conviction apart from his own experience."[58]

---

53. Krentz, "Military Language," 126, suggests that ὑπέρ is used of the one on whose behalf one fights; Geoffrion, *Rhetorical Purpose*, 49, notes that εὐαγγελίον was a technical term used in a military sense, but specifically regarding the Roman emperor's birth or accession to the throne.

54. Not that God condones suffering *per sē*, but that suffering for God's cause receives his approval. God's authoritative permission or approval of a kind of suffering makes it valid.

55. Holloway, *Consolation*, 116.

56. Bloomquist, *Suffering*, 157–60.

57. Oakes, *From People to Letter*, 79.

58. Geoffrion, *Rhetorical Purpose*, 76.

In Bitzer's language, what specific condition or situation invites Paul's utterance that suffering is God's gracious gift to the Philippians?[59] In a fresh approach, N. Walter proposes that the specific condition which invited utterance was the Philippians's view, influenced by their pagan background, that the Deity would not require his worshippers to willingly undergo suffering.[60] In proposing this, Walter attempts to address the significance of divine approval of suffering in the context of the epistle. That Paul saw fit to include the converse of this sentiment lends support to Walter's proposal, and is a strong indication that there might have been disagreements among the Philippians about how to respond to suffering. A brief analysis of Phil 1:29bc seems to support this view.[61]

In Phil 1:29 where Paul describes the Philippians's suffering, the emphatic use of ἀλλὰ καί, and therefore the rhetorical force of the phrase οὐ μόνον ... ἀλλὰ καί has been overlooked by most commentators. For example, Lightfoot considers οὐ μόνον τὸ εἰς αὐτὸν πιστεύειν an after-thought and drops ἀλλὰ καί from his analysis.[62] Silva does not include the phrase in his exegesis.[63] Fee's explanation that οὐ μόνον ... ἀλλὰ καί can be accounted for simply as the result of interrupted dictation does not account for the emphatic use and seemingly deliberate choice of the term.[64] O'Brien is closer when he sees ἀλλὰ καί as providing a balance, but it is doubtful that οὐ μόνον simply introduces a fresh thought of believing in Christ,[65] rather than conveying the idea of deliberate contrast along with ἀλλὰ καί. Paul's admonition is that there is more to gospel citizenship than professed faith—you must suffer too, because God has granted it. The suggestion that Paul's use of οὐ μόνον ... ἀλλὰ καί, with respect to faith and suffering respectively, suggests a corrective for those Philippians who rejected suffering as concomitant with gospel citizenship can be based on the adversative force of ἀλλὰ καί. In the clause, ἀλλὰ καί is used to introduce an additional point in an emphatic way.[66] Contrary to the view that "only faith" has been given freely as a favor by God, faith *and suffering* have been given freely as a favor by God. But the

---

59. Bitzer, "Situation," 250.
60. Walter, "Die Philipper und das Leiden," 417–34.
61. Phil 2:14 and 4:2 are suggestive of disagreement in the community.
62. Lightfoot, *Philippians*, 106–7.
63. Silva, *Philippians*, 83–85.
64. Fee, *Philippians*, 171.
65. O'Brien, *Philippians*, 159.
66. BDF §448; see Phil 1:18: ἐν τούτῳ χαίρω. ἀλλὰ καὶ χαρήσομαι.; Loh and Nida, *Handbook*, 44, probably overstate the case for a *strictly* additive meaning (see below).

phrase is still used with adversative force[67]—although not negating God's gift of faith, ἀλλὰ καί suggests that Paul intends to introduce, emphatically, suffering in a way that *counters* faith as the *only* issue in the argument. Michaelis rightly recognizes the contrast: "it [πάσχειν] is a privilege, a special grace (ὑμῖν ἐχαρίσθη) which surpasses even the grace of being able to believe in Christ."[68] Suffering (and faith), in contrast to faith-only, is the *surprising* element of God's gracious bestowal. An appropriate paraphrase would be: "God has not gifted you (those who are disinclined to accept suffering as part-and-parcel of gospel partnership) faith *only*, but (contrary to your current way of thinking), suffering *also*." The double-emphatic use of μόνον, appearing twice in Phil 1:27–29 and forming a loose *inclusio* around the subject of what it means to live as citizens of the gospel, offers a hint that the problem in Philippi involves differing responses to conflict, with some disinclined to accept suffering. Gnilka puts it well: "And perhaps it needs time to pass from resistance or avoidance of suffering to the realisation that it is grace that one has received."[69] *The theme of God's sanctioning of suffering, experienced on account of Christ and his gospel, is therefore crucial to Paul's argument because he uses it to legitimize his exhortation to persevere.*

Conclusions

In Phil 1:27–30, Paul perceives the Philippians to be in a situation where they are suffering at the hands of their adversaries because of their commitment to the gospel. The real exigencies of fear, adversaries, suffering and conflict, and the rhetorical constraints of faith, citizenship, the gospel of Christ, eschatological salvation and destruction, and God's approval of suffering for the sake of Christ are prominent in the passage. Based on our exegesis of Phil 1:27–30, it is difficult to see how "unity" is the problem Paul confronts through his rhetoric, despite the scholarly consensus. The shocking disclosure of God's approval of suffering in the cause of Christ implies an alternative communicative intention. Therefore, our initial suggestion at this stage is that the controlling exigency that most economically accounts for Paul's language relates to the notion that some Philippians challenged the idea that God would approve of suffering for the sake of Christ. This

---

67. See BDF §448 for ἀλλὰ καί as the contrary to the preceding οὐ μόνον. Cf. Loh and Nida, *Handbook*, 44, who rightly advise against direct negation, but lessen the adversative force with the paraphrase, "you may serve Christ by believing in him, and you may also serve him by suffering on his behalf."

68. Michaelis, "πάσχω," 920.

69. Gnilka, "Philippians," 31.

controlling exigency is presupposed in Paul's admonition:[70] "for to you it has been graciously granted for Christ's sake, *not only* to believe in him, *but also* to suffer for his sake." God's approval is the rhetorical constraint that Paul brings to bear on this exigency—their suffering is by divine authority and is therefore valid as a defining characteristic of their citizenship. We suggest that this rhetorical situation is within the bounds of textual plausibility and can be reasonably inferred from our exegesis of the text. We will now investigate whether these conclusions can be supported by, developed from, or refuted by an analysis of Phil 2:1–4; 2:5–11, 14 and 3:1–21.

THE RHETORICAL SITUATION IN PHIL 2:1–4

The second passage selected in which Paul's injunctions may offer insights into the rhetorical situation is Phil 2:1–4. In fact, this part of the rhetorical unit contains an imperative (πληρώσατε) that several commentators have found difficult to explain in the context of Paul's argument. Most scholars argue that the main theme of Phil 2:1–4 is unity.[71] Two reasons are offered for this; firstly, the theme of unity is anticipated, or even established, in Phil 1:27–30 by the terms ἐν ἑνὶ πνεύματι, συναθλοῦντες and μιᾷ ψυχῇ;[72] secondly, Phil 2:1–4 forms a *renewed* appeal to unity as conveyed through Paul's use of the terms τὸ αὐτὸ φρονῆτε, τὴν αὐτὴν ἀγάπην ἔχοντες, σύμψυχοι and τὸ ἓν φρονοῦντες, which describe the general disposition of harmony.[73] Once again, the influence of terms carrying the sense of "oneness," "togetherness" or "sameness" predominates. But, as we have shown, a re-evaluation of the rhetoric of Phil 1:27–30, challenges the view that unity (as the main theme) is anticipated or established in the passage. Furthermore, the terms used by Paul in Phil 2:1 are those we would expect in a context of relieving sorrow and want, not necessarily unity; namely, comfort (παράκλησις), consolation (παραμύθιον), tender mercies (σπλάγχνα), and compassions (οἰκτιρμοί). Similarly, in Phil 2:3, 4, the terms and phrases used by Paul contrast selfishness and selflessness, and not necessarily division in the community; namely, selfish ambition (ἐριθείαν), self-interest (κενοδοξίαν), humility (ταπεινοφροσύνῃ) and concern for the welfare of others (μὴ τὰ ἑαυτῶν ἕκαστος σκοποῦντες ἀλλὰ [καὶ] τὰ ἑτέρων ἕκαστοι). We will aim

---

70. Culler, *Pursuit*, 111, who proposes that a logical presupposition is anything implied to be true by a sentence, whether the sentence is affirmed or denied.

71. For example, Black, "Paul and Christian Unity," 301; Fowl, *Story of Christ*, 88; Marshall, *Philippians*, 41; Oakes, *From People to Letter*, 178; Peterlin, *Disunity*, 61.

72. Marshall, *Philippians*, 41; Silva, *Philippians*, 85; O'Brien, *Philippians*, 166.

73. See Black, "Paul and Christian Unity," 302; Fee, *Philippians*, 175.

to establish Paul's argument through his use of these terms by answering the question: for which specific situation could Phil 2:1–4 be a fitting response? Since Phil 2:1–4 is a single sentence, we will start with a structural layout intended to identify which units of text are subordinate to others and therefore which ones convey the primary idea in Paul's rhetoric.

The Literary Structure of 2:1–4

Phil 2:1–4 has been subjected to form-critical analysis (although not to the same degree as Phil 2:6–11) with several proposals about literary structure and strophic arrangement—but as with Phil 2:6–11, there is a lack of consensus about the structure of the passage.[74] Below is a structure which follows the grammar of Paul's wording:[75]

a. therefore	if any (and there is) comfort in Christ,	
b.	if any (and there is) consolation of love,	
c.	if any (and there is) fellowship in the Spirit,	
d.	if any (and there are) affections and mercies, [then]	
e.	make my joy complete by (ἵνα)	
f.	thinking the same thing,	
g.	having the same love,	
h.	united in mind, thinking the one thing,	
i.	[thinking] nothing according to selfish ambition	
j.	nor according to excessive selfishness, but	
k.	considering, according to humility of mind, one	
l.	another as more important than one's self	
m.	each one not looking out for the things of one's	
n.	self but	
o.	each one [looking out for] the things of the other	

The ἵνα clause (e) governs a principal clause (f) which is modified by a series of subordinate clauses (g–o). The principal clause states how the imperative will be fulfilled—Paul's joy will be completed by the Philippians "thinking the same thing." Phrases g–o elaborate the principal clause by describing what is involved in "thinking the same thing"—"think the same thing,

---

74. See Lohmeyer, *Kyrios Jesus*, 80–81; Gnilka, *Der Philipperbrief*, 102–3; O'Brien, *Philippians*, 164–65; Silva, *Philippians*, 85–86.

75. See Fee, *Philippians*, 176.

namely ... " With this structure, we can now proceed to a verse-by-verse exegesis of Phil 2:1-4.

The Theological Grounds for the Response to Suffering

Verse 1 states the grounds for the imperative in verse 2—inferred from Phil 1:27-30 by the conjunction οὖν (for this reason). It is generally accepted that the fourfold use of the particle with the indefinite relative pronoun, εἴ τις/τι does not suggest doubt but refers to realities experienced by the Philippians[76]—"for this reason *since there is* comfort in Christ, *since there is* consolation of love, *since there is* fellowship of the Spirit and *since there are* affections and mercies, make my joy complete ... "[77] There is less agreement however on the meaning of the terms that follow.[78] O'Brien has argued convincingly for the meaning comfort in Christ (παράκλησις ἐν Χριστῷ) and consolation of love (παραμύθιον ἀγάπης) referring to the consolation or solace in God's or Christ's[79] love. The former refers to suffering on behalf of Christ,[80] and the latter term refers to "the consolation which Christ's love for them has brought to them in their dangers and sufferings."[81] This is a justifiable interpretation given the immediately preceding verses, which emphasize the shared suffering of Paul and the Philippians (Phil 1:29f). The third phrase, κοινωνία πνεύματος probably means the fellowship created by the Spirit, or refers to the Spirit as the agent through whom the fellowship is realized.[82] The fellowship (κοινωνία)[83] is the partnership of common interest

---

76. Silva, *Philippians*, 90; Fee, *Philippians*, 177; Black, "Paul and Christian Unity," 301.

77. Silva, *Philippians*, 88, is correct to point out that Paul's choice of words arose out of particular shortcomings in the Philippian community, although he believes "since" weakens the rhetorical force (ibid., 90).

78. See the thorough explanation by O'Brien, *Philippians*, 167-76.

79. Fee, *Philippians*, 180-81, prefers God's love, in line with his Trinitarian substructure of the passage.

80. See also ibid., 179-80, where he suggests that what Paul writes about Christ in Phil 2:1 "responds directly to the motif of suffering just mentioned."

81. Beare, *Philippians*, 71; cf. Lightfoot, *Philippians*, 105, who interprets the word as "exhortation."

82. Taking πνεύματος as a subjective genitive and referring to the Holy Spirit (so, Schweizer, "πνεῦμα," 434 and Collange, *Philippians*, 78). Although we do not see any reason why the objective genitive sense cannot also apply—namely, the fellowship is created by the Spirit, yet those for whom the Spirit creates fellowship have fellowship *with* the Spirit.

83. κοινωνία can mean "having *something* in common with *someone*" with the ideas of participation and association present.

or shared experience—we take this to refer to what Paul has just written in Phil 1:29f, namely suffering.[84] Thus, association with Christ brings suffering, through which Paul and the Philippians have the fellowship of the Spirit. This seems to be what Paul has in mind in Phil 3:10, where κοινωνία is used in terms of Paul sharing in Christ's suffering. Thus, gospel partnership is defined, in this context, as sharing the common interest of suffering for Christ's sake—suffering is the *means* of the fellowship *grounded in and created by* the Holy Spirit.

Following the threefold exhortation that grounds the appeal to the Philippians theologically (Christ's comfort, God's love, the Spirit's fellowship), Paul's fourth appeal seems to be rooted in community sympathy.[85] σπλάγχνα καὶ οἰκτιρμοί can refer to Christ's tender mercy and compassions,[86] but also to the compassion and pity that the Philippians have toward one another.[87] Considering the close connection with Phil 1:29f, in which Paul reminds the Philippians of the suffering and conflict they are sharing, it is reasonable to propose that Phil 2:1 links the theme of suffering in Phil 1:29f to 2:2-4 and describes the grounds upon which the following instructions rest.

Joy as the Response to Suffering

It has been noted that the only imperative in the paragraph, πληρώσατε, relates to Paul on a personal level (make my joy complete). Hawthorne claims the imperative is prefatory to the main idea of unity coupled with humility.[88] Fee also recognizes the difficulty of making sense of the imperative in the context of Phil 2:1-4. Recognizing that the imperative seems unnecessary, and in an effort to resist brushing it aside, he suggests it reveals Paul's "pastoral heart," and is fitting content for a letter of friendship.[89] Similarly,

---

84. If so, then the Spirit's fellowship should be a decisive factor in their acceptance of suffering. This is not to deny that fellowship can be realized through other shared experiences, but in this context Paul has in mind, suffering as the bond of fellowship. See Phil 1:5, 7.

85. Fee, *Philippians*, 182. His reasons are: the absence of a genitive qualifier (cf. the first three appeals) and the consistency of a direct appeal with the following imperative.

86. O'Brien, *Philippians*, 175–76, argues for the tender mercies and compassions of Christ experienced by the Philippians when they became Christians.

87. Fee, *Philippians*, 182; Köster, "σπλάγχνον," 555-56, translates the phrase σπλάγχνα καὶ οἰκτιρμοί as "love from the heart" and "personal sympathy."

88. Hawthorne, *Philippians*, 67.

89. Fee, *Philippians*, 183.

O'Brien's explanation of the imperative is to call it a "tactful expression."[90] Silva claims that the main verb of a sentence does not necessarily convey the writer's main concern—the Philippians's unanimity of mind, not Paul's personal yearnings for joy, is the primary thought of the whole passage as expressed in the *subordinate* clauses that follow.[91] But these interpretations fail to explain Paul's rhetoric, as well as lightening the force of his imperative and ignoring the "background" function of the subordinate clauses. The ideas expressed in the subordinate clauses ("sameness" and "oneness") complement the imperative. Paul's joy should be accounted for in the context of Phil 1:29f and 2:1 which describe the realities of Paul's and the Philippians's suffering. In Phil 1:17f Paul expresses joy in the context of a response to those who intend to increase his suffering, and he repeats the sentiment in Phil 1:18f, anticipating that his imprisonment will turn out for his salvation. In Phil 2:17f Paul conveys his joy when faced with the possibility of his death exhorting the Philippians to do likewise (either rejoice at the prospect of his death or theirs). Phil 1:4 describes the joy the Philippians have brought Paul in spite of his afflictions.[92] Considering these occurrences of the joy motif in the letter, and the immediate context of Phil 1:27–30, πληρώσατε μου τὴν χαράν probably relates, rhetorically, to Paul's attitude as it finds expression in his response to his suffering and possible death—the significance of the phrase immediately following Phil 2:1 is that it connects Paul's response to suffering with the realities of the Philippians's suffering (Phil 2:1 and 1:29f). We suggest that the response to suffering (his own and theirs) is the main point Paul wants to convey by the imperative.

The ἵνα clause which follows is best taken as indicating the method by which the action of the verb is achieved—"Make my joy complete *by* having the same mind."[93] Thus ἵνα τὸ αὐτὸ φρονῆτε functions as an adverbial clause of manner describing how Paul's joy will be made complete. This principal clause is then modified by two participial phrases:[94] τὴν αὐτὴν ἀγάπην ἔχοντες and σύμψυχοι τὸ ἓν φρονοῦντες. The subordinate clauses continue the expression of means (how Paul's joy will be made complete) indicated by the preposition *by*—"think the same thing *by* having the same love, and *by* thinking the one thing." Alternatively, they might function "causally," providing the reason why the Philippians should think the same thing—

---

90. O'Brien, *Philippians*, 176.
91. Silva, *Philippians*, 86. Emphasis his.
92. Silva, *Philippians*, 86.
93. Loh and Nida, *Handbook*, 50.
94. Not three, since σύμψυχοι goes with τὸ ἓν φρονοῦντες—"with harmony of soul cherishing the one sentiment." See Meyer, *Philippians and Colossians*, 73.

"make my joy complete *because* you think the same thing *because* (like me) you have the same love, and united in soul, you think the one thing."⁹⁵ On balance, it is preferable to interpret the phrases to refer to an expression of means that describes what the Philippians have to do to make Paul's joy complete (his imperative serves as a "reminder").

The following modifying clause (μηδὲν κατ' ἐριθείαν μηδὲ κατὰ κενοδοξίαν) amplifies τὸ ἓν φρονοῦντες in Phil 2:2c—"thinking the one thing, *namely*, '[thinking] not according to selfish ambition nor according to vainglory.'"⁹⁶ It is this, and the positive expressions of it which follow in v. 3, that Paul desires of the Philippians. Paul desires the Philippians to think the same way about *something* or share a common orientation towards *something*—this orientation is common because it is *the same* for everyone. Few commentators ask about the nature or content of the "sameness" that Paul desires from the Philippians—what is it that he wants them to agree on, or be united around? As Bockmuehl writes, "The actual *content* of this 'sameness' of mind is about to be spelled out in Phil 2:6–11, which recounts the 'mind' of Christ (v. 5)."⁹⁷ If the "sameness" Paul urges has content, then there might be an alternative to the popular understanding of the terms τὸ αὐτό, τὴν αὐτήν, σύμ- and τὸ ἕν as being used in an absolute way to convey unity.⁹⁸ Paul is using the terms because he desires the Philippians to be "characterized by a common orientation"⁹⁹ that is explicated elsewhere in the text—but what is it? It might refer to what Paul has written before (the realities about suffering in v. 1) or after (the renunciation of self-centeredness in vv. 3–4). This is corroborated by other occurrences of τοῦτο with the verb φρονεῖν in the letter—where they do not speak of unity in an abstracted sense, but refer to the surrounding context. For example in Phil 1:7, τοῦτο φρονεῖν refers backwards to verse 6 as Paul thinks in a particular way about God completing the good work he has begun in the Philippians. In Phil 2:5, τοῦτο φρονεῖτε relates to an attitude expressed in the preceding or following verses (Phil 2:2–4: the attitude of selflessness or Phil 2:6–11: the attitude/

---

95. Loh and Nida, *Handbook*, 50–51.

96. O'Brien, *Philippians*, 179, suggests that the one thing "describes the one aim on which the readers ought to focus." He proposes that the one thing requires them to be gospel oriented.

97. Bockmuehl, *Philippians*, 109. Italics his.

98. Cf. Barth, *Philippians*, 53–54, who admits that it (*to auto*) is not empty of content, yet suggests it refers to something general, not specific: "It is to be supposed, although the concrete details are all hidden from us, that it was also in Philippi a case of radical disunity."

99. Fowl, *Story of Christ*, 88, recognizes that a common orientation should define or establish the Philippians's unity, but concludes by stating that this is "unity" itself.

story of Christ). Likewise, in Phil 3:15, the phrase, τοῦτο φρονῶμεν, used with εἴ τι ἑτέρως φρονεῖτε, refers to alternative ways of thinking about death and resurrection. In each of these instances, the "sameness" has a specific content which differs from context to context. In Phil 4:2, Paul's appeal to Euodia and Syntyche (τὸ αὐτὸ φρονεῖν) is modified by ἐν κυρίῳ—they are to have the same mind, or think the same way *in the Lord*. This latter example might encourage Euodia and Syntyche to have the common disposition of mind towards *all things* as the Lord would. But it might equally refer to a way of thinking about a particular issue, such as renouncing status that affords protection from suffering and death, as typified by the Lord (Phil 2:6–8).[100] In this case, thinking the "same thing" refers to Christ's self-renouncing attitude and behavior that led to his suffering and death. Thus "sameness" is not an abstract concept of unity but a specific expression of conformity and solidarity to be shared by all, with regard to suffering.

From the preceding analysis, we are therefore justified in taking the phrases τὸ αὐτὸ φρονῆτε and τὸ ἓν φρονοῦντες to refer forward to the following, subordinate, verses (3–4 and 3a respectively)—the Philippians are to think, with humility, of others as more important than themselves, the practical outworking of which will result in them looking out for the welfare of others ahead of themselves. This view is corroborated by the recurrence of verbs of mental attitude (ἡγέομαι and φρονεῖτε) in vv. 3–5. Verse 2 thus reaches forward to vv. 3, 4 (and beyond to vv. 6–8) which elaborate on the common orientation that Paul desires for the Philippians.

Self-sacrifice and Self-preservation Contrasted

Verse 3 has no verb, so like Meyer, we take the verse not as a prohibition on its own, but depending on φρονοῦντες in v. 2c,[101] since verbs of mental attitude permeate the passage. This views v. 3a as subordinate to v. 2c and providing explanation of it, as proposed above. Until this point Paul has been somewhat general in his instructions, but now specifies what he suspects to be the problem in Philippi. He uses two terms in a negative injunction, followed by two in a positive. ἐριθεία can mean "base self-seeking" or "self-interest" and need not necessarily refer to strife or contention between groups.[102] This

---

100. See also τὸ αὐτὸ ... φρονοῦντες in Rom 12:16 (in a context of haughtiness of mind), and τὸ αὐτὸ φρονεῖν in 15:5 (in a context of perseverance).

101. Meyer, *Philippians and Colossians*, 74; cf. Fee, *Philippians*, 186, and Lightfoot, *Philippians*, 106 who views the verbless phrase carrying imperatival force (Gal 5:13), so provides ποιοῦντες. See also NASB, NRSV, NIV.

102. Büchsel, "ἐριθεία," 661: "The admonitions of Phil 2:3–4 are against self-seeking

meaning can also apply to 2 Cor 12:20; Gal 5:20; Phil 1:17 and Jas 3:14, 16.[103] Thus selfish ambition is not necessarily over against others as Fee claims[104] nor does it convey the nuance of "party spirit."[105] The second negative term, κενοδοξία, can mean "boasting," "vainglory"[106] or "excessive ambition."[107] In Gal 5:26 the cognate κενόδοξος is used to describe those who "talk big, who are boastful and vainglorious." In 4 Macc 2:15 it means "empty boasting." The BADG meaning supports κενοδοξία as an amplification of ἐριθεία—an expression of extreme self-interest.[108] The extreme nature of the self-interest implies a neglect of others, which is precisely the idea that Paul develops in the following clauses of the sentence. Paul is advising the Philippians not to let their thinking (φρονοῦντες) be governed[109] by selfish ambition. Instead, their thinking is to be governed by a humility (ταπεινοφροσύνη) of mind that regards (ἡγούμενοι) others as more important (ὑπερέχοντας) than themselves (Phil 2:3b). Here, two terms are set against the negatives above—"humility" that results in regarding others as "excelling or surpassing oneself."[110] This language goes beyond a call to unity, which does not necessarily require treating others as more important than oneself, although this attitude could contribute to the nurturing of community harmony. Indeed, instructing dissenters and disputers to treat others as more important than themselves might be considered an odd way of encouraging them to iron out their differences: we do not think that deferring to another's view, to foster community unity, requires the deep sense of self-abnegation that these verses suggest. Instead, Paul's language seems more like a strong admonition to renounce the mindset of self-preservation in favor of one of self-sacrifice. This view is corroborated by verse 4—"each one is not to look out for the things of one's self, but the things of the other." This is more than

---

and vanity." He points out that ἐριθεία in Rom 2:8, does not refer to strife or contention, but selfish ambition.

103. In 2 Corinthians and Galatians, Paul uses other terms for strife, dissensions and factions (ἔρις, διχοστασίαι, αἱρέσεις) so ἐριθεία meaning "strife" or "disputes" would be redundant.

104. Fee, *Philippians*, 186.

105. Lightfoot, *Philippians*, 106–7, who seems to draw the meaning from Gal 5; Peterlin, *Disunity*, 63.

106. Oepke, "κενοδοξία," 662.

107. BADG, 538.

108. As BADG above; cf. Peterlin, *Disunity*, 64.

109. This seems to be the use of κατά—the majority text substitutes "or" for μηδὲ κατά.

110. See Delling, "ὑπερέχω," 524.

just a restatement of verse 3,[111] since Paul moves from verbs of thinking to verbs of action—they are to look out for the needs of others or take care of others.[112] This seems to be the meaning of σκοπέω in the LXX of 2 Macc 4:5[113] in which Onias's motive for appealing to the king is revealed: " . . . but having in view the welfare, both public and private, of all the people" (τὸ δὲ σύμφορον κοινῇ καὶ κατ' ἰδίαν παντὶ τῷ πλήθει σκοπῶν). Paul is clearly urging care for others. In the context of Phil 1:27-30 and 2:1-3, and seeking the situation for which the verses are a fitting response, we are justified in proposing that Paul wrote these words because there were Philippians who were in need of help,[114] which might not have been forthcoming from some quarters of the community.[115]

Conclusions

From the preceding exegesis, we can now propose the rhetorical situation for which Paul's communicative intentions, included in Phil 2:1-4, could be a possible response. The content of Phil 2:1 links the realities of shared suffering and conflict with the theological explanation of suffering in Phil 1:27-30,[116] and thus provides the grounds for what follows. Phil 2:2 conveys Paul's attitude to suffering and conflict, amplified in an imperative about his joy, and in a call for solidarity. Verses 3 and 4 reveal the common orientation that Paul desires for the Philippians—the renunciation of an attitude of self-preservation reflected in excessive selfishness and a concern for one's own interests. Paul's instructions presuppose the problem of some in the community not getting the care they need from others during the conflict. Those who are disinclined to stand together with their suffering partners in the gospel, perhaps distancing themselves for fear of opposition and hardship, have an attitude of self-preservation antithetical to how citizens should live in response to the gospel. Paul therefore calls for solidarity among the community, that they might stand firm, and together, not being divided over

---

111. Some see synonymous and antithetical parallels in Phil 2:1-4. See below on the authorship of Phil 2:5-11.

112. BADG, 931; Fee, *Philippians*, 190.

113. LEH, Part II, 430.

114. Perhaps Euodia and Syntyche are among them: ναὶ ἐρωτῶ καὶ σέ, γνήσιε σύζυγε, συλλαμβάνου αὐταῖς (4:2).

115. This is probably why he includes the details of Phil 1:15-17 and 2:21.

116. Cf. Fee, *Philippians*, 175. The main point in the preceding paragraph (Phil 1:27-30) is not, as Fee claims, the exhortation to live as citizens as opposed to the theological explanation of suffering, but to live as citizens *in a way that takes account of the theological explanation of suffering*.

the consequences of gospel citizenship—opposition, suffering and perhaps death. Consequently, "comfort in Christ," "consolation of love," "fellowship in the Spirit," compassion, humility of mind and self-sacrifice are rhetorical constraints employed by Paul to commend the response of joy in communal suffering. We suggest that, in the rhetoric of Phil 2:1–4, Paul seeks to correct an attitude of self-preservation that resulted in a neglect of others during conflict.

THE RHETORICAL SITUATION IN PHIL 2:5–11

The third passage where Paul's explicit injunctions might inform us of the situation in Philippi is Phil 2:5–11 in which he commands[117] the Philippians to orient their thinking. The text has been the subject of much attention and rigorous debate, with critical focus on authorship, whether the text should be interpreted soteriologically or ethically, whether it describes a pre-existent Christ or a human Jesus, and the relationship of vv. 9–11 to vv. 6–8. These four issues will be addressed in turn, before examining the situation for which vv. 5–11 seems to be a fitting rhetorical response.

Authorship

The question of authorship is of particular importance to our study because the intertextual methodology used emphasizes the role of the author in text production. Our thesis is that Paul is a sophisticated interpreter who intentionally alludes to Scripture texts which support his argument in Philippians. The presence of Isa 45:23 in Phil 2:6–11 raises an important question for our study because the majority of scholars suggest that Phil 2:6–11 is a pre-Pauline hymn which the apostle inserted into his letter to the Philippians;[118] how could Paul be the author of the alleged intertextual relationships between Isa 45:23 and other parts of the letter if he did not author Phil 2:10–11? Some scholars have noted that Paul's use of the "hymn" demonstrates his approval and agreement with its content, therefore his authorship of Phil 2:6–11 might not be particularly crucial for an exegesis of Philippians.[119] The problem remains, however, for any exegesis pursuing an

---

117. The imperatival form (φρονεῖτε) can be taken to mean "Do this!" See O'Brien, *Philippians*, 204.

118. See Martin, *Carmen Christi*, 24–62.

119. Hooker, "Philippians 2:6–11," 152, writes, "even if the material is non-Pauline, we may expect Paul himself to have interpreted it and used it in a Pauline manner."

intertextual study using the diachronic, text-production approach.[120] The issue of authorship of Phil 2:6–11 is therefore broached as a result of an exegesis which recognizes that the text of Isa 45:23 has been reproduced in Phil 2:10–11 by the author of Phil 2:6–11. To our knowledge no attention has been paid to the mechanics of Scripture citation as a means of exploring authorship of Phil 2:6–11, and we suggest that this might be more fruitful than some of the form-critical approaches[121] which have gained acceptance since Lohmeyer's groundbreaking monograph in 1928.[122] We will offer two new categories of evidence that draw on biblical parallelisms and a comparison of recurring citation technique in two undisputed Pauline letters (Rom 14:11 and Phil 2:10–11) where the author(s) allude(s) to Isa 45:23.

Critique of non-Pauline Authorship

There are four categories of evidence offered against Pauline authorship of Phil 2:6–11; stylistic, linguistic, contextual and theological. The stylistic evidence is founded on the view that stylistic abnormalities point to redactional activity on a pre-existing text. The linguistic argument is founded on a statistical analysis of vocabulary with some words identified as uncharacteristically Pauline. The theological argument attempts to show that the absence of "expected" Pauline theology and the presence of "foreign" theology

---

120. This approach views Paul, in a strict sense, as the creator of all of the intertextual relationships in Philippians. The idea that another author has used Isa 45:23 in the "hymn" in the intertextual way I suggest that Paul does cannot be ruled out at this stage. Neither can the possibility that Paul has detected the intertextuality of the previous author and concurred with it and been influenced by it. It might also be argued that the intertextuality that exists between Isa 45:23 and other texts in Philippians (other than Phil 2:10–11) is synchronic (assuming pre-Pauline authorship of Phil 2:10–11) because the author would have had no knowledge of Paul's letter to the Philippians (and thus, for example, of the possible allusion to Ps 2:11 in Phil 2:12) when he wrote the "hymn." Thus an intertextual study involving analyses of, say, Isa 45:23 with Phil 2:10–11 *and* Ps 2:11 with Phil 2:12 could proceed on a synchronic, text reception basis.

121. In saying this we do not doubt the value of source/form-critical methodologies, only how they have been applied in determining authorship of Phil 2:6–11.

122. Lohmeyer, *Kyrios Jesus*. See Martin, *Carmen Christi*, 256: "The influence of Isaiah in the Philippians-psalm is unconscious and is not shown as an acknowledged quotation"; Nagata, *Philippians 2:5–11*, 88–89: "Thus, since it is an accepted fact that the hymn in Phil 2:6–11 is composed independently and prior to the writing of the surrounding epistolary context, the question of the authorship of the hymn bears no primary importance for the formal analysis of the hymn: therefore, one can speak of the original hymn and its later redaction as incorporated into the letter, regardless of one's position on the Pauline authorship of the hymn." Such a view does not adequately account for the intertextuality that is clearly present in Phil 2:10–11. Moreover, we argue that this intertextuality is deliberately intended.

undermine Pauline authorship. The contextual argument considers the text as a self-contained unit which does not fit the context of the surrounding verses. Of these, the stylistic evidence proves more pernicious to the argument for Pauline authorship and will be treated at length.

The Linguistic Argument

The idea that a statistical analysis of vocabulary can determine authorship is inconclusive and raises doubts about how different two texts can be before their common authorship is disputed. The basic assumption seems to be that two works are necessarily more similar if they are by the same author than if they are not.[123] This leaves no scope for different vocabulary to enter in (by the same author) based on subject matter, context, or rhetorical exigency. Moreover, shorter letters, in general, have less repetitive and more specialized vocabulary.[124]

The Theological Argument

The view that "expected" Pauline theology is missing from Phil 2:6–11 does not take into account the size of the text (6 verses, 76 words) which would limit the doctrines the author could include anyway. This seems a particularly odd viewpoint given that the text is replete with Pauline theology (Christ coming in the flesh; the cross; Christ's obedience; Jesus as crucified Lord; the thoecentrism of Phil 2:9a, 11; the distinction between Jesus as Lord and God). The claims of the presence of "foreign" Pauline theology can be accounted for by appealing to the distinctiveness of the rhetorical exigency. The specifics of the Philippian situation would naturally result in a particular expression of Paul's theology. For example, to modify the exigency of a rejection of divinely-approved self-abnegation, an author might appeal to the alleged "foreign theology" of Jesus' equality with God and incarnation as an example of divine self-renunciation of privileges that culminates in death.

---

123. Metzger, "Reconsideration," 92.

124. See Yule, *Statistical Study*, 281, who argues that a solid basis for word-count statistical analysis requires a text of about ten thousand words. Since Philippians has only 1625 words, with 2:6–11 comprising a mere 76, use of the statistical method to determine authorship is prone to untrustworthy results.

The Contextual Argument

The claim that Phil 2:6–11 interrupts the paranetical context in the letter[125] and is too lofty for its immediate context will be addressed at the end of this section in which we argue that Christ's pre-existence, his equality with God, his voluntary abasement and death, and God's exaltation of him, are all fitting components of Paul's argument. Indeed, far from being a "'purple patch' stitched into the fabric of the exhortation,"[126] Phil 2:5–11 is the centerpiece of a rhetorical tapestry and serves as the climax of the whole argument.

The Stylistic Argument

The arguments about abnormal style are closely connected with the idea that Phil 2:6–11 exhibits the style of a hymn or poem,[127] such texts being characterized by an abundant use of participles, the presence of parallel phrases and the rhythmic quality of the sentences.[128] However, certain elements of hymnody are missing from Phil 2:6–11,[129] and the use of διὸ καί, ἵνα and ὅτι in vv. 9–11 suggests the style of epistolary argumentation.[130] Moreover, Phil 2:6–11 does not have syllabic rhythm, that is, metrical lines containing the same number of syllables in a regular rhythmical pattern. Indeed, all attempts to restructure the strophic arrangement of Phil 2:6–11 to achieve the desired metrical symmetry have failed, casting doubts on whether there is meter in the text.[131] This takes us to an important issue that Kugel has

125. Stanley, *Christ's Resurrection*, 102; Hengel, "Song," 288.

126. Hunter, *Paul and His Predecessors*, 42.

127. Martin, *Carmen Christi*, 45: "The designation of the section as a Christological tribute has a distinct bearing on the matter of authorship"; Minear, "Singing and Suffering in Philippi," 203; Fee, *Philippians*, 193: "The steps towards the denial of authenticity are easy to discern: first, the passage is understood to be a hymn; if so, then it is probably pre-Pauline."

128. Harrington, *Interpreting the New Testament*, 60. The absence of the definite article and the frequent or recurring use of the relative pronoun ὅς are also used as evidence of hymnody.

129. There is no address to God, the elements of praise (with its motive) are absent and there is no concluding prayer of petition commonly found in hymns. See Fowl, *Story of Christ*, 31–45; Lattke, *Hymnus*, 233; Berger, "Hellenistische Gattungen im Neuen Testament," 1151; cf. Krentz, "Epideiktik and Hymnody," 89–93, who proposes that the texts in the NT are incomplete hymns, and that the absence of introductory invocations, petitions for aid and concluding prayers are not grounds for rejecting the text as a hymn. But he argues based on what is in, *and* not in, the text.

130. Fee, *Philippians*, 193.

131. See the attempts by Jeremias, "Zur Gedankenführung in den paulinischen Briefen"; Talbert, "Pre-existence," 141–53; Howard, "Phil 2:6–11," 376; Martin, *Carmen*

observed and which relates to the designation of Phil 2:6-11 as a hymn; that classification of a text as being poetic or having metrical or rhythmic patterns is an *interpretation* of parallelism. According to Kugel, "Metrical speculation usually depends on 'parallelism' for its lineation, and is not a wholly independent principle."[132] It is to the issue of parallelism that we now turn because much of the authorship debate depends upon it, and there is no denying that Phil 2:6-11 contains parallel clauses or phrases.

Parallelism in Phil 2:6-11

Jeremias thought that the substructure to Phil 2:6-11, as a hymn, is built up in couplets, in a device known as *parallelismus membrorum*.[133] Hofius suggested the passage was made up of a series of parallel couplets in metrical order.[134] Hengel, concurring with Jeremias that Lohmeyer's arrangement of the verses partially destroyed the parallelism, prefers a pattern of seven double verses arranged in Semitic *parallelismus membrorum*.[135] Longenecker includes "the presence of parallel structures (*parallelismus membrorum*) that reflect Jewish or Hellenistic poetic conventions" as the first of his criteria for the identification of early Christian hymns.[136] Parallelism clearly figures prominently in the classification of Phil 2:6-11 as a pre-Pauline hymn, especially the concept of *parallelismus membrorum*. The origin of the term can be traced back to R. Lowth who, in 1753, introduced the terminology of *parallelismus membrorum* (the parallelism of the clauses) which defined all parallelism under three broad "types": synonymous, antithetical and synthetic.[137] Synonymous parallelism came to mean, "saying the same thing twice" and antithetical parallelism had a second clause acting as a negative complement to a first clause. By identifying these types of parallelisms in a

---

Christi, 36-38; Gundry, "Style and Substance"; Fitzmyer, "Aramaic Background of Philippians 2:6-11," 483. According to Fitzmyer, the hymn has no metrical symmetry in Aramaic either; Clarke, *New Testament Problems*, 148; Eckman, "Metrical Analysis," 266, in which she concedes that meter can only be achieved by deleting or emending anomalous phrases.

132. Kugel, "Biblical Style," 113; Gray, *Forms of Hebrew Poetry*, 47: "I treat of parallelism before metre: parallelism is unmistakable, metre in Hebrew literature is obscure"; Gloer, "Homologies and Hymns," 126-27.

133. Jeremias, "Zur Gedankenführung in den paulinischen Briefen," 152-54.

134. Hofius, *Der Christushymnus Philipper 2, 6-11*, 8-9.

135. Hengel, "Song," 288-89.

136. Longenecker, *New Wine Into Fresh Wineskins*, 10. Also Martin, *Carmen Christi*, 12-13.

137. Lowth, *De Sacra Poesi Hebraeorum Praelectiones Academicae Oxonii Habitae*.

text Lowth not only defined the convention for future scholarship, his work prepared the way for the general acceptance that parallelism was a literary means of distinguishing prose from poetry;[138] the presence of parallelism in a text meant that the text was poetry. Lowth's work has had a significant impact on the scholarly approach to classification and interpretation of Phil 2:6–11 as a hymn. However, use of *parallelismus membrorum* has produced contradictory conclusions and disagreements over which lines in Phil 2:6–11 are parallel and in what way they are parallel; the same pairs of lines in the "hymn" can be interpreted as synonymously parallel *and* antithetically parallel by different scholars! At least eight different structures for Phil 2:6–11 have been proposed alerting us to question the concept of *parallelismus membrorum* as a means of structuring and interpreting a text.

Although Lowth's system of *parallelismus membrorum* has been widely accepted, it was challenged as early as the turn of the last century by Budde.[139] More recently, Kugel doubted that any of Lowth's examples of antithetical parallelism shows the second clause in a couplet as a negative complement of the first. Instead, the supposed negation creates agreement not contrast.[140] He also noted the effect of imposing synonymity on a text when it did not exist, with the real nature of biblical parallelism condemned to a perpetual "falling between two stools."[141] Kugel identifies a greater variety of parallelisms in the Bible than Lowth first proposed—at least eight forms spread across various genres:

> [parallelism] was an extraordinarily versatile and popular form of expression, one that almost anyone could use almost anywhere. Parallelistic lines appear throughout the bible, not only in 'poetic' parts but in the midst of narratives (especially in direct discourse), in detailed legal material concerning the sanctuary and the rules of sacrifices, in genealogies, and so forth.[142]

One of Kugel's most important findings was that it was wrong to suggest that the presence of parallelism in a text classifies it as poetry. Rather, parallelism is the primary rhetorical way of producing a heightened persuasive

---

138. Kugel, "Biblical Style," 109.

139. Quoted by Kugel, *Idea of Biblical Poetry*, 15: "By distinguishing three kinds of parallelism, synonymous, antithetic, and synthetic, as well as by the very name 'parallelism,' he [Lowth] contributed at the same time to encourage too narrow a conception of the phenomenon."

140. Ibid., 14.

141. See also Gray, *Forms of Hebrew Poetry*, 49.

142. Kugel, *Idea of Biblical Poetry*, 3–7; Watson, "Review of Kugel's Idea," 90–91, who lists even more types of parallelisms than Kugel.

effect and is used in prose and poetry (although poetry uses it more often than prose). Kugel's view that parallelism in the Bible is more numerous and varied than Lowth proposed in the eighteenth century has found favor in recent scholarship. For example, Watson writes: "Of itself, of course, parallelism is not indicative of poetry since prose, too, uses parallelism." He cites 1 Sam 26:12 as an example of parallelistic prose:[143]

> No one saw;
>
> no one noticed;
>
> no one woke—
>
> for they were all sleeping;
>
> for a dead sleep had fallen on them.

In similar vein, Landy writes: "there is no absolute dividing line between poetry and prose in the Bible,"[144] and that the presence of parallelism is "not a mandatory marker of poetry." He goes on to provide an example of poetry that has no parallelisms (Ps 23) and prose that does (Gen 22). In Gen 22, he describes prose in terms of parallel couplets that interrupt the temporal flow, such as:

> And the Lord visited Sarah as he had said
>
> and the Lord did for Sarah as he had spoken (Gen 21:1)[145]
>
> Stretch not your hand against the lad
>
> And do nothing whatsoever to him (Gen 22:12)

Landy goes as far as to argue that parallelism in poetry can be distinguished from parallelism in prose; the former exploits disjunction whereas the latter supports conjunction.[146] In prose, the parallelism helps the narrative to move forward by small and interconnected steps. In this type of parallelism the second phrase (B) of a "parallel couplet" adds something to the first phrase (A). In Kugel's terminology: "A is so, and what's more, B is so" or "not only A, but B." The second clause (B) intensifies or emphasizes the first. With this kind of "seconding," the B clause particularizes, defines or expands the meaning of the A clause and is not merely a restatement of it (cf. "synonymous parallelism"). This is very similar to Lohmeyer's ap-

---

143. Watson, *Classical Hebrew Poetry*, 50.

144. Landy, "Poetics and Parallelism," 66–67.

145. There is more than simple repetition in these couplets because *doing* for Sarah is a progression on *visiting* Sarah.

146. Ibid., 79.

proach to the "hymn" where he saw a logical progression that links the sections—incarnation; humiliation and death; exaltation. Brown calls this logical progression a *sorites*—"a chain of propositions in which the predicate of a statement forms the subject of the next, and the conclusion unites the subject of the first proposition with the predicate of the last."[147] We suggest that the style of parallelism characteristic of prose described above is present in Phil 2:6-11 and can be recognized without the need to excise content or distort and separate connecting phrases. The following structure of Phil 2:6-11 has parallel couplets set out in prose fashion:

(A) [6]who in the form of God existing
(B) did not consider equality with God a thing to be exploited,

(A) [7]but He emptied himself
(B) taking the form of a bondservant, being made in the likeness of men;

(A) and being found in appearance as a man [8]he humbled himself
(B) becoming obedient to the point of death, even death on a cross.

(A) [9]for this reason also God highly exalted him
(B) and bestowed on him the name which is above every name,

(A) [10]so that at the name of Jesus every knee shall bow
(B) of those in heaven and on earth and under the earth

(A) [11]and every tongue shall confess
(B) that Jesus Christ is Lord to the glory of God the Father.

It is not our intention to offer yet another arrangement of the hymn[148] but merely to show that parallelism in Phil 2:6–11 can be accounted for using concepts advanced by Kugel, Landy and Watson. With this style of parallelism, the B clause "develops" the A clause in each parallel couplet producing the contiguity that Landy identifies as supportive of parallelism in prose

147. Brown, "Ernst Lohmeyer's Kyrios Jesus," 9.
148. It can be seen that this arrangement follows the versification (NA^{26}, UBSGNT^4) closely, with each couplet comprising a verse, and aligned with a verse beginning (exception is Phil 2:8). There is no violation of sentence structure or Greek punctuation. The arrangement is not far off Lohmeyer's in logical flow—six couplets vs. six triplets. See also Fee, "Hymn" 39, who also begins by following the structure of Paul's Greek sentences.

form. What's more, the narrative progression of events is also present in the conjunctive sense described by Landy; the parallelism supports a sequence of activities by using conjunctions between and within the couplets (such as "and," "but," "for," "so that") to introduce the consequent action.

The distinctiveness of Phil 2:6–11 can therefore be explained without recourse to hymnody. It is the stylistic feature of parallelism which is at the heart of the text's classification, we suggest wrongly, as poetry or hymn. Parallelism is an emphatic feature of a text designed to produce a heightened effect in both prose and poetry. It is partly due to the failure to recognize *parallelistic prose* that has led to Phil 2:6–11 being classified as a hymn, and consequently pre- and un-Pauline. Likewise, the *rhythmical quality* of the sentences in Phil 2:6–11 is the result of the parallelisms in the text, not metrical symmetry. Consequently, because the parallelisms in Phil 2:6–11 fit very well the form of prose that Kugel, and others, have described, Martin's claim should be reconsidered:

> It has become a *sententia recepta* of literary criticism that Philippians ii. 6–11 is clearly to be distinguished from the neighbouring verses of the Epistle; *and its language and style must be treated as totally unlike the language and style of epistolary prose.*[149]

The implication of our analysis for Pauline authorship need not be seen as obvious—if Phil 2:6–11 is not a hymn that has been inserted by Paul into his letter, then its parallelistic prose style can be credibly attributed to him. That Paul had the literary talent to compose "poetic" prose is evident from texts such as Rom 11:33–36 which is not only "poetic" material, but seems to have been composed with the rest of the epistle.[150] Clearly, use of parallelism was a common stylistic device of Paul,[151] as Hunter states:

> St. Paul when he "took fire," could produce exalted prose-poetry almost *currente calamo*—witness 1 Cor 13 and Rom 8:31ff—prose-poetry possessing many of the features of a carefully-composed hymn.[152]

---

149. Martin, *Carmen Christi*, 28. Italics mine.
150. Fowl, *Story of Christ*, 38–39.
151. See also Rom 2:7ff.; 1 Cor 1:18; 4:10ff.; 2 Cor 6:4ff.
152. Hunter, *Paul and His Predecessors*, 38; Grant, *Historical Introduction*, 71: "Parallelism is also common in the letters of the apostle Paul." He cites 2 Cor 9:6; 1 Cor 10:23 and 12:4–6 (Ibid., 62); Taylor, *Person of Christ*, 63, cites 1 Cor 1:26–31 and 2 Cor 9:21–29 as having rhythmical style; Caird, *Apostolic Age*, 113, recognizes " . . . Paul's propensity to break forth into lyrical and rhythmical prose"; Hengel, "Song," 289: "One cannot prove—as is often claimed upon stylistic grounds—that Paul cannot have composed the hymn."

In summary, when evaluating Phil 2:6-11 as a pre-Pauline hymn, the following must be noted: the text has not been found anywhere outside of an undisputed Pauline letter; as we shall see, the text fits well with Paul's overall argument; the text lacks key elements of hymnody; there is no consensus on either the strophic arrangement of the hymn or the source of the hymn; traditional arguments based on linguistics, theology and style are inconclusive and lack methodological rigor (for example, the use of statistical analysis of vocabulary). Moreover, we suggest that an investigation into how Isa 45:23 has been reproduced in Phil 2:10-11 strengthens the case for Pauline authorship. This approach, which might be considered a development of the stylistic argument, will now be presented.

Authorship Determined from Citation Technique

In his comparative study of Paul's citation technique with that of contemporary Greco-Roman literature and early Judaism, Stanley concludes:

> In adapting the language of Scripture to reflect his own interpretation of a given passage, Paul was simply following the normal literary conventions of his day. Nevertheless, there remain certain areas where Paul has left his own personal stamp on the way he employs these techniques in his letters.[153]

Stanley is correct to highlight the stylistic convention of *citation technique* as a means of identifying the author of a text since the editorial activity outlined below is detailed and specific enough to allow comparisons with other texts and authors. Examination of citation technique offers a better arena for stylistic comparison than hymnody because the data available to us for this task is substantial, having three texts to investigate—Isa 45:23, Isa 45:23 reproduced in Rom 14:11 and Isa 45:23 reproduced in Phil 2:10-11.[154]

Six identifiable textual adaptations of Isa 45:23 can be attributed to the author of Phil 2:6-11. These are: the replacement of ἐμοί with ἐν τῷ ὀνόματι Ἰησοῦ, the alteration of the two verbs in Isa 45:23 from future indicative to aorist subjunctive, the reversal of the word order of verb and subject in both clauses, the insertion of ἐπουρανίων καὶ ἐπιγείων καὶ καταχθονίων between πᾶν γόνυ κάμψῃ and καὶ πᾶσα γλῶσσα ἐξομολογήσηται, the insertion of ὅτι κύριος Ἰησοῦς Χριστὸς εἰς δόξαν θεοῦ πατρός and the omission of τῷ θεῷ.[155]

---

153. Stanley, *Paul and the Language of Scripture*, 348.

154. Contrast with the unknown author of the "hymn" for whom we have no data whatsoever.

155. Here, we take ὅτι κύριος Ἰησοῦς Χριστὸς εἰς δόξαν θεοῦ πατρός to be an

Similarly, there are two identifiable adaptations of Isa 45:23 which can be attributed to Paul in Rom 14:11. These are the replacement of κατ' ἐμαυτοῦ ὀμνύω with ζῶ ἐγώ, λέγει κύριος and the reversal of πᾶσα γλῶσσα and ἐξομολογήσεται. In both replacement adaptations a juxtaposition of YHWH and Jesus takes place, and in both reversal adaptations there is a disruption of the parallelism that associates "bowing of the knee" and "confessing of the tongue" with God—the former is now assigned to Jesus, the latter to God. Thus, in their references to Isa 45:23, the authors of Phil 2:10-11 and Rom 14:11 seem to offer a christologically-motivated interpretative rendering of a distinctly Jewish monotheistic text using identical citation technique.

In addition to the substitutions and word order reversal described above, the author of Phil 2:10-11 makes three other adaptations to the text of Isa 45:23. He disrupts the flow of the verbatim citation of Isa 45:23 by inserting the phrase ἐπουρανίων καὶ ἐπιγείων καὶ καταχθονίων in between πᾶν γόνυ κάμψῃ and πᾶσα γλῶσσα ἐξομολογήσηται,[156] he omits τῷ θεῷ and he adds ὅτι κύριος Ἰησοῦς Χριστὸς εἰς δόξαν θεοῦ πατρός. If the author of Phil 2:10-11 intends to associate κάμψει πᾶν γόνυ with Jesus and ἐξομολογήσεται πᾶσα γλῶσσα with God, or at least break the two phrases's close association with God in the text of Isa 45:23, then these three adaptations to the text would achieve this. It is worth recalling the parallel structure of Phil 2:10-11 suggested above:

(A^1) ⁹for this reason also God highly exalted him
(B^1) and bestowed on him the name which is above every name,

(A^2) ¹⁰so that at the name of Jesus every knee shall bow
(B^2) *of those in heaven and on earth and under the earth*

(A^3) ¹¹and every tongue shall confess
(B^3) *that Jesus Christ is Lord to the glory of God the Father.*

It is the two insertions (*italicized*) that create the parallelisms in the last two couplets of the passage—the insertion of ἐπουρανίων καὶ ἐπιγείων καὶ καταχθονίων creates a "parallelism"[157] where the B^2-clause develops and completes the A^2-clause; thus the author is *amplifying the extent* of homage

---

expression of the *content* of the confession (as in Isa 45:24).

156. Ibid., 344, 349. Stanley notes that additions to "time-honoured" text are more numerous in Paul.

157. Contrary to the opinion that ἐπουρανίων καὶ ἐπιγείων καὶ καταχθονίων is a Pauline gloss that disrupts the original parallelism of the "hymn," it in fact creates the parallelism with the A2-clause, and separates the second and third couplets.

to Jesus. The addition of ὅτι κύριος Ἰησοῦς Χριστὸς εἰς δόξαν θεοῦ πατρός creates a second "parallelism" which develops and completes the A³-clause by describing the *content* and *result* of the confession. The two insertions achieve the same result as the word order change in Rom 14:11—they disrupt the association of both universal submission and universal confession with God.[158] If we accept the parallel structure suggested above, the two insertions cause "bowing of every knee" to be in a separate couplet from "confessing of every tongue." What's more, these two insertions are consistent with Stanley's observations about the reasons why Paul "adds" to a cited text—he is "injecting interpretative elements into the wording of a quotation."[159] If so, the three adaptations *operate in conjunction with* the first two, and are part of an overall interpretive strategy to include Jesus in the divine identity whilst distinguishing "Lord" and "God."[160] Such a literary style that marks a desire to distinguish Lord from God as designations of Jesus and the Father respectively is decidedly Pauline.[161]

According to Stanley, among the citation techniques which signal possible Pauline authorship (where he left his stamp) are the substitution and addition of phrases and shifts in word order in the cited text. Stanley goes on to describe other ways of adapting the language of Scripture that Paul shared with his contemporaries (omissions and grammatical adjustments, and combining and conflating citations).[162] We should therefore not be surprised when we observe these literary conventions used in one citation (of Isa 45:23) in an undisputed Pauline letter (Rom 14:11). But when these citation techniques are repeated in two separate, undisputed Pauline letters which cite the same scriptural text, in different contexts, the case for Pauline authorship is surely strengthened. We therefore propose that Paul's author-

---

158. According to Capes, *Yahweh Texts*, 127–28, the intention to identify Jesus with Lord, yet to distinguish Lord from God also explains another of Paul's adaptations of the text of Isa 45:23 in Rom 14:11—the reversal of ἐξομολογήσεται and πᾶσα γλῶσσα. He suggests that the reversal disrupts the parallelism which would naturally identify both phrases with God (τῷ θεῷ) in the second line, thus creating a chiasmus:

Christ (Lord)   a   κάμψει
                     b   πᾶν γόνυ
                     b¹   πᾶσα γλῶσσα
God   a¹   ἐξομολογήσεται

159. Stanley, *Paul and the Language of Scripture*, 347.

160. It is feasible that the author of Phil 2:9–11 omits τῷ θεῷ from Isa 45:23 *in conjunction with adding* εἰς δόξαν θεοῦ πατρός as the concluding doxology. If τῷ θεῷ was retained in the A3-clause it would result in a tautology: "and every tongue shall confess *to God*, that Jesus Christ is Lord *to the glory of God the Father*."

161. See esp. 1 Cor 8:6 and his epistolary greetings in Rom 1:7; 1 Cor 1:3; 2 Cor 1:2f.; Gal 1:3; Phil 1:2; 1 Thess 1:1; and Philemon 1:3.

162. Stanley, *Paul and the Language of Scripture*, 348–50.

ship of Phil 2:6-11 can be argued through a consideration of how the text of Isa 45:23 is reproduced in Phil 2:6-11 with reference to how it is reproduced in Rom 14:11.[163] If citation technique informs us of an author's style when he/she quotes from another source then its merits should be considered alongside other stylistic arguments.

To summarize the case for Pauline authorship of Phil 2:9-11 and therefore 2:6-11, we propose the following points: using Isaiah in his letters is characteristically Pauline; using Isa 45:23 in his letters, is uniquely Pauline; the use of Isa 45:23 in Phil 2:9, 10 follows a similar citation technique to its undisputed Pauline use in Rom 14:11; the use of Isa 45:23 in Phil 2:10-11 is a christological interpretative rendering of a Jewish monotheistic text; the use of Isa 45:23 in Rom 14:11 is a christological interpretative rendering of a Jewish monotheistic text; christological interpretative rendering of Jewish monotheistic texts is characteristically Pauline;[164] the citation adaptations can be explained better as being integrated with the citation itself and being connected to an application the author has in mind.

Conclusions

Our investigation follows a diachronic, text-production approach to intertextuality, which emphasizes the intentionality of the author. This has led us to re-examine the arguments for non-Pauline authorship of Phil 2:6-11 on the basis of either eliminating or validating the author-oriented approach to an intertextual study of Phil 2:10-16. Having done this, and closely investigated the use of parallelistic prose and citation techniques that reproduce Isa 45:23 in Phil 2:10-11, we conclude that a diachronic, text production approach to Phil 2:10-16 can proceed on the grounds that Paul is probably the author of Phil 2:6-11.

Ethics or Soteriology?

The arguments proffered about whether Phil 2:5-11 should be interpreted ethically or soteriologically have proved inconclusive.[165] We will offer a

---

163. Our argument is not dependent on the chronology of Paul's epistles. If Paul wrote Romans before Philippians, the citation technique in the "hymn" could not be described as pre- or un-Pauline. But, since the dating of the hymn has never been concerned with citation technique anyway, it will suffice for us to propose the presence of Paul's citation style in Phil 2:6-11.

164. See Capes, *Yahweh Texts*, 114.

165. See Käsemann, "Critical Analysis," 83-84; Losie, "Note," 53; Barth, *Philippians*,

summary view. There seems to be a strong contextual case for an ethical interpretation when we note Paul's other appeals to attitude and imitation found in the immediate literary context (Phil 1:27–30; 2:1–4; 2:12–18, 21 and 3:15–17). On the other hand, the mention of the cross, salvation and Jesus as savior (Phil 1:19, 28; 2:6; 3:20) suggests a soteriological element to Phil 2:6–11. It might be argued that soteriology and ethics are present at the level of Christ's achievement and example respectively. Phil 2:5–11 can therefore be understood as a salvation-ethics text; the way in which God saves helps to define the ethics of the beneficiaries of that salvation. It is therefore prudent to leave open the possibility that the verses contain an interweaving of soteriological and ethical elements—Paul seems to be exhorting the Philippians to the same mindset that Christ had and which led to his actions in the salvation event. This mindset is defined by Phil 2:3 (*regarding* others as more important) and the actions by Phil 2:4 (*look out for* the interests of others).

Pre-existent Christ or Human Jesus?

At the heart of the exegetical problem in Phil 2:6 is how to understand the *hapax legomenon* μορφή and ἁρπαγμός, and the term ἐκένωσεν. How these terms are understood determines whether the attitude and actions described are those of a divine, pre-incarnate Christ or a post-incarnate Christ in his earthly ministry. Our goal is to seek an answer to the question of whether Paul's description of a pre-incarnate or post-incarnate Christ in his letter is a fitting response to his perceived exigency. Before analyzing the text, we include a brief survey of how two methodological approaches have been used by some scholars to conclude that Phil 2:6–8 describes the choices and actions of the human Jesus and not Christ in pre-temporal existence.

The Role of Parallelismus Membrorum in Interpretation

Several writers have used synonymous and antithetical parallelisms to reject pre-existence in the passage. Talbert proposes that the hymn is structured as four strophes, the first two being synonymously parallel and referring to the same thing—the earthly Jesus. Since the second strophe (commencing at Phil 2:7b) clearly refers to the earthly Jesus (being made in the likeness of men) and is the "same as" the first strophe, then the latter also refers to

---

59; O'Brien, *Philippians*, 204; Fee, "Hymn," 37; Morgan, "Incarnation, Myth, and Theology," 56.

the earthly Jesus (being in the form of God and taking the form of a slave). Thus, Talbert has used synonymous parallelisms to determine the meaning of the verses, which he argues contrast Adam with the human Jesus.[166] But, as we have argued above, successive lines of Phil 2:6-11 might not restate or negate preceding lines, but describe a progression of events involving Christ and God. Therefore "being made in the likeness of men" is a *progression* from "existing in the form of God," and not a simple restatement of a condition. In other words, Christ's existence in the form of a man *comes after* his existence in the form of God (see exegesis below).

The Role of Conceptual Allusion in Interpretation

Several writers, accepting Phil 2:6-11 as previously composed, see a latent contrast with another human figure through conceptual parallels with Jesus.[167] Dunn appeals to the workings of allusion in support of his view that the "hymn" was written and intended to be read through the grid of Adam theology, and therefore does not describe Christ's pretemporal existence. However, his attempt to interpret the "hymn" using Adam Christology relies upon an imprecise definition of allusion (seemingly more conceptual than literary) where multiple texts (Genesis, Wisdom of Solomon, Romans, 1 Corinthians, Galatians and Hebrews) are evoked through conceptual parallels which ultimately identify Adam as the figure of comparison with Christ. For example, Christ's humility and death correspond to Adam's subjection to death (Gen 2:7; 3:22-24). He also appeals to *clear* echoes and *clear* allusions designed to contrast Christ with Adam, again without defining what these terms mean or how they would trigger the connotations claimed for Paul or the Philippians.[168] Dunn concludes by identifying "several points of contact" between Phil 2:6-11 and Adam tradition and Adam theology.[169] An immediate problem with this approach is seen when alternative figures are identified with Jesus using nuanced concepts. For example, some propose that Phil 2:6-11 "alludes" to the so-called servant of Isaiah. In this case, Christ's humility and death correspond to the derision, rejection and death

---

166. Talbert, "Pre-existence," 141-53; Howard, "Phil 2:6-11," 376; R. B. Strimple, "Philippians 2:5-11," 247-68.

167. For example, Alexander the Great (Ehrhardt, "Jesus Christ and Alexander the Great," 45-51). See also Furness, "Behind the Philippian Hymn," 178-82.

168. See also Hooker, "Philippians 2:6-11," 160-64, who suggests echoes of Gen 1:26.

169. Dunn, "Christ, Adam, and Pre-existence," 76.

of the servant (Isa 53:3, 8, 12).¹⁷⁰ In similar vein, O'Connor notes that the humility and obedience of Christ are salient traits of the righteous man of *Wisdom*. He claims Phil 2:6b implies Christ's sinlessness and incorruptibility which are paralleled in Wis 2.23 which provides insight into the divine intention for man.¹⁷¹ Clearly, more precise definitions of "points of contact," "parallels" and "allusion" are necessary along with an explication of why and how the alleged, evoked texts would be activated through tacit reference.

The Form of God

Deciding the meaning of μορφή on lexical grounds alone proves difficult since appeals to Classical Greek,¹⁷² Hellenistic Greek¹⁷³ and LXX¹⁷⁴ usage of the term all yield different results. Consequently, in our investigation into the meaning of μορφή, we consider its use in two parallel phrases (μορφῇ θεοῦ and μορφὴν δούλου). Additionally, we are helped by the context of τὸ εἶναι ἴσα θεῷ (equality with God) as it elaborates on μορφῇ θεοῦ, and ἐν ὁμοιώματι ἀνθρώπων γενόμενος· καὶ σχήματι εὑρεθεὶς ὡς ἄνθρωπος (being made in the likeness of men and being found in appearance as a man) as it elaborates on μορφὴν δούλου. Appealing beyond the lexical study to the context, what seems to be in view is a *change* in form; an initial state, described as "form of God," is followed by a "self-emptying action" that results in, or is coincident with, a new state described as "form of a slave."¹⁷⁵ Phil 2:6-8 suggests a movement from a divine to a human state, which Christ did not have, but took (λαβών). Whatever "form" is, it appears to be both changeable and concrete (Jesus as μορφὴν δούλου was subservient to the point of death, which was a real death).

Bockmuehl suggests a helpful *prima facie* definition of μορφή: "the visible identifying features of a person or object."¹⁷⁶ The suggestion here is that μορφή refers to that "which truly and fully expresses the being which

---

170. Although not all adherents to this view reject pre-existence in the passage. We include the viewpoint here to highlight another application of the methodology of conceptual allusion.

171. Murphy-O'Connor, "Christological Anthropology," 40–42. Elsewhere he argues that Wis II.23 alludes to Gen 1–3 ("Christological Anthropology," 34–35).

172. μορφή in classical Greek from Homer onwards meant "outward appearance." See Plato, *Republic*.

173. Where it can mean the visual sphere only.

174. In the LXX it means visible shape or appearance or visible form.

175. Braumann, "μορφή," 706.

176. Bockmuehl, "Form of God," 11.

underlies it."[177] Form is a true expression of being, but not exactly the same as it. This is useful because it allows ontological consistency across changing conditions or states. So, Christ can be God even though he has adopted a condition (human slave) that might be uncharacteristic of his being. The condition or state (form of God or form of slave) is real but changeable. We might suggest that Christ is immutable ontologically, but mutable in μορφή. The "form of God" can thus be defined as: "The visible divine beauty and appearance which Christ had in his pre-incarnate state, before taking on the visible form and appearance of a slave."[178]

Equality with God

The second expression in the passage is perhaps one of the most difficult in the whole of the NT to understand—"did not regard equality with God a thing to be grasped." "Being equal with God" (τὸ εἶναι ἴσα θεῷ) would seem to be a further expression of the deity of Christ—that Christ is both fully God and God in his totality (not a part of God). According to Stählin, ἴσα (and ἴσος) expresses neither likeness nor identity, but equality of dignity, will and nature. The term denotes a qualitative and quantitative equality which is both essential and perfect.[179] Use of the definite article, τό (*the* being equal with God) confirms that the expression is related to the previous expression (μορφῇ θεοῦ)—the sense would therefore be: "did not consider (this circumstance of being in the form of God, in other words) equality with God ἁρπαγμόν." With this interpretation, τὸ εἶναι ἴσα θεῷ refers epexegetically to ἐν μορφῇ θεοῦ ὑπάρχων, *elaborating* on the pre-existence of Christ in a form equal to God.[180] The idea of Christ's pretemporal being seems also to be conveyed in the participle ὑπάρχων, if given its full lexical meaning—to be inherently (so) or "be really"[181] as opposed to a substitute for εἶναι. The participle stands in contrast with λαβών and γενόμενος in Phil 2:7 (taking the form of a slave and being made in the likeness of men) so the contrast

---

177. MM, 417.

178. Bockmuehl, "Form of God," 23.

179. Stählin, "ἴσος," 353; BDAG, 480–81—being equivalent in number, size, quality.

180. Cf. Martin, *Carmen Christi*, 148–49, who makes a distinction between μορφῇ θεοῦ and ἴσα θεῷ, and proposes that Christ was in the form of God, but this did not mean equality with God. Martin is guided by ὑπερύψωσεν used comparatively and signaling an elevation to equality. But the term can also be interpreted superlatively, meaning "raised to the loftiest height" as a position once held. See Barth, *Philippians*, 62.

181. BDAG, 1029–30.

among these participles is weakened if the timeless existence of Christ is not in view.

Refusal to Exploit Privilege

The word ἁρπαγμός can mean "robbery,"[182] which renders the awkward phrase: "did not consider equality with God robbery." O'Neill proposes this meaning but, recognizing the awkwardness of the interpretation, suggests that scribes replaced a second negative (μή) with τό in the expression τὸ εἶναι. The phrase should then have read, οὐχ ἁρπαγμὸν ἡγήσατο μὴ εἶναι ἴσα θεῷ—did not consider it robbery not to be equal with God.[183] O'Neill prefers to emend the text to make sense of the literal definition of ἁρπαγμός, but perhaps alternatives to the strict lexical meaning are worth exploring. One option is to take the meaning of ἁρπαγμός as approaching that of ἅρπαγμα. This offers two possibilities, namely, "booty claimed by grasping," or "a windfall or prize." In both cases, the issue of whether the booty or prize is already possessed by Jesus raises differences.[184]

Perhaps the most promising interpretation has been proposed by R.W. Hoover. Hoover's philological study concluded that ἁρπαγμός (with the meaning approaching that of ἅρπαγμα) taken in the passive voice, should be understood in an idiomatic way when used with ἡγήσατο. He discovered that in every instance when ἅρπαγμα was used as a predicate accusative (as ἁρπαγμόν in Phil 2:6) with ἡγήσατο, it conveyed the meaning: "something to use (exploit) for one's own advantage." If so, then the issue is not whether one possesses something but whether one chooses to exploit something already possessed.[185] Hoover seems to have discovered a consistent and legitimate idiomatic use that fits the context and recognizes that ἁρπαγμός is contextually bound up with μορφῇ θεοῦ and τὸ εἶναι ἴσα θεῷ.[186] By accepting

---

182. BDAG, 133; Foerster, "ἁρπαγμός," 473: "What is seized, plunder, booty."

183. O'Neill, "Hoover on Harpagmos," 449; O'Neill, "Goethe and Philippians 2:6," 359.

184. See the discussion in Martin, *Carmen Christi*, 138–43, where he uses the terminology "res rapta" for equality with God already possessed and "res rapienda" for equality with God not possessed.

185. Hoover, "Harpagmos Enigma," 118; cf. Dunn, "Christ, Adam, and Pre-existence," 77, who argues that a sense of "retaining" does not inhere in the word. But there is an inherent sense of retention in the idiomatic usage—*exploitation* implies possession.

186. See also Glasson, "Two Notes On The Philippians Hymn," 133–34.

this idiomatic use of ἁρπαγμός, we conclude that equality with God is something that Jesus already possessed, but refused to exploit.[187]

Kenosis

The aorist ἐκένωσεν (from κενόω) means "emptied." There are four occurrences in the LXX: Gen 24:20 (Rebecca empties the water), 2 Chr 24:11 (the king's scribe and high priest's officer emptied the box), Jer 14:2 (Judea's gates are emptied), and Jer 15:9 (she [a widow] that bore seven is empty). In four other Pauline NT references the sense is of something being made void or of no effect.[188] The difficulty is whether to adopt a metaphorical or literal (metaphysical) meaning.

Various kenotic Christologies describe Jesus emptying himself, in a metaphysical sense, of the form of God or equality with God.[189] Given the Pauline usage of κενόω and the context of Phil 2:6, we suggest that it is more likely that he intends a metaphorical meaning for ἐκένωσεν. Because the verb has no object (what did he empty himself of?) some have suggested that the object is μορφῇ θεοῦ or ἴσα θεῷ. But this proves difficult on exegetical grounds. Firstly, μορφῇ θεοῦ is part of the participial phrase ἐν μορφῇ θεοῦ ὑπάρχων which modifies the relative pronoun ὅς ("who, in the form of God existing"). Secondly, this participial phrase is the subject of the verb ἡγήσατο (it is the one who exists in the form of God who is doing the regarding/considering). How then can μορφῇ θεοῦ be the object of the verb ἐκένωσεν?[190] Secondly, as we proposed above, if τὸ εἶναι ἴσα θεῷ refers epexegetically to ἐν μορφῇ θεοῦ ὑπάρχων, can it function as the object of ἐκένωσεν?[191] In addition, the fact that ἐκένωσεν is separated from μορφῇ θεοῦ and ἴσα θεῷ by the adversative conjunction ἀλλά,[192] mitigates against an emptying of form or equality.

Perhaps the question is better asked: how did Jesus empty himself? (as opposed to the metaphysically-loaded question: what did Jesus empty himself of?) The answer might lie with the two participial phrases that follow and modify ἐκένωσεν, namely: μορφὴν δούλου λαβών and ἐν ὁμοιώματι

---

187. See Wright, *Climax of the Covenant*, 62–98, for a detailed treatment of the meaning of ἁρπαγμός.

188. Rom 4:14; 1 Cor 1:17; 1 Cor 9:15; 2 Cor 9:3.

189. See Macquarrie, "Pre-existence of Jesus Christ," 199; Müller, *Philippians*, 83–86.

190. Feinberg, "Kenosis and Christology," 41.

191. Ibid., 41.

192. BDF §447 and §448. Emphasizing ἀλλά as expressing direct contrast.

ἀνθρώπων γενόμενος.[193] Some take the aorist participles λαβών and γενόμενος to denote action prior to the main verb (ἐκένωσεν),[194] thus advancing the view that taking the form of a slave and being made in the likeness of men took place *before* the emptying—this view found favor with Jeremias who thus interpreted Phil 2:7a as referring to the crucifixion and Phil 2:7b, c to the incarnation. However, interpreting the two participial phrases as aorists of antecedent action (but emptied himself having [already] taken the form of a slave, and having [already] been made in the likeness of men) is grammatically valid *when time sequence is in view*. But this does not seem to be the case in Phil 2:7 which describes the event of self-emptying, not the sequence of steps involved in this event.[195] If the participles are interpreted as circumstantial/modal participles coincident with ἐκένωσεν, then how Jesus emptied himself was *by* "taking the form of a slave" and "being made in the likeness of men."[196]

Moule cites 2 Cor 8:9 (Jesus, though he was rich, yet he became poor) as an example of an ingressive aorist where the action of becoming poor takes place at a definite point in time as opposed to describing a series of past actions viewed in their entirety (constative).[197] Phil 2:6-7 is similar to 2 Cor 8:9 in the sense that both passages speak of a state in the present (ὑπάρχων in Phil 2:6, and ὤν in 2 Cor 8:9) which leads to the assumption, in the aorist (*emptied* and *became* respectively), of a subsequent state.[198] If μορφὴν δούλου λαβών and ἐν ὁμοιώματι ἀνθρώπων γενόμενος are interpreted as modal participial phrases coincident with ἐκένωσεν, the latter verb being an ingressive aorist, then Paul would seem to have in mind the point in time when Jesus became a man—the incarnation.[199]

What, then, is Paul describing for the Philippians? There has been a tendency in some quarters of recent scholarship to downplay the "preexistence" motif and to interpret Phil 2:6-11 in terms of Christ's earthly

193. BDF §339. Describing the aorist participles λαβών and γενόμενος as expressing coincident action.

194. Moule, *Idiom*, 99; BDF §339.

195. See Käsemann, "Critical Analysis," 70.

196. See Fee, "Hymn," 40; Feinberg, "Kenosis and Christology," 42; Barth, *Philippians*, 64.

197. Moule, *Idiom*, 11; see also *Proleg.*, 109; cf. Dunn, *Christology In The Making*, 122. Dunn interprets Phil 2:6f. as describing the actions of the earthly Jesus rather than the preexistent Christ. He also parallels Phil 2:7 and 2 Cor 8:9, understanding both ἑαυτὸν ἐκένωσεν and ἐπτώχευσεν to refer to the crucifixion. Because the *kenosis* is not coincident with taking the form of a slave and being made in the likeness of men, ἐκένωσεν is a constative, rather than ingressive aorist.

198. Hurst, "Christ, Adam, and Pre-existence Revisited," 87.

199. So too, Käsemann, "Critical Analysis," 67; Fowl, *Story of Christ*, 58-59.

history.[200] On the contrary, White notes that pre-existence does seem to be a necessity for the measure of Christ's humility to have the full force of Pauline thought:

> If Christ was not equal with the Father but was in some sense a subordinate created being, the illustration of humility involving the voluntary renunciation of rights so as to serve others is abrogated. There is no humility in a creature, who is intrinsically inferior to God, not seeking after equality with Him.[201]

However, we should go further and ask how the deity of Christ might function as a constraint brought to bear upon the Philippians. According to Bitzer, every rhetorical situation contains a set of constraints made up of persons, events, objects, and relations capable of constraining decisions and actions needed to modify the exigency.[202] Rhetoric provides important constraints that act as logical proofs in the argument. Paul seems to be describing how the self-renouncing attitude of the preexistent Christ becomes concrete in the act of incarnation. But Paul's argument does not champion self-renunciation of rights in an absolute sense. The self-renunciation of rights results in death for Jesus—Phil 2:5-8 describe Christ's attitude and actions in the renouncing of the privileges of his deity so that he could die. The death of the deity is the ultimate goal of the kenosis. Certainly, Jesus' death can be interpreted soteriologically as a saving act, but for it to function rhetorically, as a situational constraint, his self-renunciation of rights to the point of death must address the controlling exigency, as we shall see.

The Relationship of Phil 2:6-8 to Phil 2:9-11

Parallelismus Membrorum has contributed to an unnecessary "partitioning" of Phil 2:6-11 into two halves, with abasement (vv. 6-8) and exaltation (vv. 9-11) viewed as "opposites."[203] Those advancing a soteriological interpretation consider the "hymn" to describe a divine drama containing contrasts. But we have argued that the parallelisms in Phil 2:6-11 support a progression of activities and not a restatement or negative complement of preceding clauses. With this view, the exaltation in Phil 2:9-11 is not antithetical

---

200. Wegener, "Philippians 2:6-11," 511; Talbert, "Pre-existence," 141; O'Connor, "Christological Anthropology," 25-50; Dunn, *Christology In The Making*, 119; Bakken, "The New Humanity," 71-82; Howard, "Phil 2:6-11," 368-87.

201. White, "Beyond the Veil of Eternity," 35.

202. Bitzer, "Situation," 254.

203. Martin, *Carmen Christi*, 28; See also, Stauffer, *New Testament Theology*, 339.

(or the negative complement) to Phil 2:6–8, nor does it primarily function as a depiction of the "reversal of Christ's fortune."[204] Rather, it is a positive progression that demonstrates God's response to Christ's abasement; exaltation is not antithetical to abasement, but the consequence of it. The question is how are we to understand the progression from abasement to exaltation as a *positive* progression? Those advancing an ethical interpretation have taken the view that vv. 9–11 are a positive progression on vv. 5–8 in the sense that God vindicates Christ.[205] However Park has rightly called this interpretation into question, pointing out that vindication, as a wrong that has been righted, is incongruous with the positive view of humility and self-sacrifice encouraged in Phil 2:1–4.[206] Park notes that *God's approval of Christ's actions* is more in line with the immediate context.[207] This is confirmed in Phil 1:29f, where God sanctions the suffering of the Philippians (for the sake of Christ). Phil 2:5–11 therefore carries both soteriological and ethical weight—although exaltation is not prototypical for Christians, God's approval of suffering and death (in the salvation event) is.

Conclusions

Duane Watson noted that "the more elevated Paul's style, the more important to the rhetorical situation."[208] If so, then Phil 2:5–11, suggested as one of Paul's most sublime compositions in the style of elevated prose, would be essential to Paul's argument. From the preceding analysis, we can now consider the situation which might have invited the discourse of vv. 5–11. The divinity of Jesus, his refusal to exploit privileged status and his willingness to embrace death on a cross are crucial constraints incorporated by Paul in vv. 6–8. God's approval of Jesus' attitude and actions are additional constraints expressed in the response of vv. 9–11 in which God elevates Jesus as the object of universal submission. As rhetorical discourse, Phil 2:5–11 is a fitting response to the exigency of claiming immunity from suffering and death on the grounds of status (vv. 6–8), that the deity would not approve (vv. 9–11). There may be other situations for which the passage could have been written, but it is plausible that it functions as a proof from *logos*[209] in that God is justified in sanctioning his people's suffering and death because

204. Martin, *Carmen Christi*, 244.
205. Fee, *Philippians*, 220; Bockmuehl, *Philippians*, 141.
206. Park, *Submission*, 26–31, 65–66.
207. Ibid., 32.
208. Watson, "Contributions," 149.
209. Bitzer, "Situation," 254. Also Watson, "Contributions," 137.

he participates in suffering and death in the salvation of his people[210]—thus, the idea of the death of the deity addresses the exigency. Phil 2:5–11 is Paul's *tour de force* (rhetorical constraint) that conveys God's participation in, and approval of, the suffering and death paradigm. It is also the second occurrence of the argument that God approves of suffering (Phil 1:27–30) with a development that includes the divine death. Moreover, Christ's self-renunciation of the privileges of deity in order to participate in death is antithetical to, and a constraint that addresses, the exigency proposed in our exegesis of Phil 2:1–4, namely, self-preservation. Gospel citizenship is grounded in Christ and his paradigm and is characterized by the attitude of self-renunciation. But this self-renunciation is not an abstract quality—it shows itself in the abnegation of status that affords survival and suffering-free living (Phil 2:5–8 and 3:7–11). It looks as if God's approval of the suffering paradigm can be thought of as an unwritten intertext that unifies Phil 1:27–30, 2:1–4 and 2:5–11.

THE RHETORICAL SITUATION IN PHIL 2:14

The fourth passage in which Paul's explicit injunctions inform us of the situation in Philippi is Phil 2:14 where he instructs the Philippians to "do all things without grumblings and disputes." There is no consensus about the object of γογγυσμῶν καὶ διαλογισμῶν. Some suggest these terms are directed against God,[211] others against people in the community.[212] An argument used by several scholars against Godward grumblings in Phil 2:14 is that "there has been no hint in the letter so far of this kind of rebellious attitude towards God on the part of the Philippians."[213] Yet, as we have seen above, Phil 1:29 contains an explicit instruction about God's active role in the Philippians's suffering—this clearly could be construed as providing grounds for Godward grumblings. Additionally, it is worth considering whether other passages might carry the sense that Paul is addressing actual complaints against God, or a latent tendency. For example, if we accept that Phil 1:19 contains an echo of Job 13:16,[214] then we have an OT context where

---

210. Christ is an example, known to the Philippians, whose attitude and actions are being paralleled only by some. See ibid., 137.

211. Vincent, *Philippians*, 67; Lightfoot, *Philippians*, 115; Müller, *Philippians*, 93; Fowl, *Philippians*, 123.

212. Kennedy, *Philippians*, 441; Collange, *Philippians*, 111; Plummer, *Philippians*, 52; Moule, *Philippian Studies*, 112; Loh and Nida, *Handbook*, 69.

213. O'Brien, *Philippians*, 291; Kennedy, *Philippians*, 441.

214. See Hays, *Echoes*, 21–24.

God's people/servant are registering complaints against him based on the hardships he has permitted in their lives.[215] Although both Job and Paul are confident of deliverance from their respective trials (Job 13:16; Phil 1:19), the wider context of Job's misery might serve as a foil for Paul's joy—two contrasting responses to God-approved suffering. The theme of rejoicing in Philippians has been well noted, but it is worth pointing out that many of these references describe a response to hardship,[216] which, at least on a conceptual level, would be consistent with an apostolic interest in correcting Godward grumbling. There is therefore at least a hint that a negative attitude towards God could lie behind Paul's rhetoric. We will now explore this possibility.

Complaint against God?

γογγυσμός is normally taken to mean grumbling or murmuring carrying the sense of "muted complaining,"[217] but it can also mean overt confrontation (see below). διαλογισμός can refer to the "verbal exchange[s] that takes place when conflicting ideas are expressed"[218] conveying the sense of arguments or disputes. But διαλογισμός can also mean evil thoughts, doubting or questioning.[219] This latter meaning seems closer to Paul's other usage in Romans and Corinthians. In Rom 1:21 Paul describes those who know God, yet refuse to give him honor and thanks—they became διαλογισμός (futile in thought/evil speculations). Here, a Godward orientation is certainly in view. In Rom 14:1, Paul uses the term to advise against passing judgment on others's opinions and has a man-ward orientation. In 1 Cor 3:20, Paul's use of διαλογισμός is part of a citation of Ps 94:11 (LXX),[220] in the context of the Corinthians being deceived into thinking themselves wise by human standards: "The Lord knows the διαλογισμός (futile thoughts/reasonings) of the wise, that they are useless." Williams suggests that Ps 94:11 "also functions as a rebuke to those who are deserting the Lord because they believe that he does not understand or perceive their plight."[221] Thus, both contexts (Ps 94:11 and 1 Cor 3:20) would seem to support a Godward orientation. Although both terms could have man or God as object, we suggest that the

---

215. This is clearly the case with Job (1:12; 2:3–6).
216. Phil 1:18; 2:2, 17–18; 4:1, 4.
217. BDAG, 204.
218. BDAG, 232–33.
219. Schrenk, "διαλογισμός," 98.
220. According to Williams, *Wisdom*, 303.
221. Ibid., 306.

balance swings in favor of Godward attitudes because this is Paul's predominant use, and the OT parallels with γογγυσμός presented below.

"Murmuring" in the LXX

In the LXX, γογγύζω is translated from לון, and is used to describe the grumblings of the Israelites in the wilderness (Exod 16:7-12; 17:3; Num 14:27-29; 16:41; 17:5, 10).[222] The term might have had a theological character, carrying the sense of tempting or scorning God (cf. Exod 17:2; Num 14:2, 11; Ps 78(77):40, 41).[223] In his monograph, Coats observes that although the object of the murmurings is commonly Moses and Aaron (Exod 16:2; Num 14:2; 16:3; 17:6, 7; 20:2), in other texts it is God (Exod 16:7, 8; Num 14:27, 29, 35; 16:11; 17:20; 27:3).[224] Moses, understanding their (his and Aaron's) authority as delegated from God, is recorded as saying that God is ultimately the object of the murmuring:

> And Moses said, "When the Lord gives you meat in the evening to eat and bread in the morning to the full, because the Lord heard your complaining (τὸν γογγυσμὸν ὑμῶν) which you complain against us (ὑμεῖς διαγογγύζετε καθ' ἡμῶν), then we, what are we? For not against us is your complaining (ὁ γογγυσμὸς ὑμῶν), but rather against God. (Exod 16:8)

In the LXX, then, the murmuring motif introduced by γογγύζω characterizes a tradition about the rebellion of Israel against God.[225] Is this tradition likely to have influenced Paul in his choice of γογγυσμός in Phil 2:14? Although the other three occurrences of γογγύζω (the meaning being the same as γογγυσμός) in the NT[226] do not carry the theological sense, there is reason to believe that Paul is influenced by the Israelite wilderness experience, as we shall see.

Paul's Use of "Murmuring" in 1 Cor 10:10

Paul's only other use of this term is the cognate verb, γογγύζω, used in the imperative in 1 Cor 10:10. Here, Paul uses γογγύζω to refer to the Israelites's grumbling because of their hardships in the wilderness: γογγύζετε, καθάπερ

---

222. Smith, "לון," 781.
223. Rengstorf, "γογγύζω," 730.
224. Coats, *Murmuring Motif*, 27.
225. See ibid., 249.
226. John 7:12; Acts 6:1; 1 Pet 4:9.

τινὲς αὐτῶν ἐγόγγυσαν καὶ ἀπώλοντο ὑπὸ τοῦ ὀλοθρευτοῦ ("we must not grumble as some of them grumbled and were destroyed by the destroyer"). Paul is referring to one or other of the narratives where God responds in judgment to the Israelites's grumblings (e.g., Num 14:27–29; 16:41–49).[227] In these narratives God destroys those who have grumbled against him. God's response to the grumblings, both positively in the provision of food (Exod 16:8), and negatively in the form of judgment, suggests that he is, ultimately, the object of the murmuring. According to Rengstorf, Paul's use of γογγύζω in 1 Cor 10:10 is consistent with the readoption of the theological assessment of grumbling (against God) abandoned by later Judaism.[228] If so, Paul's choice of this term in Philippians to refer to grumblings against God would be congruent with his only other use of the term.[229]

Conclusion

Grumbling is a rhetorical exigency that Paul seeks to overcome through his discourse; his imperative "do not grumble" presupposes that some Philippians were grumbling. We have argued that this grumbling was God-ward, its concrete ground probably being suffering at the hands of adversaries. In the LXX, not only did "murmuring" have a theological connotation, it "always had some concrete ground, namely, hunger or thirst in the desert (Exod 15:24; 16:3), or the proximity and yet apparent unattainability of the promised land (Num 14:1)."[230] In proposing that Paul uses the murmuring motif in Phil 2:14, we suggest that the γογγυσμός in Philippi were complaints against God, because of his apparent passivity in relation to the Philippians's suffering. The διαλογισμός were either the ensuing disagreements among the community about God's apparent passivity in relation to their suffering for the gospel, or doubts about his integrity to "complete the good work he had begun"—the disagreements were therefore over the legitimacy of

---

227. See Fee, *First Epistle to the Corinthians*, 457–58.

228. Rengstorf, "γογγύζω," 733, notes that the Rabbis, when referring to the murmuring tradition, used a different word, which meant dissatisfaction in general (murmuring before God as opposed to murmuring against God), and removed the theological thrust of לין.

229. Another reason for understanding Paul's choice of γογγυσμῶν as being influenced by the tradition of the rebellious Israelites is the concentration of allusions found in the immediate context of Phil 2:14. Although this anticipates our argument in chapter 4, it is worth highlighting the possibility of the wilderness tradition of Godward grumbling connoted by the three terms, "murmurings" (v. 14), "children of God" (v. 15) and "crooked and perverse generation" (v. 15).

230. Rengstorf, "γογγύζω," 730.

suffering. Such an interpretation coheres with our ongoing development of the argumentative complex of the letter. Paul seems to be reminding the Philippians that their suffering is for Christ's sake, and is graciously granted as a privilege by God. Paul's own response to his suffering is joy, not complaint—joy therefore, as a key motif in Philippians, is not only exemplary, but grounded in the specifics of the Philippian situation. Suffering for the gospel is evidence of God's salvation, so should be greeted with perseverance and joy—not grumbling.

Hitherto, we have identified the following controlling exigencies for Phil 1:27-30, 2:1-4, 5-11 and 14 respectively: the refusal to accept that God would approve of his people's suffering for the sake of Christ; an attitude of self-preservation that resulted in a neglect of others during conflict; claiming immunity from suffering and death on the grounds of high-status and that God would not approve; grumbling against God because of suffering inflicted by adversaries.

THE RHETORICAL SITUATION IN PHIL 3:1-21

The fifth part of the rhetorical unit under investigation is Phil 3:1-21. In this passage Paul seemingly issues a threefold warning to the Philippians (Phil 3:2) using autobiographical data as part of his argument (Phil 3:4-11). He then reiterates, in three consecutive verses, the idea of his non-attainment and pressing towards a future goal (Phil 3:12-14), which relates to a knowledge of Christ through his resurrection, suffering and death. After this he instructs the Philippians on the eschatological implications of attitude and conduct (Phil 3:15-21). Our main question as we attempt to determine Paul's epistolary argument is: What does Paul see as the central issue in Phil 3:1-21, and subsequently, how does he address it? To answer this question we must, in part, engage with two hotly debated issues, namely "letter integrity"[231] and "opponents,"[232] although neither will shape the structure of

---

231. The seemingly awkward transition from chapter 2, the sudden change of tone at verse 2 and the apparent introduction of different subject matter have fuelled debates on the integrity of the letter. See Dalton, "Integrity of Philippians," 97–102; Watson, "Rhetorical Analysis of Philippians," 57–88; Pollard, "Integrity." 57–66.

232. Holladay, "Paul's Opponents in Philippians 3," 77–90; Klijn, "Paul's Opponents in Philippians III," 278–84; Grayston, "Opponents in Philippians 3," 170–72; Mearns, "Identity of Paul's Opponents at Philippi," 194–204; Tyson, "Paul's Opponents at Philippi," 82–95; Bateman IV, "Were The Opponents At Philippi Necessarily Jewish," 39–61; Robinson, "We are the Circumcision," 28–35; See also Jewett, "Conflicting Movements," 362–90; Lüdemann, *Opposition to Paul in Jewish Christianity*; Hooker, "Phantom Opponents."

our argument. We have argued that Philippians is a letter of communication between partners sharing a common experience, and that the controlling exigency which prompted the writing can be identified. Consequently, we begin by asking the question: What is the controlling exigency in Phil 3:1–21?

The Controlling Exigency in Phil 3:1–2

To identify the source of the controlling exigency as perceived by Paul in Phil 3:1–2, we will investigate three interpretive issues—what does τὰ αὐτά refer to? Who are the "dogs," the "evil workers" and the "false circumcision"? What is the nature of the threat they pose? A simple paraphrase of Paul's forceful rhetoric in Phil 3:1–2 would seem to justify this approach: "I'm writing to you to safeguard you against the dogs!" The biting sarcasm in his reference to them hints that they are somehow central to his argument; identifying them and their role in the argument should assist in determining the rhetorical situation.

A Recurring Rhetorical Situation Spoken About?

There is no consensus among scholars on the referent of τὰ αὐτά in Phil 3:1 with two main lines of argument offered; firstly, that it refers to something previously *spoken* to the Philippians; secondly, that it refers to something previously *written* to the Philippians. Following his report on, and commendation of, Epaphroditus in Phil 2:25–30, Paul seems to prepare to close his letter, yet moves on to a new subject: "Finally, my brethren, rejoice in the Lord. To write the same things (τὰ αὐτά) to you is not irksome to (for) me, and is a safeguard for you." There are two views of what τὰ αὐτά refers to in this verse. Firstly, τὰ αὐτά refers to things that the Philippians received orally from Paul before he wrote the letter.[233] Fee claims the accent falls on τὰ αὐτά and not γράφειν, and that Paul is referring to the many times he had previously *told* them about such things. As such, "it is pedantic to think this emphasis must include former communications by letter."[234] The repetition inherent in τὰ αὐτά is thus accounted for by something Paul said previous to writing. It is here that appeal is made to Phil 3:18 which clearly describes something said formerly (ἔλεγον ὑμῖν) by Paul to the Philippians. Furnish takes a somewhat different approach by proposing that τὰ αὐτά refers to

---

233. Mackay, "Further Thoughts," 164; Garland, "Composition and Unity," 164.
234. Fee, *Philippians*, 292–93.

oral instructions already delivered by Timothy and Epaphroditus to the Philippians.²³⁵

Three points can be raised against the views that τὰ αὐτά refers to oral communications. Firstly, these proposals neglect the written nature of τὰ αὐτά—τὰ αὐτά are written (γράφειν) not spoken (cf. λέγω in Phil 3:18). Secondly, Paul had spoken about something previously in Phil 3:18 with sadness and regret, whereas in Phil 3:1 the potential for "arousing dislike or displeasure"²³⁶ is in view. This should caution us against equating the two verses uncritically—the content of the written and spoken messages of Phil 3:1 and Phil 3:18 might be different; or at least reflect different aspects of the same problem. Thirdly, the appeal to previous oral communication does not explain why the repetition described in Phil 3:1 could be construed as irksome *for Paul*. Since he had, unapologetically, repeated himself often in spoken address to the Philippians (Phil 3:18; cf. Gal 1:9; 5:29), why is there the potential for a sense of hesitation or shrinking away *on his part* in Phil 3:1?²³⁷ We suggest that it is more likely that Paul is not irked by having to write *again*²³⁸ to address a controversy that has plagued his ministry, a specific aspect of which *now* threatens the Philippians. Also, if we can identify the previous written source in question, it might provide clues relevant in determining the nature of the threat perceived by Paul.

A Recurring Rhetorical Situation Written About?

There are two variations on the notion that τὰ αὐτά refers to things Paul has previously written about to the Philippians. These views respect the written nature of τὰ αὐτά and propose that the referent is either to something written in *this* letter, or in a previous letter to the Philippians. We will examine these views in turn.

---

235. Furnish, "Place and Purpose of Philippians III," 86. He is followed by Jewett, "Conflicting Movements," 383.

236. See Hauck, "ὀκηνρός," 167. τὰ αὐτὰ γράφειν ὑμῖν . . . ὀκνηρόν does not convey the same emotions as ἔλεγον ὑμῖν, νῦν δὲ καὶ κλαίων λέγω. Although this does not rule out a common reference between what was written in Phil 3:1 and what was said in Phil 3:18, it does draw attention to the different mode and manner of communication that might be indicative of related, yet dissimilar subject matter.

237. Cf. Mackay, "Further Thoughts," 164, who suggests that Paul is apologizing for repeating himself *to the Philippians*.

238. Cf. Fee, *Philippians*, 292, who questions a former communication by letter which would have been better explained by Paul's use of πάλιν. But this assumes that Paul is repeating himself *in writing, to the Philippians*.

Firstly, τὰ αὐτά refers to what had been written in a former letter to the Philippians, but which has been lost.[239] This view assumes the repetition inherent in τὰ αὐτά is best explained by an assumed πάλιν (again)—thus Paul had written to the Philippians on a previous occasion. Appeal is also made to Polycarp's reference to Paul having written ἐπιστολάς (Pol. Phil. 3.2).[240] Against this view, it must be noted that the word πάλιν does not appear in the text, and its assumed presence could have colored later interpretations including Polycarp's.[241] Even though no other extant source has been found, it must be conceded that Paul might have written a previous letter to the Philippians, but we suggest a better explanation for the repetition inherent in τὰ αὐτά below.

Secondly, Paul uses the phrase τὰ αὐτά to refer to the call to rejoice in *this* letter to the Philippians (Phil 2:18; cf. 1:4; 2:17, 18, 28, 29).[242] This view interprets the repetition inherent in τὰ αὐτά to refer to something written in chapters 1 or 2. Bockmuehl is representative of this view. He notes that Judaizers are not mentioned in chapters 1 or 2, therefore τὰ αὐτά refers to Paul's constant exhortation to joy in the midst of affliction.[243] Bockmuehl follows Caird, and others, in proposing that joy is the backward referent of τὰ αὐτά (Phil 2:18, 29), despite O'Brien's critique that it is difficult to see how joy can be a safeguard for the danger of selfish ambition and disunity which Paul addresses earlier in the letter.[244] Bockmuehl's solution is to remove the specificity of selfish-ambition and disunity and suggest that there is no particular danger in the preceding context for which joy could not be considered a safeguard. Instead, joy becomes an *inherent* safeguard against all manner of dangers.[245] Against this view, four points can be raised. Firstly, τὰ αὐτά is plural, which is an odd choice if Paul had "rejoice" as the antecedent. Secondly, it is difficult to see why, if Caird's joy doesn't combat selfish ambition, Bockmuehl's joy can be an "inherent" safeguard in every situation—every situation would surely include selfish ambition. Thirdly, it is debatable that the preceding context does not refer to dangers for which joy seems an inappropriate safeguard—since every occurrence of joy in the

---

239. Vincent, *Philippians*, 91; Herklots, *Philippians*, 86.

240. Polycarp, *Philippians*, 287.

241. See Lightfoot, *Philippians*, 136–40; Garland, "Composition and Unity," 154, suggests that Polycarp inferred multiple letters from τὰ αὐτά in Phil 3:1. Unfortunately, NIV and NASB add "again" giving the sense that Paul had already written to the Philippians about "these things."

242. Bruce, *Philippians*, 102.

243. Bockmuehl, *Philippians*, 180.

244. So too, Lightfoot, *Philippians*, 123.

245. Bockmuehl, *Philippians*, 181.

immediate context is connected with the suffering or death of either Paul or Ephaphroditus (Phil 2:17, 18, 27–30; cf. 1:17–18, 21–25). Fourthly, it is doubtful that Paul would consider it a potentially onerous and unpleasant task for him to repeat an exhortation to rejoice.

We conclude that Paul's opening words in Phil 3:1 need not require him to have written to the Philippians in a previous letter, nor that the repetition inherent in τὰ αὐτά be explained from content in previous chapters. What we can say is that he had evidently written on a previous occasion about a similar matter—but if so, to whom did he write these things?

A Proposal: Gal 6:12-18 is the Persistent Rhetorical Situation

According to Bitzer, some rhetorical situations mature and decay, others persist in spite of repeated attempts at modification.[246] Rhetorical forms are born and special vocabulary, grammar, and style are established due to recurring rhetorical situations. He cites Lincoln's Gettysburg Address as a fitting response to an historical situation, elements of which persist today (for example, the legitimacy of struggling to ensure "government of the people, by the people, for the people").[247] Our proposal is that Philippians is a fitting response to a situation, elements of which Paul might have observed and recorded previously in Galatians. With this proposal, we do not claim that the context of Galatians can be used simply to explain the context of Philippians. Rather, we recognize that both situations might involve the interaction of several complex elements, *some of which are common to both*. Our proposal is that Paul, desiring to avoid a recurrence of a specific exigency in Galatia, issues a warning to the Philippians using the same rhetorical forms, special vocabulary, grammar and style. Consequently, τὰ αὐτά refers to what follows in Phil 3:2ff[248] and to the content of a previous letter Paul had written to another church (Galatia)[249]—in particular, Paul is recalling Gal 6:12–18[250] in which he reveals the motivation of Judaizers who boast in the Galatians's conversion to circumcision in order to avoid persecution for the cross of Christ.[251]

---

246. Bitzer, "Situation," 258–59.

247. Ibid., 256.

248. Silva, *Philippians*, 152.

249. See Müller, *Philippians*, 105, who advocates the same position, although he identifies the threat from false teachers of Judaism.

250. For the importance of Gal 6:11–18 in interpretation see Betz, *Galatians*, 313; Deissmann, *Bible Studies*, 347–48; Weima, "Pauline Letter Closings," 177–98.

251. Taking τῷ σταυρῷ τοῦ Χριστοῦ as a dative of cause, so the cross was the cause

The rhetorical forms, special vocabulary, grammar and style common to Phil 3:1–21 and Gal 6:12–18 can now be sketched out. Firstly, Paul's vocabulary in both passages includes all of the following terms and phrases: γράφω (Phil 3:1; Gal 6:11), σαρκί (Phil 3:3, 4; Gal 6:12, 13), ἡ περιτομή (Phil 3:3, 5; Gal 6:12, 13 (x2), 15), τῷ σταυρῷ (τοῦ σταυροῦ) τοῦ Χριστοῦ (Phil 3:18; Gal 6:12), νόμον (Phil 3:6, 9; Gal 6:13), καυχήσωνται (Phil 3:3; Gal 6:13, 14), διώκων (Phil 3:6, 12, 14; Gal 6:12), στοιχεῖν (Phil 3:16; Gal 6:16), and σῶμα (Phil 3:21 (2); Gal 6:17). This demonstrates a high degree of lexical similarity and is especially significant since all of the Galatian references are concentrated in Gal 6:12–17. Secondly, the following contextual and conceptual similarities can be noted: the notion of a rejection of earthly advantage for a heavenly gain is common to both passages (Phil 3:7–11; cf. 3:19d; Gal 6:14, 15); in both passages, the phrase τοῦ σταυροῦ τοῦ Χριστοῦ modifies the description of those whom Paul opposes; only in Galatians and Philippians does Paul describe himself as a "persecutor of the church" (διώκων) in the context of renouncing past Jewish privileges (Gal 1:13, 23; Phil 3:6); describing converts to Christ using Jewish epithets as part of an anti-Judaizing argument is common to both passages (Phil 3:3; Gal 6:16). Although the presence of similar vocabulary in Philippians, in and of itself, need not necessarily mean that Paul is recalling the Galatian situation, the similarity in concepts and context adds weight to the argument. In each epistle, these terms and phrases form a regular pattern of words and ideas repeated in an argument against Judaizers. Moreover, the argument seems to spiral around the subjects of circumcision, persecution and the cross of Christ.

Following his assessment of the attitude of the Judaizers, and the reason behind their boasting, Paul contrasts the object of his own boasting in Gal 6:14: "the cross of our Lord Jesus Christ." Paul seems to have used the phrase to contrast two viewpoints—that of the Judaizers who desire to avoid persecution,[252] and Paul who embraces, indeed boasts in, persecution. This is not to deny that other rhetorical and/or theological aspects of boasting may qualify the Judaizers as Paul's "opponents," but in Gal 6:12–14 Paul has in mind the specific motivation of avoiding persecution. This is consistent with how he describes the marks of his own persecution[253] in the immedi-

---

of the persecution. See BDF §196; Moule, *Idiom*, 45.

252. Longenecker, *Galatians*, 292, suggests non-believing Jews or zealots were the source of the persecution. Regardless of the source, Paul presents persecution as factual in Gal 6:12.

253. So Fung, *Galatians*, 313: τὰ στίγματα refers to "the wounds and scars left in Paul's body as a result of his sufferings for the gospel"; Ciampa, *Presence and Function of Scripture*, 371, writes, "The marks of Jesus he bears on his body (6:17b) show that

ate literary context: "from now on let no one cause trouble for me, for I bear on my body the brand-marks of Jesus" (Gal 6:17). This interpretation supports our proposal that τὰ αὐτά refers to the Judaizers's motivation to avoid persecution for the cross of Christ. It is the danger of imitating this attitude that Paul presents as the threat to the Philippians. τὰ αὐτά thus refers to a recurring rhetorical situation;[254] the Judaizers, opponents whom Paul previously wrote about to the Galatians and frequently spoke about to the Philippians, serve as a negative paradigm[255] of self-preservation.

The Prominent Rhetorical Constraint in Phil 3:4–21

Several scholars treat Philippians 3 as polemical, believing Paul to be addressing some kind of perfectionism in the Philippian community (see the survey below). However, no consensus has emerged about the specific problem Paul seems to be addressing. Treating Philippians as rhetorical discourse, our aim shifts focus from identification of opponents, to identification of the controlling exigency and its modification using the prominent rhetorical constraint determined from the text. We will first examine representative views of the dominant interpretation of Phil 3:11–14, then offer our own interpretation with particular focus on the meaning of τελειόω, in the phrase "not that I have now been made perfect," and εἴ πως in the phrase "if perhaps I may obtain the resurrection from the dead." Then we will suggest how our interpretation coheres with the surrounding context of Philippians 3.

Schmithals

Schmithals suggests the theme of Phil 3:12–14 is Paul's denial that he has reached "perfect" Christian status.[256] He proposes that the concept of τέλειος (perfect) is to be understood from the perspective of a Gnostic background,

---

unlike others he has not taken the cowardly route of avoiding persecution for the cross of Christ (cf. 6:12c)." See also 2 Cor 11:23–30.

254. Ibid., 367. Ciampa suggests that Gal 6:11–18 "... coheres around the contrast between those who are compelling the Galatians to be circumcised (to avoid suffering, 6:11–13) and those who, like Paul, follow the rule that says circumcision is not a significant issue (and suffer for their conviction, 6:14–17)."

255. See Kilpatrick, "ΒΛΕΠΕΤΕ," whose findings corroborate Phil 3:2 as the introduction of a negative paradigm.

256. Schmithals, *Paul and the Gnostics*, 95.

the term τέλειοι being a Gnostic catchword, *terminus technicus*,[257] referring to spiritual perfection. In addition to this lexical evidence, Schmithals suggests examples of Gnostic perfectionism in some of Paul's other letters. The most obvious examples of this "spiritual perfection" are found in the Corinthian epistles (1 Cor 4:7ff; 4:10; 5:2; 2 Cor 3:4ff; 4:2-5; 5:11-15; 10:4-5; 10:12ff; 12:11; 13:93) which contain the idea of being already filled, already rich, already kings and superiority over others—these are Gnostic reflections of having reached the goal. Schmithals then imports what he considers to be the same background from Corinthians into the Philippian context. This can be observed in his comparison of Phil 3:2b and 2 Cor 11:13. Because both verses describe Paul's opponents as ἐργάται, Schmithals proposes that the same people are in view. Schmithals refers to the use of ἐργάται as a "precise parallel."[258] He concludes that Phil 3:14-16 is a polemical text in which Paul disassociates himself from those Gnostics who claim perfect status. Schmithals interprets Phil 3:12-14 to be the concrete expression of "rejection of human boasting before God."[259]

Köster

Köster interprets Phil 3:12-15 as a polemic against perfectionism.[260] Appealing to its Hebrew equivalent and its Hellenistic usage, he defines τέλειος as meaning, "the possession of the qualities of salvation in their entirety, the arrival of heaven itself." In Phil 3, this is represented by both a religious and moral perfectionism based on circumcision and the Law[261]—this is how he links the alleged perfectionism of Phil 3:12-15 with Phil 3:2.[262] But Köster also suggests that Phil 3:10-11 is Paul's refutation of claims to eschatological perfection[263]—this is how he links Phil 3:12-15 with Phil 3:10-11. He thus attempts contextual cohesion through religious, moral and eschatological perfectionism. Köster's interpretation of τέλειος, as we shall see, goes beyond what can reasonably be claimed for the term. He follows Schmithals in using verbal parallels between Philippians and 2 Corinthians to support his theory about perfectionism—"the occurrence of the catchword καυχᾶσθαι

---

257. Ibid., 100.
258. Ibid., 85.
259. Ibid., 98.
260. Köster, "Polemic," 331.
261. Ibid., 322.
262. Ibid., 331.
263. Ibid., 322. Paul is arguing against opponents who believe they have already achieved resurrection as opposed to those who deny resurrection (ibid., 323).

in the next phrase (Phil 3:3) again points to II Corinthians, where the controversy concerning the necessity of boasting in order to give evidence of true apostleship and the possession of the spirit dominates the discussion."[264] Köster considers the situation to be the same in Philippi.

Lincoln

Lincoln "mirror-reads" τελειόω (understanding Paul's use of τέλειοι in Phil 3:15 as ironical) as a favorite term of Paul's opponents.[265] He suggests that in Phil 3:12–16, Paul refers to Philippians with a perfectionist viewpoint, liable to succumb to propaganda. Lincoln assumes this Judaizing propaganda has a "perfectionist" element to it, not from the text of Phil 3:12–14, but 2 Corinthians. With Schmithals and Köster, he proposes that in Phil 3, Paul is attacking opponents similar to those in 2 Cor 11:13–15—"Jewish Christian missionaries willing to accommodate themselves to "Hellenistic" emphases and perfectionist interests."[266] He justifies this by noting the strikingly similar terms used.[267] Lincoln therefore believes the threat to the Philippians is being taken in by perfectionist propaganda, which they are already prone to. But he does not explain in what way the Philippians could be taken in when they are already "leaning that way." However, we suggest that consideration be given to the more striking verbal similarities between Galatians and Philippians and also the conceptual and contextual similarities in both letters that are absent in 2 Corinthians.

Lüdemann

Lüdemann helpfully distinguishes between Galatian and Corinthian anti-Paulinists.[268] Although he notes the similarities between Galatians and Philippians, he seems to favor the historical connection between Corinthian anti-Paulinists in 2 Cor and Phil 3. He supports this from the literary evidence of the occurrence of ἐργάτας in both epistles, similarities in Pauline autobiography (Phil 3:4f and 2 Cor 11:13), with the suggestion that the mention of circumcision in Philippians sheds further light on the Co-

---

264. Ibid., 321.
265. Lincoln, *Paradise Now*, 93.
266. Ibid., 94–95.
267. The reference seems to be to ἐργάτας, which appears in Phil 3:2 not Phil 3:12–16, the passage under scrutiny.
268. Lüdemann, *Opposition to Paul in Jewish Christianity*, 108–9.

rinthian anti-Paulinists. There are two key points than can be raised against this viewpoint; firstly, Paul seems to be defending himself against agitators in 2 Cor 10–13, but he is comparing himself with them in Phil 3; secondly, circumcision, as it relates to boasting, is a key element of the comparison and should not be retrospectively applied to the Corinthian context. As we shall see, by making the historical connection between Galatian anti-Paulinists, the way is prepared for an investigation of the *text* of Galatians (esp. Gal 6:12–18), which we propose is significant for understanding the nature of the threat posed in Phil 3.

Park

Park argues that "the central issue in Phil 3:2–9 is one of boasting in privileges and accomplishments first before God and second before others (by implication)."[269] Differing in the designation of the opponents as Judaizers, she follows Schmithals in linking boasting in Phil 3:2 to the theme of selfish ambition mentioned in Phil 2:3–13, 20–21 and 2:30. Park argues that self-abnegation (Christ's in Phil 2:6–11 and Paul's in Phil 3:4–11) is used to contrast the Judaizer's self-promotion.[270] She understands the offence of the Judaizers to be that of self-promotion before God and others with Paul's list of rejected privileges supporting this. She concludes that self-promotion is not only the central issue in Phil 2:1–5, but also Phil 3:4–11.[271] Park, however, does not analyze Phil 3:12–16 and seems to rely on the idea of Paul's self-renunciation of privileges in Phil 3:2–9 to interpret Phil 3:11ff. Following Garland, she takes the two references to "perfection" and "maturity" in Phil 3:12 (τετελείωμαι) and Phil 3:15 (Ὅσοι οὖν τέλειοι) to be read as references to the issue of self-ambition in Phil 3:2–9.[272] As we shall see, this is incongruent with the substance of Phil 3:12–16 which focuses on resurrection and non-attainment of a desired goal. Self-renunciation, as a counter to boasting, is not in view in Phil 3:12–16, rather self-renunciation as a counter to self-preservation.

---

269. Park, *Submission*, 74.

270. Ibid., 61–62, 77–78.

271. Ibid., 76. In Phil 2:1–5, the immediate application of Phil 2:6–11 is to address self-promotion on the inter-believer level, whereas in Phil 3:2–11 it is on both God and human level.

272. Ibid., 55–56; Garland, "Composition and Unity," 171.

DeSilva

DeSilva interprets Phil 3:11 as a polemic "primarily against Christian forms of fleshly confidence and claims to privilege before God, among which over-realized eschatology may be secondarily included."[273] He argues that Phil 3:12–16 develops the rejection of confidence in the flesh and the negation of claims on God presented in Phil 3:2–11. DeSilva believes Paul is reflecting on his experience with the Corinthians who mistakenly understood their new life in Christ as the full possession of the resurrected life—as a result, they had become boastful. In Phil 3:12–16, Paul counters their boasting with an instruction about the futurity of the attainment of the resurrection.[274] DeSilva's interpretation is thus characterized by a dependence on 1 Corinthians for an explanation of the nature of boasting, and the presumption that Phil 3:11 emphasizes *certain futurity of*, rather than *desire for*, the attainment of resurrection.

Exegesis of Phil 3:11–14

All of the scholars surveyed identify Phil 3:1–14 as part of Paul's counter-argument to boasting. In critiquing this viewpoint, we will examine three interpretive issues in turn: firstly, the lexical analysis of τελειόω; secondly, the dependency on the Corinthian correspondence in comparative word studies; thirdly, whether or not Paul has doubts about attaining to the resurrection from the dead.

Lexical Analysis of τελειόω

Although his thesis on Gnosticism is no longer accepted, Schmithals's evaluation of the role of perfectionism and boasting in Phil 3 has exercised a crucial influence on exegesis and interpretation. Because he is representative of the dominant interpretation of Phil 3:12–14, three general objections to his viewpoint can be raised before we commence our exegesis. Firstly, as we shall see, there are other meanings for τελειόω which fit the context of Philippians better than a "Gnostic catchword." Secondly, τελειόω is not associated with boasting in Phil 3:12, but the non-attainment of something desired.[275] Interestingly, the Gnostic catchword τελειόω does not occur in the

---

273. DeSilva, "No Confidence in the Flesh," 47.
274. Ibid., 47.
275. This is not to deny that boasting is relevant in the overall context, but that Schmithals has not developed the link between boasting in Phil 3:3 and τελειόω in Phil

Corinthian texts that Schmithals and others cite as parallels to Philippians. Thirdly, Paul is speaking about himself, and has been throughout Phil 3:4–14, so the text could just as well be exemplary rather than polemical.

τελειόω can mean "to make perfect in the moral sense, to make perfect, to perfect, causing perfection."[276] This meaning provides the background to the many mirror-reading interpretations about "perfectionist" opponents in Philippi. But the word can also mean "to bring to completeness, wholeness,"[277] "finish," "accomplish." For example, BADG offers one meaning of τελειόω as "the perfection of upright persons who have gone on before"—that is, who have completed their work and died.[278] Alternatively, in Sir 50:19b, τελειόω means to finish service to the Lord—τὴν λειτουργίαν αὐτοῦ ἐτελείωσαν.[279] These different meanings simply confirm that any individual word has a limited semantic range that can be shaped or modified by its context. A brief examination of usage of the term in several LXX and NT passages may shed light on its meaning in the context of Phil 3:1–20.

In the LXX, τελειόω can refer to the "seal of martyrdom completed," describing those who have completed a life of fidelity. For example in 4 Macc 7:15, Eleazar is described as "O man of blessed age, venerable gray hair and law-observant life, whom the faithful seal of death has perfected (ἐτελείωσεν)." In Wis 4:16, a comparison is drawn between the righteous who die young and who are perfected by their death and the unrighteous who live longer: "But the righteous who are dead will condemn the impious who are living, and youth that is quickly made perfect (τελεσθεῖσα), the prolonged old age of the unrighteous." Philo also uses τελειόω in terms of the achievement of death as well as moral perfection; in *Leg.* 3 (45), he describes Aaron's death as completely asserting the truth.

τελειόω occurs in several NT texts where it can mean "to complete an activity," "bring to an end," "finish," "accomplish." In Heb 11:40, it refers to that which has not been attained by those OT saints who rested wholly on faith and who have died: " ... apart from us they would not be made perfect (τελειωθῶσιν)." τελειόω can also mean, "to fulfill," or "to carry out a course of action in the sense of a received commission." In Luke 13:32 Jesus describes how his work is brought to conclusion, in response to those Pharisees urging him to escape death at the hands of Herod: "I cast out

---

3:12 through the Gnostic understanding of the term.

276. See Louw and Nida, *Greek-English Lexicon of the New Testament*, 88.38, 747.

277. Delling, "τελειόω," 80.

278. BADG, 996. See also Greenlee, "Saint Paul—Perfect but not Perfected," 53–55.

279. See Delling, "τελειόω," 84, who notes that, in the writings of the Post-Apostolic Fathers, τελειόω could mean "to carry out one's ministry."

demons and accomplish healings today and tomorrow, and on the third day I will reach my goal (τελειοῦμαι)." Joel Green writes: "The report of Herod's design provides Jesus with the opportunity to remind all who hear him that his divine mission actually involves the violent fate of a prophet."[280] Here, τελειόω refers to Jesus' death[281] (note also Jesus' exclamation from the cross in John 19:30: τετέλεσται—"it is finished").[282] Green notes the parallel between Luke 13:32 and Acts 21:12-14 where Paul is urged, by Luke among others, to avoid persecution by not going to Jerusalem. This parallel is made more stark when it is noted that in Acts 20:24, Paul describes the completion of the ministry he received from Christ using the word τελειόω: "But I do not consider my life of any account as dear to myself, so that I may finish (τελειῶσαι) my course and the ministry which I received from the Lord Jesus . . . "—this is clearly a reference to his death. Finally, notwithstanding disputes about authorship, it is worth noting that in 2 Tim 4:6-8, τελέω is used to describe Paul's death in terms of the completion of his ministry: "I have fought the good fight, I have finished (τετέλεκα) the course."[283]

Of particular relevance to our argument are the LXX and NT usage of τελειόω (τελέω) in a context where death is described as instrumental in reaching the goal or completing the mission. We suggest that Paul's use of τελειόω in Phil 3:12 is consistent with these meanings. He has not become perfect because he has not completed his labors on behalf of Christ and arrived at the point of death. This interpretation of τελειόω as referring to Paul's death coheres with his attitude to his death in other parts of the letter. In chapter 1, Paul expressed his confidence that his incarceration would not result in his death (Phil 1:21-26; also 2:24). Although he desired death, and considered it gain, because of its immediate[284] and eschatological benefits, he reassures the Philippians that he will continue in ministry for their sake.

---

280. Green, *Luke*, 538.

281. Ibid., 536-38.

282. According to Delling, "τελειόω," 84, the verbs τελέω and τελειόω coincide in the NT. See also Brawley, "Absent Complement," 427.

283. Here, precise verbal, conceptual and contextual parallels spiraling around a description of Paul's struggle and death can be made with Philippians: σπένδομαι (Phil 2:17; 2 Tim 4:6), ἀναλύσεως (Phil 1:23; 2 Tim 4:6), ἀγῶνα (Phil 1:30; 2 Tim 4:7), τετέλεκα (Phil 3:12 [τελειόω]; 2 Tim 4:7).

284. Paul's use of ἀναλῦσαι in the phrase ἀναλῦσαι καὶ σὺν Χριστῷ εἶναι in Phil 1:23 refers metaphorically to his death, and perhaps, proleptically, to resurrection. See Palmer, "To Die is Gain," 207, who interprets σὺν Χριστῷ εἶναι as referring to the intermediate state (pre-resurrection) of being a dead Christian. For discussions on the intermediate state see Hanhart, "Paul's Hope in the Face of Death," 445-57; Dailey, "To Live or Die," 18-28; De Vogel, "Reflexions on Philipp. I 23-24," 262-74; Croy, "To Die is Gain," 517-31.

He also refers to his attitude when faced with the possibility of his death in Phil 2:17, rejoicing at the prospect of "being poured out as a libation." That he didn't consider himself to have reached the point of death also explains his two denials of having obtained the resurrection from the dead in Phil 3:12 ("I have not attained it"), and v. 13 ("I do not consider myself as having laid hold of it"). The recurrence of the theme of death in chapters 1, 2 and 3[285] further justifies our suggestion that τελειόω as referring to Paul's death is congruent with the immediate and wider context of the epistle.

Dependency on the Corinthian Correspondence

Sandmel cautioned against the methodological error of assuming that the presence of parallels between texts meant that there was dependency between the texts.[286] This methodological error of "parallelomania" has been used in some exegetical treatments of Philippians 3. As we have seen, several scholars argue that "boasting," "confidence in the flesh," and "evil workers" point to similar backgrounds for Corinthians and Philippians, namely, the presence of anti-Paulinist perfectionists. But it should be noted that the boasting in Philippians is of an altogether different nature from 2 Corinthians. The description of boasting in Philippians 1 takes place within the immediate context of Paul surviving death in his present incarceration (Phil 1:25, 26) and sharing in the Philippians's experience, which is followed by his instructions on suffering and perseverance (Phil 1:27–30). The description of boasting in Philippians 3 takes place within the immediate context of circumcision (Phil 3:2–5). However, in 2 Corinthians, boasting relates to appearances (2 Cor 5:12), apostolic authority (2 Cor 10:12–17) and the distinguishing conduct of true apostolic ministry (2 Cor 11:12—12:9).[287] Schmithals's claim of a "precise parallel" between Phil 3:4–6 and 2 Cor 11:18, 21ff and between Phil 3:2 and 2 Cor 11:13 is overstated.[288] His methodology of conflating a Gnostic understanding of τελειόω with the presumption of Gnostic boasting in Corinth, to arrive at the perfectionist polemic in Phil 3:12–14 is questionable on both lexical and contextual grounds. As we have shown above, there is not only an alternative understanding of τελειόω, but when lexical, and conceptual parallels as well as the "boasting context" are

---

285. Christ's death is mentioned three times (Phil 2:8 (x2); 3:10), Epaphroditus's death once (Phil 2:30) and resurrection from the dead twice (Phil 3:10–11).

286. Sandmel, "Parallelomania," 2. His principle can be applied to comparisons made between texts written by the same author.

287. See also Garland, "Composition and Unity," 168.

288. Schmithals, *Paul and the Gnostics*, 89.

considered, 2 Corinthians might not be the most apt background to Philippians 3.[289]

Furthermore, it is difficult to see how boasting, as the main issue in Phil 3:4–11, coheres with the central exhortation and content of Phil 1:27–30, which focuses on suffering and perseverance.[290] Additionally, there is no mention of boasting in Phil 3:11–16 and it is not clear how the passage can be considered as a development of Paul's argument about boasting before God. Finally, most proposals assume that Paul is countering boasts in something already achieved by contrasting his "not yet" eschatological expectation. But this latter point rests on a disputed exegetical examination of Phil 3:11. We will offer an alternative interpretation of Phil 3:11 and challenge the notion that Paul contemplates future certainty of resurrection from the dead. It would then be appropriate to ask why Paul would use a statement about the *possible non-attainment of a desired goal to counter claims from opponents of having reached that goal*. We argue that boasting is not the primary threat to Philippian behavior, but is a manifestation of a particular attitude that does concern Paul.

Certain Futurity of, or Desire for, Resurrection

The third exegetical issue germane to the interpretation of chapter 3 is Paul's attitude to his attaining resurrection from the dead. In Phil 3:11, Paul writes: "if perhaps (εἴ πως) I may attain to the resurrection from the dead." There are few exceptions to the view that Paul does not express doubt about attaining to the resurrection in verse 11.[291] This view rests on an understanding that Paul uses *present non-attainment of (yet future certainty of) resurrection to combat his opponents's presumption of present attainment of resurrection*. This view, in turn, depends upon an interpretation of the phrase εἴ πως as not carrying any sense of doubt—εἴ πως does not refer to Paul's doubts about resurrection but his different view of the resurrection and his lack of presumption to have experienced it already.

This interpretation of εἴ πως also affects how other parts of the letter are read. For example, Paul's expectancy, but his present non-attainment, of resurrection facilitates a link with the theme of self-renunciation (demonstrated by Christ in Phil 2:6–11 and contained in Paul's autobiography of

---

289. Ciampa, *Presence and Function of Scripture*, 371–72, notes the connection in Gal 6:12–18 between avoiding persecution and boasting in the circumcision of the Galatians.

290. Composite letter theorists would not share this view.

291. For example, Perriman, "Pattern of Christ's Sufferings," 62–79.

Phil 3:4–11). Paul and Christ renounce privileges in contrast to those who engage in self-promotion and boast in privileges and achievements. Boasting in privileges and achievements might be a tendency in Philippi that Paul desires to correct by his example of humility—so he does the opposite of his opponents and denies achievement of what they boast in. Alternatively, Bockmuehl links Phil 3:11 to Judaizers by suggesting that Paul's emphatic phrase, "resurrection from the dead,"[292] implicitly denies an opposing alternative to a future resurrection. Then he suggests that since Judaizers believe in a future resurrection, their opposition would be to a future resurrection for Gentiles. According to Bockmuehl, Paul's emphatic statement about resurrection should be seen to reinforce the conviction that this assurance does indeed belong to the Gentiles by faith in Christ.[293] Thus we see how the interpretation of εἴ πως influences broader understanding of the epistle.

However, if Paul's doubts about attaining the resurrection are genuine, it is difficult to see how he would use it to combat Judaizing claims of Gentile exclusion since he himself might be excluded. Similarly, if Paul expresses real doubt about attaining to the resurrection from the dead, this would lead us to ask why he would use future expectation of resurrection to combat opponents's boasts of present achievement, when he himself had doubts about attaining it. The interpretation of εἴ πως is therefore crucial to how we interpret the "opponents" and the threat they pose. In examining the meaning of εἴ πως in Phil 3:11, we will engage with the views of Judith Gundry Volf who has succinctly stated the main arguments against the phrase conveying a sense of doubt.[294]

Gundry Volf

Gundry Volf adopts a mirror-reading approach to Phil 3:11 suggesting that Paul argues against perfectionist theology in Philippi by maintaining that final salvation is yet future.[295] She suggests that εἴ strengthened by πως expresses expectation not doubt. In support of this view, she notes other expressions of expectation that use the combination εἴ πως in the NT and the LXX: Rom 1:10; 11:14; Acts 27:12 and 2 Sam 14:15. None of these, she claims, contains the element of doubt. Gundry Volf argues that Paul uses εἴ πως for the expectation of divine working. For example, in Rom 1:10 Paul

292. The emphasis is because of the double occurrence of ἐκ in the phrase τὴν ἐξανάστασιν τὴν ἐκ νεκρῶν.

293. Bockmuehl, *Philippians*, 219–20.

294. She is followed by Fee, *Philippians*, 335–36, and Park, *Submission*, 66.

295. Gundry Volf, *Paul and Perseverance*, 259.

writes "if perhaps (εἴ πως) now at last by the will of God I may succeed in coming to you." According to Gundry Volf, the phrase does not describe Paul's doubt, but the "divine possibility" of his visit to Rome. Similarly, in Rom 11:14 Paul hopes that God will save Israel: "if perhaps (εἴ πως) I might move to jealousy my fellow countrymen and save some of them." Here, εἴ πως denotes Paul's hope and expectation in God's fulfillment.[296] In similar vein, she writes, "By introducing his hope to 'attain to the resurrection from the dead' with εἴ πως, Paul removes the realization of this hope from the realm of human possibility and confesses it to be only a 'divine possibility.'" Accordingly, "The εἴ-clauses in Phil 3:11, 12, therefore, do not suggest that Paul doubted his final salvation."[297]

Two aspects of Gundry Volf's analysis merit closer examination. Firstly, in the verses cited in support of her argument, the sense of doubt is stronger than she claims. Randall Otto has argued convincingly that εἴ πως carries a sense of doubt in *all* of the NT and LXX passages in which the phrase occurs.[298] In Rom 1:10 where Paul uses εἴ πως in reference to his visiting the church in Rome, the phrase is part of a prayer petition characterized by the term δεόμενος (making request or asking). The verb δέομαι is translated "earnest asking" or "begging" in four other occurrences in Paul's letters.[299] Its occurrence in verse 10 reflects Paul's strong desire, yet his uncertainty about how God will respond to his prayer. This interpretation coheres with verse 13 in which Paul admits that previous plans to visit Rome had been thwarted; "that often I have planned to come to you and have been prevented thus far." In light of verse 13, εἴ πως in verse 10 hardly indicates certainty or even expectancy of divine working (positive). Paul is more likely expressing a *desire* to visit Rome, whether or not he succeeds in doing so.

Similar objections can be raised against Gundry Volf's interpretation of εἴ πως in Rom 11:14 in which Paul does not doubt God's power to convert many Jews, but does doubt the impact of his own ministry in effecting those conversions. In this passage Paul desires the Jews to be saved through jealousy provoked by his ministry to the Gentiles. Gundry Volf claims εἴ πως is an expression of hope in God's power. But Paul is talking about his ministry to the Gentiles and its relation to the place of the Jews in God's plan, not God's power. As Otto notes: "While Paul may have a great expectation for

---

296. Ibid., 257.

297. Ibid., 258.

298. Otto, "Resurrection," 324–40. He includes Rom 1:10; 11:14; Acts 27:12; 4 Kgdms (2 Kgs) 18:13ff.; 3 Kgdms 21:31 (1 Kgs 20:31); Jer 28:8. We would add 2 Sam 14:15 to this list.

299. See Dunn, *Romans 1—8*, 29, who notes 2 Cor 5:20; 8:4; Gal 4:12; 1 Thess 3:10.

the *eventual* conversion of many Jews to the gospel, he does not seem at all certain of the impact his own ministry will have in effecting that change."³⁰⁰ This coheres with Luke's recording of Paul turning to the gentiles following a failed ministry to his own people. Desire rather than expectancy seems to be in view. The same arguments can be marshaled in favor of εἴ πως expressing doubt in Acts 27:12; 2 Sam 14:15; 4 Kgdms 18:13ff.; 3 Kgdms 21:31 and Jer 28 (51). From this survey we conclude that NT and LXX usage "preponderates in favour of εἴ πως having a strong element of doubt or uncertainty."³⁰¹

Another aspect of Gundry Volf's analysis that pertains to her interpretation of εἴ πως is the role that a theology of assurance plays in her argument. She believes there can be no uncertainty about Paul's persevering in the faith and obtaining final salvation. She draws on Phil 3:10 to support this: "Because of Christ's prior action towards him, Paul pursues expecting to obtain."³⁰² In Gundry Volf's analysis, both phrases, "Christ's seizing of Paul" (Phil 3:12) and "being found in Christ" (Phil 3:9) correlate to "resurrection from the dead." If these terms reflect Paul's assurance of salvation, then Paul can have no doubts about resurrection. But this position does not leave open the possibility that there is a distinction in this passage between resurrection from the dead and final salvation—it is possible for Paul to be certain about the latter (assurance of salvation) yet have doubts about experiencing the former (if he is alive at the Parousia), as we shall see. In similar vein, O'Brien and Bockmuehl³⁰³ propose that εἴ πως expresses expectation, since Paul elsewhere writes of resurrection as a "certain hope for the Christian" (for example, 1 Cor 15:20; 2 Cor 5:1). Although support for this position is garnered from BDF,³⁰⁴ we suggest that the actual "uses" of εἴ πως argued for above show that the phrase always denotes doubt and uncertainty.³⁰⁵ According to Paul, resurrection is a certain hope for the *dead* Christian *only* therefore doubts about participating in the resurrection from the dead can cohere with a confident expectation of final salvation.

Some scholars accept that some kind of hesitancy is implied in the term, but consider the doubt to refer to the means or method relating to events leading to resurrection,³⁰⁶ or the manner of Paul's death.³⁰⁷ These

---

300. Otto, "Resurrection," 327.
301. Ibid., 328.
302. Gundry Volf, *Paul and Perseverance*, 256.
303. O'Brien, *Philippians*, 412; Bockmuehl, *Philippians*, 217.
304. BDF §375.
305. Otto, "Resurrection," 326.
306. Motyer, *Philippians*, 170.
307. Koperski, *Knowledge*, 281.

views interpret εἴ πως to mean "somehow" or "by any means."³⁰⁸ But the idea of instrumentality is missing from all the other uses of the term, where it means "whether or not."³⁰⁹ Others suggest that εἴ πως refers to humility or self-distrust, which precludes doubt.³¹⁰ But if Paul, as a former Pharisee, believed in an eschatological resurrection of both the wicked and the righteous (Acts 24:15; cf. Dan 12:2), then εἴ πως as an expression of humility makes little sense—he does not wish to presume he will attain to the resurrection, which will certainly take place! Given the uses of the phrase in the NT and the LXX, and the use of the subjunctive as the mood of doubtful assertion (καταντήσω—"I might arrive at" or "I might attain to") we conclude that the phrase εἴ πως conveys a sense of doubt. It is therefore an odd choice if Paul intended to describe the certainty of future resurrection as a counter claim to present possession of resurrection life made by his opponents.

Paul's Doubt and the Parousia

The reason for Paul's doubt can be determined from the immediate context (Phil 3:10 and 3:12). The phrase "if perhaps I might attain to (or reach) the resurrection from the dead" is part of a conditional clause which describes Paul's resurrection as contingent upon conformity to Christ's death—a process currently taking place for Paul at the time of writing (συμμορφιζόμενος in v. 10).³¹¹ Self-evidently, Paul's resurrection from the dead is contingent upon Paul's death. In v. 12 the adverb ἤδη occurs twice and can be translated "now" as opposed to "already."³¹² "It is not the case that I have *now* attained it or have *now* become perfect." This is its meaning in Phil 4:10 in which Paul describes the timing of his receipt of the Philippians's gift: "*now* at last you have revived your concern for me." This translation is also consistent with its occurrence in 2 Tim 4:6, where it is used to convey the sense that Paul has arrived at the point of death: "for I am *now* being poured out as a drink offering, and the time of my departure has come."³¹³ From this brief analysis, we offer our rendering of Phil 3:12 as follows: "It is not the case that I have now attained to the resurrection from the dead or have now reached

---

308. NIV, NRSV (cf. RSV).

309. Otto, "Resurrection," 329.

310. Vincent, *Philippians*, 106. Osiek, *Philippians*, 95, who suggests that Paul doubts his own fidelity.

311. συμμορφιζόμενος adverbially modifies τοῦ γνῶναι. See O'Brien, *Philippians*, 412; Koperski, *Knowledge*, 281, 284; Perriman, "Pattern of Christ's Sufferings," 73.

312. BDAG, 434; Perriman, "Pattern of Christ's Sufferings," 74.

313. The word also occurs in Rom 1:10 where it clearly refers to the present.

the point of death by completing my ministry (τετελείωμαι) since I have not yet been conformed to Christ's death." By recognizing that the process which leads to the resurrection of the dead is συμμορφιζόμενος τῷ θανάτῳ αὐτοῦ, we find an explanation for εἴ πως in the *temporal* aspect of Paul's death.[314] Paul can express doubt that he will achieve resurrection from the dead if, in relation to his current circumstances, survival and being alive at the Parousia are a possibility.

This interpretation is supported by the occurrence of the phrase τὴν ἐξανάστασιν τὴν ἐκ νεκρῶν which contains an unusual emphasis because of the double ἐκ stressing the resurrection *out from among the dead*.[315] Gnilka observes that the emphasis in the phrase only makes sense if it is distinguished from another interpretation. He considers this to be "a participation in the resurrection already in this life."[316] According to Gnilka, Paul uses the phrase to distinguish between his expectation of a future resurrection and the views of his opponents who believed resurrection life could be experienced before death. Notwithstanding our analysis of εἴ πως above, Gnilka's interpretation might account for the reference to the dead, but not the emphasis given to the sphere of the dead by the double ἐκ. Our alternative proposal is that Paul is contrasting *resurrection out from among the dead* with *transformation of the living* at the Parousia.[317]

Interpretation of Phil 3:11–14

We have argued that τελειόω relates to the completion, or perfecting, of Paul's ministry by the means of his death, and that he has expressed uncertainty that he will achieve the resurrection from the dead because he does not know if the Parousia will prevent his death. Phil 3:12–14 contains a repeated emphasis on Paul's non-attainment of, yet strong desire for, resurrection from the dead. He seems to want to convey his unfulfilled desire for conformity with Christ which includes suffering, death then resurrection. He is willing to embrace suffering to the point of death and death itself as perfecting or completing his response to Christ. This perfecting is ultimately realized through resurrection which Paul has already described in terms of God's approval of the pattern of suffering and death (2:9; 3:9, 10; cf. 1:29).

---

314. Ibid., 70.

315. The majority text has τῶν νεκρῶν instead of τὴν ἐκ νεκρῶν, which is attested in 𝔓[16] 𝔓[46] ℵ A B D P Ψ 33 81 and Latin and Sahidic versions. τῶν νεκρῶν is considered less likely—so, O'Brien, *Philippians*, 382.

316. Gnilka, *Der Philipperbrief*, 197.

317. Perriman, "Pattern of Christ's Sufferings," 71.

From this we conclude that the emphasis in vv 11–14 is *Paul's attitude to persevere to the point of death, in order to conform to the pattern of Christ*. This is consistent with how he presents his, Christ's and Epaphroditus's attitude to death in Phil 1:21–26, 2:5–8 and 2:30 respectively. We could say that Phil 3:11–14 is Paul's argument for his preference for, and the virtue of, death.

Phil 3:11–14 in the Context of Phil 3:4–10

Hawthorne notes the difficulty of explaining Phil 3:12–16 in the context of Phil 3:4–11: "One can only hope, therefore, to make an intelligent guess as to how vv. 12–16 fit with vv. 4–11."[318] His dilemma results from what Riffaterre and Wakefield describe as a mimetic or surface reading of the text. But if we accept that vv. 11–16 represents Paul's example of a correct attitude to suffering, death and resurrection, there is no puzzle about how they fit with vv. 4–11. Verses 4–11 describe Paul's recognition that soteriology is the basis for accepting suffering: "Christ's resurrection is the proof of God's approval that indeed, the believer's fellowship or salvation, wrought by suffering, is the one determined by God as appropriate."[319] Paul recognizes the approval and righteousness of God in the Christ event (Phil 3:9), therefore conformity with Christ is what Paul presses towards—obedience to the point of death receives God's approval marked by resurrection. Paul's self-renouncing of privileges in Phil 3:5–8 can therefore be viewed as a self-renouncing of status that provides protection from persecution and avoidance of suffering. Phil 3:4–16 is Paul's counter to some Philippians's attitude of avoiding suffering, since it is antithetical to how they have been saved, and how they are thinking about life as a believer. What's more, this interpretation of Phil 3:11–16 explains the "content of the imitation" in Paul's mimetic injunction in the following verses.

Phil 3:11–14 in the Context of Phil 3:17–21

The call to imitate Paul in Phil 3:17 follows logically from the attitude and behavior he "models" in Phil 3:11–14, namely his preference for death and resurrection, even while expecting release from prison. The idea of imitation is anticipated by ἐφθάσαμεν . . . στοιχεῖν (to arrive at a standard) in Phil 3:16, and περιπατοῦντας . . . τύπον (walking according to a pattern), which

---

318. Hawthorne, *Philippians*, 149.

319. Park, *Submission*, 74: "knowing God's sovereign power and approval in the resurrection event leads to knowing that the believer's fellowship with Christ is one effected by Christ's sufferings."

then prepares for the contrast in Phil 3:18—πολλοὶ γὰρ περιπατοῦσιν (the many who walk ...). According to Brandt, "Scholars who have examined these texts tend to focus upon the object of the mimesis rather than the process or activity in which Paul exhorts his reader to engage."[320] Brant's view of mimesis is helpful because it reminds us that Paul need not be instructing the Philippians to be a mirror-image of their object of imitation, but that he exhorts them to imitate him *in respect of a particular exigency*. But what aspect of himself does Paul want the Philippians to imitate? O'Brien notes the urgency in Paul's admonition because others have set an example that is the absolute antithesis of the Pauline model.[321] He identifies that the immediately preceding verses are particularly in view when Paul issues this call to imitation: "However, one cannot properly understand vv. 12–16 apart from what has been stated as their basis, namely vv. 8–11 ... "[322] According to O'Brien, Paul's appeal to imitation begins at Phil 3:8 or even earlier. He concludes that what should be imitated is, "gaining Christ, possessing the righteousness of God, knowing Christ through the power of his resurrection and the fellowship of his sufferings and ... laying hold of Christ."[323] O'Brien seems to have overlooked the content of the mimesis in Phil 3:12–16, namely, *be like me, embrace suffering and persevere to the point of death, in conformity with Christ, for this will bring the approval of God through resurrection from the dead*. Paul's desire to complete his ministry for Christ through death and resurrection explains his focus on the benefits of the Parousia for those who will die—τὸ σῶμα τῆς ταπεινώσεως (Phil 3:21) probably refers, specifically, to the dead.[324] This interpretation coheres with Paul's repeated mention of death (Phil 1:20, 21, 23; 2:8, 30) and especially resurrection (from the dead: Phil 3:10–14, 21; cf. 2:9). That Paul is describ-

---

320. Brant, "Place of *Mimēsis* in Paul's Thought," 285. See esp. Castelli, *Imitating Paul*. Contra Castelli, Paul seems to be specific about the content of the imitation in Philippians, and desires to alter attitudes and behaviors with his rhetoric, rather than using it to reinforce his own power over the Philippians. See also Stanley, "Become Imitators of Me," 861; Clarke, "Be Imitators of Me," 329–60.

321. O'Brien, *Philippians*, 444.

322. Ibid., 447.

323. Ibid.

324. Cf. Lincoln, *Paradise Now*, 102, who thinks μετασχηματίσει corresponds to the concept of being changed by putting on the additional clothing of immortality, this being suggestive of a living body being translated. But μετασχηματίσει can mean to change the form of something (BDAG, 641) as in the LXX (4 Macc 9:22) where it refers to the transforming of the martyrs into incorruptibility at death (Schneider "μετασχηματίζω," 957). Also, why would Paul use a term that seemed to exclude those who would be dead when Christ returns, when he has expressed a desire to be one of them?

ing the Parousia in a context of suffering and death is corroborated by his use of πολίτευμα which refers back to Phil 1:27–30—heavenly citizenship involves a present conformity to suffering and death (Phil 1:29, 30; 3:8, 10; 4:14) and a future conformity to glory (Phil 3:21), with Christ as the referent of both.

Conclusions

In this section we have argued that Paul uses his self-renunciation of privileges and willingness to embrace death (in order to experience resurrection) to combat the inimical exigency of self-preservation, exemplified by the Galatian Judaizers. In renouncing his privileged status as the persecutor, Paul takes on the role of the persecuted in a reversal that enables him to counter the rhetorical exigency of self-interest. He achieves this by using the rhetorical constraints of self-renunciation, fellowship of Christ's suffering, being conformed to Christ's death, expectation of Parousia and belief in eschatological resurrection. Phil 3:10–14 contains the prominent rhetorical constraint that Paul uses to address the controlling exigency—his desire to complete his ministry for Christ through death and resurrection. Phil 3:10–14 is therefore Paul's argument for his preference for death, and its virtue as the prerequisite for resurrection. We therefore propose that the most economical explanation for Phil 3:1–21 as rhetorical discourse is to be found in Paul's intention to correct an imperfection in the Philippian community summed up as, "the desire to avoid death for the sake of Christ instead of desiring resurrection as God's approval of death for the sake of Christ." We can now consider if a single theme can bring the exigencies and constraints of Phil 1:27–30, 2:1–4, 2:5–11, 14 and 3:1–21 into a unity and significance.

CONCLUSIONS: THE MATRIX

Most NT exegetes who have analyzed the five passages in the rhetorical unit broadly agree on the summary of their meaning as follows. Phil 1:27–30—"unity"; Phil 2:1–4—"unity"; Phil 2:5–11—"vindication"; Phil 2:14—"manward/Godward grumbling"; Phil 3:1–21—"boasting." As argued in our exegesis, these summaries do not adequately account for Paul's rhetoric and his broader interests in the epistle, nor do they offer an explanation for the cluster of Scripture references in Phil 2:10–16. Our exegesis has produced an alternative set of "summaries." We have identified five controlling exigencies derived from a rhetorical exegesis of Phil 1:27–3:21:

the refusal to accept that God would approve of his people's suffering for the sake of Christ; an attitude of self-preservation that resulted in a neglect of others during conflict; claiming immunity from suffering and death on the grounds of high-status and that God would not approve; grumbling against God because of suffering inflicted by adversaries; the desire to avoid death for the sake of Christ instead of desiring resurrection as God's approval of death for the sake of Christ. Our conclusions suggest a unifying theme for Philippians that spirals around "God's approval." Allowing for variations and emphases in the progression of an argument, Paul's rhetoric seems designed to address the attitude of self-preservation evinced in those with a tendency to avoid suffering and death for the sake of Christ. Consequently, the matrix sentence which we propose as most economically accounting for the greatest number of formal and semantic features in Phil 1:27–3:21 is: *God approves of suffering and death for the sake of Christ*. We believe this matrix sentence is an expression of the epistolary argument, central theme or rhetorical situation and brings the passage into unity and significance. It gives an account of the spread of stylistic, linguistic, grammatical and theological elements highlighted in our exegesis of Phil 1:27—3:21, and which we offer as a yardstick for judging the plausibility of the proposed rhetorical situation. Before we investigate the possibility that the alleged literary allusions to Scripture in Phil 2:10–16 are variants of this matrix, a hypothetical construction of the historical situation in Philippi can be put forward.

A Hypothetical Construction of the Historical Situation of Philippians

While in prison, Paul had learned from Epaphroditus that the Philippians were being persecuted because of their confession of Christ as the one and only Lord, and their refusal to participate in the imperial cult of Philippi. The opposition and conflict caused disagreement within the Philippian Church over the role of suffering, with some Philippians being disinclined to accept it as a legitimate consequence of gospel citizenship approved by God. The division left some within the community bearing the burden of persecution more than others. Epaphroditus also reported that those Philippians with a tendency to promote suffering-free gospel citizenship were questioning the community's continued patronage of Paul since they perceived his imprisonment as an impediment to gospel mission and something which God would not sanction. In Paul's view, their attitude of self-preservation induced a wrong assessment of hardship and disdaining of a God who appeared indifferent to the apparent failure of his people. Paul writes to instruct and warn the Philippians that the avoidance of suffering resulting from a loyalty to Christ would require rejection of submission, obedience and self-renunciation—in fact, those things Christ did to achieve their salvation. Paul's letter is therefore intended to exhort the Philippians to persevere, and not capitulate in the face of suffering and death, since God indeed approves of their circumstances in advancing the gospel.

CHAPTER 4

Intertextual Allusion in Phil 2:10–16

IN CHAPTER 2, WE laid out the methodological framework for our analysis of Paul's use of Scripture in Phil 2:10–16. We examined various theories of intertextuality and allusion, concluding that a diachronic, text production approach to analysis of Philippians would be viable. We discovered that considering the role of an author who makes tacit references to precursor texts (pretexts or intertexts) is compatible with theories of intentional allusion. We not only examined the mechanics of how the elements of a single, evoked text might be activated (actualizing of the allusion), but also the possibility that successive allusions are all variants of a rhetorical situation which can be proposed from an analysis of the text of Philippians itself. Moreover, we argued that this rhetorical situation might have been used to control which elements of an evoked text were activated by the author, during composition, and the reader, during reception, of the text. Consequently, in chapter 3, we set out to construct the rhetorical situation for which Philippians seems a fitting response. In this chapter we will use Ben-Porat's model to test the plausibility of literary allusion based on congruence with the elements of the rhetorical situation constructed in the previous chapter. We should recall that, in an effort to verify or falsify the presence and functioning of Scripture, Bormann offered four "themes" to test for congruence between Philippians and OT texts: Paul's imprisonment, his relationship with the Philippians, Christology, and the problem with opponents.[1] We have already appraised Bormann's benchmark as too narrow and advocated a test for congruence that conceives of a more expansive rela-

---

1. Bormann, "Triple Intertextuality in Philippians," 93.

tion between texts consonant with value, purpose, viewpoint, tone, feeling, and predicament.² With this in mind our rhetorical-exegetical approach has unveiled several exigencies and constraints that constitute the rhetorical situation, and which may yield different results in a test of congruence between Philippians and the OT:

> a) acceptance of a pattern of conduct that flows from belonging to a particular commonwealth, and having allegiance to its ruler (a crucified Lord)
>
> b) the disinclination to accept suffering as a requirement of gospel citizenship
>
> c) God's sanction of suffering in the cause of Christ
>
> d) injunctions to share a specific expression of conformity and solidarity with regard to suffering
>
> e) self-preservation exemplified in self-interest and the neglect of others
>
> f) self-renunciation of privileged status that provides immunity from persecution, suffering, and death
>
> g) God's approval of suffering and death in the salvation event
>
> h) complaints against God whilst enduring suffering at the hands of adversaries
>
> i) preference for death because of its eschatological benefits and conformity to Christ's pattern.

We suggest that these are elements of the argumentative complex of the epistle and variants of the rhetorical situation which can be summarized as: "some Philippians were disinclined to accept that God approves of suffering and death in the cause of Christ." We will use the test of congruence to investigate whether it is plausible that Paul evoked the wider context of the texts of Scripture or simply echoed their language.

As we have argued previously, there is little to be gained by using scientific criteria to prove the presence of allusion because the ultimate test of allusion requires congruence between texts, and a plausible suggestion that elements in one text connote elements in another. Congruence between texts can be present or absent regardless of the probability of allusion established using criteria—a poorly-denoted allusion is still an allusion. Therefore, like Jauhiainen, we will not use scientific criteria to assess the probability of allusion but take, as given, a list of allusions already compiled from various sources. With this in mind we should recall that the first stage of Ben-Porat's process of allusion is the recognition of the allusion marker

---

2. Alter, *Pleasures*, 131.

as belonging to, or closely related to, another independent text. The second stage is identification of the evoked text. Thus, accepting the list of suggested allusions mentioned above is equivalent to completing Ben-Porat's first and second phases—the allusion markers and evoked texts have already been identified. Nevertheless, we will provide some rationale for accepting this list, drawing mainly on the probability of allusion determined from the denotative function of the alleged allusion marker. Such an approach yields varying degrees of certainty and cannot solely be relied upon as the test for allusion. Consequently, we will also perform the more sophisticated analysis of the connotative function of the allusion device by testing the suggestion of allusion using rhetorical situation as an hermeneutical constraint—this could be thought of as another way of calculating the probability of allusion. In our "case study" approach to a detailed analysis, we will use the following cluster of allusions identified by various scholars: Isa 45:23 in Phil 2:10-11; Ps 2:11 in Phil 2:12; Deut 32:5 in Phil 2:15; Dan 12:3 in Phil 2:15; Isa 49:4 in Phil 2:16.[3] We will test our hypothesis by asking two questions for each alleged allusion: In what way could the alleged alluded-to text be a variant on the rhetorical situation? Why does Paul use this particular alluded-to text?

ISA 45:23 IN PHIL 2:10-11

Exegesis of Phil 2:9-11

⁹διὸ καὶ ὁ θεὸς αὐτὸν ὑπερύψωσεν καὶ ἐχαρίσατο αὐτῷ τὸ ὄνομα τὸ ὑπὲρ πᾶν ὄνομα, ¹⁰ἵνα ἐν τῷ ὀνόματι Ἰησοῦ πᾶν γόνυ κάμψῃ ἐπουρανίων καὶ ἐπιγείων καὶ καταχθονίων ¹¹καὶ πᾶσα γλῶσσα ἐξομολογήσηται ὅτι κύριος Ἰησοῦς Χριστὸς εἰς δόξαν θεοῦ πατρός.

In chapter 3, we challenged the almost universal agreement that has dominated exegesis of Phil 2:6-11 since Lohmeyer first advanced the idea in 1928—that Phil 2:6-11 constitutes an early hymn of the Christian church.[4] Now we will examine the key exegetical issues surrounding the "second half" of the passage and its predominant interpretation. Phil 2:9-11 comprises a single sentence in which God is the subject of the main verbs ὑπερυψόω and χαρίζομαι with Christ the passive recipient. The transition from humiliation (vv. 6-8) to exaltation is denoted by the inferential conjunction διό followed by καί indicating God's response to Jesus' prior action

---

3. Hübner's list is the most comprehensive (*Vetus Testamentum*, 490) but see also UBSGNT⁴, 893, 895, 897.

4. Lohmeyer, *Kyrios Jesus*, 4ff.

of self-humbling, which reached its climax in his death on the cross. The debates concerning God's response as a consequence of,[5] or reward[6] for, Jesus' voluntary abasement should not detract from the divine approval clearly conveyed by the phrase.[7] As a result of Jesus' abasement, then, God highly exalted (ὑπερύψωσεν) him and bestowed on him the name above every name; ὁ θεὸς αὐτὸν ὑπερύψωσεν καὶ ἐχαρίσατο αὐτῷ τὸ ὄνομα τὸ ὑπὲρ πᾶν ὄνομα, [10]ἵνα ἐν τῷ ὀνόματι Ἰησοῦ πᾶν.... Two issues arise from Paul's phrase; the nature of the exaltation and the name bestowed on Jesus. The force of the prefix in ὑπερύψωσεν (ὑπέρ—meaning "over/beyond")[8] has been understood (comparatively) as meaning that Jesus has been elevated *beyond* a previously held rank.[9] Alternatively, ὑπερύψωσεν can be used in the superlative sense, meaning "raised to the loftiest height."[10] This is consistent with Paul's description of Jesus' equality with God and our interpretation of ἁρπαγμός as it describes Jesus' refusal to exploit this equality. Thus, the result, or consequence, of Jesus' divesting himself of exalted status is his restoration by God to the loftiest height—a height which, *positionally*, he occupied before, albeit in a non-incarnational mode of existence. There has been considerable debate concerning which name God bestowed on Jesus. Some understand the name to be the personal name "Jesus"[11] whereas the majority of scholars accept the name "Lord" as a periphrasis of Yahweh.[12] The latter is preferable for several reasons. It removes the awkwardness of God bestowing a name already borne by Jesus throughout his incarnation. Additionally, the inclusion of the definite article (*the* name) in v. 9, the use of the genitive to refer to the name *belonging* to Jesus in v. 10[13] and the confession of v. 11 that "Jesus Christ is Lord" are in keeping with the idea of Jesus being exalted to the highest place and sharing in the divine dignity (v. 6—"the being equal with God"). The purpose or result of the exaltation is introduced by the expression which includes the proposed allusion marker to Isa 45:23: ἵνα ἐν τῷ ὀνόματι Ἰησοῦ πᾶν γόνυ κάμψῃ ἐπουρανίων καὶ ἐπιγείων καὶ καταχθονίων καὶ πᾶσα γλῶσσα ἐξομολογήσηται. Two prominent

---

5. Michael, *Philippians*, 93; Collange, *Philippians*, 105.

6. Meyer, *Philippians*, 99; Silva, *Philippians*, 109.

7. BDF §442: διὸ καί introduces a result.

8. Riesenfeld, "ὑπέρ," 507.

9. See Bostock, "Origen's Exegesis of the Kenosis Hymn," 538.

10. BDAG, 1034. See also Beare, *Philippians*, 85.

11. Moule, "Further Reflexions on Philippians 2:5–11," 270; Silva, *Philippians*, 110–11.

12. For example, Fee, *Philippians*, 221–22.

13. Hawthorne, *Philippians*, 92; Contra Silva, *Philippians*, 110, who notes other uses of the genitive, but overlooks context.

exegetical issues arise; whether the homage offered to Jesus is voluntary or involuntary and the identity of those paying it. It is generally accepted that ἐπουρανίων καὶ ἐπιγείων καὶ καταχθονίων refers, respectively, to heavenly beings, angels and demons; those living on earth at the parousia; those who are dead but awaiting resurrection at the parousia—essentially, the whole of created beings.[14] The inclusion of demons has led to the suggestion that Phil 2:9–11 conveys the idea of universal salvation.[15] But in light of the eschatological destruction explicit in Phil 1:28 and 3:19 this is untenable. Consequently, the homage paid to Jesus indicated by the phrase πᾶν γόνυ κάμψῃ ... καὶ πᾶσα γλῶσσα ἐξομολογήσηται is not in acknowledgment of his salvation for them but his sovereignty over them. This is consistent with the only other occurrence of the phrase in extant Greek literature[16] (found in Rom 14:11) where Paul adapts his citation of Isa 45:23 in an argument to remind the Romans that God is the supreme and final authority in matters of judgment. In his interpretation of Rom 14:11, Moo evokes the wider content of Isa 45:23 (v. 22b and 24a) because of the appropriateness of the Lord's unique sovereignty to the matter discussed in Rom 14:1–12.[17] In similar vein, Dunn uses Isa 45:23 to interpret Rom 14:11 as part of Paul's argument directed against those who, by setting themselves as judge over one another, usurp the sovereignty that belongs to God alone. Dunn also evokes the wider context of Isa 45:23 (v. 21) claiming that "the citation of one of the most powerful monotheistic passages in the scriptures (Isa 45:23) would have a powerful effect particularly on those seeking to be loyal to Jewish traditional beliefs."[18] Thus, Phil 2:5–11 describes the abasement and exaltation of Jesus and the universal submission owed to him as one who shares in the divine identity, dignity, and sovereignty of the God of Israel. But how does this rhetoric function in the epistolary argument?

On the basis of the foregoing exegeses, most historical scholars summarize or reduce the meaning of Phil 2:5–11 to a phrase or sentence. For example, Silva suggests that Phil 2:5–11 is about "Christian humility,"[19] whereas Hawthorne argues that the hymn means that "self-sacrifice [comes]

14. See O'Brien, *Philippians*, 244.

15. See Fee, *Philippians*, 224.

16. Determined by using the Online TLG® database to search Greek literature predating or contemporaneous with Paul from the third century BCE through the first century CE.

17. Moo, *Romans*, 847.

18. Dunn, *Romans 9–16*, 809, 815; Neither Dunn nor Moo argues for a christological interpretation of Isa 45:23 in Rom 14:11, suggesting instead that Paul uses κύριος with reference to God not Christ.

19. Silva, *Philippians*, 92.

first before the self is exalted by God."[20] With particular reference to vv. 9-11, Fee interprets the passage as proof of Jesus' vindication by God and as paradigmatic for God's response to suffering believers.[21] Specifically, in terms of the role of Isa 45:23 in vv. 10-11, Oakes argues that the purpose of the phrase is to present the triumph of Christ over the Roman Empire.[22] But none of these explanations requires the language of Isa 45:23. Fee and Hawthorne are typical of those who advance the preeminent interpretation that argues for vv. 9-11 as paradigmatic for the suffering believer whom God will exalt in an act of vindication. Although we agree that Christ's self-renunciation is paradigmatic (vv. 6-8), we have argued that vindication of suffering does not cohere with the idea of God's approval and is contrary to the positive view of humility and abasement communicated elsewhere in the letter (for example, Phil 1:29; 2:5-8). In relation to the hermeneutical importance of Isa 45:23 in Phil 2:10-11, Hawthorne reaches the logical conclusion that the nature and scope of Christ's sovereignty expressed by the phrase πᾶν γόνυ κάμψῃ . . . καὶ πᾶσα γλῶσσα ἐξομολογήσηται, although of great christological significance, is incidental to the point Paul wishes to drive home to the Philippians.[23] In similar vein, O'Brien suggests a christological focus for Isa 45:23 in Phil 2:10-11 viewing Christ's exaltation as exemplary for his followers. What happens to Jesus will happen to believers—the Philippians will be exalted when Jesus "transforms them into his own likeness."[24] Once more Isa 45:23, beyond its christological significance, is inconsequential in its functioning as the second half of the humiliation-exaltation motif. The problem with these interpretations is that Isa 45:23, although supporting a radically Christ-centered re-affirmation of Jewish monotheism, is incidental to the rhetoric of vindication—essentially, the passage can function in *only* a christological way. As a result of this, and especially since "vindication" is inconsistent with the injunction to have the same (correct) attitude that produces abasement (Phil 2:5), we suggest an alternative interpretation should be sought. That Paul intended to present Jesus as universal sovereign is clear, but is it possible that Paul intended to allude to the wider context of Isa 45:23? To answer these questions we will investigate the possibility of intertextual allusion and of another interpretation that might shed new

20. Hawthorne, *Philippians*, 96.

21. Fee, *Philippians*, 219, 228; Bockmuehl, *Philippians*, 148.

22. Oakes, *From People to Letter*, 150-51, who sees Phil 2:9 as primarily a gaining of authority. He prefers the background of Roman ideology as influencing Paul and his Gentile readers, ruling out Jewish influence and the OT as a source of "logic" for Phil 2:9-11 (159). See also Hellerman, *Reconstructing Honor*, 152.

23. Hawthorne, *Philippians*, 96.

24. O'Brien, *Philippians*, 243, 253.

light on the role Isa 45:23 plays in Paul's argument—an interpretation which coheres with patterns of rhetoric found throughout the wider context of the letter (Phil 1:27-30; 2:1-4, 14; 3:1-21).

The Probability of Allusion

The presence of Isa 45:23 in Phil 2:10-11 is suggested by the occurrence of the phrase κάμψει πᾶν γόνυ καὶ ἐξομολογήσεται πᾶσα γλῶσσα which appears in both texts (with slight variations):

Phil 2:10-11 NT ἵνα ἐν τῷ ὀνόματι Ἰησοῦ <u>πᾶν γόνυ κάμψῃ</u> ἐπουρανίων καὶ ἐπιγείων καὶ καταχθονίων <u>καὶ πᾶσα γλῶσσα ἐξομολογήσηται</u>[A]

Isa 45:23 LXX^OG ὅτι ἐμοὶ <u>κάμψει πᾶν γόνυ καὶ ἐξομολογήσεται</u>[B] <u>πᾶσα γλῶσσα</u> τῷ θεῷ

A. Several MSS (A, C, D, F, G, Ψ) have the future indicative ἐξομολογήσεται, but this was considered an assimilation to the indicative ὀμεῖται in the LXX of Isa 45:23 according to Metzger's commentary (Metzger, *TCGNT*, 546). As we have seen, the verb ὄμνυμι/ὀμνύω is missing from Isa 45:23 LXX^OG. See below.

B. Following Ziegler, *Isaias*, 295. Cf. Kreitzer, "When He at Last Is First," 120, who follows Codex Vaticanus.

Although not preceded by a so-called introductory formula, the verbatim repetition of seven, uniquely distinct words from Isa 45:23 LXX^OG signals the presence of an allusion marker. As we have seen, the divergence from the text of Isaiah can be understood as Paul's interpretive adaptations, this being consistent with Stanley's and Ben-Porat's observation that textual elements which make up the citation/allusion marker can be arranged differently in the alluding text. Since the only other occurrence of the phrase in extant Greek literature is Rom 14:11, we are justified in accepting Isa 45:23 LXX^OG as the evoked text in Phil 2:10-11. Moreover, given the distinctiveness of the marker and the verbal similarities with Isa 45:23, it is reasonable to consider πᾶν γόνυ κάμψῃ ... καὶ πᾶσα γλῶσσα ἐξομολογήσηται in Phil 2:10-11 as an *overt* allusion to Isa 45:23. Indeed, the probability that Paul intended a literary allusion to Isa 45:23 in Phil 2:10-16 can be supported by an appeal to the majority of historical, exegetical analyses of the passage. For example, Bockmuehl considers Phil 2:10-11 to be a midrash on Isa 45:23 in which Paul transfers universal rule from God to Jesus.[25] Fee understands Phil 2:9-11 as a formulation intended to echo the oracle in Isa 45:18-24 where Yahweh, Israel's savior, declares his exalted status over all

---

25. Bockmuehl, *Philippians*, 145.

gods and nations.[26] O'Brien argues that "bending of the knee" and "confessing of the tongue" are dependent on Isa 45:23 and should be understood as expressions of universal homage to Jesus.[27] Essentially, these scholars have concluded that a reference to Isa 45:23 is present from the quality of the denotative function of the allusion marker. Therefore, we will continue on the basis of a "strong probability" that πᾶν γόνυ κάμψῃ . . . καὶ πᾶσα γλῶσσα ἐξομολογήσηται in Phil 2:10–11 is a literary allusion to Isa 45:23.

Modification of the Initial Local Interpretation

The third stage in Ben-Porat's process is "modification of the initial local interpretation of the signal." This happens when the context of the marker in the alluded-to text is recognized and its interpretation "impinges upon" the alluding text. This patterning of the two independent interpretations yields a modified interpretation of the alluding text.[28] Before actualizing the allusion to Isa 45:23, the phrase πᾶν γόνυ κάμψῃ . . . καὶ πᾶσα γλῶσσα ἐξομολογήσηται is meaningful "in its own right" because it portrays Jesus as the object of universal submission—this constitutes the initial local interpretation of the marker and could be the sole interpretation if the allusion was missed. However, when Isa 45:23 is recognized and its context recalled, this initial interpretation is modified. This is because the same marker in the alluded-to (evoked) text acquires different denotations. The denotations are the referents belonging to the reconstructed world of the evoked text and are independent of the reconstructed world of the alluding text. In Isa 45:23, the phrase denotes the universal submission and confession directed towards the God of Israel. In alluding to Isa 45:23 in Phil 2:10–11, Paul forms an initial intertextual pattern through the association, or substitution, of God with Jesus. This modifies the initial interpretation, because Jesus is not merely the object of universal submission, but he is now the object of *that* universal submission reserved and predicted for the God of Israel. Without the allusion, this interpretation would not have been possible, even though Jesus' deity can be argued from the local interpretation of Phil 2:6–11. We have suggested that the deity of Christ functions as a constraint brought to bear on the Philippians in order to modify the rhetorical exigency—the tendency to avoid suffering as a God-endorsing expression

---

26. Fee, *Philippians*, 220.

27. O'Brien, *Philippians*, 241–43. The presence of Isa 45:23 in Phil 2:10–11 is widely accepted. See also Collange, *Philippians*, 107; Bratcher, *Old Testament Quotations*, 58; Court, *New Testament Writers*, 123; Childs, *Isaiah*, 356.

28. Ben-Porat, "Allusion," 110–11.

of faith. So, the modified interpretation of Phil 2:10–11 that the allusion to Isa 45:23 activates is found in the declaration that Jesus shares in the divine sovereignty of God (or is sole possessor of this sovereignty), which is a *development* or *progression* of/on the thought of his deity, on Paul's part. This is consistent with our view that Phil 2:6–11 is not a hymn or poem but parallelistic prose, in which "the form of God," "equality with God" and now, participation in the divine sovereignty of God are not restatements of the same thing (synonymous parallelism) but logical progressions in Paul's argument. According to Ben-Porat, the completion of this stage is enough to determine the existence of a literary allusion. This is once again borne out by the scholarly consensus; by recognizing that in Phil 2:10–11 universal homage is transferred from God to Jesus, Bockmuehl, Fee, and O'Brien affirm that Paul is referring to the wider context of Isa 45:23, since God's role as one-time object of this universal homage is not mentioned in the text of Philippians—the substitution of ἐμοί with ἐν τῷ ὀνόματι Ἰησοῦ confirms this. Thus, the allusion marker connotes God as one-time object of universal homage. So, we have an early indication from Paul's text that he intended at least one reference to the wider context of Isa 45:23. We will now use stage 4 of Ben-Porat's theory to investigate other denotations that the allusion marker (referring to the sovereignty of God) might acquire from its original context.

Activation of the Evoked Text as a Whole—Intertextual Patterning

The fourth and final stage of the allusion process is the "activation of the evoked text as a whole in an attempt to form maximum intertextual patterns." In the allusion process, the marker is used to activate independent elements from the evoked text which are never referred to directly.[29] So how can we identify elements of the evoked text and argue for their plausibility? For an allusion to be present congruence between texts must exist— this being the yardstick used by traditional historical exegetes, as we have seen.[30] But the formal indications of the allusion marker may not provide guidelines/clues to what elements of the evoked text are consonant with the alluding text[31]—in Ben-Porat's method, verbal similarity is necessary for the denoting function of allusion, but not between exigencies, constraints, and other components of the argument connoted by the textual marker.

---

29. Ben-Porat, "Allusion," 108–9.

30. For example, Fowl, "Use of Scripture in Philippians," 13; Reed, *Discourse Analysis of Philippians*, 291–92; Reumann, *Philippians*, 402–3.

31. Alter, *Pleasures*, 129.

Consequently, in our test for intertextual linkages in Phil 2:10–16, we seek to discover plausible degrees of congruence by comparing OT contexts and the rhetorical situation of Philippians. To achieve this we used Bitzer's theory to identify several exigencies and constraints, exegetically and logically inferred from Phil 1:27—3:21; these are summarized in the opening to the chapter and will be included as elements for comparison with the context of Isa 45:23.

The Context of Isa 45:1–25

The immediate context of Isa 45:23 is the response of universal acknowledgement of, and submission to, the unique God of Israel as savior. The setting is the Babylonian captivity of Israel; Jerusalem has fallen, but despite the disasters of 586, God still delivers oracles of future restoration and salvation through his prophet. Isa 45 is a description of God and his anointed agent Cyrus who is chosen to bring salvation to God's people: "for the sake of my servant Jacob, and Israel my chosen I will call you [Cyrus] by my name." The phrase, κάμψει πᾶν γόνυ καὶ ἐξομολογήσεται πᾶσα γλῶσσα, occurs within a trial speech where God invites the defeated Babylonians (Isa 45:20) to turn to him and be saved (Isa 45:22) because the very defeat they have suffered at the hands of Cyrus was foretold (Isa 45:21), proving him to be the one, true God (Isa 45:21–22). Yet, God's judgment is questioned by his people. Deutero-Isaiah describes the disputation of God's people concerning God's appointment of Cyrus as liberator and their passive role in deliverance (Isa 45:9–13)—God will save his chosen people with no military action on their part. The trustworthiness of God's predictions is emphasized by the phrase "By myself I swear, 'Verily righteousness shall go forth from my mouth; my words shall not be turned back . . . '" which immediately precedes the prediction of interest, "to me every knee will bow, every tongue will confess." God is predicting that a future universal submission to him will take place—he has announced it, therefore it will come to pass. He has demonstrated his trustworthiness before since it was he who prophesied the fall of Babylon (Isa 45:21). Also clearly present in the context of Isa 45:23 is the theme of judgment; "all who oppose him shall be ashamed and disgraced" (Isa 45:16) and "all who separate themselves shall be ashamed" (Isa 45:24). Moreover, within the broader context of God's restoration of Israel and the rebuilding of Jerusalem, is the offer of salvation to the Gentiles. As Clements notes:

> In the greatest and most openly evangelical invitation which the Old Testament anywhere contains, God makes his own appeal to all nations and peoples to turn to him: "Turn to me and be

saved, all the ends of earth! For I am God, and there is no other" (Isa 45:22).[32]

From this brief overview of Isa 45:1-25 we will select elements of context that can be considered congruent with the argument of Philippians. If the intertextual connections proposed are within the bounds of imaginative possibility and could reasonably be connoted by a tacit reference to Isa 45:23 in Phil 2:10-11, then the probability of a literary allusion that activates the wider context of Isa 45:23 is strengthened. Additionally, the framework which defines and delimits "congruence" will have been extended to include epistolary argument.

Salvation and Identity

As stated above, salvation is key to Deutero-Isaiah. Westermann writes: "... the oracle concerning Cyrus [Isa 44:24—45:8], which is the pivot on which all that is said in the book turns, is integrally related to the message of salvation."[33] Salvation is mentioned repeatedly throughout chapter 45 (vv. 15, 17, 20, 21, 22)[34] with God referred to as savior twice (vv. 15, 21). Thus, the text of Isa 45 places God's sovereignty, and the universal recognition of it, firmly within a salvation context. There are several reasons to suggest that, in Phil 2:10-11, Paul might be evoking the broader context of Isa 45 and activating salvation and identity themes. Firstly, the association of Jesus with God in Phil 2:9-11[35] and Paul's designation of him as savior in Phil 3:20 are congruent with God's repeated designation as savior in Isa 45 (for example, Isa 45:15: "O God of Israel, savior"; Isa 45:21: "I am God and there is no other besides me, there is no righteous one or savior except me"; Isa 45:22: "Turn to me and you shall be saved"). In identifying Jesus with, or as, God, through the allusion to Isa 45:23, Paul associates the universal acknowledgement of Jesus' Lordship with universal acknowledgement of him as God *and* savior of his people—*the bowing of the knee and confessing of the tongue are therefore responses to the saving acts of God.*[36] This soteriological

---

32. Clements, "Isaiah 45:20-25," 393.
33. Westermann, *Isaiah 40-66*, 10.
34. See also Isa 46:4, 13.

35. As we argued above, it is widely accepted that the "name of Jesus" in Phil 2:10 is the name that belongs to Jesus, namely LORD. See De Lacey, "One Lord," 191ff.; Kramer, *Christ, Lord, Son of God*, 156; Dunn, *Jews and Christians*, 189.

36. So Phil 2:9-11 describes universal submission, not universal salvation—even those who are not God's people will confess that he is both God and savior of his people. Thus, it is unlikely that Paul uses ἐξομολογήσηται in the sense of "a solemn statement

emphasis is consonant with the rhetorical situation of Philippians. As Bitzer points out, sources of rhetorical constraint include beliefs, attitudes, documents, facts, traditions, images, interests, and motives.[37] Salvation and the identity of the savior certainly qualify as rhetorical constraints or "artistic proofs" managed by Paul to modify the Philippians's attitude and actions. He uses these constraints in four verses which describe the eschatological hope of believers who are experiencing conflict (Phil 1:19, 27–28; 2:12; 3:20–21). All four contexts suggest God's salvation as motivation for Paul's ethical exhortations as well as conveying God's approval of the circumstances in which his people suffer hardship.

Additionally, unique identity is clearly important in Phil 2:10–11 and Isa 45:1–25. The personal name "Jesus" has material significance; it means YHWH-is-salvation.[38] Although the name was common among Jews up to the beginning of the second century CE[39] its material significance is surely accentuated in the context of Phil 2:9–11 ("the name which is above every name"; "at the name of Jesus") and Phil 3:20 ("we eagerly wait for a Saviour, the Lord Jesus Christ"). The sense of Phil 2:10–11 would therefore be: "at the name YHWH-is-salvation every knee shall bow ... and every tongue shall confess that YHWH-is-salvation [the Christ] is YHWH." In Isa 45, the refrain "I am God and there is no other besides me" occurs no fewer than seven times in the chapter (Isa 45:5, 6[x2], 14, 18, 21, 22) resulting in the text being classified as the distinctive prooftext for Jewish monotheism.[40] Additionally, the context is replete with the emphatic "I am" declarations of identity:

Isa 45:3, 5, 6, 7	ἐγὼ κύριος ὁ θεός
Isa 45:8	ἐγώ εἰμι κύριος
Isa 45:18	Ἐγώ εἰμι

---

of faith" (cf. Rom 10:9–10). The term can mean "to admit," "to concede," "to make a statement." Contra Michel, "ὁμολογέω," 214.

37. Bitzer, "Situation," 254.

38. Foerster, "Ἰησοῦς," 284–93. He describes the name (יְהוֹשֻׁעַ) as a "sentence name" containing subject-verb represented in Hebrew as יהוה ישע.

39. France, *Matthew*, 78, associates the giving of Jesus' name in Matt 1:21 with the etymology, "Yahweh is salvation" or "O save, Yahweh" which also serves to explain (αὐτὸς γάρ)—that "he will save his people from their sins." Hagner, *Matthew 1–13*, 19, writes: "The αὐτός is emphatic: it is *he* who will save his people," and again, "The reader's knowledge of the meaning of Ἰησοῦς via its Hebrew meaning is assumed by the γάρ without further explanation, indicating that this early Hebrew etymology had already become a part of the common tradition of the Greek-speaking church."

40. Mach, "Concepts of Jewish Monotheism," 23.

| Isa 45:19 | ἐγὼ εἰμί ἐγὼ εἰμί κυριός |
| Isa 45:22 | ἐγὼ εἰμί ὁ θεός^A |

A. See also Isa 45:11—κυριός ὁ θεός; Isa 45:13, 14—κυριός σαβαωθ.

According to Zimmerli, "The statement 'I am Yahweh' contains the element of self-introduction by means of the use of the personal name in its pure form."[41] He goes on to qualify some uses as independent statements of self-introduction (Isa 45:6–7, 18) and statements of recognition (Isa 45:3, 49:23).[42] In Isa 45:3 YHWH is recognized (by Cyrus) through his actions: "so that (ἵνα) you may know that I am the Lord God, the God of Israel." Commenting on Zimmerli's seminal work, Walter Brueggemann writes, "Yahweh's self-disclosure is not a matter of casual interest, but a matter of life and death" because "[God's] sovereignty is always known as *judgment and salvation*."[43] God's work of salvation is inextricably linked to his identity through his self-disclosure as YHWH.

Paul creates additional intertextual patterns by alluding to Isa 45:23 in Phil 2:10–11. He allows the identity and salvation motifs of Isa 45 to converge on Jesus by activating elements of the text that are independent of the marker. As Bauckham writes, "The identity of God—who God is—is revealed as much in self-abasement and service as it is in exaltation and rule."[44] With such an intertextual reading of Phil 2:10–11, the διὸ καί of Phil 2:9 does more than introduce the result, or consequence, of Jesus' obedience and death on the cross as exaltation, it links the identity of the God of Israel with his chosen means of providing salvation—God is identified as crucified savior. The presence of Isa 45:23 in Phil 2:10–11 allows Paul to frame the relationship between Phil 2:6–8 and Phil 2:9–11 within salvation and identity, rather than vindication, categories,[45] allowing us to suggest that Jesus' actions are not vindicated by God, but approved by God as the means of revealing his identity.[46]

This suggests a soteriological content for Phil 2:6–8, affirmed by Paul's mention of the cross in Phil 2:8.[47] Every knee *should* bow to Jesus, not sim-

41. Zimmerli, *I am Yahweh*, 4.
42. Ibid., 4.
43. Ibid., xv. His italics.
44. Bauckham, *God Crucified*, 61.
45. See also Park, *Submission*, 77.
46. Cf. Nagata, *Philippians 2:5–11*, 265; Fowl, *The Story of Christ*, 66; Oakes, *From People to Letter*, 201–4; Fee, "Hymn," 38.
47. Cf. O'Brien, *Philippians*, 231–32.

ply because he has been exalted (that would be an obligatory response to exalted power more akin to the imperial cult),[48] but because he is revealed as the crucified savior of God's people. Thus, in Phil 2:9-11, the aspects of God's identity and God's act of salvation coalesce in Jesus, and require Isa 45:23 and its surrounding context to enable the fusion to take place in the mind of Paul and his implied audience.

The Divine Name and God's Approval of His Christ

The probability of allusion is strengthened when rarely-occurring elements of congruence between texts can be identified and/or there is an accumulation of elements unique to specific texts. This would seem to be the case with the idea of God's bestowing of the divine name on his chosen agent of salvation (the Christ). Phil 2:10-11 and Isa 45:1-25 both describe God identifying with his agent of salvation by the bestowing of the divine "name." In Phil 2:10-11 Paul describes Jesus as recipient of both "the name" and submission offered by "every knee" and "every tongue." As we argued above, "name" with the definite article refers to "the well-known" name and probably reflects an OT phenomenon in which "the name" was a periphrasis for Yahweh.[49] Isa 44:24—45:8 contains the royal oracle of Cyrus,[50] in which he is described as God's chosen agent of salvation for Israel, in a political and military context. In Isa 45:1 God anoints Cyrus, addressing him as τῷ χριστῷ μου, and confirms him in royal office (cf. κύριος Ἰησοῦς Χριστός in Phil 2:11). In Isa 45:4b, God legitimates Cyrus's task by giving him an honorific title or throne name[51]—he calls him by God's own name (ἐγὼ καλέσω σε τῷ ὀνόματί σου; cf. ὁ θεὸς ... ἐχαρίσατο αὐτῷ τὸ ὄνομα τὸ ὑπὲρ πᾶν ὄνομα in Phil 2:9). And in Isa 45:1b-3, God empowers Cyrus by granting him dominion over the nations whom God will subdue for him (cf. Phil 2:10-11). Certainly, the notion of a single person who incorporates the title of Christ, is called by the divine name and exercises rule over submitting powers is congruent in both passages. It is noteworthy that in the immediate literary context of the alleged allusion to Isa 45:23, Paul describes God's approval of both agent and manner of salvation in language similar to Isa 45:1-5. If, as our methodology permits, every conceivable relation to the

---

48. Cf. P. Oakes, "Re-mapping the Universe," 319-20.

49. Fee, *Philippians*, 221-22.

50. Westermann, *Isaiah 40-66*, 153-54. See Thomas, *Documents from Old Testament Times*, 92-94.

51. Westermann, *Isaiah 40-66*, 159, "grasping the right hand indicates confirmation of the royal office."

evoked text consonant with value, purpose, viewpoint, tone, feeling, and predicament can be evoked,[52] it is not beyond the bounds of plausibility that the approval and commissioning of God's Christ were in Paul's mind as he composed Phil 2:6–11 and considered πᾶν γόνυ κάμψῃ . . . καὶ πᾶσα γλῶσσα ἐξομολογήσηται an appropriate expression of Jesus' sovereignty. Perhaps most significantly, there are only two extant Greek texts that express the idea of God's Christ receiving the divine name concomitant with universal submission conveyed by the terms "every knee will/should bow . . . every tongue will/should confess"—Phil 2:9–11 and Isa 45:1–23. This, we suggest, is further evidence that Paul had in mind the wider context of Isa 45:23.

The Complaint Against God

We have argued that Paul's letter to the Philippians is a fitting response to a rhetorical situation in which there was division over a particular issue— the legitimacy of suffering and death as consequences of faith in Christ. One manifestation of the division is the complaint (against God) that Paul records in Phil 2:14. In proposing that Paul uses the murmuring motif in Phil 2:14, we suggested that the γογγυσμός in Philippi were complaints against God, because he seemed to let his people suffer at the hands of their adversaries (Phil 1:29). The διαλογισμός were either the ensuing disagreements among the community about God's apparent passivity in relation to their suffering for the gospel, or doubts about his integrity to "complete the good work he had begun." The complaint against God is a constituent of the rhetorical situation which Bitzer labels a rhetorical exigency.[53] As we consider how much of the evoked text should be activated in a literary allusion, we encounter this recurring rhetorical exigency in Isa 45:9–11. The wider contexts of Isa 45:23 and Phil 2:9–11 thus share the rhetorical exigency of disputation against God.

In Isa 44:24—45:25, God's sovereignty, which encapsulates his freedom to decide what is right, is demonstrated in his choice of a pagan king to deliver his people from Babylonian captivity. That a non-Jewish monarch, Cyrus, was described as messiah and that his commissioning follows the pattern of a prophetic, royal oracle would have shocked the Israelites.[54] In an

52. Alter, *Pleasures*, 131.

53. Bitzer, "Situation," 252–53. An exigency which can be modified through rhetoric is a rhetorical exigency.

54. Brueggemann, *Isaiah 40–66*, 78: "It makes most sense that Israel in exile responded negatively and resistantly to the Cyrus announcement of a non-Jewish messiah"; Westermann, *Isaiah 40–66*, 165, writes, "the actions are his actions towards Israel through the instrumentality of Cyrus, which greatly offended his chosen people." But

anticipated response, God emphasizes his sovereign right to raise up Cyrus as his instrument to rebuild Jerusalem and free the people of Israel (Isa 45:9–13). In terms of Israelite disputation and rejection of God's appointed agent, Ogden identifies correspondences between Moses and Cyrus: "just as the people of Israel refused to accept Moses (Exod 6:9), so the exiles refused to accept the news that Cyrus was their savior."[55] Ogden attributes the woe-oracle of Isa 45:9–13 as the prophet's response to the Jewish exiles's protest that a foreigner was to be the savior of Israel.[56] Ogden rightly seeks an explanation for the vehement response of God in Isa 45:9–13 which does seem to answer the surprising question, "What are you doing (in raising up Cyrus)?" Certainly, God's appointment of Cyrus as savior of Israel was unexpected from the nation's perspective.

The legitimacy of Cyrus as Israel's messiah is therefore grounded in God's sovereign approval of him. The universal acknowledgement of God's sovereignty as described by the phrase "every knee shall bow and every tongue shall confess" is contextually related to the Israelites's questioning his choice of a Persian king as the instrument of salvation for Israel. The phrase is capable of connoting God's sovereign approval of persons and methods, the rightness and validity of which were not easily discernible, nor accepted, by his own people or others.

Conclusions

We have sought to test the suggestion of a literary allusion to Isa 45:23 in Phil 2:10–11 using Ben-Porat's theory to determine plausible levels of congruence between the texts. We can now draw several conclusions from our investigation. By identifying Jesus as the saving God of Israel, in a development of Isa 45, Paul has reflected christologically and theologically before reproducing the text of Isa 45:23 in his letter to the Philippians.[57] Including an intentional allusion to Isa 45:23 would seem particularly fitting because the God of Israel is identified with the method of salvation that reveals his universal sovereignty—the crucifixion of Jesus. As argued in chapter 3, there may have been an underlying tendency of some Philippians to be disinclined to accept suffering as intrinsic to gospel-advancing Christian life,

---

see Koole, *Isaiah III*, 448, who see the dispute as between YHWH and the nations.

55. Ogden, "Literary Allusions in Isaiah," 322.

56. Ibid., 317.

57. Contra Stanley, *Paul and the Language of Scripture*, 29. See also Hays, *Conversion of the Imagination*, 48, who writes, "Paul's primary interest in his actual *use* of Isaiah does not seem to be Christological." Italics his.

and consequently as an expression of Christian identity.[58] By alluding to Isa 45:23, Paul evokes God's call to the peoples of the world to come together to dispute the true identity of deity.[59] Commenting on Isaiah, Westermann writes, "that a god should prove his divinity by letting his own people be defeated was something the ancient world had never even dreamt of!"[60] Commenting on Philippians, Walters argued that the notion that a deity might require his or her worshippers to undergo suffering willingly was inconceivable.[61] So, Isaiah and Philippians not only share a recurring exigency, the latter is a *progression* on the former in that Paul seems to address the conundrum—*the* god proves his identity through *his own* abasement, with his expectation that those loyal to him should follow suit. It seems that Paul wanted to identify God through the obedient suffering and death of Christ, because God's sovereignty and righteousness are bound up with his approval and legitimizing of his people's suffering for the sake of Christ. Isa 45:23 in Phil 2:6–11 therefore helps Paul to explain the salvation-basis of God's approval of self-renunciation, suffering, and death (God-crucified). Isa 45:23 in Phil 2:6–11 also helps to provide the salvation-based paradigm for Christian conduct—self-abnegation as a response to God's salvation (rather than, or not merely, God's power). Living as God's people involves responding to God, primarily because he is savior. Phil 2:6–11 is therefore a kind of apocalyptic theodicy which exonerates God in the suffering of his people—God is justified in sanctioning and approving suffering for the sake of Christ because he participates in it in the salvation (Christ) event. Philippians can therefore be considered as a continuation of the recurring rhetorical situation in which God identifies himself with, and approves of, that which is objectionable to his people—Cyrus, a non-Jewish messiah and the paradigm based on Jesus, a suffering and death-embracing messiah. Both texts are appropriate to an implied audience who need reminding that God's identity is bound-up with his saving activity (in the Cyrus and Christ events respectively). What seems to be important for Paul is salvation, the paradigm it offers and the response it elicits. This leads us to suggest that the description of the history of Jesus described in Phil 2:6–11 is *interpreted* by Paul as the salvation event authored and promised by God in Isa 45. We conclude that Deutero-Isaiah is an intertext, or hypogram, that is a variant on the rhetorical situation of Philippi, and was chosen by Paul for this reason. We should also recall that Ben-Porat defines two types of literary

---

58. Chapple, *Local Leadership in the Pauline Churches*, 341.
59. See Oswalt, *Isaiah*, 221, referring to Isa 45:20.
60. Westermann, *Isaiah 40–66*, 15.
61. Walter, "Die Philipper und das Leiden," 428.

allusion: metaphorical and metonymical. In metaphorical allusion, only the marker is common between texts that appear unrelated. In metonymical allusion the marker is a product of the link between the texts—the texts are linked because of their explicit relatedness.[62] The congruence identified between Phil 1:27—3:21 and Isa 45:1-25 above increases the probability that πᾶν γόνυ κάμψῃ . . . καὶ πᾶσα γλῶσσα ἐξομολογήσηται in Phil 2:10-11 is an intertextual, metonymical allusion to Isa 45:23.[63]

PS 2:11 IN PHIL 2:12

Exegesis of Phil 2:12-13

[12] Ὥστε, ἀγαπητοί μου, καθὼς πάντοτε ὑπηκούσατε, μὴ ὡς ἐν τῇ παρουσίᾳ μου μόνον ἀλλὰ νῦν πολλῷ μᾶλλον ἐν τῇ ἀπουσίᾳ μου, μετὰ φόβου καὶ τρόμου τὴν ἑαυτῶν σωτηρίαν κατεργάζεσθε· [13]θεὸς γάρ ἐστιν ὁ ἐνεργῶν ἐν ὑμῖν καὶ τὸ θέλειν καὶ τὸ ἐνεργεῖν ὑπὲρ τῆς εὐδοκίας.

Immediately following the description of Christ's exaltation and cosmic rule (Phil 2:9-11), Paul exhorts the Philippians to be obedient, while he is absent from them, by working out their salvation with "fear and trembling" (Phil 2:12). The phrase φόβου καὶ τρόμου, as it describes the manner of working out salvation, contributes to a controversial exegetical puzzle which invites investigation. We will now engage with this controversy in testing the suggestion of an allusion to Ps 2:11.

Although there is no object with the verb, the initial obedience of the Philippians commended by Paul (καθὼς πάντοτε ὑπηκούσατε) is best understood as their first response to the demands of God in the gospel and the apostolic teaching—therefore Christ and Paul were the objects of this past obedience.[64] Paul's instruction to continue in this obedience *now* (ἀλλὰ νῦν) presupposes a new challenge arising during his absence from the Philippian community (μὴ ὡς ἐν τῇ παρουσίᾳ μου μόνον ἀλλὰ νῦν πολλῷ μᾶλλον ἐν τῇ ἀπουσίᾳ μου—see also his concern about their conduct during his absence in Phil 1:27). The idea of a continued obedient response to a new exigency is consistent with his exhortation in Phil 1:29; "for to you it has

---

62. Ben-Porat, "Allusion," 117.

63. Contra Hays, who argued that Paul distorted the original sense of Scripture using metaphorical echo.

64. Paul frequently uses ὑπακούω to refer to obedience to Christ, the gospel and apostolic teaching; Rom 1:5; 5:19; 6:16, 17; 10:16; 15:18; 16:19, 26; 2 Cor 10:5, 6; 2 Thess 1:8; 3:14.

been graciously granted for the sake of Christ, not only to believe in him [which you have already done through your initial obedience] but also to suffer for his sake [now continue in this other expression of obedience]."

Undoubtedly, understanding of Phil 2:12–13 hinges on the meaning of τὴν ἑαυτῶν σωτηρίαν κατεργάζεσθε and resolution of the paradox of divine sovereignty and human responsibility created by the following verse—θεὸς γάρ ἐστιν ὁ ἐνεργῶν ἐν ὑμῖν καὶ τὸ θέλειν καὶ τὸ ἐνεργεῖν ὑπὲρ τῆς εὐδοκίας. Some have argued that the verses should be understood in a sociological rather than theological sense, Paul being concerned with the well-being of the community and not with individual salvation. To support this interpretation, appeal is made along several exegetical lines. Firstly, ἐν ὑμῖν should be translated "among you" as it refers to the corporate life of the community. Secondly, σωτηρία can refer to "health" or "well-being" [of the community] and not individual salvation. Thirdly, ὑπὲρ τῆς εὐδοκίας should be taken to mean goodwill in the community. Thus, "working out salvation" is part of an appeal for communal harmony.[65] In response, it should be noted that ἐν ὑμῖν probably should be translated "in you" similar to ἐν ὑμῖν in 2 Cor 4:12 where the same verb is used (θάνατος ἐν ὑμῖν ἐνεργεῖται). Furthermore, σωτηρία, in the vast majority of occurrences in the Pauline corpus, has the theological sense, as it does in Phil 1:28. Additionally, ὑπὲρ τῆς εὐδοκίας can refer to the subject of the sentence (God's good pleasure) since the insertion of the article with an abstract noun following a preposition can be understood reflexively.[66] Finally, the striking verbal correspondence between Phil 1:6 and Phil 2:13 tips the balance in favor of a theological sense—God began the good work and will complete the good work of salvation, the knowledge and acceptance of which produces a conscious effort from the Philippians. God is clearly the subject of the actions ἐνεργέω and θέλεω in Phil 2:13 as Paul seems to be crediting him with producing the salvation-confirming κατεργάζεσθε (Phil 2:12) in the Philippians. Volf gives a concise explanation of this verse: "Divinely-inspired impulses and actions in the Christian life confirm God's faithfulness to God's intent to finish God's salvific purpose begun in believers (cf. Phil 1:6)."[67] The use of the two conjunctions in Phil 2:12 ("Ὥστε) and Phil 2:13 (γάρ) also suggest that Paul is arguing for a correct response to God's actions in Phil 2:6–11 and Phil 2:13 respectively. Thus Vincent connects the ὥστε of v. 12 with ὑπήκοος in Phil 2:8,[68] whereas O'Brien claims the conjunction reaches back, beyond Phil 2:6–11, to Phil

65. Collange, *Philippians*, 108–9; Beare, *Philippians*, 91.
66. Silva, *Philippians*, 131.
67. Gundry Volf, *Paul and Perseverance*, 270.
68. Vincent, *Philippians*, 64.

1:27.⁶⁹ Consequently, "work out your own salvation," is generally accepted as a suggestive way of expressing the idea of obedience⁷⁰—make your eternal salvation fruitful in the here and now. This brings us to the phrase which has been suggested as an allusion marker to Ps 2:11 (φόβου καὶ τρόμου) and which modifies τὴν ἑαυτῶν σωτηρίαν κατεργάζεσθε as it describes how the Philippians are to obey.

Noting the emphasis of the preceding analyses, it is not surprising that exegesis of the phrase has become polarized around the issue of God-ward or man-ward attitude. For example, Fee admits that it is not at all certain what Paul means by the phrase and suggests the OT background (Exod 15:16; Isa 19:16; Deut 2:25; 11:25; Ps 54:6) calls for understanding it as describing "awe in the presence of God."⁷¹ Barth argues that φόβου καὶ τρόμου are the decisive and most emphatic words of the whole complex, partly because they make little sense in the context of the passage. However, unlike Fee, he seeks to solve the puzzle of their meaning by drawing on Paul's parallel usage in 1 Cor 2:3, 2 Cor 7:15 and Eph 6:5, concluding that the expression φόβου καὶ τρόμου denotes humility before man, not God.⁷² Clearly, a surface-level, or mimetic, reading of the passage cannot resolve the hermeneutical puzzle which has left traditional historical exegetes seeking answers from other texts and contexts (OT and NT)—this is essentially an intertextual approach to exegesis.

In the main, both sets of interpreters view Phil 2:12–13 as an injunction to the Philippians to work out their salvation (be obedient to Christ), either by showing respect towards one another or in response to God's mighty acts. But both interpretations fall short of explanations that do much more than discover human or divine orientation in the phrase φόβου καὶ τρόμου. In doing so, the rhetorical and semantic force of φόβου καὶ τρόμου is reduced to a "stock meaning."⁷³ Such an approach might be valid, but considering the substance and nature of the rhetoric in Phil 2:5–11 and the admission of an exegetical conundrum in Phil 2:12–13, coupled with Paul's propensity to allude and cite from Scripture, we seek to investigate what φόβου καὶ τρόμου might connote if it functions as an allusion marker. Our approach is further justified since, surprisingly, most scholars have abstracted the obedience demonstrated by Jesus in Phil 2:8 in its application to

69. O'Brien, *Philippians*, 273–74.
70. Silva, *Philippians*, 118.
71. Fee, *Philippians*, 236.
72. Barth, *Philippians*, 71.
73. Hawthorne, *Philippians*, 100. He claims that φόβου καὶ τρόμου was a "stock phrase" that meant something less forceful than the individual terms might convey.

Phil 2:12–13. Thus, Vincent interprets "work out your own salvation" in Phil 2:12 to refer to the "spirit of obedience" of the Philippians.[74] Fee suggests that "working out their common salvation" means for the Philippians to continue in their obedience to Christ.[75] Yet, the obedience of Christ is an obedience that, specifically, produced a self-renunciation of high status in order to embrace death. From a rhetorical perspective, it is therefore possible that φόβου καὶ τρόμου might modify a kind of obedience that responds to this or some other facet of Jesus' person recorded in Phil 2:5–11. It is worth recalling Schweizer's suggestion regarding Phil 2:6–11 and its possible application to Phil 2:12–16: "The meaning of obedience in this passage is: acceptance of suffering."[76] Considering the impasse in NT scholarship, we are justified in asking if there might be a literary, rhetorical, or theological relationship between the humiliating death, exaltation, and universal sovereignty of Jesus and the manner in which the Philippians are to respond to it that might give an alternative, plausible explanation for the rhetorical use of φόβου καὶ τρόμου.

The Probability of Allusion

Given that an allusion to Ps 2:11 is catalogued by several scholars and considering Paul's propensity to allude to the Scriptures, we initially note the verbal similarity between Phil 2:12 and Ps 2:11 through the occurrence of the two words φόβος[77] and τρόμος[78] ("fear" and "trembling"):

Phil 2:12 NT   μετὰ φόβου καὶ τρόμου τὴν ἑαυτῶν σωτηρίαν κατεργάζεσθε

Ps 2:11 LXX^OG   δουλεύσατε τῷ κυρίῳ ἐν φόβῳ καὶ ἀγαλλιᾶσθε αὐτῷ ἐν τρόμῳ

As before, if an allusion to Ps 2 is present the divergence from the text can be explained as Paul's interpretive adaptation. In this case, Paul had elided the phrase ἀγαλλιᾶσθε αὐτῷ, perhaps for syntactical reasons. An allusion is certainly possible although verbal similarity as a necessary condition for allusion is not a sufficient condition. Yet, investigating the probability of allusion becomes more inviting if mimetic or surface-level interpretations

---

74. Vincent, *Philippians*, 64.
75. Fee, *Philippians*, 235–36.
76. Schweizer, *Lordship and Discipleship*, 62.
77. BDAG, 1062: also, "reverence, respect"; LEH, Part II, 506.
78. BDAG, 1016; LEH, Part II, 482.

prove unsatisfactory. We have argued that past exegeses of φόβου καὶ τρόμου have not adequately explained the meaning of the phrase as the modifier of τὴν ἑαυτῶν σωτηρίαν κατεργάζεσθε—at least not in terms of how it functions argumentatively beyond man-ward or God-ward disposition as obedient response. Nevertheless, identifying φόβου καὶ τρόμου in Phil 2:12 as an allusion to Ps 2:11, is less straightforward than the previous example. In the NT, the phrase appears four times, and only in the Pauline literature (1 Cor 2:3; 2 Cor 7:15; Phil 2:12; Eph 6:5). In 1 Cor 2:3, Paul writes that he was with the Corinthians "in weakness and in fear and in much trembling," as he describes the manner in which he proclaimed the message of the gospel. Fee admits that it is not at all clear what the two words (φόβος and τρόμος) mean, concluding that they express the idea of Paul being overwhelmed by the task of evangelizing the notorious city.[79] Morris proposes a God-ward interpretation for the phrase: Paul "feared" God because of an anxious desire to fulfill his duty.[80] In 2 Cor 7:15, Paul reminds the Corinthians of how they greeted Titus with "fear and trembling" following Paul's description of their sorrowful response to his "severe letter" (2 Cor 7:8). The phrase is used in terms of the Corinthians's obedient response to the gospel message/apostolic ministry[81] and has been variously understood as referring to "respect shown to Paul and Titus,"[82] "respect for Paul and his apostolic team,"[83] and "eschatological dread of separation from Paul's apostleship."[84] In Eph 6:5, slaves are instructed to be obedient to their masters "with fear and trembling." Although the repeated refrain ὡς τῷ Χριστῷ and ὡς τῷ κυρίῳ καὶ οὐκ ἀνθρώποις in verses 5 and 7 respectively may suggest an obedience and service that involve a God-ward element, Lincoln argues that "fear and trembling" is used to intensify the attitude of respect owed to human masters, not to God or Christ.[85] Again, exegesis has focused on whether man-ward or God-ward orientation is in view. There is thus no consensus on the meaning of the phrase in these other letters, with most scholars recognizing some kind of dependency on the OT. The phrase's popularity with Paul might suggest that its use in Philippians is a transformation of a cliché or hypogram hinting at some significance beyond the mimetic reading.[86]

---

79. Fee, *Corinthians*, 93–94.
80. Morris, *1 Corinthians*, 51.
81. Barnett, *The Second Epistle to the Corinthians*, 385.
82. Martin, *2 Corinthians*, 244.
83. Kruse, *2 Corinthians*, 147.
84. Barnett, *The Second Epistle to the Corinthians*, 385.
85. Lincoln, *Ephesians*, 420.
86. Namely, "respond to the salvation of God in this way ... with fear and

Interestingly, Hübner lists the occurrence of the terms φόβος καὶ τρόμος in 1 Cor 2:3 and Eph 6:5 as "idiomatic Septuagint phrases," rather than deliberate allusions to Ps 2:11, whereas in 2 Cor 7:15 and Phil 2:12 the latter designation is preferred.[87] Along similar lines, Leddy notes that, in shifting circumstances, the same words may or may not count as an allusion.[88] A logical consequence of this is that the same word or string of words might be an allusion in one circumstance and not in another, and that the same string of words can allude differently.[89] He provides an example of the conventionalized phrase "that is the question." The phrase is "conventionalized" because of its occurrence in Shakespeare's Hamlet soliloquy.[90] A teacher, pointing in turn to blackboard examples of indicative, interrogatory, and exclamatory sentences, declares, "this is the statement (indicative), that is the question (interrogatory), that one over there is the exclamation" (exclamatory). The conventionalized phrase is an allusion to Shakespeare's play in the teacher's literature class, but not her grammar class. This insight is appropriate to Paul's use of the "conventionalized" phrase "fear and trembling" in his other letters, where it might function as an allusion in all, some or none of the texts. Furthermore, it might allude differently in any two texts where it does allude. Consequently, a comparative study of how the phrase was used in Paul's other letters has limited benefit,[91] since the evoked text might be a variation on a rhetorical exigency or constraint in Philippians only. To complicate matters further, variations of the textual marker appear in several other precursor texts opening up the possibility that any one of them was Paul's source for the allusion.[92] In this case, the guidelines/clues provided by the allusion marker are not specific enough in themselves to identify one of many texts.[93] If, with several scholars, φόβου καὶ τρόμου is probably an

trembling."

87. Hübner, *Vetus Testamentum*, xvii, 234–35, 372–73, 468–69, 490.
88. Leddy, "Limits," 112.
89. This might be the case with Paul's allusion to Isa 45:23 in Rom 14:11.
90. Leddy, "Limits,"112. He states that "no word or string of words is an allusion by convention."
91. Cf. Fee, *Philippians*, 236, who claims that the phrase's meaning in 1 Cor 2:3 should direct our understanding of it in other places.
92. Using the Online TLG® database, a total of thirty-three examples were found (four in the NT) of the character string combination φοβ . . . and τρομ . . . within a span of twenty words of each other.
93. According to Ben-Porat, allusion is the simultaneous activation of *two* texts. When the allusion marker appears in multiple texts, the question is—which text is being alluded to? See Hübner, *Vetus Testamentum*, xvii: "When the author quoted a passage he wanted to bring out this one passage, and it alone." Cf. Brown, "Ernst Lohmeyer's Kyrios Jesus," 27, who claims that words and phrases may contain multiple allusions.

allusion marker, how probable is it that it alludes to Ps 2:11? Patently, verbal parallels are only the initial indicator of allusion, the ultimate test requiring congruence between texts, and a plausible suggestion that elements in one text connote elements in another. Since it would not be practical to use Ben-Porat's theory in a thorough test of every one of 29 texts, we will survey all the (extant) Greek texts that Paul could have intended to evoke, and compare their immediate context. This initial filtering exercise should help reinforce or undermine the case for including Ps 2 in our case study for testing the suggestion of an allusion in Phil 2:12.

φόβος and τρόμος in Scripture

In Scripture, the two nouns φόβος and τρόμος appear together twelve times: in Gen 9:2; Exod 15:16; Isa 19:16; 54:14; Ps 2:11; 54:6; Job 4:14; Deut 2:25; 11:25; Dan 4:19, 37; 10:12. An allusion to any one of these texts is therefore possible. Gen 9:2 describes the post-diluvian "fear and trembling" of the animals towards Noah and his sons.[94] Exod 15:16 is part of the first song of Moses[95] in which the phrase φόβου καὶ τρόμου is used to describe the terror of Israel's opponents to God's power.[96] In Isa 19:16, the prophet uses the phrase to describe the dread and terror that befall the Egyptians in battle (against God) and in Isa 54:14 it is the experience that God's people will avoid if they keep away from injustice. In Ps 54:6, the phrase refers to David's reaction to his enemies. In Job 4:14 it is part of Eliphaz's rebuke of Job and refers to the fear and trembling before the Lord's anger. In Deut 2:25 and 11:25 it is the response of the land to Israel if they obey God's commandments. In Dan 4:19 the terms refer to Daniel's reaction to contemplating the interpretation of Nebuchadnezzar's dream and in 4:37 to Nebuchadnezzar's repentance and his confession to God. In Dan 10:11–12, the words appear in close proximity and refer to Daniel's fear and trembling at his vision of a heavenly agent.

φόβος and τρόμος in the OT Apocrypha

In Jdt 2:28 the word combination "φόβος" and "τρόμος" is used to describe the fear and dread of the inhabitants of Sidon, Tyre, Sour, Okina, and Lemnaan towards Olophernes, second in command to king Nebuchadnezzar.

---

94. Wenham, *Genesis 1–15*, 192.
95. Also recorded in Ode 1:16.
96. Durham, *Exodus*, 208.

In Jdt 15:2, the phrase refers to the response of the Assyrians to Judith's beheading of Olophernes. In 1 Macc 7:18 the words are used of the emotions felt by the Israelites towards Alcimus and Bacchides following their murder of a company of scribes, and in 1 Macc 13:2 it refers to the people's reaction to Trypho's threatened invasion of Judah. In 4 Macc 4:10, it is the response of Apollonius and his army to angels. The phrase also occurs in Ode 1:16, which is the first song of Moses and is a repeat of Exod 15:16.

φόβος and τρόμος in the OT Pseudepigrapha

In 1 En. 1:5, the terms "φόβος" and "τρόμος" describe the response of universal fear to God's appearance on the earth and the "quaking" of the watchers.[97] In 1 En. 13:3, the words are ascribed to Asael and his fallen angels following God's judgment on them. In 1 En. 14:13 both terms appear in close proximity describing Enoch's "fear and trembling" at approaching God's throne room.[98] In *T. Ab.* 16:1,[99] the words describe "Death's" response to being summoned by God to bring Abraham to heaven.

φόβος and τρόμος in Philo

In *Flacc.* 176, Philo uses both terms to describe Flaccum's soul trembling with terror at his anticipation of the retribution that awaited him from the hands of avengers.

φόβος and τρόμος in Ancient Hellenistic Texts

Homer uses the word combination to describe Hector's fear and trembling at the sight of Achilles (Hom. *Il.* 22, verses 136–37). In the *Rhesus*, Euripides uses the phrase as part of Hector's rebuke of the soldiers of the Trojan and Thracian armies who left their post. The terms are also used by Aristotle (*Probl.* 11, 906a) to account for trembling in the voices of those who are old, nervous, and frightened. In *Ant. Rom.* 5.54.2, Dionysius Halicarnassus uses the phrase to describe the response of slaves to demonic dreams and visions. Hippocrates applies the phrase in his diagnosis of the causes of "tremors of the body in shivers" (*Flat.* 8). Finally, Plutarch describes his opponents's

---

97. See Nickelsburg, *1 Enoch 1*, 140.
98. Ibid., 263.
99. See Davila, "Old Testament Pseudepigrapha," 57. He considers it to be a Christian composition.

reaction of "fear and trembling" to his criticism of their use of euphemisms (Plut. *Mor.* 449a).

Conclusions

In all these texts, except one, the terms for "fear" and "trembling" refer to the emotional dread and terror of animals, human beings, and fallen angels towards either man or angels or God. Only in Dan 4:37, in which Nebuchadnezzar expresses a sense of serving God, do the words "φόβος" and "τρόμος" combine to convey the notion of worship or service to God. This is also the sense carried by the phrase in Ps 2:11 where it describes a disposition of loyalty towards God.[100] Like Dan 4:37, Ps 2:11 includes a variation that marks a significant difference from the other passages:

Ps 2:11 LXX^OG   δουλεύσατε τῷ κυρίῳ ἐν φόβῳ καὶ ἀγαλλιᾶσθε αὐτῷ ἐν τρόμῳ
Be subject to the Lord with *fear,* and rejoice in him with *trembling.*

Dan 4:37 LXX^OG   ἀπὸ τοῦ νῦν αὐτῷ λατρεύσω, καὶ ἀπὸ τοῦ φόβου αὐτοῦ τρόμος εἴληφέ με
From now on I will serve him, and *trembling* has gripped me from *fear* of him

Thus, it can be argued that Ps 2:11 and Dan 4:37, as the evoked text in a literary allusion, are better candidates than the others because of the positive disposition towards God connoted by the combination of the terms "φόβος" and "τρόμος" which they share with Phil 2:12 (see below). Yet, a literary allusion is the simultaneous activation of *two* texts, so either Ps 2 or Daniel can be the alluded-to text. In this case, the recognition of an intertextual connection has been made in addition to the identification of verbal parallels between texts but Ps 2 has still not been distinguished (by us) as the probable, evoked text. Linguistically, Ps 2:11 has a greater concordance with Phil 2 through the use of δουλεύσατε and κυρίῳ. Conceptually, the presence of "rejoice" resonates more greatly with Philippians. Perhaps Dan 4:37 itself contains a literary allusion to Ps 2:11, given that there is a clear analogy to be drawn between Nebuchadnezzar and the repentant kings of Ps 2:1-2, 10.

To summarize, in Ps 2:11, "fear" and "trembling" are positive characteristics of service to God with the sense of allegiance (δουλεύσατε),[101] and

---

100. For fear as a correlative of faith, see Balz, "φοβέω," 213–14.

101. LXX translates the Hebrew Qal imperative עִבְדוּ (עָבַד—work, serve) as δουλεύσατε confirming that "fear and trembling" are to characterize the service offered to the Lord.

cooperation (ἀγαλλιᾶσθε αὐτῷ) present in the exhortation. Although Ps 2 is addressed to the nations and kings who oppose God and his anointed king (Ps 2:1-2, 10), "fear and trembling" is not an expression of dread experienced at the presence of the living God (for example, Exod 15:16; Isa 19:16). Rather, it is the response of rebels following a change of allegiance. In Phil 2:12, φόβου καὶ τρόμου qualifies *how* the Philippians are to work out their own salvation. The case for the phrase referring to a God-ward attitude of obedience and allegiance is strengthened in two ways. Firstly, Paul has already claimed that salvation (σωτηρία) comes from God (Phil 1:28). Secondly, the account of the apostolic call to obedience which appeals to Christ's obedience in the form δούλου (Phil 2:7; which God approves of and responds to in Phil 2:9) corresponds to the psalmist's command to serve (δουλεύσατε) the Lord. Bockmuehl seems closest to the mark when he states that the phrase φόβου καὶ τρόμου in Phil 2:12 connotes "the response of due reverence in face of a major challenge, and especially in the presence of God and his mighty acts."[102]

Despite these perceptions, detecting allusions is a matter of intuition, guesswork, and our own and others's insights.[103] We have depended upon the insights of Hübner and others to identify a possible allusion. Nevertheless, we have followed a rationale that justifies our testing of Paul's use of the formulaic expression,[104] φόβου καὶ τρόμου, as a possible literary allusion to Ps 2:11.

Modification of the Initial Local Interpretation

An initial local interpretation of Phil 2:12 might render a meaning in line with several modern writers: "work out your salvation with 'holy awe and wonder' before God."[105] If Ps 2's presence is recognized this interpretation can be modified as the evoked text impinges on the alluding text. In Ps 2, "fear and trembling" denotes the positive disposition towards YHWH that accompanies obedient service (δουλεύειν) to him.[106] However, this service

---

102. Bockmuehl, *Philippians*, 153. The OT evidence also suggests that φόβου καὶ τρόμου refers to a sense of awe and reverence in the presence of God. See Van Pelt and Kaiser, "ירא," 527.

103. Jauhiainen, *Use of Zechariah in Revelation*, 27. See also McLean, *Citations and Allusions to Jewish Scripture*, 2: "The identification of allusions and verbal parallels is, to a great extent, a matter of interpretation."

104. O'Brien, *Philippians*, 282, calls it a "stereotyped expression."

105. Fee, *Philippians*, 237; O'Brien, *Philippians*, 284; Bockmuehl, *Philippians*, 153.

106. See Rengstorf, "δοῦλος," 267-68. In the LXX, δουλεύειν is the most common term for the service of God.

includes the sense of extreme power demanded and exercised by a king, and extreme subjection and bondage of his citizens.[107] Furthermore, the threat of punishment hangs over those refusing to pay homage to the ruler (Ps 2:12). Thus, the phrase "fear and trembling" denotes new referents belonging to the reconstructed world of Ps 2; namely, compulsory allegiance to the king and the threat of opposing him. Although these referents are independent of the reconstructed world of Philippians, Paul might face a situation in which Ps 2 presents itself as a "model of achievement"[108] in exhorting allegiance to an opposed king. If so, we should not be surprised if he thought Ps 2 contained worthy material to include in a literary allusion. The phrase "fear and trembling" as a literary allusion to Ps 2, not only connotes God as the object of fear and trembling, but also compulsory allegiance and service to a monarch, which, if withheld, results in punishment (Ps 2:12). In our opinion, these connotations augment the plain meaning of "fear" and "trembling" in a way lacking in the common surface-level interpretations discussed above, such as "reverence and awe with respect to God and/or man." If the probability of allusion is increased with such a modification of the initial local interpretation, then it is not unreasonable to examine ways in which intertextual patterns can be formed as the allusion marker in Phil 2:12 (referring to the allegiance to a king) acquires further denotations in its original context.

Activation of the Evoked Text as a Whole—Intertextual Patterning

As before, in our test for intertextual linkages between Philippians and Ps 2, we seek to discover plausible degrees of congruence by comparing OT context and the rhetorical situation of Philippians, along with more obvious surface-level themes and motifs. Ben-Porat's method admits intertextual patterns formed from the activation of elements in Ps 2 that might not have the marker as their components. For example, "kingship" can be evoked by "fear and trembling" in Ps 2:11 even though the phrase is not a component of verse 6—"But I was established king by him on Sion, his holy mountain." This is because "fear and trembling" denoted a disposition towards the king. The test for congruence in this case incorporates at least persons (God and king) and events (coronation), but should be expansive enough to include all aspects of the rhetorical situation such as objects, actions, relations, ideas, beliefs, values, attitudes, documents, facts, traditions, and images shared by

---

107. Rengstorf, "δοῦλος," 266–67.
108 Alter, *Pleasures*, 132.

both texts.[109] As the density and quality of interconnections between the contexts increase so too does the plausibility of intertextual allusion. In proposing those elements of Ps 2 actualized by Paul in creating the allusion, and recovered by his audience in successfully interpreting the allusion, we first need to identify the elements of Ps 2 consonant with the rhetorical situation of Philippians.

Paul and Ps 2

Paul's specific interest in Ps 2 can be noted in his introductory salutation to the Romans, where he describes Jesus in language derived from Ps 2:2, 7:

> Paul, a servant of Christ Jesus, called as an apostle, set apart for the gospel of God, which he promised beforehand through his prophets in the holy Scriptures, concerning his Son, who was born of a descendant of David according to the flesh, who was declared the Son of God with power by the resurrection from the dead, according to the spirit of holiness, Jesus Christ our Lord (Rom 1:1–4)

As God's Christ, descended from David according to the flesh, and declared[110] Son of God through his resurrection, Paul describes Jesus in terms of Ps 2.[111] That Paul equates the enthronement of the Davidic king in Ps 2 with the resurrection of Jesus is further borne out in Luke's record of Paul's sermon commencing in Acts 13:16. The enthronement perspective runs throughout verses 22 to 37 in which Paul speaks about the "raising up" of David and Jesus, quoting directly from Ps 2:7 in Acts 13:33:

> After he has removed him (Saul), he raised up David to be their king (v. 22).

> From the descendants of this man (David), according to promise, God has brought to Israel a saviour, Jesus (v. 23).

> But God raised him from the dead (v. 30).

> that God fulfilled this promise to our children in that he raised up Jesus, as it is also written in the second Psalm, "You are my son; today I have begotten you" (v. 33)

---

109. See Bitzer, "Situation," 254.

110. Some prefer "appointed" (Dunn, *Romans 1–8*, 13), others "determined" (Moo, *Romans*, 47–48).

111. Ibid., 48. Moo states that Rom 1:1–4 is probably an allusion to Ps 2:7.

> As for the fact that he raised him up from the dead, no longer to return to decay (v. 34)
>
> But he whom God raised did not undergo decay (v. 37)

In this last mention of the "raising up" of Jesus in Acts 13:37, Luke records Paul comparing David's death, burial, and decay with Jesus' resurrected status. Paul appears to contrast the temporary raising up of David as king with the permanent raising up of Jesus at his resurrection; in fact, he cites two psalms (Pss 2 and 16) within three verses of Acts 13:33, to argue that the resurrection of Jesus is the fulfillment of a promised king who would rule in the sovereignty of God. Thus in the NT we have a spoken address and a written record of Paul's use of Ps 2 in an enthronement and resurrection context. According to Hayes, the close association of David and Jesus in Paul's mind is described from the perspective of an "enthronement Christology"[112] that links the coronation of the Davidic king with the resurrection of Jesus. Furthermore, Paul's understanding of Jesus as the reigning messiah expressed with the help of similar messianic, enthronement psalms (see our historical critical study below) can be noted in 1 Cor 15:25. Here, his selection of Ps 109 (LXX) is consistent with reading methods demonstrated from well-established messianic texts of pre-Christian (for example, 1QSa. 2.11–12; 4QFlor. 1.10–14) and early church (for example, Heb 1:13; 2:6–9; 5:5; Rev 2:26f) tradition. Paul's first-century reading of Ps 2 as messianic enthronement finding ultimate significance through the history of Jesus can also be considered from an historical-critical perspective.

The Context of Ps 2

"For us the Psalter largely ministers to the needs of the devotional life withdrawn into its privacy with God."[113] Vos succinctly describes a limited, yet popular, view of the psalms which "relegates" them to the sphere of the pious, devotional life. However, several writers have recognized the need to determine the *Sitz im Leben* of the psalms for proper understanding. Consequently, much effort has been spent on researching and categorizing the psalms with a view to determining their original setting. For example, Westermann comments: "To interpret a particular psalm, without giving attention to the class to which it belongs, is methodologically without

---

112. See Hayes, "Resurrection as Enthronement," 333–45.
113. Vos, *Pauline Eschatology*, 323.

justification."[114] As a result, there is almost universal agreement that Ps 2 is a royal psalm,[115] the central character being God's anointed king, and that it originates from, and is dependent on, the prophecy of Nathan given to David described in 2 Sam 7:12–14 (MT) and 2 Reigns 7:12–14 LXX[OG]:

2 Reigns 7:12–14	And it will be if your days are fulfilled and you lie down with your fathers, that I will raise up your offspring after you who shall be from your belly, and I will prepare his kingdom; he shall build me a house for my name, and I will restore his throne for ever. I will be a father to him, and he shall be a son to me . . .[A]
Ps 2:6, 7	But I was established king by him, on Sion, his holy mountain, by proclaiming the Lord's ordinance: The Lord said to me, 'My son you are; today I have begotten you . . .'[B]

A. McLean and Taylor, "2 Reigns," 281.
B. Pietersma, "Psalm 2," 548.

It has been noted that the royal psalms used in songs, prayer, and ritual are similar to those found in the ANE literature of Mesopotamia and Egypt. For instance, Eaton writes of Psalm 2: "Restrained comparison with foreign rituals of kingship is supported by the fact that the psalm, thoroughly Israelite as a whole, yet preserves a considerable foreign inheritance. This could well descend from the rites of pre-Davidic kings in Jerusalem, influenced in turn by the great empires of Egypt, the Hittites, and Mesopotamia."[116] It is within this ANE setting that the concept of world-wide sovereignty (Ps 2:8), the title deeds of divine sonship (Ps 2:7), the figure of the pots (Ps 2:9), and the kiss of submission arose (Ps 2:12—MT).[117] In these traditions, the psalm was used specifically during the ritual inauguration of a new king, thus the classification of royal psalm can be qualified further as coronation or enthronement psalm.[118] In the ANE tradition, the accession to the throne of

114. Westermann, *Living Psalms*, 9.

115. This taxonomy derives from the work of Gunkel, who classified ten psalms as "royal" pertaining to the kings of the Davidic dynasty (Pss 2; 18; 20; 21; 45; 72; 89; 101; 110; 132). Gunkel has been challenged by Eaton, *Kingship and the Psalms*, 2 and Johnson, *Sacral Kingship in Ancient Israel*, who extend Gunkel's list substantially.

116. Eaton, *Kingship and the Psalms*, 113.

117. Ibid., 113; Cf. Kraus, *Theology of the Psalms*, 107–8, 113, who doubts that the Israelite king was associated with divinity, and emphasizes that the king in Israel was not the son of God by nature but by adoption. Also Dahood, *Psalms I 1—50*, xxvi–xxvii, who sees the influence of kingship tradition from mostly Ugaritic sources.

118. Craigie, *Psalms 1—50*, 64.

the new king involved two ceremonial acts. Firstly, the new king was given a ruling mandate or decree from the deity, along with the bestowal of a throne name,[119] the purpose being to legitimate the new king's rule. Ps 2 conforms to this format since the decree in Ps 2:7 is taken to be a "royal document of legitimation,"[120] with the title "son of God" acting as the throne name. Secondly, the king ascended his throne to proclaim the commencement of his rule and to give an ultimatum to the nations[121]—from the outset his speech was intended to issue a warning.[122] In Ps 2, the proclamation of the decree is contained in Ps 2:8, 9 with the ultimatum delivered in Ps 2:11, 12. The threatening tone of Ps 2:12 is a clear warning of the consequences of refusing allegiance to the new king, and brackets the psalm with the admonition of the futility of opposing him recorded in Ps 2:1–5. The key elements of coronation depicted in Ps 2 are: anointing (Ps 2:2), installation (Ps 2:6), legitimating (Ps 2:7), and empowering (Ps 2:8–9).

From this analysis of Ps 2 we will select components that can be considered consonant with Paul's argument in Philippians. As before, if the intertextual connections proposed are within the bounds of imaginative possibility and could reasonably be connoted by a tacit reference to Ps 2:11 in Phil 2:12, then the probability of a literary allusion that activates the wider context of Ps 2:11 is strengthened.

The Coronation Drama

There are good reasons to suggest that, in using the phrase φόβου καὶ τρόμου in Phil 2:12, Paul might be alluding to Ps 2:11 and intending to evoke the broader context of Ps 2:6–9, thus activating the coronation ritual of the Messiah. The probability of an intertextual relationship between Phil 2:12 and Ps 2:11 is strengthened when we consider the likelihood that Christ's exaltation described in Phil 2:9–11 includes resurrection, ascension, and enthronement—a "raising up" to a position of authority. Interestingly, Maile notes that Rom 1:3–4 can be understood in terms of messianic enthronement only, with the references to "his son," "power," and "Lord" pointing to the exaltation of the pre-existent son to the status of Lordship, closely paralleling Phil 2:6–11.[123] Maile was not the first to recognize that Phil 2:6–11 contained the elements of messianic enthronement. Käsemann ar-

---

119. So Kraus, *Theology of the Psalms*, 112–13.
120. Eaton, *Kingship and the Psalms*, 112.
121. Mays, *Lord Reigns*, 111.
122. Eaton, *Kingship and the Psalms*, 111.
123. Maile, "Exaltation and Enthronement," 278.

gued that the ὑπερυψόω of Phil 2:9 includes the scheme of Christ's heavenly enthronement in the salvation drama of Phil 2:5–11.[124] He particularly noted the "bestowal of the name" (Phil 2:9) as part of the presentation ceremony before the divine court assembly.[125] Moreover, Phil 2:10–11 describes the transfer of power to Jesus at his enthronement (not parousia) in terms of the confession, proclamation, and public recognition of him as Lord by the cosmic powers.[126] Martin describes the prominent imagery in Phil 2:9 as that of the enthronement of the divine king in ancient Egyptian ceremony which encompassed the triple-action of elevation, proclamation of the name, and homage to the enthroned one by gesture and confession.[127] Yet none of these scholars considered Ps 2 to be the precursor text or tradition behind Paul's enthronement Christology in Phil 2:9–11, despite his recurring interest in it as he contemplated the Davidic covenant and the arrival of a promised king who would rule in the sovereignty of God. The formal or structural components of enthronement identified in Ps 2 are also present in Phil 2:6–11—in this case we are less interested in verbal agreement and more in whether the concepts of anointing, installation, legitimating, and empowering are plausibly conveyed, even by diverse terms.[128] In Philippians, Paul concludes the story of Christ by describing his installation as cosmic ruler by God (Phil 2:9a, b), the giving of his throne name (YHWH: Phil 2:9c, 10a), and the emphatic legitimating of his rule (Phil 2:10–11). He then exhorts the Philippians to work out their salvation with "fear and trembling" in response to this exaltation drama. In Ps 2, the psalmist describes the installation of God's anointed king (Ps 2:6), the giving of his throne name (son of God: Ps 2:7), and the emphatic legitimating of his rule (Ps 2:8, 9). He then instructs the kings of the earth to respond to the king's enthronement with "fear and trembling." From this brief comparison, two points merit consideration. Firstly, these parallels are precise enough to suggest more than mere coincidence. Secondly, despite enthronement patterns being more widespread,[129] it is noteworthy that the phrase φόβου καὶ τρόμου only appears in the im-

124. Also Bertram, "ὑψόω," 611.

125. Käsemann, "Critical Analysis," 76. He, famously, viewed this as a variation of the *Urmensch*-Saviour myth.

126. Ibid., 80.

127. Martin, *Carmen Christi*, 242–43.

128. In Ben-Porat's model, the allusion marker is used to activate independent elements from the evoked text which are never referred to directly. In other words, the phrase φόβου καὶ τρόμου can, in theory, evoke every conceivable relation to Ps 2 consonant with value, purpose, viewpoint, tone, feeling and predicament.

129. Hawthorne, *Philippians*, 78. He suggests the Jesus tradition of John 13:3–17 is the background to the "hymn."

mediate, literary context of messianic enthronement in two extant Greek texts, namely Ps 2 and Philippians. Considering its position following the rhetoric of Phil 2:9–11, which describes the exaltation of the crucified Christ, it is not beyond the bounds of imaginative possibility that the phrase in Phil 2:12 could connote the enthronement of the messiah by evoking its formal or structural components—anointing, installation, legitimating, and empowering. Additionally, the terms φόβος and τρόμος, in both Phil 2:12 and Ps 2:11, share the same hortatory context as they either modify or immediately follow an injunction to obey an enthroned monarch.[130] It can therefore be argued that in both texts φόβος and τρόμος combine to function as part of the correct response to the rhetorical constraint of the enthronement of God's anointed king.

It is certainly possible that when composing Phil 2:12 (and Phil 2:5–11), Paul was recalling the inauguration of Christ as God's anointed king by alluding to Ps 2:11. The semiotic grid, or intertextual field created by Paul for his implied audience in the allusion to Ps 2:11 envelops the full drama of the Davidic king's accession to the throne. This is what Alter referred to as a "part to whole" logical relationship between the alluding and evoked texts, with every conceivable relation to the evoked text consonant with value, purpose, viewpoint, tone, feeling, and predicament being activated.[131] We have argued that whether an allusion is whole-to-part, part-to-whole, or part-to-part can be determined by the intertextual matrix (Riffaterre) or the rhetorical situation (Bitzer). Ps 2 seems to be a variant on the rhetorical situation in Philippi as it brings to bear upon the Philippians the identity and sovereignty of the king as the object of obedience (Phil 2:9, 10a, 12 and Ps 2:6, 7, 11). If so, φόβου καὶ τρόμου does not merely convey either a God-ward or man-ward disposition of reverence but a specific type of God-ward orientation, garnered from the wider context of Ps 2, that incorporates subjection to an enthroned monarch.

The Threat of Eschatological Destruction

As we consider degrees of congruence between texts as the decisive test for allusion, it is notable that Ps 2 and Philippians share an interest in opposition to God, and its eschatological consequences. As we have shown, opposition (resulting in suffering) is an exigency that Paul uses in Phil 1:27–30 to encourage perseverance. We have argued that the Philippians were

---

130. In Phil 2:12—Ὥστε . . . τὴν ἑαυτῶν σωτηρίαν κατεργάζεσθε; in Ps 2:11— καὶ νῦν . . . δουλεύσατε τῷ κυρίῳ.

131. Alter, *Pleasures*, 129–31.

facing opposition and suffering, because of their allegiance to Christ—the enemies of the king are the enemies of his people. Opponents or enemies are explicitly mentioned in Phil 1:28 (τῶν ἀντικειμένων) and Phil 3:18 (τοὺς ἐχθρούς). Not only is Paul concerned about how the Philippians respond to opposition (Phil 1:28; 2:15; 3:2), but he also shares with the psalmist an eschatological interest. In Ps 2:2–3, the psalmist records the opposition to God's (already) anointed king. This opposition seems to surface *after* the king's enthronement. In fact, rather than signaling the end of rebellion, the king's enthronement is the *cause* of rebellion.[132] Despite the opposition, the futility of the rebellion is recorded in the outcome of a refusal to submit to the king in Ps 2:12: " . . . and you will perish (ἀπόλλυμι) from the righteous way, when his anger quickly blazes out." Both Paul and the psalmist are confident about the eventual destruction of opposing forces—the psalmist describes the overthrow of all opposition to the Davidic king and Paul anticipates a future time when Jesus will exert power to subject all things to himself (Phil 3:21). In Phil 1:27, Paul describes the eschatological destruction (ἀπόλλυμι) that awaits the Philippians's opponents. Moreover, although identification of the "enemies of the cross," in Phil 3:18, has proved a thorny issue in NT scholarship, their final outcome is undoubtedly "destruction" (ἀπόλλυμι). The Hebrew אָבַד refers to divine judgment against the ungodly nations allied against Israel[133] and is translated ἀπόλλυμι[134] in the LXX of Ps 2:12. The sense in all three cases is one of eternal destruction.[135] Hence, the eschatological dimension of divine dealings with enmity is clearly a rhetorical constraint used by Paul and the psalmist.[136] The possibility that Paul intended to evoke Ps 2:12 (the immediately following verse) and thus draw an analogy between the enemies of the Davidic king, who are perishing from *the way of righteousness*, with the enemies of the cross who are *"walking a path that leads to utter ruin"*[137] cannot be ruled out. Paul might be challenging the Philippians to demonstrate obedience by working out their own salvation (with fear and trembling) which involves a loyalty and commitment to a once-abased king whose dominion is yet unrealized, but who currently reigns amidst his enemies—these enemies appearing to have the "upper hand" in the conflict.

---

132. Bentzen, *King and Messiah*, 17; Eaton, *Kingship and the Psalms*, 112.

133. Van Dam, "אבד," 224. See also Kraus, *Theology of the Psalms*, 125: "First of all, we must note the way in which Israel's foes are regarded as Yahweh's foes."

134. LEH, Part I, 53: to destroy utterly.

135. Oepke, "ἀπόλλυμι," 394–97.

136. Craigie, *Psalms 1–50*, 69.

137. Bockmuehl, *Philippians*, 231.

The Exhortation to Allegiance

Phil 2:12 and Ps 2:11 share a common purpose: to command obedience to God's enthroned ruler. In Ps 2:10, καὶ νῦν (now then, come now, now therefore), as a translation of וְעַתָּה[138] is assertive:[139] "The earthly kings and rulers, who at the opening of the psalm were acting rashly and arrogantly (Ps 2:1–3), are now admonished and told to think very carefully (v. 10) of the implications of the coronation which has just transpired."[140] The earthly kings are brought to a decisive crisis point—they will either perish or be happy, depending on their continued rebellion against, or submission to, the anointed king (Ps 2:12). Just as the rebellious earthly rulers in Ps 2 must respond to the king's enthronement, so too must the Philippians (albeit from a different loyalty position). In Phil 2:12, Paul uses the inferential conjunction ὥστε (so then) to introduce an independent sentence[141] ("so then just as you have always obeyed") and indicates that an inference is to be made from what has just been said about Christ and God in Phil 2:6–11. Paul often uses this conjunction when he wants to apply an exhortation to a specific situation,[142] so he is probably concerned with the Philippians's obedience (otherwise the inference made, through the use of ὥστε, to Christ's obedience to the point of death is surely weakened). However, an allusion to Ps 2:11 in Paul's description of the *manner* of obedience (fear and trembling) is capable of shifting the emphasis from a response to Christ's humble obedience in the salvation event, to a response to Christ's rule. Although this emphasis is already present in the local interpretation of Phil 2:9–11, the universal submission to Jesus as God and savior of his people described in Phil 2:10–11 (with the help of Isa 45:23) does not of necessity include allegiance of his people. Psalm 2's presence is capable of developing cosmic submission to Christ by evoking the Davidic kingship, service to God, and activating the warnings of Ps 2:12. This is not to minimize the exhortation to *willful* obedience based on Christ as savior and exemplar, but to stress the *obligatory* allegiance that the king demands. If the act of obedience of the Philippians finds an exemplar in Christ's obedience (Phil 2:6–8), then the grounds of their obedience is the allegiance owed to him as anointed king (Phil 2:9–11). In this way, Ps 2 is a *progression* on the Isa allusion in Phil 2:10–11.

---

138. See BDB 774: וְעַתָּה often expresses an informal inference, or consequence, *so, then*, esp. at the beginning of a speech.

139. BDF §442.

140. Craigie, *Psalms 1—50*, 68.

141. BDF §391.

142. cf. 1 Thess 4:18; 1 Cor 3:21; 4:5; 10:12; 11:33; 14:39; 15:58; Phil 4:18.

Moreover, Paul repeatedly brings the rhetorical constraint of citizenship to bear on the problems facing the Philippians (Phil 1:27; 3:20). Previously, we suggested that the Philippians's Christian identity and witness were the causes of opposition, perhaps from emperor cult practitioners. Additionally, the tendency to avoid conflict and suffering (akin to the Galatian Judaizing group) brought pressure to change allegiance and membership. As we argued in chapter 3, the imperative, πολιτεύεσθε, defines how the Philippians are to live, and is a technical term which Paul uses in a distinctive way in reference to their earthly existence in the Roman colony (Phil 1:27; 3:20a). Paul's use of this term suggests he is not simply concerned with moral behavior (cf. περιπατέω, his usual word for this) but the pattern of conduct that flows from belonging to a particular commonwealth, and having allegiance to its ruler (Phil 3:20b, c). The Philippians's citizenship is bound up with their identity in Christ as enthroned monarch, and the allusion to Ps 2 enables Paul to connote the cosmic kingship of God's Christ as a proof in his argument.

Conclusions

In this section we have sought to test the suggestion that the phrase φόβου καὶ τρόμου in Phil 2:12 is an embedded fragment of an OT text (Ps 2:11) that functions as a literary allusion. Certainly, several commentators have identified the possible allusion to Ps 2, but none has given it the significance proposed in this investigation.[143] In contrast to the majority of scholars, our conclusion is that the "fear and trembling" which the Philippians are to demonstrate is not merely a man-ward or God-ward expression of respect, but is characteristic of an act of allegiance to an enthroned king whose enemies did not recognize or submit to his rule. The king shares in the divine sovereignty and identity of YHWH, and reigns with an invincible mandate. Paradoxically, he is the same Jesus who was overcome to the point of death, but has been raised up and declared the son of God in the tradition of the David dynasty. The king is, however, an absentee monarch who seems to have left his subjects to fend for themselves, resulting in Paul's apostolic call to allegiance. This act of allegiance is to be characterized by "fear and trembling" which recognizes the king's reign amidst the apparent domination, yet eschatological futility, of those who oppose him. The Philippians

143. For example, Weber, "Philipper 2,12–13," 35–36, recognizes the allusion to Psa 2.11, but settles for the sociological interpretation. Bormann, "Triple Intertextuality in Philippians," 92, omits the allusion from his list of significant, three-word, two-word and one-word allusions.

are reminded of the exemplary obedience and enthroned status of the king and the eschatological outcome of the rebellion against him—the reminder takes the form of a veiled threat or warning as the Philippians are confronted with the pressure to change allegiance, perhaps to avoid suffering and opposition. Thus, we propose that Ps 2 is an intertext, or hypogram, that is a variant on the rhetorical situation of Philippians, capable of bringing to bear three rhetorical constraints on the audience. Firstly, identity of the king (Phil 2:9, 10a and Ps 2:6, 7)—the identity of Jesus as God and king is amplified by Ps 2's presence in Phil 2:12, and is a progression on his identity as God and savior evoked from Isa 45:23 in Phil 2:10–11. Secondly, eschatological victory of the king (Phil 2:10–11; 3:21b and Ps 2:8, 9). Thirdly, allegiance to the king (Phil 1:27; 2:12ff and Ps 2:10ff). With these elements of congruence, it is feasible that Ps 2 has been intentionally chosen by Paul to contribute, as a fitting response, to the problems faced by the Christian community in Philippi. Consequently, the phrase φόβου καὶ τρόμου in Phil 2:12 can be thought of as an intertextual, metonymical allusion to Ps 2:11. If so, questions are raised about how and why Paul uses Scripture. From the analysis above we have proposed that the wider context of Ps 2:11 and its *Sitz im Leben* are important to Paul, because Philippians and Ps 2 have come into existence due to some specific condition or situation which invites utterance—namely, opposition to Christ and his people. Paul seems to be using *all* of Ps 2 in an intertextual field of coronation drama and rebellion-crushing which fit his overall argumentation. His purpose in using the expression "fear and trembling" is therefore to evoke Ps 2 to emphasize the call to allegiance in the face of opposition. Allegiance to Christ requires his followers to take up their own cross in the pattern of their salvation. Thus, the rhetorical exigency of Philippians is addressed through the allusion to Ps 2 allowing Paul's use of Scripture to be considered as rhetorical and christological.[144]

DEUT 32:5 IN PHIL 2:15

Exegesis of Phil 2:15 a,b

¹⁵ἵνα γένησθε ἄμεμπτοι καὶ ἀκέραιοι, τέκνα θεοῦ ἄμωμα μέσον γενεᾶς σκολιᾶς καὶ διεστραμμένης

---

144. See Martin, *Carmen Christi*, 74–84, for the various settings advanced as possible "background" to Phil 2:6–11. The Jewish Psalter does not feature prominently. But see, Hengel, *Between Jesus and Paul*, 85.

The purpose clause of Phil 2:15 provides the reason for the imperative in v. 14 (Do all things without grumbling). The Philippians are to stop grumbling (against God) "so that (ἵνα) they might become blameless and pure amidst a crooked and perverse generation." The key exegetical issues in the passage revolve around the present or future reference of γένησθε ἄμεμπτοι καὶ ἀκέραιοι, the identity of the "crooked and perverse generation," and the role of Deut 32:5 in interpretation.

Paul uses the term ἄμεμπτος (blameless)[145] in 1 Thess 3:13 where it refers to a future blamelessness of believers at the parousia and accompanies a temporal reference ("at the coming of our Lord Jesus"). See also his similar use of the adverb, ἀμέμπτως, in 1 Thess 5:23. He also uses the adverbial form to refer to present conditions such as in 1 Thess 2:10 (his present, blameless behavior with the Thessalonians). His second use of the term, also with γίνομαι, in Phil 3:6 refers to his self-assessment of a past blamelessness. Therefore, in the absence of a temporal reference, Paul probably points out the Philippians's present freedom from blame as they do all things without grumbling; this offers an appropriate rendering of γένησθε in the ἵνα clause after a command to do something in the present (ποιεῖτε in v. 14).[146] The second word in the compound, ἀκέραιος, can mean "pure, unmixed."[147] Paul uses the word figuratively in Rom 16:19 to mean "innocent"; "be innocent with regard to evil." Martin notes the term's usage in first-century literature to describe wine which is undiluted or metals which contain no weakening alloy.[148] The combination of these ethical terms develops the idea that the Philippians are to be above reproach and remain pure by not syncretising with the surrounding unbelieving community; such an interpretation dovetails with the setting of "children of God without blame" being amidst a "crooked and perverse generation." Furthermore, as a result of not grumbling against God, not only are the Philippians blameless and pure, they can be recognized as obedient "children of God." Paul uses this term of believers in Rom 8:16, 21 and in Rom 9:8 (τέκνα τοῦ θεοῦ) to refer directly to the OT story of God's promise to Abraham (Gen 18:10, 14). As we shall see below, the probability that he evokes the wider context of Deut 32:5 in Phil 2:15 is reinforced by his usage of this "Abrahamic terminology."[149]

The language of Deut 32:5 is recognized by most interpreters, some discerning a typology between Paul and Moses (similarity between

---

145. BDAG, 52.
146. O'Brien, *Philippians*, 293.
147. BDAG, 35.
148. Martin, *Philippians* (TNTC), 118.
149. Fee, *Philippians*, 245.

authors/rhetors),[150] others between the Israelites and Philippians (deliberate contrast).[151] Interestingly, for both of these interpretations, broader aspects of Deut 32:5 must be evoked because the textual marker alone (γενεᾶς σκολιᾶς καὶ διεστραμμένης in Phil 2:15) cannot denote Moses or the Israelites. Once again, traditional historical exegetes draw on unstated material in the OT to interpret rare phrases in Paul's rhetoric (our investigation can be considered an expansion of this approach). Indeed, several decades before Hays proposed that Paul tacitly likened himself to Job (through the intertextual relationship of Phil 1:19 with Job 13:16), Beare argued for Paul's conscious analogy between himself and Moses through the reproduction of Deut 32:1–5 in Phil 2:15.[152] Furthermore, he suggested that in Phil 2:14f, Paul adapted phrases from the Song of Moses (Deut 32:1–43) because he was thinking of the failings of the Israelites in their wilderness journey.[153] Michael seems to suggest that the Song of Moses is the centerpiece of Phil 2:12–18.[154] O'Brien suggests that Paul deliberately contrasts the Philippians with the wilderness generation of Moses' day, using the phrase from Deut 32:5 to indicate that Christians have replaced Israel as God's children.[155] Alternatively, Bockmuehl repudiates the idea that γενεᾶς σκολιᾶς καὶ διεστραμμένης might refer to the wholesale dismissal of Judaism, on the questionable grounds that the Philippians would not have been aware of the link to Deut 32:5.[156] Thus, the "crooked and perverse generation" has been variously interpreted as: the wilderness generation of Moses' day applied to the whole unbelieving world,[157] pagan Philippi,[158] non-Christian contemporaries (rather than Jews),[159] and the adversaries of Phil 3:2ff, proud of their Jewish descent.[160]

Hence, the focus of interpretation has been on making a direct correspondence with a group of opponents (whether unbelieving Gentiles, Jews, or Jewish Christians) in order to establish a contrast with the Philippians.

150. Loh and Nida, *Handbook*, 69; Beare, *Philippians*, 88.
151. Witherington III, *Friendship*, 72.
152. Beare, *Philippians*, 88–90.
153. Ibid., 92.
154. Michael, *Philippians*, 99–106; See also Reumann's comments (*Philippians*, 402–3).
155. O'Brien, *Philippians*, 294. Following Collange, *Philippians*, 112.
156. Bockmuehl, *Philippians*, 157. Also Reumann, *Philippians*, 403.
157. O'Brien, *Philippians*, 294.
158. Fee, *Philippians*, 244.
159. Bockmuehl, *Philippians*, 157.
160. Collange, *Philippians*, 112.

On the one hand those interpreters who reject a link with Deut 32:5 (beyond the mere borrowing of words) reduce the pejorative force of the phrase to simple group identification and contrast; but in what way would "non Christian contemporaries" be deserving of the derisive designation, "corrupt and perverted" in terms of the exigencies facing the Philippians? On the other hand there is no consensus among those who recognize the link to Deut 32:5, their exegeses of the allusion marker being more intuitive than analytical[161]—what is the nature of the link, which elements in Deuteronomy should be evoked (Moses and/or Israelites) and how do they contribute to Paul's argument? In summary, it must be noted that there is general agreement that Deut 32:5 is present in Phil 2:15 and the wider context of the allusion marker contributes to interpretation of the passage in most analyses. Therefore, we will test the suggestion of an allusion to discover if Paul's argument might become clearer through an intertextual reading that looks deeper into plausible connotations of the deprecatory phrase γενεᾶς σκολιᾶς καὶ διεστραμμένης.

The Probability of Allusion

The possible presence of a literary allusion to Deut 32:5 in Phil 2:15 is signaled by the occurrence of the rare, four-word phrase γενεᾶς σκολιᾶς καὶ διεστραμμένης:

Phil 2:15 NT	ἵνα γένησθε ἄμεμπτοι καὶ ἀκέραιοι, τέκνα θεοῦ ἄμωμα μέσον <u>γενεᾶς σκολιᾶς καὶ διεστραμμένης</u>
Deut 32:5 LXX^{OG}	ἡμάρτοσαν οὐκ αὐτῷ τέκνα μωμητά, <u>γενεὰ σκολιὰ καὶ διεστραμμένη</u>.[A]

A. Brenton, *The Septuagint with Apocrypha*, 275–76, translates as "They have sinned, not pleasing him; spotted children, a crooked and perverse generation." But see Wevers, *Notes on the Greek Text of Deuteronomy*, 511, who takes οὐκ αὐτῷ as modifying τέκνα which is the subject of the verb.

Only two other texts, predating or contemporaneous with Paul, contain the phrase:[162] Ode 2[163] and Philo's *De Sobrietate*. Philo's reference is to Deut 32:5 or Ode 2:5 and is not a literary allusion. Rather, he makes explicit refer-

---

161. Beare, *Philippians*, 88–90, and Silva, "Old Testament in Paul," 635, could be considered exceptions.

162. Found by using the Online TLG® database; See also Bell, *Provoked to Jealousy*, 209–85, who catalogues the Song's occurrences in Jewish and Christian tradition.

163. The second Song of Moses which is a repeat of material in Deut 32:1–45. According to Swete, *Introduction to the Old Testament*, 253–54, the Odes were later Christian writings.

ence to Moses' "great song" to draw an analogy between the relationships of a child to a man and a sophist to a wise man (*Sobr.* II.9). The "crooked and perverse generation" are those men who deserve to be called children because they have committed many errors through folly and senselessness. According to Philo, this explains why Moses designates a whole people as children (*Sobr.* III.10). The absence of literary allusion in Philo notwithstanding, Paul does not interpret "crooked and perverse generation" in the same way, since he exhorts the Philippians to be "blameless and innocent" *and* "children of God."

The case for a literary allusion to Deut 32:5 is strengthened when we consider the proximity of the phrase "children of God" to "a crooked and perverse generation." A variation on this phrase also occurs in the immediate context of Deut 32:5:

| Phil 2:15 | τέκνα θεοῦ ἄμωμα |
| Deut 32:5 LXX^{OG} | οὐκ αὐτῷ τέκνα μωμητά |

This pattern of words, preceding γενεᾶς σκολιᾶς καὶ διεστραμμένης, is unlikely to be coincidental, and although the words are not quoted verbatim, there is an unmistakable syntactical pattern:

| Phil 2:15 | Children | of God | without blemish |
| Deut 32:5 LXX^{OG} | Children | not of him (God) | Blemished |

The phrase "children of God without blemish amidst a crooked and perverse generation" (Phil 2:15) resonates with "blemished children, not his, have sinned, a generation, crooked and perverse" (Deut 32:5 LXX^{OG}). The contrasting elements "of God/not of him (God)" and "without blemish/blemished" as they qualify τέκνα, in conjunction with the verbatim phrase "a crooked and perverse generation" strengthen the case for lexical dependency of Phil 2:15 on Deut 32:5. Moreover, the distinctive subject matter of children, designated by their filial status, classified morally, and excluded from, or included with, contemporary, perverse society would seem to support the case for a literary allusion to Deut 32:5. Additionally, Paul's recurring interest in Deuteronomy is also noteworthy—of the eight citations in his other epistles, three are from the Song of Moses (Deut 32:1–43).[164] Therefore, we will continue on the basis of a "strong probability" that γενεᾶς σκολιᾶς καὶ διεστραμμένης in Phil 2:15 is a literary allusion to Deut 32:5.

---

164. Rom 10:19; 12:19; 15:10.

Modification of the Initial Local Interpretation

If the allusion to Deut 32:5 was missed by Paul's implied audience, a local interpretation of Phil 2:15 might point to his use of the phrase as deliberately contrasting the Philippians and the unbelieving world.[165] In this case, the "crooked and perverse generation" in Phil 2:15 might be either pagan Philippi or corrupt humanity in general[166] which the Philippians are not to emulate—a kind of "negative typology." However, when the text of Deuteronomy is recalled, the local interpretation is modified. The phrase γενεᾶς σκολιᾶς καὶ διεστραμμένης is no longer used, merely, to distinguish the Philippians from their surroundings, but to connote the disobedience of Israel and their relinquished filial status.[167] With this modification of the initial local interpretation, most analyses of Paul's use of Deut 32:5 in Phil 2:15 are content to see a contrast between the disobedient Israelites and the Philippians.[168] However, the "crooked and perverse generation" of Deut 32:5 are those Israelites who abandoned God, their father and creator (Deut 32:6), and departed from God, their savior (Deut 32:15). It is these extremes of unfaithfulness which warrant their assessment as a "crooked and perverse generation." The pejorative force of the phrase would therefore connote more than simple contrast to an implied Philippian audience capable of actualizing this initial intertextual pattern from a rudimentary knowledge of Deuteronomic teaching. Indeed, the phrase separated from its original context will always present a puzzle, to reader and exegete alike. We will now investigate whether more scripturally-informed members of Paul's implied audience might have formed additional intertextual patterns by actualizing parts of Deuteronomy consonant with the rhetorical situation in Philippians, and which Paul activated as he composed Philippians.

Activation of the Evoked Text as a Whole—Intertextual Patterning

Silva correctly notes that Paul's use of the phrase "crooked and perverse generation" could serve as a powerful reminder of the dangers created by

---

165. O'Brien, *Philippians*, 294.

166. Watson, *Paul and the Hermeneutics of Faith*, 443, 445. Although, see Bertram, "σκολιός," 407, where he views the crooked and perverse generation in Philippi as Jews.

167. Cf. Basser, *Midrashic Interpretations of the Song of Moses*, 105–10, who notes Rabbi Meir's midrashic interpretation in which the Israelites are children of God whether they behave as children or not.

168. Bell, *Provoked to Jealousy*, 256. Like most others who recognize the allusion, he looks for a direct correspondence with a group present in Philippi—unbelieving Gentiles or *possibly*, Jewish Christian opponents.

a disobedient life. He then suggests that the phrase is an allusion to Paul's Judaizing opponents in Phil 3:2 ("the dogs"). The setting is one in which the Philippians's stand against their Jewish opponents must not be threatened by a type of behavior that has been characteristic of the Jewish nation throughout its history. Despite his plausible explanation of the tacit reference to Deut 32:5, Silva advises against "pressing the nuance" because the Judaizers are not the primary object in view.[169] But has he prematurely dismissed as "nuance" rhetorical constraints used by Paul elsewhere in the letter—the dangers of disloyalty or attitude of opponents? Exploring the possibility of deeper intertextual connections between Philippians and Deuteronomy requires an analysis of the wider context of Deut 32:5.

The Context of Deut 32:5

The phrase γενεὰ σκολιὰ καὶ διεστραμμένη occurs in Deut 32:5 which is part of the "Song of Moses" (Deut 32:1–43). The place of the song in the historical setting of Deuteronomy can be briefly explained.[170] While gathered on the plains of Moab, Moses renews the covenant (Horeb) in three spoken addresses, and delivers his final Torah teaching in a prophetic song which God commissions him to write. The song's composition was occasioned by Moses' anticipated death and the transference of the leadership to Joshua (Deut 31:16; 31:7, 8; 34:9). It was written as a witness against the Israelites whose future disobedience, while resident in the promised land, was predicted by Moses as inevitable. The song was written to remind the Israelites that when "many evils and troubles came upon them" (Deut 31:17, 21) they would recall that it was because God was not among them (Deut 31:17), because they had broken the terms of his covenant. Thus, the song is mostly a proclamation of judgment on disobedient Israel, and takes the form of covenant lawsuit.[171] It begins with Moses' pronouncement to the heavens and earth, about the greatness, faithfulness, and righteousness of God (Deut 32:1–4) followed by a summary account of the disobedience of the Israelites who have not responded correctly to God's faithfulness: "a generation, crooked and perverse. Do you thus repay the Lord these things, O people, foolish

---

169. Silva, *Philippians*, 125.

170. For authorship, and dating of the Song of Moses in the Mosaic period, see Kline, *The Structure of Biblical Authority*; Craigie, *Deuteronomy*, 29; Albright, "Some Remarks on the Song of Moses," 339–46. For a pre-exilic dating, see Sanders, *Provenance of Deuteronomy 32*. For a seventh century BCE dating (the majority opinion) see Driver, *A Critical and Exegetical Commentary on Deuteronomy*.

171. Niehaus, "Deuteronomy: Theology of" in *NIDOTTE*, 4:539. Wright, *Deuteronomy*, 297–98, suggests that Deut 32:1–4 follows the structure of a deliberative lawsuit.

and not wise?" (vv. 5-6). In vv. 6-14 Moses recounts the benefits of covenant relationship with God—the verses seem to offer a compact historical review chronicling God's provision through the Exodus. In vv. 15-18, the idolatry and disobedience of the Israelites highlights the extent of their ingratitude: "he [Israel] abandoned God who made him, and he departed from God his saviour" (v. 15). Israel's response provokes God's judgment on them, and he inflicts them with conquering adversaries, famine, and pestilence (vv. 19-26). God, however, did not allow the total destruction of Israel because he did not want her enemies to misinterpret her downfall as being outside of his sovereignty (vv. 26-27). The adversaries's lack of discernment is described in vv. 28-30—they should have known that God was ultimately behind the misfortunes of his people.[172] The song closes with God assessing and judging the enemies of Israel, and vindicating his people (vv. 31-43).

Thus, the "Song of Moses" previews the apostasy of the nation of Israel. The "crooked and perverse generation" refers to apostate Israel who rejected YHWH by turning to other gods, despite his benefaction towards them. Vv. 6b-18 describe *why* the nation of Israel is branded a "crooked and perverse generation." The principal cause of the apostasy was idolatry (vv. 16-17). The Israelites were not disobedient in a vacuum, but struggled to live as a distinctive community regulated by the laws of God in a promised land full of idolatry and wickedness. They became a "crooked and perverse generation" because they succumbed to the snares of the surrounding religion. The ongoing recital of the song of Moses was intended to serve as a stark reminder of their failed allegiance to God as they engaged with a Canaanite culture that was both hostile (to God) and enticing (to them).[173] With this characterization of the disobedient Israelites of Deut 32, we can proceed to consider ways in which the "Song of Moses" in Deuteronomy might be congruent with the rhetorical situation of Philippians—remembering that our test for congruence should take account of facets of the rhetorical situation such as persons, events, objects, actions, relations, ideas, beliefs, values, attitudes, documents, facts, traditions, images, interests, and motives.

A Warning Against Disloyalty

There are several elements of Deut 32 that are congruent with Philippians and that might plausibly be evoked in the test for a literary allusion. Firstly, like Moses, Paul provides reasons why his congregation should obey and show loyalty to God. The call to obedience in Phil 2:12 is the desired response to

172. Hab 1:12-17.
173. Wright, *Deuteronomy*, 9.

Paul's declaration of who God is and what God has done for the Philippians as described in Phil 2:6-11. Phil 2:6-11 thus provides the grounds for the Philippians's obedience— "Ὥστε, ἀγαπητοί μου, καθὼς πάντοτε ὑπηκούσατε. This is consonant with Moses' declaration of who God is and what God has done for the Israelites in Deut 32:3-4 and 6-14. In Deut 32:5, γενεὰ σκολιὰ καὶ διεστραμμένη denotes the status of those who have denounced God whose identity is revealed through his name (ὄνομα κυρίου: Deut 32:3) and his perfect work (θεός, ἀληθινὰ τὰ ἔργα αὐτοῦ: Deut 32:4). Paul uses the same rhetorical constraints in his letter to identify God's name with Jesus (τὸ ὄνομα τὸ ὑπὲρ πᾶν ὄνομα, ἵνα ἐν τῷ ὀνόματι Ἰησοῦ ... κύριος Ἰησοῦς Χριστός: Phil 2:9-10), and God's work in and for the Philippians which he will perfect (ὁ ἐναρξάμενος ἐν ὑμῖν ἔργον ἀγαθὸν ἐπιτελέσει: Phil 1:6; see also Phil 2:13). The obedience and loyalty owed to God in response to his perfect work on behalf of his people resonates in both rhetorical situations.[174] Just as God's detailed requirements of Israel are founded on his graceful action demonstrated throughout their history (particularly the exodus),[175] his requirements of the Philippians are founded on his graceful action demonstrated in Christ's condescension, obedient life, death, and exaltation.

Secondly, like the Israelites, the Philippians were in the midst of a culture that was hostile and perhaps enticing—the enticement might have been assimilation to the culture to assuage the hostility and thus avoid persecution for the cross of Christ.[176] For, as Walter noted, the surrounding pagan culture would consider the concept of a crucified deity who expected his followers to endure hardship to be inconceivable.[177] Thus, we argued in chapter 3 that the Philippians were facing the pressures of pagan culture (Phil 1:27-30) because of their citizenship of a particular commonwealth, having allegiance to its ruler (a crucified Lord). Yet we also argued that the Philippians were to consider the attitude of the Galatian Judaizers ("the dogs") who boasted in the Galatians's conversion to circumcision in order to avoid persecution for the cross of Christ.[178] We have proposed that it was the danger of imitating this attitude that Paul presents as the threat to the Philippians in Phil 3:2ff. With the Judaizers's *attitude* as the primary object

---

174. The "Song of Moses" is rhetorical discourse written to address a specific situation.

175. Thomson, *Deuteronomy*, 13.

176. The nature of the capitulation in Deut 32:6b-18 might be different to that in Philippians. But since capitulation means to surrender under specific conditions, it remains a danger for those being persecuted or enticed.

177. Walter, "Die Philipper und das Leiden," 426.

178. Taking τῷ σταυρῷ τοῦ Χριστοῦ as a dative of cause, so the cross was the cause of the persecution. See BDF §196; Moule, *Idiom*, 45.

in view, then our rhetorical exegesis of Phil 3:1–21 lends support to Silva's conjecture that "crooked and perverse generation" warns against a type of behavior that has been characteristic of the Jewish nation throughout its history. So, it can be argued that two disparate groups pose problems for the Philippians and it is noteworthy that both disdain the notion of a suffering deity.

Actually, commentators's interpretations of "crooked and perverse generation" in Phil 2:15 have been preoccupied with identifying the culture/group for which the phrase is a referent. One reason for the resulting impasse in NT scholarship described above is the simple transference of the referent from either Jew to Jew or Jew to pagan. But, as we have shown, using the phrase as a mere assignation of ethnicity has proved inconclusive. Alternatively, in Ben-Porat's model a precise transference of referents is not the necessary outcome of allusion; even though "crooked and perverse generation" referred to Jews in Deut 32:5, it need not necessarily refer to Jews in Phil 2:15. By the same token, it need not refer to pagans either. In fact, the phrase denotes Jews in Deut 32:5, but also denotes the relationship between Jews and pagan culture in Deut 32:16–18. Indeed, "disloyalty by succumbing to pagan influence" might be considered intrinsic to its meaning. "Disloyalty" is certainly conveyed through the forceful rhetoric of Deut 32:6—"Do you thus repay the Lord these things, O people, foolish and not wise?"[179] Moreover, the phrase denotes God's judgment on Israel in Deut 32:20; a "crooked and perverse generation" is one that incurs God's displeasure because they have been disloyal by succumbing to pagan influence (cf. Deut 7:16; 8:19f). Can the phrase, in Phil 2:15, connote the disastrous relationship between Jews and pagan culture described in the song of Moses, and so function as a rhetorical device, or more particularly a literary allusion, that conveys a veiled threat or warning? To suggest such connotation is simply to extend the exegetical technique employed by most traditional historical scholars who have already imbued the term with "Jewishness" because of its links with Deuteronomy 32. We suggest that, in Phil 2:15, γενεᾶς σκολιᾶς καὶ διεστραμμένης not only connotes ethnicity, but the actions of those Israelites who have benefited from the works of God (chronicled in Deut 32:6b–14), and God's response (Deut 32:20). But how might the phrase function, as a literary allusion, in Paul's argument?

A mimetic reading of Phil 2:15 seems to convey the idea of an exhortation to distinctiveness as a rhetorical constraint that addresses the dangers of assimilation to an ungodly culture: "so that you will prove yourself to be blameless and uncontaminated (ἀκέραιος), children of God above

---

179. Cf. Ps 77:7f (LXX).

reproach in the midst of a crooked and perverse generation, among whom you shine like stars." Therefore, it is not implausible that Paul is evoking the capitulation of the Israelites as characteristic of the dangers posed by the surrounding culture of Philippi. The difficulty of holding fast to a faith that is opposed by a hostile (or enticing) culture can be easily understood as a recurring rhetorical exigency addressing the children of God throughout their history (as we shall see in the next allusion to Dan 12:3). Paul's choice of γενεᾶς σκολιᾶς καὶ διεστραμμένης would be apt if he perceived that some Philippians were in danger of emulating the capitulation of Israel described in Deut 32:6b-18. If the "crooked and perverse generation" in Paul's letter has the same characteristics as that in Deuteronomy, the Philippians are not simply outnumbered by pagans who oppose them (a mimetic reading of "crooked and perverse generation"), they are in the midst of a group of people who have disobeyed God and rejected him as creator and savior, *having once shown him allegiance*. The idea that the "crooked and perverse generation" in Philippi comprised those who had once claimed allegiance to Christ might also explain Paul's reference to those "enemies of the cross of Christ" over whom he wept (Phil 3:18; cf. Rom 9:2-4). Paul's weeping might be better interpreted as his sadness and disappointment about those who capitulated from a faith-professing position. In this case, "crooked and perverse generation" does not refer to pagan Philippi, or the unbelieving world, but those like the Jewish apostates of Moses' day who are used as a warning against disloyalty and disobedience.

The Impending Death of Moses

As we have seen, several exegetes have evoked the wider context of Deut 32:5 in their interpretation of Phil 2:15. For example, Beare introduces his analysis of Phil 2:12-18 as "The Apostle's Farewell Appeal," proposing that Moses' farewell charge to the Israelites in Deuteronomy 32 lies behind Paul's thought.[180] It would not be the first time that Paul had compared his ministry with Moses; in 2 Cor 3:12f., he writes: "Since we have such a hope, we are very bold, not like Moses, who put a veil over his face so that the Israelites might not see the end of the fading splendour."[181] There are clear correspondences between Moses and Paul which are capable of being connoted through a literary allusion to Deuteronomy 32 in Phil 2:12. For example, Paul and Moses share the burden of leadership which often arouses resent-

---

180. Beare, *Philippians*, 88. Also Silva, *Philippians*, 130-31.

181. For Paul's illustrative, typological and theological uses of Moses in his letters, see Belleville, "Moses," 620-21.

ment and dissension. As Paul instructs the Philippians in the manner of their obedience, he commands them to "do all things without grumbling or disputing." As we have shown, the word translated grumbling (γογγυσμός) is the same as that used in Exod 16:7, 8, 9, 12 (LXX) to describe the grumbling of the Israelites against God and his appointed leaders (Moses and Aaron). Paul has had his fair share of detractors (cf. the Corinthian correspondence) and even during his imprisonment, there are those within the church community who were seeking to cause him distress (Phil 1:15–17). Grumbling, either against[182] or within[183] the leadership structure of the church has been identified as a possible issue in Philippians (Phil 1:1; 4:2).

Notwithstanding these correspondences between Moses and Paul, there is perhaps a dominant constraint that links them both through the *Sitz im Leben* of Deuteronomy 32 and Philippians—impending death and the call to obedience. Moses repeatedly informs the Israelites of his anticipated death (Deut 3:26, 27; 4:21, 22; 31:2, 14, 16, 29) that very day (Deut 32:48–52) and so, concerned for the ethical conduct of the people in his absence (Deut 31:27), he delivers an hortatory address designed to move them to obedience and commitment to the Lord of the covenant.[184] Moses, before reciting his song, commissioned Joshua, and then commanded the Levites to place the book of the law in the Ark of the covenant as a witness against the people (Deut 31:23–26). We should note, however, that the book of the law was to be a witness against the Israelites in Moses' absence. He saw the rebellion of the Israelites while he was with them, and anticipated the same thing when he would be absent from them following his death: "For I know your rebelliousness and your hard neck. For, while I am still alive among you today, you are being fractious concerning the things of God, how not also after my death?" (Deut 31:27). Thus, the approaching death of Moses serves as the initial basis for the renewal of the covenant, the commissioning of Joshua as the new leader, and the encouragement to wholehearted obedience to God. In Bitzer's terminology, Moses' anticipated death is the situation that has invited the rhetorical discourse of Deut 32:1–43.

Hence, we can consider certain rhetorical exigencies and constraints that Paul has in common with Moses[185] and which should be considered in the test of congruence. Both men share in a moment of crisis—facing death and concerned about the ethics of their people in their absence. Paul

---

182. Silva, *Philippians*, 144.

183. Peterlin, *Disunity*, 105.

184. Craigie, *Deuteronomy*, 17.

185. At least three commentators have noted the correspondence between Moses and Paul: Beare, *Philippians*, 88; Michael, *Philippians*, 99; Craddock, *Philippians*, 44.

also exhorts his congregation to obedience in his absence, unsure whether his trial will result in life or death (Phil 1:21–24; 2:17). Either way, his imprisonment prevents him being present with the Philippians: "Only conduct yourselves in a manner worthy of the gospel of Christ, so that whether I come and see you or remain absent . . . " (Phil 1:27). But, unlike Moses, he is confident that their obedience is not dependent on his presence: "just as you have always obeyed, not as in my presence only, but now much more in my absence, work out your salvation with fear and trembling" (Phil 2:12). Whether Moses is alive or dead, the Israelites are factious; whether Paul is absent or present, the Philippians are to obediently work out their salvation. Whereas Moses used the book of the law as a witness against the inevitable disobedience of the Israelites, Paul uses God's action as, and for, Christ (Phil 2:6–11) as witness in favor of the obedient Philippians. So, although Moses and Paul are authors of an hortatory call to obedience to their respective congregations, whilst contemplating death, there is a definite antithetical aspect to their shared historical experience. Yet, facing death, the concern of both is for the well-being of their communities. This is demonstrated in Moses' closing exhortation to the Israelites. At the end of his farewell speech (Deut 32:43), he issues a double imperative (εὐφράνθητε—be glad/rejoice!) commanding the Israelites to respond to God's avenging of them and repaying of their enemies. Paul, too, issues a "double rejoice" (χαίρω/χαίρετε) following the implication that he is facing the prospect of death (Phil 2:17f). Despite the difference in lexical terms used, the point of congruence that links Philippians and Deuteronomy in this instance is the command to rejoice in the face of death. Recalling that our test for congruence should take account of all aspects of the rhetorical situation including persons, events, attitudes, and motives, it is not unreasonable to suggest that Paul is evoking the impending death of Moses as part of his exhortation to obedience.[186] Philippians is replete with references to "death" and "attitude to death" as exigencies and rhetorical exigencies respectively (Phil 1:20–23; 2:5–8, 17, 30). As Bitzer points out, not all exigencies are rhetorical, for example death and winter. Although death, as an exigency, can be modified by God through resurrection (Phil 3:10f, 21), it cannot be modified by rhetoric. However, *the attitude to impending death* is a rhetorical exigency that can be modified with the assistance of discourse. Both Moses' and Paul's acceptance of impending death, in God's service, could act as a rhetorical constraint brought to bear upon the Philippians in their current situation. Such an interpretation coheres better with the wider interest of the epistle as laid out in chapter 3 than those which essentially reduce "crooked and perverse generation" to

---

186. Houlden, *Letters*, 85.

a stock phrase used to identify ethnicity. By evoking the wider context of Deut 32, Paul recalls the death of Moses and his exhortation for joy, even as he faced death.

Conclusions

In this section, we set out to test the suggestion that γενεᾶς σκολιᾶς καὶ διεστραμμένης in Phil 2:15 is a literary allusion to Deut 32:5. Again, we used Ben-Porat's theory to determine plausible levels of congruence between the texts. We conclude that the "Song of Moses" recorded in Deut 32:1–43 can be considered a variation on the rhetorical situation of Philippians in at least two aspects; firstly, as a warning against disloyalty: secondly as an exhortation to obedience in the face of death. If, as we have argued, Paul's letter to the Philippians is a fitting response to the danger of capitulation (in order to avoid persecution and possible death), the covenant renewal speeches of Moses, as instruction on the dangers of assimilation, would therefore commend themselves to him as worthy precursor sources of literary allusion. The "crooked and perverse generation" in Philippi is an exigency which Paul cannot modify through his rhetoric. But the "crooked and perverse generation" of Deut 32:5 becomes a *rhetorical constraint*, connoted in Phil 2:15, because their capitulation can be used as a warning, or a bad example, that Paul brings to bear on the Philippians. Furthermore, γενεᾶς σκολιᾶς καὶ διεστραμμένης denotes Moses' branding of the Israelites in his death speech. We have argued that a wrong attitude to suffering and death is the controlling exigency in Philippians. By creating intertextual patterns that connote the death of Moses, Paul invites his implied audience to discover the correspondences that link him to the OT prophet. Paul mentions his impending death tacitly and directly, and conveys his joy at the prospect of being with Christ his savior (Phil 1:21, 23; 2:27; 3:10). Neither Moses nor Paul blames God for their impending death: rather they rejoice that God is the savior of his people (Deut 33:29; Phil 3:20). Thus, γενεᾶς σκολιᾶς καὶ διεστραμμένης in Phil 2:15 can be considered as a literary, metonymical allusion used to convey the idea that Paul participates in the tradition of the Mosaic warning of the dangers of capitulation, and the acceptance of death by God's leader as he exhorts his congregation to obedience and loyalty.

DAN 12:3 IN PHIL 2:15

Exegesis of Phil 2:15c–16a

ἐν οἷς φαίνεσθε ὡς φωστῆρες ἐν κόσμῳ, ¹⁶λόγον ζωῆς ἐπέχοντες

Paul develops his description of how the Philippians are to live amidst a crooked and perverse generation using two clauses that have divided scholarly opinion. As with the phrases "fear and trembling" and "crooked and perverse generation," several exegetical difficulties have resulted in two predominant, contrasting interpretations—Paul is either exhorting the Philippians to moral conduct or evangelism. As we shall see, both of these are problematic, inviting the consideration of our alternative interpretation.[187]

In the first clause, Paul exhorts[188] the Philippians to φαίνεσθε ὡς φωστῆρες ἐν κόσμῳ. The phrase has been variously translated: "shine as lights in the world,"[189] "shine like stars in the universe,"[190] "appear as lights in the world."[191] The combination φαίνεσθε ὡς φωστῆρες does not occur elsewhere in Paul's letters and the middle/passive deponent φαίνομαι can mean "to shine" when referring to heavenly bodies or "to become visible" when referring to persons.[192] As a result, some understand it to mean "appear"[193] because it takes that meaning in 2 Cor 13:7 and Rom 7:13.[194] In the NT φωστῆρ only occurs in Phil 2:15 and Rev 21:11 where it refers to the brilliance or radiance of a jewel (Jerusalem). In the LXX it can denote the shining heavenly bodies such as the sun, moon, and stars which God created on the fourth day (Gen 1:14, 16; Wis 13: 2; Sir 43:7). It can thus mean "light" or "light-giving body."[195] A further exegetical challenge is whether κόσμος refers to the natural, physical order of creation[196] or "the world" in its ethical and religious sense.[197] If it refers to the physical world or universe,

---

187. Although an emphasis could be given to either evangelism or moral conduct in a given situation, Paul viewed them as inseparable. See for example 1 Thess 1:5; 2:8.

188. φαίνεσθε can be taken as indicative (Vincent, *Philippians*, 69) or imperative (Hawthorne, *Philippians*, 103).

189. KJV; RSV.

190. NIV.

191. NASB.

192. Bultmann and Lührmann, "φαίνω," 1–2. See also LEH, Part II, 499.

193. Lightfoot, *Philippians*, 117.

194. The word probably means "shine" in Isa 60:2 and "flash" in Matt 24:27.

195. BDAG, 1073.

196. BDF §253. See also its use in 2 Cor 5:19, John 3:16 and 12:46.

197. For example, Lightfoot, *Philippians*, 118, connects ἐν κόσμῳ with φαίνεσθε, not

then "stars" would be an appropriate rendering of φωστῆρες and "shine" for φαίνομαι—a figurative or metaphorical description of the Philippians. Alternatively, an ethical understanding of κόσμος could render φωστῆρες as "light-bearers" and φαίνομαι as either shine or appear—the notion of the Philippians as appearing as light bearers to a dark, perverse world would be well suited to the context. Finally, scholars are also divided on the meaning of the second, participial clause λόγον ζωῆς ἐπέχοντες.[198] ἐπέχω can mean "hold out/proffer" or "hold fast," whereas λόγον ζωῆς, with no precise parallels in Paul's other letters, is universally understood to refer to the gospel.[199] Whether the passage denotes the evangelistic influence of the Philippians on their surrounding culture or proper moral conduct depends largely on the meaning of this second clause. If ἐπέχω is interpreted as "holding out," the Philippians could be thought of as offering the word of life for acceptance. However, as "hold fast" the idea of constancy is conveyed, and this is also consistent with Paul's injunction to perseverance.

The preceding exegetical challenges have produced various interpretations. For example, Collange suggests the Philippians are to "bear light to the world by conveying God's word."[200] In similar vein, Fee concludes the phrase describes the Philippians's role in pagan Philippi as those who "bring the word of life to the dying," in other words, those who evangelize. In contrast, Hawthorne suggests that φαίνεσθε ὡς φωστῆρες refers to people who know God's truth and who live in accordance with that truth.[201] Likewise, Silva proposes that proper moral conduct not evangelism is the real point of the passage.[202] So, once again, an odd phrase (contained within a cluster of odd phrases) in Paul's rhetoric produces diverse interpretations.

Although it is possible that Paul instructed the Philippians to "shine like stars" *by* spreading the gospel, such an interpretation does not offer an economical account of the range of formal, semantic, and linguistic conventions in Phil 1:27—3:21. In particular, Paul's injunctions, as they reflect his

---

with φωστῆρες alone, thus "the world" is pleonastic after "among whom"—the crooked and perverse generation (also Collange, *Philippians*, 111).

198. Most interpreters understand the phrase as a modal qualifier: shine like stars *as* you hold fast the word of life, rather than linking the participle with ἵνα γένησθε to describe how the Philippians can behave as God's children (O'Brien, *Philippians*, 297). Therefore, ἐπέχοντες is not imperatival, starting a new sentence at v. 16 (cf. Hawthorne, *Philippians*, 103).

199. For example, Hawthorne, *Philippians*, 103; Bockmuehl, *Philippians*, 158: "God's word in the life-giving gospel."

200. Collange, *Philippians*, 112.

201. Hawthorne, *Philippians*, 102.

202. Silva, *Philippians*, 127.

concern for the Philippians, do not seem to have an evangelistic thrust. For example, "having the same attitude as Christ Jesus" (Phil 2:5) does not refer to evangelism. The injunctions to stop grumbling (Phil 2:14) and consider others as more important (Phil 2:3) do not seem to lie within an essentially evangelistic framework. Even conducting oneself in a manner worthy of the gospel (in a conflict and suffering context—Phil 1:27), need not necessarily mean sharing the gospel message; indeed, ἐπέχω as "hold fast" rather than "hold out," coheres more with the overall theme of perseverance in the letter (for example, "stand firm" in Phil 1:27).[203] Furthermore chapter 3 contains no mention of sharing the gospel, with Paul's mimetic injunction in Phil 3:17 following logically from the attitude and behavior he "models" in Phil 3:11–14, namely his preference for death and resurrection. It might be argued, then, that the rhetorical exigencies these injunctions address only have an indirect bearing on evangelism. It is also noteworthy that Fee sees a call to evangelism conveyed in the Hebrew version of Dan 12:3b, "and those who bring many to righteousness."[204] Fee's actualizing of a Hebrew text (Dan MT) using the allusion marker contained in a separate Greek text (namely, φανοῦσιν ὡς φωστῆρες in Dan LXX[OG]) requires a literary allusion to span two different textual traditions. This is because the LXX[OG] of Daniel (which contains the marked textual element φανοῦσιν ὡς φωστῆρες) does not contain the phrase "bring many to righteousness." This raises a key question: Did Paul intend to evoke a call to evangelism from one text (Dan MT) when he crafted a literary allusion to another (Dan LXX[OG])? From the theoretical perspective of this study, such an evocation is untenable. This is not to say that there are no denotations to evangelism in Dan LXX[OG], but that φανοῦσιν ὡς φωστῆρες does not denote them in the way Fee has stated—by way of a Hebrew text.[205] Essentially, although he recognizes an allusion to Dan 12:3 LXX[OG], Fee does not deal adequately with this text as the Septuagintal source underlying Paul's use of the OT in Phil 2:15c.

On the other hand, Paul's instructions seem to relate, directly, to moral conduct. O'Brien proposes that Paul uses a metaphor for moral conduct similar to Jesus' in Matt 5:14—"You are the light of the world."[206] Likewise, Silva suggests that the best commentary on Paul's words of moral conduct is the dominical saying in Matt 5:16: "Let your light shine before men in such

---

203. See Bockmuehl, *Philippians*, 159, who notes the absence of comparable evangelistic usage of ἐπέχω in other early Christian texts. See also Poythress, "Hold Fast," 45–53, who argues convincingly for ἐπέχω as "hold fast."

204. Fee, *Philippians*, 246–47.

205. O'Brien, *Philippians*, 296, also evokes Dan 12:3b MT.

206. Ibid., 296.

a way that they may see your good works."²⁰⁷ The problem with these interpretations is the adequacy of explaining the meaning of an odd phrase in Paul's rhetoric using dominical sayings abstracted from their original situation; essentially, what kind of moral conduct is in view and how does it connect with Paul's argument? We will therefore consider whether intertextual allusion and epistolary argument (in particular, the specificity of rhetorical situation) can contribute anything to the exegesis of Phil 2:15c–16a.

The Probability of Allusion

Beare, Hübner, O'Brien, and Fee are among those scholars who, based on verbal similarities, advance the idea that Dan 12:3 is reproduced by Paul in Phil 2:15.²⁰⁸ Consequently, the occurrence of the expression φαίνεσθε ὡς φωστῆρες (shine as stars) in Phil 2:15 and its verbal similarity to φανοῦσιν ὡς φωστῆρες in Dan 12:3 LXX^OG prompts our more theoretically-oriented investigation to test if a literary allusion is present:

Phil 2:15, 16
NT
ἵνα γένησθε ἄμεμπτοι καὶ ἀκέραιοι, τέκνα θεοῦ ἄμωμα μέσον γενεᾶς σκολιᾶς καὶ διεστραμμένης, ἐν οἷς <u>φαίνεσθε ὡς φωστῆρες</u> ἐν κόσμῳ, ¹⁶λόγον ζωῆς ἐπέχοντες

Dan 12:3
LXX^OG
καὶ οἱ συνιέντες <u>φανοῦσιν ὡς φωστῆρες</u> τοῦ οὐρανοῦ καὶ οἱ κατισχύοντες τοὺς λόγους μου ὡσεὶ τὰ ἄστρα τοῦ οὐρανοῦ εἰς τὸν αἰῶνα τοῦ αἰῶνος.^A

A. McLay, *OG and Th Versions of Daniel*, 186, thinks that, although omitted in 88-Syh, the article might have been added in Ziegler's text because it is better Greek (οἱ in φανοῦσιν ὡς οἱ φωστῆρες).

There are several reasons why the probability of an intertextual allusion to Dan 12:3 in Phil 2:15 should be considered. Firstly, deliberating an alternative interpretation is merited because previous analyses have proved to be inconclusive, failing to offer an adequate account of how the phrase φαίνεσθε ὡς φωστῆρες functions, specifically, in the epistolary argument. Secondly, the unusual phrase only occurs elsewhere in Dan 12:3 where a figurative or metaphorical usage is similar to its usage in Phil 2:15.²⁰⁹ As we have seen, given that the verb φαίνομαι is associated with φωστῆρες (stars)²¹⁰ and qualified by ἐν κόσμῳ, a figurative interpretation connoting heavenly

---

207. Silva, *Philippians*, 127.

208. Beare, *Philippians*, 92; Hübner, *Vetus Testamentum*, 490; O'Brien, *Philippians*, 296; Fee, *Philippians*, 246–47.

209. Determined from a search of the Online TLG® database.

210. Conzelmann, "φῶς," 345.

bodies should not be ruled out too quickly—the Philippians are to shine ὡς (as) stars. It is noteworthy that such figurative use of the language of heavenly bodies in epistolary argumentation is not uncommon in Paul's writing. He uses similar terminology in 1 Cor 15:40-42a where he contrasts the heavenly with the earthly as he describes the resurrection body in language reminiscent of Phil 2:15 and Dan 12:3:

> There are also heavenly bodies and earthly bodies, but the glory of the heavenly is one and the glory of the earthly is another. There is one glory of the sun, and another glory of the moon, and another glory of the stars; for star differs from star in glory. So also is the resurrection of the dead.

Thirdly, the phrase φαίνεσθε ὡς φωστῆρες seems to lie essentially within the bounds of common Jewish use in an eschatological context.[211] The only other occurrence of the word combination (although not precisely reproduced as in Dan 12:3), that pre-dates or is contemporaneous with Paul, is found in the apocalypse of Enoch, with variation: "You will shine (ἀναλάμψετε) like the lights (ὡσεὶ φωστῆρες) of heaven and will be seen (φανεῖτε), and the gate of heaven will be open to you" (1 En. 104:2). Collins notes that in 1 En. 104:2-6, "shine like stars" is an apocalyptic idiom meaning to become companions to the angelic host.[212] A similar idiomatic use can be noted in Wis 3:7 where the souls of the righteous who have died will shine (ἀναλάμψουσιν) and run around like sparks (σπινθῆρες). The idea that φαίνεσθε ὡς φωστῆρες has a Jewish apocalyptic origin is supported by the apocalypse of 2 Bar. 51:10 where the final stage of resurrection is described as follows:

> For in the heights of that world shall they dwell, and they shall be made like unto the angels, and be made equal to the stars, and they shall be changed into every form they desire from beauty into loveliness and from light into the splendour of glory.

We should therefore not be surprised at the possibility of Paul, an idiosyncratic Jew,[213] producing his text (idiolect) from this particular pool of common language (sociolect). Fourthly, the probability of a literary allusion to Daniel is strengthened when we consider the cumulative effect of several similarities between unique and rare phrases in Paul's language and language used in the immediate context of Dan 12:3. For example, Paul's only

---

211. See Newman, "כּוֹכָב," 611.
212. Collins, *Daniel*, 393.
213. Watson, *Paul and the Hermeneutics of Faith*, 1; Also Barclay, *Jews in the Mediterranean Diaspora*, 381-95, who describes Paul as an "anomalous Diaspora Jew."

use of λόγον ζωῆς ἐπέχοντες (holding fast the word of life) in Phil 2:16, as a modal qualifier of φαίνεσθε ὡς φωστῆρες ἐν κόσμῳ, might possibly result from a conflation of Dan 12:2 with 12:3:

Dan 12:2b LXX^{OG}	οἱ μὲν εἰς ζωὴν αἰώνιον some (will be raised) to everlasting life
Dan 12:3b LXX^{OG}	οἱ κατισχύοντες <u>τοὺς λόγους μου</u> those who hold fast my words[A] (the ones raised to everlasting life)
Phil 2:16a	<u>λόγον ζωῆς ἐπέχοντες</u> holding fast the word of life

A. McLay, "Daniel," 1022, translates the phrase "those who strengthen my words."

Although this phrase is unremarkable on its own, we now have an explanation, admittedly not incontrovertible, for the origin of two unusual phrases not found elsewhere in Paul's letters, λόγον ζωῆς and φαίνεσθε ὡς φωστῆρες. Not only are the terms used in both phrases found in the same book of Scripture, but in the same immediate context (Dan 12:2–3). Additionally, κατισχύοντες in Dan 12:3b LXX^{OG} can be equivalent to ἐπέχοντες in Phil 2:16a, rendering the meaning—"holding fast."[214] So, both literal and conceptual concordance between Phil 2:15 and Dan 12:2b–3b is noteworthy. Furthermore, the probability of an allusion to Daniel is reinforced when we consider Paul's reference in Phil 4:3 to those in Philippi whose names are *in the book of life* (ἐν βίβλῳ ζωῆς). The phrase βίβλῳ ζωῆς is a term based on OT sayings which speak of all the saints and faithful, and of all who fear God or await salvation, being inscribed in God's book.[215] It was popular in Jewish apocalyptic literature such as Daniel[216] where variations of the phrase appear twice: ἐν τῷ βιβλίῳ in Dan 12:1d and τὸ βιβλίον in Dan 12:4.[217] Again, a relatively rare phrase, not used by Paul elsewhere, is found in the immediate context of Dan 12:3, a Jewish apocalyptic text. Although none of this evidence proves that Paul has intentionally reproduced Dan 12:3 in Phil 2:15, their cumulative effect provides a reasonable base from which to justify the testing of the suggestion made by several scholars that Phil 2:15 contains a literary allusion to Dan 12:3.

---

214. See Grundmann, "ἰσχύω," 397. The emphasis is on power possessed. The sense of ability to prevail can be noted in its use in Dan 11:32 (κατισχύσουσι) where it means "stand firm" (see Ziegler, *Daniel*, 206; McLay, "Daniel," 1021).

215. Schrenk, "βίβλος," 620.

216. Also 1 Enoch 47:3.

217. As well as Ps 69:28; 109:13, 14; Mal 3:16; Exod 32:32, 33.

Modification of the Initial Local Interpretation

If the alleged allusion to Dan 12:3 is missed, the initial local interpretation of Phil 2:15 might render "shine like stars" as referring to Christian witness bringing God's light into a dark world,[218] or God's children living amidst a perverse society as shining stars lighting up a dark sky.[219] However, when the allusion to Dan 12:3 is recognized, the local interpretation is modified. In Dan 12:3, the expression φανοῦσιν ὡς φωστῆρες is used eschatologically as the prophet describes those who will be resurrected to everlasting life as "shining like stars" (Dan 12:2).[220] As its usage in Jewish apocalyptic literature suggests, the phrase probably connotes, first and foremost, resurrection. Thus, as the interpretation of Dan 12:3 impinges upon that of Phil 2:15, Paul creates an initial intertextual pattern by assigning resurrection status to the Philippians as he exhorts them to respond to their circumstances amidst a crooked and perverse generation. This is a radical modification of the initial local interpretation and implies the prospect of death in the tradition of the Danielic martyrs. Paul, addressing the Philippians who are currently "in the world," is using the phrase in its apocalyptic sense to describe those who have *not yet* been resurrected as if they *already* had been. Thus Paul tacitly introduces (the prospect of) resurrection as a rhetorical constraint as it relates to the *present-day* situation and conduct of the Philippians. As we have seen, Paul's interest in eschatological resurrection is recorded in Phil 3:21 where he anticipates a future resurrection for the Philippians. This follows the expression of his own desire to participate in the eschatological resurrection (Phil 3:11), following the resurrection of Christ (Phil 2:10). Furthermore, Paul states his confidence in "personal afterlife," an element which consistently surfaces in the apocalyptic genre.[221] For example, in Dan 12:2, the locus of both reward and retribution is placed in the afterlife:[222] "And many of those who sleep in the flat of the earth will arise, *some to everlasting life* but *others to shame* and *others to dispersion [and contempt] everlasting.*" Similarly, Paul argues for the virtues of "personal afterlife" in Phil 1:21, 23:

218. So, Bockmuehl, *Philippians*, 158.

219. So, O'Brien, *Philippians*, 296.

220. Contra Goldingay, *Daniel*, 306–7, and Barnes, *Notes on the Old Testament*, 258, who suggest that the expression refers, not to resurrection, but to those who are "shining" like stars under persecution. But this view does not seem to take account of the apocalyptic background to the phrase nor the presence of "everlasting" as a qualifier of the state. See Charles, *Daniel*, 323: "chapter 12 passes from temporal to eternal things."

221. Lucas, *Daniel*, 310; See also Lacocque, *Daniel*, 235: He writes: "Hope for the transcendence of death is what decisively distinguishes apocalyptic from earlier prophecy."

222. Ibid., 306.

"to die is gain," and the superior outcome of his predicament is "to depart (die) and be with Christ." At first glance, Daniel is a variant on the rhetorical situation of Philippians as it brings the constraint of hope in eschatological resurrection to bear on the Philippians's mindset: "the resurrection of Christ and the resurrection of the faithful on the last day are related, the hope of the latter being based on the certainty of the former."[223]

Activation of the Evoked Text as a Whole—Intertextual Patterning

As we have shown above, evoking the wider context of suggested alluded-to texts is "standard practice" for traditional historical exegetes. Scholars seek recourse, intuitively, to broader NT and OT contexts when faced with unique or rare puzzling phrases. For example, Bruce recognizes that Paul's Christian friends at Philippi can or should "anticipate the ministry of the resurrection life."[224] Such a commentary requires the wider context of Dan 12:3 to be evoked in order to interpret "shine like stars." In our approach, we use Ben-Porat's method, which permits a more analytical and fuller treatment of the evocation process, and rhetorical situation as a more expansive exegetical platform for congruence testing. Beyond "resurrection," what can φαίνεσθε ὡς φωστῆρες plausibly connote for Paul and the Philippians as a fitting response to their problems?

The Context of Dan 12:3

Dan 12:3 follows the prophet's prediction of a great tribulation for the Jews (Dan 12:1) and, following the intervention of their heavenly representative (the chief angel Michael), a resurrection to either everlasting life or everlasting reproach and shame (Dan 12:2). Most scholars agree that the paragraph division at Dan 12:1 is unnecessary and that the phrase "at that time" refers to the events described in Dan 11:36-45.[225] Most are also agreed that Dan 11:21-35 describes the reign of Antiochus IV Epiphanes (175-164 BC) the Seleucid king who was a vicious enemy of the Jewish people, outlawing their religion and desecrating their temple.[226] His persecution of the Jew-

---

223. Kreitzer, "Resurrection," 806.

224. Bruce, *Philippians*, 87.

225. Hartman and Di Lella, *Daniel*, 305; Anderson, *Daniel*, 144; Walvoord, *Daniel*, 282; Baldwin, *Daniel*, 203; Collins, *Daniel*, 390; Leupold, *Daniel*, 526; Beale, *Use of Daniel in Jewish Apocalyptic Literature*, 44.

226. Also in 1 Macc 1:20-64. For example, Goldingay, *Daniel*, 304-5; Anderson, *Daniel*, 129-44.

ish people is described in Dan 11:33 (LXX^{OG}): "And thoughtful ones of the nation will understand for many, and they will stumble by sword and will become old by it and by captivity, and they will be soiled by pillaging for days."[227] It is within this context of intense persecution and suffering that the prophet offers the hope of eschatological reward in the form of resurrection to those who remain faithful to God. Lacocque writes: "the real ferment of the belief in the resurrection was the persecution in the time of Antiochus Epiphanes."[228] The suffering and death for the Jew who remained faithful to God and the Torah had to be explained, within the framework of God's sovereignty—God may deliver the faithful *from* death (Dan 3)[229] or *through* death (Dan 12). Hartman and Di Lella correctly contextualize Dan 12:3, recognizing that the Antiochene persecution challenged the view that a faithful Jew could successfully serve a malevolent pagan king:

> The primary audience addressed is, therefore, the loyal group of Jews who suffered cruel persecution under Antiochus IV. These stalwart men, women and children will be vindicated by God and will be rewarded for their fidelity not here on earth but beyond the grave.[230]

With this summary of Daniel's rhetorical audience, the exigencies they faced, and the eschatological constraint of God's reward proffered as their hope, we can proceed to consider ways in which the book of Daniel might be congruent with the rhetorical situation of Philippians. As before, shades of congruence can be sought through persons, events, objects, actions, relations, ideas, beliefs, values, attitudes, documents, facts, traditions, images, interests, motives, and such like (in other words, all elements of the rhetorical situation). As before, the yardstick for judging our results should be a satisfactory interpretation of φαίνεσθε ὡς φωστῆρες in conjunction with an explanation for the presence of the cluster of OT references in Phil 2:10–16 that coheres with the broader rhetorical interests of the epistle recorded in Phil 1:27—3:21.

---

227. McLay, "Daniel," 1021.

228. Lacocque, *Daniel*, 244. Quoting Causse.

229. Daniel himself was exemplary in his refusal to capitulate while surrounded by the enticements of an alien culture.

230. Hartman and Di Lella, *Daniel*, 306.

Perseverance or Capitulation

In "modification of the initial local interpretation," an initial intertextual pattern has been proposed—belief in resurrection is a rhetorical constraint used by Paul to offer hope to those Philippians who might be facing death. However, as the wider context of Dan 12:3 is evoked, more significant connotations develop. Not least of these are the circumstances of those Jews described in Daniel, which invited use of the terminology "shine like stars." The wider context of Daniel unveils not only the nature of the Antiochene persecution, but the two polar responses to it—those who persevered to the point of death and those who capitulated to escape suffering and death. Referring to them by their common Hebrew titles, those who forsake the holy covenant are the רַבִּים (*rabbim*) and those who face persecution, have insight, give understanding to many, and fall by sword and flame are the מַשְׂכִּלִים (*maskalim*). The two groups are repeatedly contrasted in the immediate context of Dan 12:1–4 LXX^{OG}. Those who are found written in the book are exalted (Dan 12:1), resurrected to everlasting life and compared with those resurrected to everlasting contempt (Dan 12:2).[231] In Dan 12:3 LXX^{OG}, it is the wise ones (οἱ συνιέντες) who hold fast the word of life and who will "shine like stars" (the same wise ones who will fall by the sword in Dan 11:30). In Dan 12:4c LXX^{OG}, the *rabbim* are in view as the prophet describes those who will "fall away" in a future apostasy caused by an increase in persecution and injustice—the phrase ἕως ἂν ἀπομανῶσιν οἱ πολλοὶ καὶ πλησθῇ ἡ γῆ ἀδικίας refers to panic and fleeing in the face of persecution. The apostasy of many Jews during the time of Antiochenes Epiphanes was the result of state-sponsored persecution—unwilling to lose their lives or their wealth many capitulated by renouncing their covenant faithfulness and embracing his laws.[232] This interpretation makes sense in the context of the persecution and tribulations of the last times and the temptation to renounce faith when faced with persecution (Dan 11:31–35 and Dan 12:1).[233] It also assists us in understanding why the book of Daniel might have commended itself to Paul as a worthwhile source in responding to the rhetorical situation in Philippians—if, as we suspect, it addresses the same recurring exigency. It is certainly plausible that, with an intentional allusion to Dan 12:3, Paul reminds the Philippians of the resurrection fate that awaits *those who remained faithful to God and bore the brunt of persecution.*

---

231. See Jeansonne, "OG Translation of Daniel 7–12," 101–2, for details of LXX^{OG} syntax and an explanation of the "three resurrected groups." Cf. Bruce, "Oldest Greek Version of Daniel," 26.

232. Hartman and Di Lella, *Daniel*, 64. See 1 Macc 1:41–52.

233. Goldingay, *Daniel*, 303.

We have argued that Paul's letter to the Philippians is written in response to a specific situation—the threat of capitulation caused by a tendency to escape suffering. Thus, the persecution, perseverance, and capitulation passages of Daniel are congruent with the rhetorical situation in Philippi. In our exegesis of Phil 1:27–30, we presented enmity, conflict, and suffering as exigencies while God's approval as the basis for perseverance was the prominent rhetorical constraint used by Paul in his argument. The recurring rhetorical constraints of eschatological fate framed within resurrection, salvation, and destruction categories also point to shared world components between Daniel (12:2–4) and Philippians (Phil 1:28; 3:19–21). Furthermore, the recurring rhetorical exigency of avoiding persecution is prominent in Galatians (Gal 6:12) which, we have argued, Paul directly references in Phil 3:2. Here, we suggest, Paul uses those Judaizers seeking to avoid persecution ("the dogs") as a bad example, perhaps connoting their correspondence with the *rabbim* of Dan 12:3. He also offers himself as their counter-example (the *maskalim*), emphasizing his own renunciation of past allegiances for an allegiance to Christ (Phil 3:7–10) that has resulted in his captivity (Phil 1:13) and may result in his death (Phil 1:20). For Paul, in choosing allegiance to Christ over other lords, death threatens, so perseverance until resurrection is attained becomes a major rhetorical constraint. In Phil 3:10–21, he optimistically, or apocalyptically, argues for the virtue of death since it ensures eschatological resurrection. Thus perseverance requires a Jewish apocalyptic understanding that obedience might bring death (Phil 2:8), after which comes exaltation (Phil 2:9 [ὑπερύψωσεν]; Dan 12:1 [ψωθήσεται]).

The Eschatological Agent

In Dan 12:1, the prophet predicts a time when the great angel Michael will "come to the side of" God's people. This heavenly agent's arrival instigates a general resurrection followed by judgment. Michael's arrival, and his role as implied judge at the eschaton, are eagerly awaited as God's people endure a time of great tribulation. Dan 12:1–4 describes a general resurrection and judgment of the dead, and contributed to the prevailing apocalyptic view embraced by Pharisaic Judaism in the first century—bodily resurrection at the end of time. Daniel is the only book from the HB containing the following key ingredients of the Jewish apocalyptic tradition: the role of the heavenly eschatological agent (Michael in Dan 12:1), the bodily resurrection and eschatological judgment (Dan 12:2).[234] The Danielic tradition of

---

234. See Sacchi, *Jewish Apocalyptic and its History*, 43–46, for a summary of the characteristics of apocalyptic thought.

the second century BCE is reflected in the accepted Jewish apocalypses (1 Enoch, 4 Ezra, 2 Baruch) and the book was "a widely used *Vorbild* through which to understand eschatological ideas."[235] As Holleman writes:

> Dan 12:1–3 is an early example of how expectations concerning the actions of an eschatological intermediary, the eschatological resurrection, and the final judgment are related to, and harmonised with, each other. The result is a more or less systematic presentation of the eschaton.[236]

It seems reasonable to suggest that Dan 12:1–3 might have influenced Paul's thoughts as he composed Philippians, in which the same apocalyptic elements are clearly present: the intervention of the heavenly eschatological agent (Phil 1:6; 3:20),[237] his instigation of the eschatological resurrection of the dead (Phil 3:21) and his role as implied judge at the eschaton (Phil 2:9–11; 1:28; 3:19), along with repeated references to the eschaton and the parousia (Phil 1:10; 2:16; perhaps Phil 4:5). The "pessimism" of Jewish apocalypse is prevalent in the passages about death (Phil 1:20, 21, 23; 2:8, 17, 30; 3:10) and destruction (Phil 1:28; 3:19) and the apocalyptic motif of "agonised waiting"[238] (Phil 3:20b) is present alongside an apocalyptic hint of "cosmic termination" (Phil 3:21c). Paul seems to actualize the pattern of Michael's activity in his description of the parousia in Phil 3:20–21, in which he assigns the role of the eagerly-awaited heavenly eschatological agent to Jesus. On his arrival, he will resurrect those citizens of heaven who have died on earth. His arrival is eagerly anticipated (ἀπεκδεχόμαι) because of the tribulation suffered by his people in his absence. Thus, φαίνεσθε ὡς φωστῆρες is capable of connoting in Phil 2:15 what φανοῦσιν ὡς φωστῆρες denotes beyond Dan 12:3 in Dan 12:1—the future arrival of a heavenly eschatological agent, the eschatological resurrection of the dead, and final judgment. From this analysis, it is reasonable to conclude that not only is φαίνεσθε ὡς φωστῆρες in Phil 2:15 probably a metonymical allusion to Dan 12:3, but that Philippians accords with the book of Daniel in the tradition of the Jewish apocalypse.[239] Furthermore, Philippians is a development of

---

235. Beale, *Daniel*, 328.
236. Holleman, *Resurrection and Parousia*, 128.
237. Cf. 1 Cor 15:23–28 and 1 Thess 4:16–17.
238. Sacchi, *Jewish Apocalyptic and its History*, 43.
239. Barton, "Theological Ethics in Daniel," 661. He comments on apocalyptic ethics: "If apocalypticism is the literature of small, beleaguered groups looking for deliverance from oppression then the ethics of apocalypticism can be expected to manifest the characteristic mindset of such groups, with their desire to stress all that binds them together and makes them distinctive."

Daniel in that Paul identifies Jesus as the eschatological agent of general resurrection and judgment.

Paul in the Role of the Maskalim

Those described as the *maskalim* or "wise ones" of Dan 12:3 who will "shine like stars" are called wise because they possess that insight which perceives how God's cause will ultimately triumph through the suffering of his people. The ministry of the *maskalim* is not teaching in general or exhortation to faithfulness but the interpretation of the prophetic scriptures for the persecuted community[240]—they are wise because they are able to interpret the people's suffering in terms of God's sovereignty. Their knowledge of God's role in his people's suffering is then used to enlighten the multitudes, who suffer as they did.[241] From this brief analysis of the *maskalim* in the book of Daniel, the correspondences with Paul as expressed through his rhetoric in Philippians can be noted. In chapter 3, we proposed that Paul implicated God in the Philippians's suffering (Phil 1:29) to convey the idea of divine approval. Additionally, we suggested that Paul uses Isa 45:23 in Phil 2:6–11 to reveal God as suffering and death-embracing deity (which justifies his approval of suffering and death for the sake of Christ). By interpreting the crucifixion of Jesus as revealing the universal sovereignty of YHWH in an argument addressing human suffering, Paul seems to adopt the role of the *maskalim*. Not only does he interpret the Philippians's suffering in terms of God's sovereignty, he seems to imitate the *maskalim* when faced with the prospect of death himself. He welcomes death as the preferred outcome of his imprisonment and trial ("to die is gain"), and he counters the attitude of self-preservation in his renunciation of privileges in order to conform to Christ's suffering, death, and resurrection (Phil 3:4–11). Also in Phil 2:17, he rejoices at the prospect of death using cultic language in the context of sacrifice, service, and faith. Hence, the presence of an intentional, metonymical allusion to Dan 12:3 (capable of activating the role of the *maskalim* as paradigmatic for implied author and audience in a suffering community) is congruent with the rhetorical situation of Philippians.

---

240. Goldingay, *Daniel*, 303.

241. Ibid., 303. Goldingay suggests that the martyrdom of some of the *maskalim* is referred to in Dan 11:33, but that many ordinary people went through the same experiences.

Conclusions

In this section, we set out to test the suggestion that φαίνεσθε ὡς φωστῆρες in Phil 2:15 is a literary allusion to Dan 12:3. Once again, Ben-Porat's theory was used to determine plausible levels of congruence between the texts, with rhetorical situation providing the framework for comparison. Both Paul and his implied audience in Philippians would stand in the historical tradition of their day in seeking answers to what Scripture said about the fate of God's people and the end of times. This would be especially so if Scripture revealed common rhetorical exigencies that invited common rhetorical constraints brought to bear upon audiences sharing common situations. The book of Daniel and Philippians share the exigencies of persecution and the prospect of death, the rhetorical exigency of temptation to capitulate, and the rhetorical constraints of hope in resurrection and the consequences of capitulation. Both implied audiences also required direction from their wise leaders about God's seemingly passive role in their suffering. Consequently, Daniel can be considered an intertext, or hypogram, that is a variant on the rhetorical situation of Philippians, capable of bringing to bear shared rhetorical constraints on the audience. Therefore, we conclude that "shine like stars" is not an appeal to evangelism or an abstracted exhortation to moral conduct. Rather, it is an eschatological prognosis that requires a steadfast refusal to capitulate under pressure in the tradition of the Danielic martyrs. In chapter 3, we argued that the rhetorical exigency which Paul seeks to overcome is the disinclination among some Philippians to accept suffering and perhaps death as legitimate consequences of their loyalty to Christ. Paul, knowing that loyalty to Christ will result in suffering and mistreatment at the hands of his (Christ's) opponents, reveals why the Philippians should embrace suffering and persevere: God has sanctioned it, and it is a proof/sign of their salvation because God, himself, participates in suffering and death to secure their eschatological fate. The book of Daniel is an appropriate precursor text with which to convey the significances connoted by the phrase φαίνεσθε ὡς φωστῆρες: the eschatological hope for a suffering congregation—resurrection to eternal life. Consequently, φαίνεσθε ὡς φωστῆρες in Phil 2:15 can be thought of as an intertextual, metonymical allusion to Dan 12:3.

ISA 49:4 IN PHIL 2:16

Exegesis of Phil 2:16b, c

εἰς καύχημα ἐμοὶ εἰς ἡμέραν Χριστοῦ, ὅτι οὐκ εἰς κενὸν ἔδραμον οὐδὲ εἰς κενὸν ἐκοπίασα.

Phil 2:16b–c completes the single sentence started in v. 12 and contains the fifth and final alleged allusion in the compact cluster of five under test. The term κενὸν ἐκοπίασα has been variously described as "reminiscent" of Isa 49:4 and "an echo" of Isa 49:4. However, a substantive theoretically-oriented examination of a possible literary allusion to Isa 49:4 has not been undertaken until now. Despite several exegetical challenges, a general consensus prevails regarding the meaning of the passage—this will now be critiqued.

The word καύχημα can mean "boast," but also the source or ground for boasting/glorying.[242] The latter meaning is consistent with Paul's usage in Phil 1:26 and 3:3 where it refers to "boasting" or "glorying" in someone.[243] εἰς καύχημα ἐμοί probably indicates purpose[244] and can be taken with λόγον ζωῆς ἐπέχοντες or the entire passage that precedes ἵνα γένησθε ἄμεμπτοι καὶ ἀκέραιοι. . . . Thus, according to Vincent, it is the Philippians's success in "working out their own salvation" and proclaiming the gospel to others that is the cause of Paul's boasting[245] and not just "holding fast the word of life."[246] But Paul's boasting is yet future. He adds an eschatological focus through the use of the phrase, εἰς ἡμέραν Χριστοῦ ("on the day of Christ"). This refers to the point in time when Paul's boasting will take place, namely, at the parousia[247] and seems to be its meaning in Phil 1:6, 10 and also 1 Cor 1:8; 2 Cor 1:14 and 1 Thess 2:19.[248] The ὅτι that introduces v. 16c can be understood as "explicative" of the nature of Paul's glorying ("that")[249] or of its ground ("because").[250] O'Brien prefers to render ὅτι as "indicating that" or

---

242. See BDAG, 537; Bultmann, "καύχημα," 651.

243. See, for example the LXX of Jer 9:23f where boasting is in "wisdom," "might," "wealth" and "the Lord."

244. Moule, *idiom*, 70. See also Rom 10:1; 13:4; 1 Cor 14:22.

245. Taking ἐμοί in Phil 2:16b as a dative of possession.

246. Vincent, *Philippians*, 70.

247. With O'Brien, *Philippians*, 299. Cf. Vincent, *Philippians*, 70, who interprets εἰς as "against" the day of Christ; Reumann, *Philippians*, 413, prefers "towards" the Day of Christ; Fee, *Philippians*, 248, translates, "with the day of Christ in view."

248. BDAG, 438.

249. Meyer, *Philippians*, 118.

250. Vincent, *Philippians*, 70.

"as the proof that."[251] Thus the passage can be translated, "in order that I may have ground for boasting on the day of Christ as proof that I have not run nor toiled in vain." The verb τρέχω can mean "to run" or "to exert oneself"[252] in certain contexts in several of Paul's other letters. In these instances Paul seems to use the term as an athletic metaphor for his apostolic ministry in particular (1 Cor 9:24, 26 and Gal 2:2) or the Christian life in general (Rom 9:16 and Gal 5:7). In like manner, κενός can signify "empty" or (with εἰς) "in vain" to picture the eventual success or failure of the athlete.[253] In some contexts, the second verb, κοπιάω, can mean "to labour/work hard" or "to toil."[254] In the LXX, it is translated for יגע conveying the sense of the diligent efforts of the servant of the Lord on behalf of his people (Isa 49:4). Included in the meaning might be an element of eschatological hope—that present toil will be rewarded with refreshing rest in the age of salvation (Isa 65:23).[255] This is probably Paul's intended meaning when using the word of Christian ministry five times in three other letters (1 Cor 15:10; 16:16; Gal 4:11 and 1 Thess 3:5; 5:12)[256] and also in coupling the words κοπός/κοπιάω with κενόν when he seems concerned that he might lose the eschatological reward for his labors through hostile circumstances (1 Thess 3:5 and Phil 2:16). Thus, in Paul's thought the idea of "laboring in vain" is closely connected with "running in vain" (for example in Gal 2:2; 4:11 and Phil 2:16)—the athletic imagery is coupled with manual labor imagery as the eschatological prize or reward awaits those who finish the race (Phil 3:14) or work hard for the Lord (cf. Rom 16:12).

To summarize, Phil 2:16b–c contains two ideas that Paul expresses in other letters: firstly, his hope that his converts will be his grounds for glorying at the coming of Christ (2 Cor 1:14 and 1 Thess 2:19); and secondly, his concerns that his work might be futile (Gal 2:2 and 1 Thess 3:5). So, what role does the phrase, κενὸν ἐκοπίασα play in Paul's argument? Bockmuehl views the passage as referring to Paul having reason to be proud at the blamelessness and steadfastness of the Philippians—the Philippians's lives are thus proof that he did not run or toil in vain.[257] Barth claims the words refer to Paul's "success in having won men to the humility of Christ and held them

---

251. O'Brien, *Philippians*, 299.

252. BDAG, 1015; LEH, Part II, 480.

253. BDAG, 539; Oepke, "κενός," 659–60; note also 2 Cor 6:1; Gal 2:2; 1 Thess 3:5; Lev 26:20; Isa 29:8 and 65:23; Jer 6:29.

254. BDAG, 558.

255. Hauck, "κοπιάω," 828.

256. In 1 Thess 3:5 the concept of "toiling in vain" is conveyed by the noun κοπός—καὶ εἰς κενὸν γένηται ὁ κόπος ἡμῶν.

257. Bockmuehl, *Philippians*, 159.

fast in it."²⁵⁸ O'Brien recognizes an echo of Isa 49:4, but goes no further than to suggest that Paul wished to receive the reward of God's commendation for a faithful ministry.²⁵⁹ However, these interpretations pay little attention to the substance of Phil 2:5–11, 17–18 which serve as the grounds for Paul's injunctions and prognosis in Phil 2:12–16. We argued previously that the literary, theological, and rhetorical relationships of Phil 2:5–11 to the (alleged) unique concentration of OT references in its immediate literary context has never been probed. For example, φόβου καὶ τρόμου might modify a kind of obedience that responds to some facet of Jesus' person recorded in Phil 2:5–11. In like manner, is there a literary, rhetorical, or theological relationship between the humiliating death, exaltation and universal sovereignty of Jesus, the manner in which the Philippians are to respond to it and Paul's assessment of ministry effectiveness that might give an alternative, plausible explanation for the rhetorical use of κενὸν ἐκοπίασα? In our opinion, only if κενὸν ἐκοπίασα is abstracted from the substance of Phil 2:5–11 and 2:17–18, can we be satisfied that the phrase refers, merely, to the success or failure of Paul's ministry in particular or Christian life in general. Any phrase mooted as conveying an explication of perceived success or failure should relate to the epistolary argument as a whole, and to how "death" brackets not only the occurrence of κενὸν ἐκοπίασα, but the entire alleged cluster—Christ's actions and attitude to death (Phil 2:5–8), God's actions and approval of Christ's abasement and death (vv. 9–11), and Paul's contemplation of, and attitude to, his own death (vv. 17–18). Moreover, the eschatological dimension of Paul's boasting is central to the idea that he wished to present the Philippians as part of the account of his stewardship *to God* as judge of both living and dead at the parousia.²⁶⁰ Consequently, Paul might be addressing, not so much his own evaluation of ministry success, but God's (and perhaps the Philippians's) in light of his imprisonment and impending death. If so, an approach that deliberates a deeper meaning for κενὸν ἐκοπίασα seems even more plausible once it is conceded that the phrase might connote some aspect(s) of the Isaiah righteous servant (see below).

The Probability of Allusion

In addition to the various compendia that include an allusion to Isa 49:4 in Phil 2:16, several scholars have recognized a link between the texts. For example, by using the phrase "run or toil in vain," Bockmuehl suggests that

---

258. Barth, *Philippians*, 78.
259. O'Brien, *Philippians*, 301.
260. Hawthorne, *Philippians*, 103.

Paul might see his own apostolic work as partial analogy to the OT antecedent of the Isaianic righteous Servant.²⁶¹ Along similar lines, Martin claims that Paul uses language reminiscent of Isa 49:4.²⁶² A literary allusion to Isa 49:4 in Phil 2:16 is certainly suggested by the occurrence of the phrase κενὸν ἐκοπίασα which appears in both texts (with slight variation):

Phil 2:16	λόγον ζωῆς ἐπέχοντες, εἰς καύχημα ἐμοὶ εἰς ἡμέραν Χριστοῦ, ὅτι οὐκ εἰς κενὸν ἔδραμον οὐδὲ εἰς <u>κενὸν ἐκοπίασα</u>
Isa 49:4 LXX^{OG}	καὶ ἐγὼ εἶπα <u>Κενῶς ἐκοπίασα</u> καὶ εἰς μάταιον καὶ εἰς οὐδὲν ἔδωκα τὴν ἰσχύν μου

However, similar to φόβου καὶ τρόμου, variations on the word combination occur in five other passages in Scripture (Job 2:9; 20:18; 39:16; Isa 65:23 and Jer 28:58 [LXX]) opening up the possibility that any one of them was Paul's source for the allusion.²⁶³ If κενὸν ἐκοπίασα is a literary allusion, how probable is it that Paul intended to evoke Isa 49:4 and not one of these other texts? Once again, we will survey all the (extant) Greek texts that Paul could have intended to evoke and compare their immediate context, with a view to reinforce or undermine the case for including Isa 49:4 in our case study for testing the suggestion of an allusion in Phil 2:16.

In Job 2:9b, the phrase is used by Job's wife in reference to their sons and daughters. Their deaths result in her claim that her wearying over them was in vain. In Job 20:18, Sophar replies to Job that the impious and the transgressor will have toiled in vain for their wealth, since they will not enjoy it. In Job 39:16, as part of God's address to Job, the Ostrich²⁶⁴ is depicted as not caring about the fate of her young and therefore her labor is in vain. In Jer 28:58 the phrase is used of the people who will not labor in vain concerning the fall of Babylon. In Isa 49:4, the person(s) designated Israel, the slave and servant of God, assess their efforts as having toiled in vain. In Isa 65:23, God promises that his chosen ones will not labor in vain. Of these six passages, Jer 28:58, Isa 49:4 and 65:23 all include God's assessment countering a sense of futility. Of these three passages, Isa 49:4 has a greater concordance with Phil 2:16 because of the autobiographical nature of the expression of failure: that is, a *self*-assessment is in view. Therefore, because of the distinctiveness of an autobiographical element in Isa 49:4, we suggest

---

261. Bockmuehl, *Philippians*, 159.

262. Martin, *Philippians* (TNTC), 122.

263. Using the Online TLG® database, five examples of the word combination were found that could have been Paul's source.

264. ασιδα καὶ νεσσα translates as "stork and plumage."

that it might be the more likely source of Paul's use of κενὸν ἐκοπίασα in Phil 2:16.[265] Moreover, as we consider the probability of a literary allusion to Isa 49:4 in Phil 2:16, it is worth mentioning that the prophetic confession of the Servant in Isa 49:1–6 includes two ideas that recur in Paul's letters: firstly, the predestinarian idea of being called from his mother's womb (Isa 49:1, 5 and Gal 1:15)[266] and secondly, his commission to preach the gospel to the Gentiles (Isa 49:6 and Gal 1:16). Paul's particular predilection for quoting from Isaiah and Luke's record of Paul identifying himself directly with the Isaianic Servant of the Lord (Isa 49:6) in Acts 13:47 are also noteworthy.[267] Consequently, we have grounds for testing the suggestion of an allusion to Isa 49:4 in Phil 2:16.

Modification of the Initial Local Interpretation

If the alleged allusion to Isa 49:4 is missed, the local interpretation of Phil 2:16 might render "toil in vain" as merely failure. Therefore, Paul uses the phrase to convey his concerns about receiving the reward of God's commendation for a faithful ministry.[268] This mimetic reading of the text seems valid since the occurrence of the expression κενὸν ἐκοπίασα in Phil 2:16 occurs within a context of eschatological reward ("in the day of Christ I will have reason to glory/boast") and refers to Paul's goal in presenting the Philippians as mature Christians in Christ.[269] How the Philippians respond to Christ's actions seems to be the measure of success for Paul's ministry to them (Phil 1:27; 2:12–16). This is corroborated by Gal 2:2 and 4:11, where Paul writes to believers in Galatia whom he fears have rejected his message and gone back to "law observance." In this passage, he uses the same language—I have labored over you in vain (Gal 4:8–11). Thus, the idea of "toiling in vain" relates to the repudiation of Paul's message to his churches, and his subsequent self-assessment of a failed mission. But as the text of Isa 49:4 is recognized as a possible referent, the initial local interpretation is modified. The allusion marker, κενὸν ἐκοπίασα, connotes the self-assessment

---

265. Although Silva (*Philippians*, 127) and Fee (*Philippians*, 242) see a reference to Isa 65:23.

266. Cf. Jer 1:5.

267. Paul quotes from Isaiah 25 times including Isa 49:18 in Rom 14:11 and Isa 49:8 in 2 Cor 6:2. See also Bruce, "Paul's Use of the Old Testament in Acts," 73: "No matter how much the selection and application of these Old Testament texts [Isa 49:6] owe to Luke, there is no sound reason to doubt that he is reproducing the general sense of Paul's preaching."

268. O'Brien, *Philippians*, 300.

269. Hauck, "κοπιάω," 829; Col 1:28–29.

of the slave, identified as Israel, who appears despondent about failure to perform a God-given task. The apparent total failure is amplified by the evocation of the phrase Κενῶς ἐκοπίασα καὶ εἰς μάταιον καὶ εἰς οὐδὲν ἔδωκα τὴν ἰσχύν μου. Yet the servant's self-assessment is only his "first thought" on his apparent failure. The διὰ τοῦτο ("for this reason" or "through this")[270] of v. 4 introduces a "second thought" which includes his deferral to God for final adjudication (κρίσις). If he has been faithful in laboring and spending himself, perhaps a sense of dismay about his failure prompts the desire for a "second opinion." He has done all he could, has apparently failed, and therefore leaves the final judgment concerning his labors with God.[271] According to Whybray, in spite of his sense of failure, the servant remained confident that God would accept his efforts.[272] Although neither the servant's identity nor the details of his mission need be evoked in this modification of the local interpretation, an initial intertextual pattern formed by Paul and his implied audience could include God's approval of the servant despite his apparent failure. This idea is certainly denoted by κενῶς ἐκοπίασα in Isa 49:4, and is also present in Philippians (for example, Phil 1:29, 2:9–11, 16b–c and, as we shall see, Phil 1:16). It is not beyond the bounds of imaginative possibility that Paul intended tacitly to transfer to himself this signification of the Isaianic servant of Isa 49:1–6. In fact, given that he seems to have viewed his own calling as prefigured in that of the Servant (see above), it is even more likely. If so, the final say, in terms of the assessment of Paul's success or failure, *does not lie with either himself or the Philippians, but God*. Before considering the possibility that Paul and the Philippians formed other intertextual patterns by activating parts of Isaiah consonant with the rhetorical situation in the letter, the wider context of Isa 49:4 will now be investigated.

Activation of the Evoked Text as a Whole—Intertextual Patterning

The suggestion is, that by reproducing a fragment of Isa 49:4 in Phil 2:16, Paul is alluding to one of the so-called servant songs of Isa 40—55.[273] Con-

270. According to Minn, *Servant Songs*, 8–9, the Hebrew אָכֵן can be translated "beyond all doubt," thus its use corrects an erroneous inference and counters the servant's pessimism; Koole, *Isaiah III*, 16, translates the Hebrew as "but nevertheless."

271. Locative use of παρά with dative κυρίῳ. The sense is that *despite* his apparently futile efforts, his judgment rests (remains) with the Lord: διὰ τοῦτο ἡ κρίσις μου παρὰ κυρίῳ.

272. Whybray, *Isaiah 40—66*, 138.

273. The classification "servant songs" is attributed to Duhm—the four songs are: Isa 42:1–4(9); Isa 49:1–6(12); Isa 50:4–9(11) and Isa 52:13—53:12. As a result of Duhm's classification the passages have been interpreted apart from their context, as

sequently, we will first consider the immediate literary context of Isa 49:4, and then sketch out the "inner narrative"[274] of Isa 40—55 as the potential semiotic grid, or intertextual matrix capable of being actualized by a literary allusion to Isa 49:4. This approach is justified because of the centrality of the unfolding nature and mission of the servant within the narrative,[275] and the prominence of the so-called "servant passage" of Isa 49:1-6 for Paul's self-understanding of his apostolic ministry to the Gentiles (as revealed in autobiographical passages such as Gal 1:15f [see also Acts 13:47]).[276]

The Context of Isa 49:4

The historical setting of Isa 40—55 is the aftermath of the Babylonian conquest of 587 BCE which resulted in the collapse of the Davidic dynasty, humiliation of the king (Jehoiachin), and destruction of the temple.[277] The calamitous events of 587 BCE posed a major theological conundrum for the exiled Jewish people as they struggled to comprehend their national disaster within the context of their Yahwistic faith—the viability of their official national worldview had been called into question by the exile.[278] Some concluded that YHWH had abandoned Israel and consequently switched allegiance to the deity who had proven himself superior in battle.[279] But YHWH

later additions to Isa 40—55. This view was successfully challenged by North, *The Second Isaiah* and others (see Laato, *The Servant of YHWH and Cyrus*, 38). The view taken in this thesis is that we can consider Isa 49:1-6 as a servant song but that it also fits well with the context of Isa 40—55. This implies acceptance of the unity of Isa 40—55 with authorship attributed to either the historical Isaiah of the eighth century BCE or Deutero-Isaiah who wrote circa. 550-538 BCE The debate on authorship does not seriously impact the argument in this intertextual investigation. Oswalt, *Isaiah*, 305, does not restrict the material of Isa 40—66 to particular historical periods. He interprets the eighth-century prophet as describing various aspects of the distant future, both in and out of historical sequence as he develops what are primarily theological concerns. Childs, *Isaiah*, 1-5, is prepared to accept "compositional growth" or intentional expansion on the part of a redactor.

274. See ibid., 382.

275. See Hays, "Who Has Believed Our Message?" 49-50. Hays is mistaken when he claims that Paul had no conception of "the Servant Songs" as a distinct collection or genre within the Isaianic prophetic material. He may not have thought of them as "servant songs," but there is no reason to doubt his ability to evoke the "prophetic narrative of the servant" from the text of Isaiah.

276. See especially Sandnes, *Paul: One of the Prophets*, 48-76; Ciampa, *Presence and Function of Scripture*, 124-25.

277. North, *Second Isaiah*, 1.

278. Hanson, "World of the Servant of the Lord," 14-15.

279. Ibid., 14.

had a plan to restore his people. In Isa 41—48, the prophet describes God's use of the Persian emperor Cyrus to initiate the restoration of Jerusalem and the rebuilding of the temple. In Isa 42:1ff, Israel, the servant of God is called to its mission of establishing justice on earth and bringing hope to the nations. But God's choice of Cyrus was greeted with complaint from Israel, who believed her rights had been disregarded by God—consequently, Israel is described as a blind and deaf servant (Isa 42:19, 20). Following Cyrus's liberation (Isa 44:24ff) and the rendering of Babylon's deities as powerless (Isa 44—47), Israel is confronted with her unbelief in relation to the divine prophecies made to her (Isa 48).[280] She is unable to function as "servant" Israel, not being able to discern the sovereignty of God nor his methods of salvation; another servant is required. According to Childs, Isa 48 functions as the transition from Cyrus to the servant, who speaks in Isa 48:16b. Following God's command to leave Babylon under Cyrus's edict (Isa 48:20), this "new" servant (perhaps the same one announced in Isa 42:1) speaks to the nations (Isa 49:1-4).

The identification of the servant in Isa 49:1-6 has proved to be a complex and hotly debated issue of interpretation. The issue centers on whether an individual or corporate entity is being described. The case for the servant of Isa 49:1-6 as a single, historical figure is compelling and, initially, requires differentiation of the "servant passages" from the "servant songs" present in Isa 40—55. Apart from the servant songs, the word servant occurs in Isa 41:8-13; 42:18-25; 43:1-13; 44:1-5, 21, 22 and 48:20, clearly referring to Israel as a people distinctively called and assigned a special mission for God. But Israel is called the blind servant in Isa 42:18-19 who sinned against the Lord (Isa 42:24). In Isa 43:10, Israel is described as the Lord's chosen servant, yet in Isa 43:22-24 she has burdened him with sins and wearied him with iniquities. In Isa 46:3-13 God addresses a stubborn-minded Israel far from righteousness, and in Isa 48:4, 8 Israel is portrayed as obstinate and a rebel from birth—clearly filling the role of a disloyal servant. In contrast, the servant in the "servant songs" is portrayed more positively than Israel, alerting us to the likelihood that the servant in the servant songs might not be exilic-Israel. Can this distinction between a failing servant (collective Israel) and a successful servant (an individual who functions as Israel should have) be sustained from an analysis of the text?[281]

The stark individualistic imagery of Isa 49:1-6, conveying the servant as a single figure, is recognized by most scholars, initially through the first

---

280. Childs, *Isaiah*, 372.
281. See Koole, *Isaiah III*, 13.

person singular voice (see also Isa 48:16).²⁸² The challenge is then how to interpret "Israel" in Isa 49:3. Some scholars solve the problem by taking "Israel" to be a later interpolation that should be omitted,²⁸³ but there is little manuscript support for this position. Others consider Israel as a predicated name perhaps of an individual: "You are my servant, *you* are *now* Israel."²⁸⁴ This reflects the idea that something new has happened—the title and office of "servant," which were borne by the corporate nation Israel up to this point, are now carried by a single figure.²⁸⁵ The idea that a single figure is the servant of Isa 49:1-6 can also be supported from an understanding of his mission. In Isa 49:5, the servant speaks for himself and describes his charge of "bringing Jacob and Israel back to YHWH." Since it is unlikely that Israel brings back Israel,²⁸⁶ the servant of Isa 49:3, 6 cannot be Israel in the closing years of the Babylonian exile. The servant's task is different from that of Cyrus who was charged with restoring Israel to the land of Judah because this servant will restore Israel to God—the locus of the servant's mission is thus in spiritual, rather than political, restoration.²⁸⁷ Additionally, the scope of the servant's mission is considerably extended by including other nations and being salvation to the ends of the earth: ἰδοὺ τέθεικά σε εἰς φῶς ἐθνῶν τοῦ εἶναί σε εἰς σωτηρίαν ἕως ἐσχάτου τῆς γῆς (Isa 49:6). Here the servant is described as salvation (εἶναί σε),²⁸⁸ not merely an agent communicating salvation, with a remit and mission that reaches beyond Israel. Furthermore, Isa 49:8 would seem to support the view that the single figure is an eschatological agent of salvation: "In an acceptable time I have listened to you, on a day of salvation I have helped you." According to Childs, this verse speaks of the eschatological moment of salvation in God's time—indeed, vv. 8-13 are shaped to enhance a coherent description of the servant's role in the new exodus of the chosen people.²⁸⁹ We conclude that the slave (δοῦλός) who apparently fails in v. 3 and the servant (παῖδά) in v.6 are the same historical figure, not a replacement for corporate Israel, but a faithful embodiment of the nation Israel which had not performed its chosen role.²⁹⁰

282. And, later, 53:2-12, where the servant remains anonymous and is identified with the pronoun "he."

283. Westermann, *Isaiah 40-66*, 209; Whybray, *Isaiah 40—66*, 136.

284. Goldingay, *Message of Isaiah 40—55*, 369.

285. Childs, *Isaiah*, 384.

286. Cf. North, *Second Isaiah*, 189.

287. Oswalt, *Isaiah*, 298, interprets vv. 8-13 as using physical imagery to refer to spiritual blindness, desolation, disinheritance and imprisonment.

288. So ibid., 294; Motyer, *Prophecy of Isaiah*, 388.

289. Childs, *Isaiah*, 387; Oswalt, *Isaiah*, 298.

290. Whybray, *Isaiah 40—66*, 138, advances Deutero-Isaiah; Goldingay, *Isaiah*,

The developing nature and mission of the servant can be noted in the inner movement of the prophetic narrative of Isa 40—55.[291] For example, the second servant song, Isa 49:1–6, is a continuation of the first, Isa 42:1–4,[292] with Isa 49:1–6 developing the servant's (spiritual) remit to include "gathering Jacob and Israel to God." The second song forges a link with the third and fourth through the growing theme of the servant's suffering, first introduced in Isa 49:7, and reaching a climax in chapter 53. In Isa 49:7, the servant's soul will be despised, he will be abhorred by the nations, and be a slave of rulers. The language parallels Isa 53:3: "he was dishonoured and not esteemed." Childs suggests that Isa 49:7 is a careful paraphrase of Isa 52:13ff, following the servant's humiliation and abuse, his ultimate recognition by kings and rulers, and his final vindication by God.[293] In Isa 50:6–7, the servant suffers scourges, blows, and spittings, yet is confident that he "will not be put to shame" (cf. Phil 1:20). The servant's confidence, recorded in Isa 50:7, seems to be in stark contrast to the despondency expressed in Isa 49:4. However, we are reminded that even in the throes of apparent failure, he trusts that God will assess his efforts fairly. Isa 49:6c, d thus sounds a note of perseverance which is reinforced in the following verse, "I will be gathered before the Lord, and my God shall become my strength."[294] These are not the words of a defeated servant, rather a persevering one. God's response to the servant's self-assessment is immediate; in Isa 49:6 he is told, "It is a great thing for you to be called my servant." The greatness of the servant is reflected in the scope of his extended mission—to set up the tribes of Jacob, turn back the dispersion of Israel, to be a light to the nations, and salvation to the end of the earth.

Following the description of the servant's suffering and recognition (v. 7), the fruits of his work (vv. 8–13) and the exhortation to rejoice at YHWH's solution (v. 13), Zion accuses YHWH of forsaking and forgetting her (v. 14). In the phrase Εἶπεν δὲ Σιων, δέ conveys the contrast between Zion's response and the servant's: "*But* Zion said, 'The Lord has forsaken me; the Lord has forgotten me.'" The servant's acceptance of suffering in

---

373, proposes a prophet bearing the name "Isaiah"; Koole, *Isaiah III*, 14–15, suggests that the "text is referring to the great saviour of the future."

291. Childs, *Isaiah*, 382.

292. For example, the similarities in language support this idea: "I have given you as a covenant to a race" (Isa 42:6): "I gave you as a covenant to nations" (Isa 49:8); "as a light to nations" (Isa 42:6): "I have made you a light of nations" (Isa 49:6).

293. Childs, *Isaiah*, 386; Motyer, *Prophecy of Isaiah*, 390, suggests that in Isa 49:7, Isa 50:4–9 and Isa 52:13—53:12c are already casting their shadow.

294. Koole, *Isaiah III*, 13, rightly notes that Isa 49:4b conveys the perseverance of the servant.

obedience to God is in contradistinction to Zion's complaint against God. Despite YHWH's attempts to assuage her feelings of having been abandoned (vv. 15–23), Zion makes her second complaint. If v. 14 expresses Zion's lack of confidence in YHWH's *willingness* to save her, v. 24 expresses her doubts about his *ability* to save them:[295] "will anyone take spoils from a mighty one?" The challenge to YHWH's power to deliver his people from captivity is followed by the refutation of Zion's complaints (vv. 25–26), and YHWH's defense against their accusation (Isa 50:1–3). The reason for Zion's predicament was their sins ("Look, for your sins you were sold, and for your acts of lawlessness I sent away your mother"—Isa 50:1). When Isa 50:1–3 is read in the narrative context of chapters 48 and 49, the rejection of God's offer of salvation to Zion is a recurring issue. Zion refused to participate in the divine deliverance from Babylon (Isa 48:20), having complained about God's choice of Cyrus (Isa 45:9–13). She doubted God's willingness and ability to save her despite God's choice and announcement of a successful, yet suffering, servant (Isa 49:14, 24). Now, in Isa 50:2, Zion's rejection of God's offer of salvation is conveyed by YHWH's questions: "Why was it that I came and no man was there? I called and there was none to answer?" (Isa 50:2). Thus, Zion's refusal to receive God's proffered salvation serves as the bridge to the third servant song (Isa 50:4–9) where the "tongue of instruction" (Isa 50:4) parallels the "mouth like a sharp dagger" (Isa 49:2). In contrast to Zion, the servant learns obedience: "he added to me an ear to hear. And the instruction of the Lord opens my ears, and I do not disobey nor contradict" (Isa 50:4–5). Isa 50:6 reveals what the servant learned, namely, to accept the experience of suffering and shame.[296]

As we noted in chapter 1, a major inhibitor to substantive investigation into Paul's use of the OT in Philippians has been the presupposition that the epistolary argument of the letter can be defined solely, or mainly, in terms of surface-level themes, motifs, and facticities. This has resulted in a perceived lack of congruence between epistolary argument and OT contexts. In response, our investigation has sought to establish a more expansive landscape for the test of congruence between Philippians and OT texts and contexts—one more amenable to the idea that κενὸν ἐκοπίασα might be an intertextual literary allusion to Isa 49:4. The preceding analysis of the inner narrative of Isa 40—55, along with our situational-rhetorical exegesis of Phil 1:27—3:21, allow us to construe data from both texts that might appertain to the salient detail of the person of the servant, the nature of his mission, the divine criteria for success, and the role and response of Israel.

295. So, Whybray, *Isaiah 40—66*, 143.
296. Childs, *Isaiah*, 394.

God's Approval of Servant Suffering

The phrase κενὸν ἐκοπίασα in Phil 2:16 is capable of connoting the despondency of the servant in Isa 49:4 as he contemplates his apparent failure in his mission. Yet, as we have seen, even an initial modification of the local interpretation of Phil 2:16 is capable of evoking the idea of God's approval. God's approval of the servant, despite his plight, is reiterated in the divine assessment: "It is a great thing for you to be called my servant" (Isa 49:6). God's approval of the servant is also implied in the giving of God's strength and help to the servant (Isa 42:6; 49:5, 8; 50:7, 9), and God's plan of salvation bracketing the servant's suffering experience (Isa 49:6, 8) in v. 7. Not only is the sense of God's approval present in the servant songs, but in Isa 53:4-6, God is understood as the active agent in the servant's suffering: "and the Lord gave him over to our sins" (Isa 53:6).[297] The idea of God's approval of servant suffering, present in the prophetic narrative of Isa 40—55, is consonant with the rhetorical situation of Philippians. We have argued that the divine approval of suffering, as a rhetorical constraint in Paul's argument, was brought to bear on the Philippians in Phil 1:29 and 2:9 as a corrective to doubts about the legitimacy of suffering for the sake of Christ. Yet, this rhetorical constraint can be used to correct variant opinions of how suffering can be construed as a sign of failure. Paul's allusion to Isa 49:4 immediately follows his exhortation to obedience in response to God's salvation event (Phil 2:12-16), and immediately precedes an exhortation to rejoice at the possibility of his death (Phil 2:17-18). Paul's situation is the same as the servant's—he is suffering, perhaps to the point of death, but this is not a sign of failure. For Paul, accepting suffering in the cause of Christ is a sign of salvation (Phil 1:19) and probably explains his eschatological emphasis in Phil 2:16—"in the day of Christ" he will be judged, by God. Thus, a literary allusion to Isa 49:4 that connotes God's approval of servant suffering is a fitting rhetorical response to a wrong-assessment of hardship and suffering. Is this an exigency in Philippi that needs correcting? To answer this question an investigation of the circumstances (namely, his imprisonment) that prompted Paul's rhetoric in Phil 2:16 is merited.

Paul's Prison Apologia

A majority of scholars understand Phil 1:12-26 as Paul's *prison apologia*—his response to a wrong-assessment of his imprisonment which he

---

297. The MT translation has, "smitten of God, and afflicted" (Isa 53:4) and "But the Lord has caused the iniquity of us all to fall on him" (Isa 53:6).

feels warrants a rebuttal. It is reasonable to identify those detractors in Phil 1:15-17 as having their gripe against Paul in terms of his imprisonment. This is suggested by his report, in Phil 1:14, of the counter reaction of his supporters—καὶ τοὺς πλείονας τῶν ἀδελφῶν ἐν κυρίῳ πεποιθότας τοῖς δεσμοῖς μου. The term πείθω can mean "to be so convinced that one puts confidence in something."[298] Taking τοῖς δεσμοῖς as an instrumental dative (*by* my chains), and ἐν κυρίῳ as the grounds for the confidence, would render a meaning such as: "most of the brethren, being convinced by my chains [that my imprisonment is a cause of advancing the gospel], have confidence in the Lord [in his methods of progressing the gospel in surprising ways such as my evangelizing my captors—the praetorian guard and/in Caesar's household]." It may be that because Paul is "in chains" he is considered a failure by his detractors, who then seek to cause him distress. Interpreting Philippians as functional communication (a fitting response to a rhetorical situation), Paul's determination[299] to address the wrong-assessment of his incarceration suggests that some Philippians shared the rhetorical exigency with those detractors at his place of imprisonment. Knowledge of Paul's imprisonment had probably reached the Philippians and they were naturally concerned not only about his well-being (Phil 4:10) but also about the adverse effects the imprisonment might have on his missionary activities (Phil 1:12; 4:15-18). If μᾶλλον in Phil 1:12 takes a meaning of "rather"[300] instead of "more,"[301] the sense is that the resultant progress of the gospel is not what some Philippians would have expected from the imprisonment of the evangelist:[302] "Now I want you to know, brothers, that my adversities [instead of damaging the faith, as some have thought] have rather turned out for the advance of the gospel."[303] In other words, his imprisonment has not turned out to be vain toiling.

Two aspects of the servant described in the prophetic narrative of Isa 40—55 can be discerned in Paul's report of his circumstances in Phil 1:20-26. Firstly, God appoints the servant to do an important and difficult task (Isa 42:1; 49:1-3; 50:3-4; 53:4-6). According to Paul, his supporters preach Christ out of love (most likely love of Paul) and presume that Paul is

---

298. BDAG, 792.

299. Paul begins the body of his epistle with the so-called disclosure formula; Γινώσκειν δὲ ὑμᾶς βούλομαι, ἀδελφοί, ὅτι ("Now I want you to know Brethren, that"). See Mullins, "Disclosure," 44-50.

300. 1 Cor 14:1, 5.

301. BDAG, 613.

302. This view held by Vincent, *Philippians*, 16; Collange, *Philippians*, 53; Plummer, *Philippians*, 19.

303. Silva, *Philippians*, 67.

appointed by God for the defense of the gospel (Phil 1:16).[304] In Phil 1:16, the word κεῖμαι (εἰδότες ὅτι εἰς ἀπολογίαν τοῦ εὐαγγελίου κεῖμαι) probably means appointed or destined to defend the gospel[305] and is instructive in how he views God's role in his predicament; the phrase reflects a divine appointment and approval of Paul's imprisonment (see also 1 Thess 3:3).[306] Secondly, God evaluates the servant's efforts which could easily be interpreted as defeat in human terms. Paul's confidence that God will deliver a positive verdict on his efforts can be compared with Isa 49:4:

Phil 1:19   ὅτι τοῦτο μοι ἀποβήσεται εἰς σωτηρίαν
            that this (my "live or die" predicament) will turn out for my salvation

Isa 49:4   διὰ τοῦτο ἡ κρίσις μου παρὰ κυρίῳ, καὶ ὁ πόνος μου ἐναντίον τοῦ θεοῦ μου.
            through this (toiling in vain) my judgment is with the Lord, and my toil before my God

The ὅτι τοῦτο of Phil 1:19 and διὰ τοῦτο of Isa 49:4 refer to apparent failure and act as a "bridge" to what turns out to be God's eventual judgment. God's positive assessment of the servant's suffering, connoted by Isa 49:4, at the conceptual level in Phil 1:19, is also connoted, by Isa 50:7 at the literary level in Phil 1:20:[307]

Phil 1:20   ἐν οὐδενὶ αἰσχυνθήσομαι
            I will not be put to shame in anything

Isa 50:7   ὅτι οὐ μὴ αἰσχυνθῶ
            I would not be put to shame[A]

A. Although the servant would be "shamed" (αἰσχύνης ἐμπτυσμάτων) by others (Isa 50:6), he would not be put to shame by God.

In the LXX, αἰσχύω denotes experience brought by the divine judgment of God,[308] rendering a sense of *enforced shame* as opposed to *being ashamed of having done something*. Since the NT usage of the word is primarily determined by the LXX, the meaning "put to shame"[309] fits the juridical context of Phil 1:18-20 where Paul contemplates the outcome of his trial. With

---

304. So Fee, *Philippians*, 120.

305. BDAG, 537.

306. αὐτοὶ γὰρ οἴδατε ὅτι εἰς τοῦτο κείμεθα (for you yourselves know that we have been *destined* for this [affliction]). See Pobee, *Persecution*, 108. Suffering is by divine appointment.

307. ἐν οὐδενὶ αἰσχυνθήσομαι is probably a literary allusion to Isa 50:7.

308. Bultmann, "αἰσχύω," 189-90.

309. BDAG, 30.

the reference to σωτηρία and his contemplation of a "death sentence," it is not unreasonable to see the passage as a reference to God's eschatological judgment on Paul.

We suggest that Paul uses the exigency of his imprisonment as one part of an argument to address a wrong attitude to suffering in Philippi. The rhetorical constraint he brings to bear on his implied audience is God's approval of servant suffering. As he composes Phil 1:12–26, his *prison apologia*, he activates elements from the prophetic narrative of Isa 40—55: the servant's divine appointment, his negative self-assessment, and his confidence in God's evaluation of his efforts. In Phil 2:16, Paul creates an allusion marker to Isa 49:4 by incorporating the phrase κενὸν ἐκοπίασα into his letter. His purpose in alluding to Isa 49:4 in Phil 2:16 is to address the perception that suffering is a sign of failure.

The Complaint Against God

We have argued that Paul's letter to the Philippians is a fitting response to a rhetorical situation in which there was division over God's role in his people's suffering. Those in Philippi who lacked an understanding of servant suffering in the divine plan of redemption had to be emphatically reminded by Paul, "For to you it has been graciously granted for Christ's sake, *not only* to believe in him, *but also* to suffer for his sake." Their misconstruing of the suffering paradigm was the basis of their complaint against God (Phil 2:14). We also argued that the recurring exigency of complaint against God can be actualized in the allusion to Isa 45:23 where it concerned God's chosen agent of salvation (Cyrus). Clearly, complaint is a recurring element throughout the movement of the servant narrative in Isa 40—55. The complaints of Israel-Zion emanate from a refusal to accept God's willingness and ability to save using his chosen methods and agents. But in the latter part of the prophetic narrative, the nature of the agent of salvation becomes increasingly associated with the suffering paradigm, as Cyrus (messiah) makes way for the slave/servant.[310] Ultimately, Israel's complaint was not grounded in the ethnic origin of the messiah (Jew or Persian), but the chosen means of salvation (the suffering slave is "Israel"). The complaints in Isa 49:14, 24 are tinged with a disdaining of the suffering paradigm proffered by God for salvation (Isa 49:6–7). Those who wrongly assessed Paul's suffering could have provoked complaints against him in Philippi as they did at his place of imprisonment. If so, by evoking the complaint element of Isa 49 in his estimate

---

310. Most scholars note that Cyrus is not mentioned after Isa 48.

of his ministry to the Philippians in Phil 2:16, he tacitly admonishes those who complain about their own, or others's, hardship and suffering.

The Servant's Role in Salvation

Salvation is clearly a constraint that Paul uses in his letter to the Philippians. In Phil 1:19 he uses it to focus his response to his imprisonment; in Phil 1:29 he argues that it is signaled by the Philippians's perseverance; in Phil 2:6–11 he links the identity of YHWH with his chosen means (the crucifixion of Jesus) of providing it; in Phil 2:12, he makes it the grounds for obedience; in Phil 3:21 he identifies Jesus as its agent. Such an emphasis on salvation supports the suggestion that Paul evokes the same constraint in Isa 49. The first time that "salvation" is linked with the servant is in Isa 49:6: "See, I have made you a light of nations, that you may be for salvation to the end of the earth." Isaiah and Philippians thus share the same interest in describing the locus of salvation in an historical, individual figure. The difference between the two texts is that in Isaiah, the figure is anonymous, while in Philippians, Paul identifies him as Jesus. In Isa 49:4, the phrase κενῶς ἐκοπίασα denotes the self-assessment of the slave who is designated servant[311] and, in Isa 49:6, commissioned to be for salvation. In Isa 49:8, the servant is depicted as receiving God's help on a day of salvation. By alluding to Isa 49:4, Paul was capable of connoting the notion of an individual servant whose experience is closely linked to God's plan of salvation. The servant's experience is developed in the prophetic narrative showing him to be someone who is a slave (Isa 49:3), despised, abhorred (Isa 49:7), obedient in accepting scourges, blows, and spittings (Isa 50:5–6). His appearance is without glory, having grown up as a child, with no form, glory, beauty, or honor (Isa 52:14—53:2). He is a man in calamity, who bears the sins of others (Isa 53:3–4), yet whose suffering heals others (Isa 53:5). He was humiliated and led to death (Isa 53:8), yet he will be exalted (Isa 52:13) and kings and rulers will pay homage to him (Isa 49:7). The similarities between the servant's experience and Paul's description of Jesus' experience in Phil 2:6–11 are unmistakable. Paul clearly draws an analogy between the redemptive activity of the Isaianic servant and the passion and death of Jesus Christ.[312] The intertextual patterns

---

311. Contra Hooker, *Jesus and the Servant*, 120. Although Jesus is referred to as δοῦλος, not παῖς, in Phil 2:8, the connection between him and the servant can be made intertextually through δοῦλος in Isa 49:3, 5.

312. Childs, *Isaiah*, 422–23. Like Childs, we resist the temptation to claim that the suffering servant theme of Isa 53 was only a messianic prophecy predicting the future passion of Jesus. Rather, Jesus follows in the pattern of the Isaianic servant. The connection between Jesus and the suffering servant is ontological, or discovered in the

formed by Paul's allusion to the servant narrative tacitly link God's salvation to abasement, suffering, and death.

Conclusions

In this section we investigated the probability that elements of the wider context of Isa 49:4 could be considered congruent with the epistolary argument of Philippians, as constructed, thus justifying κενὸν ἐκοπίασα in Phil 2:16 as a literary allusion. In our estimation, the general consensus that the phrase refers, merely, to the success or failure of Paul's ministry in particular or Christian life in general does not adequately explain Paul's rhetoric nor cohere particularly well with the broader interests of his letter. Instead, we have argued that the prophetic narrative of the servant of Isaiah and Philippians share the rhetorical exigencies of the wrong assessment of suffering, with consequent complaint. Furthermore, they share the rhetorical constraints of the acceptance of suffering as the paradigm of obedience and God's approval of servant suffering in a salvation context. In this way, Isa 40—55 can be considered as an intertext which is a variant of the rhetorical situation in Philippi. As with the other literary allusions, we suggest that Paul wrote Philippians with Isa 40—55 in mind. In Riffaterre's model, the intertext is a *hypogram* which serves as a "thematic complex" already set in Paul's mind when he wrote and capable of being recalled by his implied audience when they read. The intertexts are recognized by words embedded in a sentence (κενὸν ἐκοπίασα) and are components and variants of a matrix which is determinate for the text to be interpreted. Isa 40—55, especially the prophetic narrative of the servant, is a component and variant of a matrix which might be reduced to the following matrix sentence: "God approves of suffering and death for the sake of Christ." As such it is a worthy source of literary allusion for Paul as he writes a fitting response that addresses the exigencies in Philippians. Thus, we recognize the relatedness between Philippians and Deutero-Isaiah, not only in terms of shared recurring exigencies and constraints, but also in the way that Paul interprets the experience of the servant as analogous to Jesus and himself.

---

substance of their experience.

CHAPTER 5

Conclusions

THE PURPOSE OF THIS study has been to test the suggestion that a cluster of tacit references to the OT in Phil 2:10–16 functions as a group of literary allusions that are integral or foundational to Paul's epistolary argument. The test for the presence and functioning of literary allusions centers on establishing congruence between the contexts of Philippians and Scripture. Until now, scholarly efforts to discover congruence have rested on a heuristic approach focusing on surface-level themes and facticities recorded in Paul's text, with mixed results. There has been little or no engagement with available theoretical or methodological platforms to assist exegesis. In this investigation we have set forth a new exegetical framework for testing the claims and assumptions made about Scripture's presence in Philippians. Our framework emerged from six questions prompted by the cluster of embedded fragments of Scripture in Phil 2:10–16 and NT scholars's previous attempts to solve the puzzle of tacit references to the OT. We draw on insights from theories of intertextuality, allusion, and rhetorical situation and are unique in using the latter as a hermeneutical constraint in the interpretation of intertextual allusions to Scripture in Phil 2:10–16. We set out to establish if the relationship between the fragments of OT language and the text of Philippians could somehow be illuminated by initially considering the fragments as literary allusions all of which are variants of the epistle's deeper argument-complex. Consequently, the first stage of our investigation involved a construction of the epistolary argument or rhetorical situation. This was necessary in order to establish which elements in Paul's rhetoric could link together with elements of Scripture to form plausible intertextual patterns.

For each suggested literary allusion to Scripture we have shown that the rhetorical exigencies and constraints that constitute a rhetorical situation were consonant with those in Philippians, albeit with varying degrees of plausibility. In Phil 2:10–11, Paul's statement of the universal submission to Jesus shared what Ben-Porat called "world components" with Isa 45:23 such as salvation and identity, the divine name and God's approval, and disputation among God's people. The activation of these elements produces intertextual patterns which are capable of conveying divine identity and sovereignty bound to a suffering paradigm. This resulting intertextuality corroborates Isa 45:23 and its surrounding context as a variant on the rhetorical situation of Philippians. In Phil 2:12, Paul's exhortation to obedience shared "world components" with Ps 2 such as response to the coronation drama of the Messiah, eschatological destruction of those opposing the king, and allegiance. The activation of these elements forms intertextual patterns that can emphasize the call to allegiance in the face of opposition. This intertextual reading verifies Ps 2:11 and its surrounding context as a variant on the rhetorical situation. In Phil 2:15, Paul's assessment of the surrounding culture shared "world components" with Deut 32:5 such as warnings against disloyalty and exhortations to obedience in the face of death. The activation of these elements can evoke intertextual patterns that convey the danger of capitulation and the positive response to death of God's leaders. The intertextuality proposed supports Deut 32:5 and its surrounding context as a variant on the rhetorical situation. Also in Phil 2:15, Paul's assigning resurrection status to the living shares "world components" with Dan 12:3 such as perseverance rather than capitulation during times of persecution, the identity and actions of the apocalyptic agent of salvation, and the understanding of God's role in his people's suffering. The activating of these elements produces intertextual patterns able to carry the meaning that resurrection to eternal life is the eschatological hope of a suffering congregation. The intertextual patterns formed validate Dan 12:3 and its surrounding context as a variant of the rhetorical situation. In Phil 2:16, Paul's self-assessment of his ministry shares "world components" with Isa 49:4 such as God's assessment and approval of servant suffering, complaint against God, and the servant's role in salvation. By activating these elements, intertextual patterns can be created that communicate God's approval of suffering as a paradigm of obedience. The intertextuality produced corroborates Isa 49:4 and its surrounding context as a variant of the rhetorical situation.

We have argued that all of the intertexts selected by Paul in Phil 2:10–16 are variants of a determinate structural matrix formed in his mind as he contemplated composing Philippians. The structural matrix is his perception of the situation that he seeks to address through rhetoric, and it can be represented by a matrix sentence: "God approves of suffering and death for the sake of Christ." The matrix sentence is a grammatical expression of a singular truth, principle, or constraint that Paul intends to use to alter the situation in Philippi. It is the starting point from which he creates a "fitting response" to a controlling exigency in Philippi, namely, the disinclination to accept suffering and death as intrinsic to gospel citizenship. There are several conclusions that can be drawn from this investigation, and several implications for future investigation of Philippians and Paul's other letters.

METHODOLOGICAL

An obvious conclusion drawn from our study is that Scripture is present in Philippians. Using Ben-Porat's theory of literary allusion, we challenged the validity of distinguishing between quotation and allusion. In contrast to other scholars, we have differentiated the denoting function of the allusion marker from the connoting function of the allusion device. Such an approach can avoid the mistake of determining the presence of Scripture from the style of the allusion marker alone—something which Philippians has suffered from in New Testament scholarship. We have shown that the absence of a formal introductory formula cannot be taken to mean that Scripture is not present in Philippians, or indeed any letter. Subsequently, investigations of Paul's use of the OT that focus exclusively on formal citations omit relevant data that might affect the conclusions reached about his thought, theology, ethics, eschatology, and hermeneutics to name but a few.

A corollary of this particular contribution is our finding that the competence of an audience cannot be determined from the style of allusion marker alone. By appealing to theories of allusion advanced by Ben-Porat and Irwin, we were able to distinguish between the presence of a literary allusion and the successful activation of that allusion. Furthermore, by considering the notion of successful and unsuccessful activation, alongside the aesthetics of allusion, and the rhetorical concept of the implied author and audience, it has been possible for us to posit a competent audience in Philippi. Moreover, at least two reasons, not comprehensive, can be offered explaining why Paul alludes to Scripture. Firstly, he invites his (implied) audience to discover the intertextual patterns he produced at the time of composition. This is designed to encourage creativity in, and nurture intimacy with, his audience. Secondly, he desires to communicate difficult instructions to an audience he is intimately connected with. Scripture is the source of literary allusions because Paul faces recurring rhetorical situations and draws on the authoritative precursor of which he had become so familiar. Our findings may lead to a revision of certain assumptions concerning the presence of Scripture in Philippians and Paul's other letters, and working hypotheses about an audience's ability to detect tacit Scripture references. For instance, the results of our study run counter to Stanley's conclusions that the presence of Scripture in Paul's letters cannot be taken as a reliable indicator of the level of biblical literacy in his congregations.

Another conclusion drawn from this study is that the allusion marker and the allusion device are the products of intentional design. Given the congruence, not only of the individual intertexts with the rhetorical situation of Philippians, but also between intertexts, it is extremely unlikely that Paul unconsciously, or loosely, referenced these texts. Rather, he carefully and deliberately crafted tacitly-referenced material to support his argument. The intentionality behind the constructing of intertextual patterns is most obvious in the relationships between the intertexts. The exigencies and constraints portrayed in these texts, when transformed into rhetorical constraints in Philippians, are equivalent and variants of a single structure capable of conveying the notion of God's approval of, and participation in, a suffering and death paradigm.

A further outcome of our investigation is the recognition that Bitzer's theory of situational rhetoric can play an important role in the interpretation of Philippians. Throughout the detailed exegetical analysis of the rhetorical unit (Phil 1:27—3:21), we attempted to answer the question: In what way can this text be a fitting response to a specific situation? To answer these questions it was necessary to consider Paul's letter to the Philippians as "functional communication" that could achieve his desired goal of altering attitudes and behavior. Philippians is argumentation directed to an (implied) audience capable of modifying a situation. This approach offers a better explanation for the rhetorical forms, special vocabulary, grammar, and style of Paul's discourse. Accordingly, exigencies (death), constraints (resurrection), rhetorical exigencies (a wrong attitude to death), and rhetorical constraints (belief in resurrection) were analyzed as they contributed to the solution to a problem. In analyzing both the rhetorical situation in Philippians and the exigencies and constraints in the alluded-to texts, our study also sheds light on how Paul uses Scripture in Philippians.

This study is different from most others of this type since it does not adopt the method of a single scholar, but attempts a complex synthesis of historical, literary, and rhetorical methods to propose a new reading of Philippians. Methodologically, the use of rhetorical situation to limit intertextual patterning in the interpretation of literary allusions is a unique aspect of our study. This distinct approach of first seeking to determine the rhetorical situation before analyzing intertextual references has helped to control the "scope of activation" of the allusion device and prevented accidental associations and mapping intertextual allusions to specific theological themes.[1] We have proposed that Riffaterre's convention for reading poems can be used when reading Philippians. Furthermore, the convention for reading Philippians is derived from the convention for writing Philippians. Just as Riffaterre argued that a poet creates the poem by taking a word or sentence and expanding it into a text using a series of hypograms, we have argued that Paul, in a similar way, addresses a controlling exigency using rhetorical discourse that contains a cluster of Scripture intertexts. Just as the reader of the poem then recognizes and activates the hypograms, so Paul's audience recognizes and activates his allusions to Scripture. An important conclusion from our analysis is that Scripture is generative for Paul's thought and formative for his audience's. This finding distinguishes our contribution from those scholars, such as Reumann and Bormann, who propose that Paul's argumentation does not depend on the allusions to Scripture. Our conclusion is that Paul could have written Philippians without using literary allusions to Scripture, but when he embedded the allusions in his text, he did so *as, or after* activating those elements of the intertext that would lend significance to his intended meaning. This leads us to consider the hermeneutical conclusions that can be drawn from this study.

HERMENEUTICAL

In Philippians, Paul does not seem to set out to reinterpret Scripture in light of Christ, nor in light of gentile inclusion in the people of God. Rather, using literary allusion, he facilitates the simultaneous activation of two texts to create intertextual patterns connoting past exigencies and constraints that are congruent with his perception of his audience's situation. So, first and foremost, Paul interprets Scripture "situationally." He selects Scripture based on shared "world components" with his audience's predicament. In particular, recurring exigencies are addressed using worthy precursors such as Isaiah, Psalm 2, Deuteronomy, and Daniel.

---

1. Cf. Hays, *Echoes*, 86, who argues that the intertextual relationships in Paul's letters function ecclesiologically.

Another hermeneutical conclusion that can be drawn from our investigation is that Paul uses Scripture analogically. By this we mean that he draws analogies, not on the basis of correspondence in some respects between things otherwise dissimilar, but on the basis of inherent similarities. For example, he uses Scripture to identify Jesus as, or associate Jesus with, YHWH, the Messiah-King, the Isaianic servant, and Michael the eschatological agent of the Danielic end-of-times. Paul also associates himself with Moses, the Isaianic servant, and the *maskalim*. Sometimes these associations are made through deictic references surrounding the allusion marker: "At the name of Jesus," "I did not (toil in vain)." At other times the associations can be evoked from the exemplary characters in the intertext prominently displaying some disposition or performing some function.

We have also argued that Paul uses Scripture typologically. In contradistinction to Hays, who advances a typological reading for Paul not necessarily concerned with historical facts, we have proposed that Paul intentionally selects Scripture intertexts because they address the same rhetorical exigencies as Philippians. God's consistent activity in the world, particularly with his chosen people, results in recurring rhetorical situations which reflect historical correspondences. It is Paul's perception of historical correspondences between the experiences of the Israelites documented in texts of Scripture and the current circumstances of the Philippians that accounts for certain textual elements in Paul's letter associated with Israelite history such as "circumcision," "murmurings," "blameless children of God," and "crooked and perverse generation." In Philippians, Paul does not seem to use Scripture allegorically or as prefigurement of something future. Rather, the typology requires real correspondence between events, persons, and institutions and presumes continuity. The notion of continuity inherent in this kind of typology[2] is consistent with our next finding, namely that Paul uses Scripture metonymically.

A distinctive finding of our investigation is that Paul pre-selects elements of Scripture and interprets them metonymically to address a specific imperfection in the Philippian community. In metonymy, an object can be made known through its components—this is the essence of the allusion device in our model. Scripture's presence need only be signaled by Scripture's components. A single, one-word, literary allusion can evoke a canon (for example, σταυρός)! We have argued that Paul uses literary allusions to evoke whole texts (Psalm 2) and discrete portions of larger works (for example, the prophetic narrative of the servant in Isaiah and the song of Moses in Deuteronomy). Furthermore, in metonymical allusion, the existence of

---

2. See Baker, "Typology," 324–28.

the allusion marker is a product of the link between the texts—the reason for linking the texts is their explicit relatedness. For every literary allusion proposed in our investigation, the context of the marked text seems to be the very reason for Paul's selection of it in the first place. Such a conclusion seriously challenges those who claim that Paul is not interested in the context of the OT when he quotes or alludes. Thus, in contrast to Stanley who argued that Paul uses Scripture consciously but unreflectively, our investigation strongly supports the view that Paul is a sophisticated interpreter of Scripture who reflects on the wider context of the texts when alluding. Furthermore, future studies in Paul's use of the OT might consider whether situational, analogical, or metonymical interpretive categories be considered before assessing his hermeneutic as either christocentric, theocentric, or ecclesiocentric. For example, contrary to Hays, the findings of our study do not support the view that Paul interpreted Scripture as metaphorical echo, nor that his use of Scripture is concentrated in places where he addresses the relationship between Jews and Gentiles as prefiguring the formation of the church (ecclesiocentric hermeneutic).

As we have shown above, it is unlikely that Paul always uses Scripture in only one way. Although the results of our study do not support the widespread notion that Paul uses Scripture to foreshadow or prefigure the gospel, we do conclude that he uses Scripture christologically. For instance, in our analysis of Isa 45:23, 49:4, Ps 2:11, and Dan 12:3, Paul seems to evoke the topics of God as savior, the servant's role in salvation, enthronement of, allegiance and opposition to, the Messiah, and the role of the eschatological agent in resurrection. The activating of these topics is obviously christological because they connote the nature, character, and work of Jesus. Yet the topics are activated as part of an argument, not as a statement of theology or doctrine. Related to this point are conclusions drawn about how Paul expresses his theology and Christology in Philippians.

In our argument for Paul's authorship of Phil 2:6–11, we suggested that Paul's theology seems to be a situational theology. In other words, his theology finds expression through the rhetorical constraints he brings to bear on the rhetorical exigencies he wants to overcome through his rhetoric. Thus, his theology surfaces in "real" constraints such as incarnation, resurrection, and parousia that are directly related to the situation. In Philippians, Paul's theology and Christology seem to be always integrated with rhetorical constraints—incarnation, as a means of participating in death, is the antithesis of self-preservation which you should avoid; resurrection is your future reward for persevering; your suffering produces an eager waiting for Jesus' return. Even if Paul's theology were completely developed, perhaps we should not expect to find it expressed *in toto* in any of his letters which are "situational."

The question concerning Paul's use of Scripture in relation to early Jewish writings merits a more comprehensive treatment that this investigation can offer. But even though we limited our examination to just five specific literary allusions, conclusions can still be drawn concerning Paul's predecessors's and contemporaries's possible use of the technique. Although most of the early Jewish usage of the phrases alleged to be Pauline literary allusions differ from Paul's usage, there are two exceptions which might qualify as intertextual, literary allusions: Ps 2:11 in Dan 4:37 and Dan 12:3 in 1 En. 104.2.

Ps 2:11 LXX^{OG}   δουλεύσατε τῷ κυρίῳ ἐν <u>φόβῳ καὶ</u> ἀγαλλιᾶσθε αὐτῷ ἐν <u>τρόμῳ</u>
Be subject to the Lord with *fear, and* rejoice in him with *trembling*.

Dan 4:37 LXX^{OG}   ἀπὸ τοῦ νῦν αὐτῷ λατρεύσω, καὶ ἀπὸ τοῦ <u>φόβου</u> αὐτοῦ <u>τρόμος</u> εἴληφέ με
From now on I will serve him, and *trembling* has gripped me from *fear* of him

The story of Nebuchadnezzar's confession of allegiance following his enmity with God is congruent with the instruction to the kings who gathered against the Lord's anointed (Ps 2:1-2) and who were invited to subject themselves to him (Ps 2:10) "with fear and trembling" (Ps 2:11). Just as God established his anointed king on the throne ('Εγὼ δὲ <u>κατεστάθην βασιλεὺς</u> ὑπ' αὐτοῦ), so he also established Nebuchadnezzar on his throne (τῇ ἡμέρᾳ <u>ἐκάθισέ</u> με ἐπὶ τοῦ <u>θρόνου</u> μου), and gave him authority to rule (Ps 2:8; Dan 4:37b). Not only is the pattern of enthronement reproduced but Nebuchadnezzar is presented as the archetype of the enemy-king turned loyal—Ps 2 was addressed to the likes of him. In terms of activating broader elements of the evoked text, at the very least, an analogy can be drawn between Nebuchadnezzar and the kings who rage and then repent (Ps 2:1-2, 10; Dan 4:30a-37).

In 1 En. 104:2, those described as shining like lights, or stars, are those who have been put to shame through ill and affliction (1 En. 104:2), and whose names will be written before the Great One (1 En. 104:1). They will become companions of the host of heaven (1 En. 104:6), and will not have to hide on the great day of judgment (1 En. 104:5). Again, the literary allusion is capable of evoking elements consonant with Dan 12:3 in a manner similar to that proposed for Paul. The writers of Dan 4:37 and 1 En. 104:2 seem to have used Scripture analogically and metonymically. This strongly suggests an early Jewish use of literary allusion, interpreted in the same way we have argued for Paul. Although too much should not be claimed from two examples, the signs are that early Jewish literature may have influenced Paul's interpretation of literary allusions.

IMPLICATIONS

This study has been both deep and narrow. The depth of coverage of several theories spanning various disciplines has enabled a thorough analysis of specific verses in Philippians and Scripture. Yet, the investigation was relatively narrow, restricted to just 5 literary allusions reproduced in 7 consecutive verses in one chapter. Clearly, there are other possible literary allusions to Scripture that were beyond the scope of this study and which might be appropriate for further investigation: Gen 31:44 in Phil 1:8; Prov 3:9 or 11:30 or 13:2 or Amos 6:12 in Phil 1:11; Job 13:16 in Phil 1:19; Ps 69:28 or Exod 32:32 in Phil 4:3; Ezek 20:41 in Phil 4:18; Isa 56:7 in Phil 4:18. Furthermore, several literary allusions to the Apocrypha are possible: Tob 11:17 in Phil 2:27; Wis 1:6 in Phil 1:8; Tob 3:6 in Phil 1:23. A substantive treatment of literary allusion in Philippians might be an ongoing project.

Moreover, this investigation has not probed the depths of a "cascading" intertextuality that might be present in Philippians. One example is worth noting. In Dan 4:37, we noted a possible candidate to which "fear and trembling" was a literary allusion. Not only can analogies be drawn between Nebuchadnezzar and the repentant kings and rulers of Ps 2, but his great confession in Dan 4:37 contains a cluster of verbal similarities with Philippians that would seem to include him in the acknowledging community of Phil 2:10–11 and the worshipping community of Phil 3:3. Acknowledging (ἀνθομολογοῦμαι/ἐξομολογοῦμαι) the exalted status of the "Most High" (τῷ ὑψίστῳ) as lord of lords (κύριος τῶν κυρίων) who is sovereign over heaven and earth and seas (τὸν οὐρανὸν καὶ τὴν γῆν καὶ τὰς θαλάσσας) is exactly what Nebuchadnezzar, one time enemy of God, does in Dan 4:37. Additionally, his conversion involves the element of worship (λατρεύω) shared with those who worship in the spirit in Phil 3:3. This relationship between these texts might be worth exploring as it reveals a "cascading or circular" intertextuality—Phil 2:12 ... Ps 2:11 ... Dan 4:37 ... Phil 2:10–11. Additionally, the similarities between the enthronement Psalms (Ps 2 and Ps 110) with Isa 45:23 and Phil 2:10–11 are striking and might unveil intriguing intertextual relationships. Of course, while this study was confined to literary allusions identified through verbal similarities, there is no reason why other types of allusion cannot be considered. For example, an analysis of conceptual allusion would necessitate an examination of Phil 2:6–11 and Isa 52–53.

Another area of future study might be in extending the rhetorical unit to include the "beginning and ending" of Philippians. As Bitzer observed, rhetorical situations can be simple or complex. Although Phil 1:27—4:3 is generally accepted as the body of the letter, we are cautioned not to neglect the introduction and closing of Paul's letters, which also contain rhetorical exigencies, constraints, and literary allusions to Scripture and other Jewish texts. Moreover, in this study we argued that a persistent rhetorical situation plagued Paul and impacted the communities in Philippi and Galatia. An examination of inter-epistle rhetorical exigencies might improve and challenge our understanding of Paul's letters. Finally, we see no reason why a similar approach taken in this study cannot be considered for some of Paul's other letters, in the hope that it will enhance our knowledge of how Paul uses Scripture.

Bibliography

Abasciano, Brian J. "Diamonds in the Rough: A Reply to Christopher Stanley Concerning the Reader Competency of Paul's Original Audiences." *NovT* 49 (2007) 153–83.

———. *Paul's Use of the Old Testament in Romans 9.1–9: An Intertextual and Theological Exegesis.* London: T. & T. Clark, 2005.

Aichele, George, and Gary A. Phillips, "Introduction: Exegesis, Eisegesis, Intergesis." In *Intertextuality and The Bible*, edited by George Aichele and Gary A. Phillips, 7–18. Semeia 69/70. Atlanta: Scholars, 1995.

Albright, William F. "Some Remarks on the Song of Moses in Deuteronomy XXXII." *VT* 9 (1959) 339–46.

Alexander, Loveday. "Hellenistic Letter-Forms and the Structure of Philippians." *JSNT* 37 (1989) 87–101.

Allen, Graham. *Intertextuality.* London: Routledge, 2000.

Allen, Leslie C. "Isaiah LIII. 11 and its Echoes." *Vox Evangelica* (1962) 24–28.

Alter, Robert. *The Pleasures of Reading in an Ideological Age.* New York: Simon and Schuster, 1989.

Anderson, Robert A. *Daniel: Signs and Wonders.* ITC. Grand Rapids: Eerdmans, 1984.

Aquinas, Thomas. *Commentary on Saint Paul's First Letter to the Thessalonians and the Letter to the Philippians.* Translated by Fabian R. Larcher and Michael Duffy. New York: Magi, 1969.

Aune, David E. *The New Testament in its Literary Environment.* Philadelphia: Westminster, 1989.

Baker, David L. "Typology and the Christian Use of the Old Testament." In *The Right Doctrine from the Wrong Texts? Essays on the Use of the Old Testament in the New*, edited by G. K. Beale, 313–30. Grand Rapids: Baker, 1994.

Bakhtin, Mikhail M. *The Dialogic Imagination.* Edited by Michael Holquist. Translated by Caryl Emerson and Michael Holquist. Austin: University of Texas Press, 1981.

Bakken, Norman K. "The New Humanity: Christ and the Modern Age. A Study Centering in the Christ-Hymn: Philippians 2:6–11." *Int* 22 (1968) 71–82.

Baldwin, J. G. *Daniel.* TOTC. Leicester: InterVarsity, 1978.

Balz, Horst. "φοβέω." In *TDNT* 9.189–97, 205–19.

Barclay, John M. G. *Jews in the Mediterranean Diaspora: From Alexander to Trajan (323 BCE–117 CE).* Edinburgh: T. & T. Clark, 1996.

Barnes, A. *Notes on The Old Testament: The Book of The Prophet Daniel.* Vol. II. London: Blackie & Son, 1851.

Barnett, Paul. *The Second Epistle to the Corinthians*. Grand Rapids: Eerdmans, 1997.
Barr, James. "Paul and the LXX: A Note on Some Recent Work." *JTS* 45 (1994) 593–601.
Barth, Gerhard. *Der Brief an die Philipper*. ZBNT. Zurich: Theologischer Verlag, 1979.
Barth, Karl. *The Epistle to the Philippians*. Translated by James W. Leitch. London: SCM, 1962.
Barthes, Roland. "The Death of the Author." In *Image Music Text*. Translated by Stephen Heath, 142–48. London: Fontana, 1977.
———. "From Work to Text." In *Image Music Text*. Translated by Stephen Heath, 155–64. London: Fontana, 1977.
———. *S/Z*. Translated by Richard Miller. London: Jonathan Cape, 1975.
———. "Theory of the Text." In *Untying the Text: A Post-Structuralist Reader*, edited by Robert Young, 31–47. Boston: Routledge, 1981.
Barton, John. "Theological Ethics in Daniel." In *The Book of Daniel—Composition and Reception, Vol. II*, edited by John J. Collins and Peter W. Flint, 661–70. Leiden: Brill, 2001.
Basser, Herbert W. *Midrashic Interpretations of the Song of Moses*. New York: Peter Lang, 1984.
Bateman IV, Herbert W. "Were The Opponents At Philippi Necessarily Jewish." *BSac* 155 (1998) 39–61.
Bauckham, Richard. *God Crucified: Monotheism and Christology in the New Testament*. Carlisle: Paternoster, 1988.
Baur, W. *A Greek-English Lexicon of the New Testament and Other Early Christian Literature*. Revised and edited by F. W. Danker, et al. 3rd ed. BDAG. Chicago: University of Chicago Press, 2000.
Beale, G. K., ed. *The Right Doctrine from the Wrong Texts: Essays on the Use of the Old Testament in the New*. Grand Rapids: Baker, 1994.
———. *The Use of Daniel in Jewish Apocalyptic Literature and in the Revelation of St. John*. New York: University Press of America, 1984.
Beale, Timothy K. "Ideology and Intertextuality: Surplus of Meaning and Controlling the Means of Production." In *Reading Between Texts: Intertextuality and the Hebrew Bible*, edited by Danna N. Fewell, 27–39. Louisville: Westminster John Knox, 1992.
Beare, Frank W. *The Epistle To The Philippians*. BNTC. London: A & C Black, 1973.
Beker, J. Christiaan. "Echoes and Intertextuality: On The Role of Scripture In Paul's Theology." In *Paul and the Scriptures of Israel*, edited by Craig A. Evans and James A. Sanders, 64–69. JSNTSup 83. Sheffield: Sheffield Academic, 1993.
———. *Paul the Apostle: The Triumph of God in Life and Thought*. Edinburgh: T. & T. Clark, 1980.
Bell, Richard H. *Provoked to Jealousy: The Origin and Purpose of the Jealousy Motif in Roman 9–11*. Tübingen: J. C. B. Mohr, 1994.
Belleville, Linda. "Moses." In *DPL* 620–21.
Ben-Porat, Ziva. "The Poetics of Literary Allusion." *PTL: A Journal for Descriptive Poetics and Theory of Literature* 1 (1976) 105–28.
Bentzen, Aage. *King and Messiah*. London: Lutterworth, 1955.
Berger, Klaus. "Hellenistische Gattungen im Neuen Testament." In *ANRW* 2.25.2 (1984) 1031–432.
Bertram, Georg. "σκολιός." In *TDNT* 7.403–8.
———. "ὑψόω." In *TDNT* 8.602–20.

Betz, Hans D. *Galatians: A Commentary on Paul's Letter to the Churches in Galatia*. Hermeneia. Philadelphia: Fortress, 1979.
Bitzer, Loyd F. "Functional Communication: A Situational Perspective." In *Rhetoric in Transition: Studies in the Nature and Uses of Rhetoric*, edited by Eugene White, 21–38. London: Pennsylvania State University Press, 1980.
———. "The Rhetorical Situation." In *Rhetoric: A Tradition in Transition: In Honour of Donald C. Bryant*, edited by W. R. Fisher, 247–60. East Lansing: Michigan State University Press, 1974.
Black, David A. "Paul and Christian Unity: A Formal Analysis of Philippians 2:1–4." *JETS* 28 (1985) 299–308.
Blass, Friedrch, and Albert Debrunner. *A Greek Grammar of the New Testament and Other Early Christian Literature*. Translated and revised by Robert W. Funk. Chicago: University of Chicago Press, 1961.
Blevins, James L. "Introduction to Philippians." *RevExp* 77 (1980) 311–24.
Bloom, Harold. *A Map of Misreading*. New York: Oxford University Press, 1975.
Bloomquist, L. Gregory. *The Function of Suffering in Philippians*. JSNTSup 78. Sheffield: Sheffield Academic, 1993.
Bockmuehl, Markus. *The Epistle To The Philippians*. BNTC. London: A & C Black, 1997.
Booth, Wayne C. *The Rhetoric of Fiction*. London: Penguin, 1991.
Bormann, Lukas. "Triple Intertextuality in Philippians: Explorations of Theory and Practice." In *The Intertextuality of the Epistles*, edited by Thomas L. Brodie et al., 90–97. Sheffield: Sheffield University Press, 2006.
Bostock, Gerald. "Origen's Exegesis of the Kenosis Hymn (Philippians 2:5–11)." In *Origeniana Sexta*, edited by Gilles Dorival and Alain Le Boulleuc, 531–47. Leuven: Leuven University Press, 1995.
Botha, Jan. *Subject to Whose Authority? Multiple Readings of Romans 13*. Atlanta: Scholars, 1994.
Brand, Peg Zeglin, and Myles Brand. "Surface Interpretation: Reply to Leddy." *The Journal of Aesthetics and Art Criticism* 57 (1999) 463–65.
Brant, Jo-Ann A. "The Place of *Mimēsis* in Paul's Thought." *Studies in Religion/ Sciences Religieuses* 22 (1993) 285–300.
Bratcher, Robert G. *Old Testament Quotations in the New Testament*. New York: United Bible Societies, 1987.
Braumann, Georg. "μορφή." In *NIDNTT* 1.705–8.
Brawley, Robert L. "An Absent Complement and Intertextuality in John 19:28–29." *JBL* 112 (1993) 427–43.
Brenton, Lancelot C. L. *The Septuagint with Apocrypha: Greek and English*. London: Samuel Bagster & Sons, 1851: Reprinted. Peabody, MA: Hendrickson, 1986–2001.
Brett, Makk G. "Motives and Intentions in Genesis 1." *JTS* 42 (1991) 1–16.
Brewer, David I. *Techniques and Assumptions in Jewish Exegesis before 70 CE*. Tübingen: J. C. B. Mohr, 1992.
Brewer, Raymond R. "The Meaning of *Politeuesthe* in Philippians 1:27." *JBL* 73 (1954) 76–83.
Brinton, Alan. "Situation in the Theory of Rhetoric." *Philosophy and Rhetoric* 14 (1981) 234–48.
Brock, Sebastian P. "The Phenomenon of the Septuagint." *OTS* 17. Leiden: Brill, 1972.

Brown, Colin. "Ernst Lohmeyer's Kyrios Jesus." In *Where Christology Began: Essays on Philippians 2*, edited by Ralph P. Martin and Brian J. Dodd, 6–42. Louisville: Westminster John Knox, 1998.

———, ed. *The New International Dictionary of New Testament Theology Vol. 1*. Exeter: Paternoster, 1975.

Brown, Francis, S. R. Driver, and Charles A. Briggs. *A Hebrew and English Lexicon of the Old Testament: with an appendix containing the biblical Aramaic*. Oxford: Clarendon, 1906.

Bruce, F. F. "The Oldest Greek Version of Daniel." *OTS* 20. Leiden: Brill, 1977.

———. "Paul in Acts and Letters." In *DPL* 679–92.

———. "Paul's Use of the OT in Acts." In *Tradition and Interpretation in the New Testament: Essays in Honor of E. Earle Ellis*, edited by Gerald F. Hawthorne and Otto Betz, 71–79. Grand Rapids: Eerdmans, 1987.

———. *Philippians*. NIBC. Peabody, MA: Hendrickson, 1995.

Brueggemann, Walter. *Isaiah 40–66*. Louisville: Westminster John Knox, 1998.

———. *The Psalms and the Life of Faith*. Edited by P. D. Miller. Minneapolis: Fortress, 1995.

Büchsel, Hermann. "ἀντίκειμαι." In *TDNT* 3.654–56.

———. "ἐριθεία." In *TDNT* 2.660–61.

Bultmann, Rudolph. "αἰσχύω." In *TDNT* 1.189–91.

———. "καύχημα." In *TDNT* 3.645–54.

Bultmann, Rudolph, and Dieter Lührmann. "φαίνω." In *TDNT* 9.1–10.

Burton, Ernest De Witt. *Syntax of the Moods and Tenses in New Testament Greek*. Edinburgh: T. & T. Clark, 1894.

Caird, G. B. *The Apostolic Age*. London: Duckworth, 1955.

Callow, Kathleen. "Patterns of Thematic Development in 1 Corinthians 5:1–13." In *Linguistics and New Testament Interpretation: Essays on Discourse Analysis*, edited by David A. Black, et al., 194–206. Nashville: Broadman, 1992.

Calvin, John. *The Epistle of Paul The Apostle to the Galatians, Ephesians, Philippians and Colossians*. Edited by David W. Torrance and Thomas F. Torrance. Translated by Thomas H. L. Parker. Grand Rapids: Eerdmans, 1965.

Campbell, J. "Allusions and Illusions." *French Studies Bulletin* 53 (1994) 18–20.

Capes, David B. *Old Testament Yahweh Texts in Paul's Christology*. Tübingen: J. C. B. Mohr, 1992.

Carpzov, Johann G. *A Defence of the Hebrew Bible*. Translated by Moses Marcus. London: Bernard Lintot, 1729.

Castelli, Elizabeth A. *Imitating Paul: A Discourse of Power*. Louisville: Westminster John Knox, 1991.

Chandler, James K. "Romantic Allusiveness." *Critical Inquiry* 8 (1982) 461–87.

Chapple, Allan L. "Local Leadership in the Pauline Churches: Theological and Social Factors in its Development—A Study Based on 1 Thessalonians, 1 Corinthians and Philippians." PhD diss., Durham University, 1984.

Charles, R. H. *A Critical and Exegetical Commentary on the Book of Daniel*. Oxford: Clarendon, 1929.

Charlesworth, James H. *The Old Testament Pseudepigrapha, Vol. 1*. London: Doubleday, 1983.

Childs, Brevard S. *Isaiah*. Louisville: Westminster John Knox, 2001.

Chrysostom, John. "Homilies on Galatians, Ephesians, Philippians, Colossians, Thessalonians, Timothy, Titus and Philemon." In NPNF Vol. 13, edited by P. Schaff. Grand Rapids: Eerdmans, 1979.

Ciampa, Roy E. *The Presence and Function of Scripture in Galatians 1 and 2*. WUNT 2/102. Tübingen: J. C. B. Mohr, 1998.

Clark, Herbert H., and Richard J. Gerrig. "Quotations as Demonstrations." *Language* 66 (1990) 764–805.

Clarke, Andrew D. "'Be Imitators of Me': Paul's Model of Leadership." *TynBul* 49 (1998) 329–60.

Clarke, W. K. Lowther. *New Testament Problems*. London: SPCK, 1929.

Clayton, Jay, and Eric Rothstein. "Figures in the Corpus: Theories of Influence and Intertextuality." In *Influence and Intertextuality in Literary History*, edited by Jay Clayton and Eric Rothstein, 3–36. London: University of Wisconsin Press, 1991.

Clements, Ronald E. *The Book of Deuteronomy*. Peterborough: Epworth, 2001.

———. "Isaiah 45:20–25." *Int* 40 (1986) 392–97.

Coats, George W. *The Murmuring Motif in the Wilderness Traditions of the Old Testament: Rebellion in the Wilderness*. Nashville: Abingdon, 1968.

Cohen, Ted. *Jokes: Philosophical Thoughts On Joking Matters*. London: University of Chicago Press, 1999.

———. "Metaphor and the Cultivation of Intimacy." *Critical Inquiry* 5 (1978) 3–12.

Collange, Jean-François. *The Epistle Of Saint Paul To The Philippians*. Translated by A. W. Heathcote. London: Epworth, 1979.

Collins, John J. *Daniel*. Minneapolis: Fortress, 1993.

Combs, J. H. "Allusion Defined and Explained." *Poetics* 13 (1984) 475–88.

Consigny, Scott. "Rhetoric and its Situations." *Philosophy and Rhetoric* 7 (1974) 175–85.

Conte, Gian B. *The Rhetoric of Imitation: Genre and Poetic Memory in Virgil and Other Latin Poets*. New York: Cornell University Press, 1986.

Conzelmann, Hans. "φῶς." In *TDNT* 9.310–58.

Craddock, Fred. *Philippians*. Atlanta: John Knox, 1985.

Craigie, Peter C. *The Book of Deuteronomy*. NICOT. Grand Rapids: Eerdmans, 1976.

———. *Psalms 1–50*, WBC Vol. 19. Waco, TX: Word, 1983.

Cross, Frank M. "The History of the Biblical Text in Light of Discoveries in the Judean Desert." *HTR* 57 (1964) 281–99.

Croy, N. Clayton. "To Die Is Gain (Philippians 1:19–26): Does Paul Contemplate Suicide?" *JBL* 122 (2003) 517–31.

Culler, Jonathan. *The Pursuit of Signs: Semiotics, Literature, Deconstruction*. London: Routledge, 1981.

Dahood, Mitchell. *Psalms I 1—50*. AB 16. New York: Doubleday, 1965.

Dailey, Thomas F. "To Live or Die" Paul's Eschatological Dilemma in Philippians 1:19–26." *Int* 44 (1990) 18–28.

Dalton, William J. "The Integrity of Philippians." *Bib* 60 (1979) 97–102.

Davila, James R. "The Old Testament Pseudepigrapha as Background to the New Testament." *ExpTim* 117 (2005) 53–57.

Davis, Casey W. *Oral Biblical Criticism: The Influence of the Principles of Orality on the Literary Structure of Paul's Epistle to the Philippians*. Sheffield: Sheffield Academic, 1999.

Day, J. "DA'AT 'Humiliation' in Isaiah LIII 11 in the Light of Isaiah LIII 3 and Daniel XII 4, and the Oldest Known Interpretation of the Suffering Servant." *VT* 30 (1980) 97–103.

Deissmann, Adolf. *Bible Studies*. Translated by A. Grieve. Edinburgh: T. & T. Clark, 1901.

De Lacey, Douglas R. "'One Lord' in Pauline Christology." In *Christ the Lord: Studies in Christology*, edited by Harold H. Rowden, 191–203. Leicester: InterVarsity, 1982.

Delling, Gerhard. "τελειόω." In *TDNT* 8.49–87.

———. "ὑπερέχω." In *TDNT* 8.523–24.

De Silva, David A. "No Confidence in the Flesh: The Meaning and Function of Philippians 3:2–21." *TrinJ* 15 (1994) 27–54.

De Vogel, Cornelia J. "Reflexions on Philipp. I 23–24." *NovT* 19 (1977) 262–74.

De Vos, Craig S. *Church and Community Conflicts: The Relationships of the Thessalonian, Corinthian, and Philippian Churches with Their Wider Civic Communities*. SBL 168. Atlanta: Scholars, 1999.

Dibelius, Martin. *An die Thessalonicher I.II, an die Philipper*. HNT 11. Tübingen: Mohr, 1937.

Dines, Jeniffer M. *The Septuagint*. London: T. & T. Clark, 2004.

Docherty, Susan E. *The Use of the Old Testament in Hebrews: A Case Study in Early Jewish Biblical Interpretation*. WUNT 2/260. Tübingen: J.C.B. Mohr, 2009.

Dodd, C. H. *According to the Scriptures: The Sub-structure of New Testament Theology*. London: Nisbet & Co., 1953.

———. "The Old Testament in the New." In *The Right Doctrine from the Wrong Texts? Essays on the Use of the Old Testament in the New*, edited by G. K. Beale, 167–81. Grand Rapids: Baker, 1994.

Donfried, Karl P. "The setting of 2 Thessalonians." In *New Testament Theology: The Theology of the Shorter Pauline Letters*, edited by Karl P. Donfried and I. Howard Marshall, 83–89. Cambridge: Cambridge University Press, 1993.

Driver, G. R. "Linguistics and Textual Problems: Isaiah I–XXXIX." *JTS* 38 (1937) 36–50.

Driver, Samuel R. *A Critical and Exegetical Commentary on Deuteronomy*. Edinburgh: T. & T. Clark, 1902.

Duncan, G. S. "Letter to the Philippians." In *IDB* 3 787–91.

Dunn, James D. G. "Christ, Adam, and Preexistence." In *Where Christology Began: Essays on Philippians 2*, edited by Ralph P. Martin and Brian J. Dodd, 74–83. Louisville: Westminster John Knox, 1998.

———. *Christology In The Making—An Inquiry into the Origins of the Doctrine of the Incarnation*. London: SCM, 1980.

———. *Jews and Christians: the Parting of the Ways A.D. 70 to 135*. Tübingen: J. C. B. Mohr, 1992.

———. *Romans 1–8*. WBC Vol. 38a. Dallas, TX: Word, 1988.

———. *Romans 9–16*. WBC Vol. 38b. Dallas, TX: Word, 1988.

Durham, John I. *Exodus*. WBC Vol. 3. Waco, TX: Word, 1987.

Eaton, John H. *Kingship And The Psalms*. SBT 32. London: SCM, 1976.

Eckman, Barbara. "A Quantitative Metrical Analysis of the Philippian Hymn." *NTS* 26 (1980) 258–66.

Ehrhardt, A. A. T. "Jesus Christ and Alexander the Great." *JTS* (1945) 45–51.

Elam, H. R. "Intertextuality." In *The New Princeton Encyclopedia of Poetry and Poetics*, edited by Alex Preminger and T. V. F. Brogan. Princeton: Princeton University Press, 1993.

Ellis, E. Earle. *Paul's Use of the Old Testament*. Grand Rapids: Baker, 1957.

Eriksson, Anders. *Traditions as Rhetorical Proof: Pauline Argumentation in 1 Corinthians*. ConBNT 29. Stockholm: Almqvist & Wiksell, 1998.

Eriksson, Anders, et al. eds. *Rhetorical Argumentation in Biblical Texts: Essays from the Lund 2000 Conference*. Harrisburg, PA: Trinity International, 2002.

Evans, Craig A. "Listening for Echoes of Interpreted Scripture." In *Paul and the Scriptures of Israel*, edited by Craig A. Evans and James A. Sanders, 47-51. JSNTSup 83. Sheffield: Sheffield Academic, 1993.

Fee, Gordon D. *The First Epistle to the Corinthians*. NICNT. Grand Rapids: Eerdmans, 1987.

———. *Paul's Letter to the Philippians*. NICNT. Grand Rapids: Eerdmans, 1995.

———. "Philippians 2:5-11: Hymn or Exalted Pauline Prose?" *BBR* 2 (1992) 29-46.

Feinberg, Paul D. "The Kenosis and Christology: An Exegetical-Theological Analysis of Phil 2:6-11." *TrinJ* 1 (1980) 21-46.

Fields, B. L. "Paul as Model: The Rhetoric and Old Testament Background of Philippians 3:1-4:1." PhD diss., Marquette University, 1995.

Fitzmyer, Joseph A. "The Aramaic Background of Philippians 2:6-11." *CBQ* 50 (1988) 470-83.

———. "The Use of Explicit Old Testament Quotations in Qumran Literature and in the New Testament" *NTS* 7 (1960-61) 297-333.

Foerster, Werner. "ἁρπαγμός." In *TDNT* 1.472-74.

———. "Ἰησοῦς." In *TDNT* 3.284-93.

Fortna, Robert T. "Philippians: Paul's Most Egocentric Letter." In *The Conversation Continues: Studies in Paul & John In Honour of J. Louis Martyn*, edited by Robert T. Fortna and Beverly R. Gaventa, 220-34. Nashville: Abingdon, 1990.

Fowl, Stephen E. *Philippians*. Grand Rapids: Eerdmans, 2005.

———. *The Story of Christ in the Ethics of Paul: An Analysis of the Function of the Hymnic Material in the Pauline Corpus*. Sheffield: Sheffield Academic, 1990.

———. "The Use of Scripture in Philippians." SBL Conference Paper (2009). Online: http://www.westmont.edu/~fisk/paulandscripture/Fowl-Use%20of%20Scripture%20in%20Philippians.pdf.

France, R.T. *The Gospel According to Matthew*. Leicester: InterVarsity, 1985.

Friedman, S. S. "Weavings: Intertextuality and the (Re)Birth of the Author." In *Influence and Intertextuality in Literary History*, edited by Jay Clayton and Eric Rothstein, 146-80. London: University of Wisconsin Press, 1991.

Fung, Ronald Y. K. *The Epistle to the Galatians*. NICNT. Grand Rapids: Eerdmans, 1988.

Furness, J. M. "Behind the Philippian Hymn." *ExpTim* 79 (1967-68) 178-82.

Furnish, Victor. "The Place and Purpose of Philippians III." *NTS* 10 (1963-64) 80-88.

Gamble, Harry Y. *Books and Readers in the Early Church: A History of Early Christian Texts*. New Haven: Yale University Press, 1995.

Garland, David E. "The Composition And Unity Of Philippians: Some Neglected Literary Factors." *NovT* 27 (1985) 141-73.

Genette, Gérard. *Palimpsests: Literature in the Second Degree*. Translated by Channa Newman and Claude Doubinsky. Lincoln: University of Nebraska Press, 1997.

Geoffrion, Timothy C. *The Rhetorical Purpose and the Political and Military Character of Philippians: A Call to Stand Firm*. New York: Edwin Mellen, 1993.

Glasson, T. Francis. "Two Notes On The Philippians Hymn (II. 6–11)." *NTS* 21 (1974–75) 133–39.

Gloer, W. Hulitt. "Homologies and Hymns in the New Testament: Form, Content and Criteria for Identification." *PRS* 11 (1984) 115–32.

Gnilka, Joachim. *The Epistle to the Philippians (New Testament for Spiritual Reading)*. Edited by John L. McKenzie. Translated by R. A. Wilson. London: Sheed and Ward, 1971.

———. *Der Philipperbrief*. HTKNT 10.3. Freiburg: Herder, 1968.

Goldingay, John E. *Daniel*. WBC Vol. 30. Dallas, TX: Word, 1989.

———. *Isaiah*. NIBC. Peabody, MA: Hendrickson, 2001.

———. *The Message of Isaiah 40–55: A Literary-Theological Commentary*. London: T. & T. Clark, 2005.

Grant, Robert M. *A Historical Introduction to the New Testament*. London: Collins, 1963.

Gray, George B. *Forms of Hebrew Poetry: Considered with Special Reference to the Criticism and Interpretation of the Old Testament*. London: Hodder and Stoughton, 1915.

Grayston, Kenneth. "The Opponents in Philippians 3." *ExpTim* 97 (1986) 170–72.

Green, Joel B. *The Gospel of Luke*. NICNT. Grand Rapids: Eerdmans, 1997.

Greenlee, J. Harold. "Saint Paul—Perfect But Not Perfected Philippians 3.12." *Notes on Translation* 4 (1990) 53–55.

Grundmann, Walter. "ἰσχύω." In *TDNT* 3.397–402.

———. "στήκω." In *TDNT* 7.636–53.

Gudas, Fabian. "Connotation and Denotation." In *The New Princeton Encyclopedia of Poetry and Poetics*, edited by Alex Preminger and T.V.F. Brogan. Princeton: Princeton University Press, 1993.

Gundry, Robert H. "Style and Substance in 'The Myth of God Incarnate' according to Philippians 2:6–11." In *Crossing the Boundaries: Essays in Biblical Interpretation in Honour of Michael D. Goulder*, edited by Stanley E. Porter, et al., 271–93. Leiden: Brill, 1994.

Gundry Volf, Judy M. *Paul and Perseverance*. Tübingen: J. C. B. Mohr, 1990.

Hagner, Donald A. *Matthew 1–13*. WBC Vol. 33a. Dallas, TX: Word, 1993.

———. *Matthew 14–28*. WBC Vol. 33b. Dallas, TX: Word, 1995.

Hanhart, Karl. "Paul's Hope in the Face of Death." *JBL* 88 (1969) 445–57.

Hanson, Anthony T. *The Living Utterances of God: The New Testament Exegesis of the Old*. London: Darton, Longman & Todd, 1983.

———. *The New Testament Interpretation of Scripture*. London: SPCK, 1980.

———. *Studies in Paul's Technique and Theology*. London: SPCK, 1974.

Hanson, Paul D. "The World of the Servant of the Lord in Isaiah 40–55." In *Jesus and the Suffering Servant: Isaiah 53 and Christian Origins*, edited by William H. Bellinger Jr. and William R. Farmer, 9–22. Harrisburg, PA: Trinity International, 1998.

Harnack, Adolf von. "The Old Testament in the Pauline Letters and in the Pauline Churches." In *Understanding Paul's Ethics: Twentieth Century Approaches*, edited by Brian S. Rosner. Translated by George S. Rosner and Brian S. Rosner, 27–49. Grand Rapids: Eerdmans, 1995.

Harris, J. Rendel. *Testimonies*. Cambridge: Cambridge University Press, 1916–1920.

Harris, William V. *Ancient Literacy.* London: Harvard University Press, 1989.
Harrington, Daniel J. *Interpreting the New Testament: a Practical Guide.* Wilmington: Glazier, 1979.
Hartman, Louis F., and Alexander A. Di Lella. *The Book of Daniel: A New Translation with Introduction and Commentary.* AB 23. New York: Doubleday, 1977.
Hatina, Thomas R. "Intertextuality and Historical Criticism in New Testament Studies: Is There a Relationship?" *Biblical Interpretation* 7 (1999) 28–43.
Hauck, Friedrich. "κοπιάω." In *TDNT* 3.827–30.
———. "ὀκνηρός." In *TDNT* 5.166–67.
Hawthorne, Gerald F. *Philippians.* WBC Vol. 43. Waco, TX: Word, 1983.
Hawthorne, Gerald F, Ralph P. Martin, and Daniel G. Reid, eds. *DPL.* Downers Grove, IL: InterVarsity, 1993.
Hayes, J. H. "The Resurrection as Enthronement and the Earliest Church Christology." *Int* 22 (1968) 333–45.
Hays, Richard B. *Conversion of the Imagination. Paul as Interpreter of Israel's Scripture.* Grand Rapids: Eerdmans, 2005.
———. *Echoes of Scripture in the Letters of Paul.* New Haven, CT: Yale University Press, 1989.
———. "On The Rebound: A Response To Critiques Of *Echoes Of Scripture In The Letters Of Paul.*" In *Paul and the Scriptures of Israel,* edited by Craig A. Evans and James A. Sanders, 70–96. JSNTSup 83. Sheffield: Sheffield Academic, 1993.
———. "'Who has believed our message?' Paul's Reading of Isaiah." In *New Testament Writers and the Old Testament,* edited by John M. Court, 46–70. London: SPCK, 2002.
Hebel, Udo J. *Intertextuality, Allusion and Quotation: an International Bibliography of Critical Studies.* London: Greenwood, 1989.
———. "Towards a Descriptive Poetics of *Allusion.*" In *Intertextuality,* edited by Heinrich F. Plett, 135–64. Berlin: Walter de Gruyter, 1991.
Hellerman, Joseph H. *Reconstructing Honor in Roman Philippi.* SNTSMS 132. Cambridge: Cambridge University Press, 2005.
Hendricksen, William. *A Commentary on The Epistle to the Philippians.* GSC. London: Banner of Truth, 1962.
Hengel, Martin. *Between Jesus and Paul.* Translated by J. Bowden. London: SCM, 1983.
———. "The Song about Christ in Earliest Worship." In *Studies in Early Christology.* Edinburgh: T. & T. Clark, 1995.
Herklots, Hugh G. G. *The Epistle of St. Paul to the Philippians.* London: Lutterworth, 1946.
Hermerén, Göran. "Allusions and Intentions." In *Intention and Interpretation,* edited by Gary Iseminger, 203–20. Philadelphia: Temple University Press, 1992.
Hezser, Catherine. *Jewish Literacy in Roman Palestine.* Tübingen: J. C. B. Mohr, 2001.
Hickling, C. J. A. "Paul's Reading of Isaiah." In *Papers on Paul and Other New Testament Authors,* edited by Elizabeth A. Livingstone, 215–23. Sheffield: University of Sheffield, 1980.
Hofius, Otfried. *Der Christushymnus Philipper 2, 6–11: Untersuchungen zu Gestalt und Aussage eines urchristlichen Psalms.* WUNT 17. Tübingen: Mohr Siebeck, 1991.
Holladay, Carl R. "Paul's Opponents in Philippians 3." *ResQ* 12 (1969) 77–90.
Hollander, John. *The Figure of Echo: A Mode of Allusion in Milton and After.* Berkeley: University of California Press, 1981.

Holleman, Joost. *Resurrection and Parousia: A Traditio-Historical Study of Paul's Eschatology in 1 Corinthians 15*. NovTSup 84. Leiden: Brill, 1996.
Holloway, Paul A. *Consolation in Philippians: Philosophical Sources and Rhetorical Strategy*. Cambridge: Cambridge University Press, 2001.
Hooker, Morna D. *Jesus and the Servant: The Influence of the Servant Concept of Deutero-Isaiah in the New Testament*. London: SPCK, 1959.
———. "Philippians 2:6-11." In *Jesus und Paulus: Festschrift für W. G. Kümmel*, edited by E. Earle Ellis and Enrich Grässer, 151-64. Göttingen: Vandenhoeck & Ruprecht, 1978.
———. "Philippians: Phantom Opponents and the Real Source of Conflict." In *Fair Play Diversity and Conflicts in Early Christianity: Essays in Honour of Heikki Räisänen*, edited by Ismo Dunderberg, et al., 377-95 Leiden: Brill, 2002.
Hoover, Roy W. "The Harpagmos Enigma: A Philological Solution." *HTR* 64 (1971) 95-119.
Houlden, James L. *Paul's Letters from Prison*. SPC. London: SCM, 1977.
Howard, George. "Phil. 2:6-11 and the Human Christ." *CBQ* 40 (1978) 368-87.
Hübner, Hans. "Intertextualität—die Hermeneutische Strategie des Paulus." *TLZ* 116 (1991) 881-98.
———. *Vetus Testamentum in Novo Band 2 Corpus Paulinum*. Göttingen: Vandenhoeck & Ruprecht, 1997.
Hunsaker, David M. and Craig R. Smith. "The Nature of Issues: A Constructive Approach to Situational Rhetoric." *Western Speech Communication* 40 (1976) 144-56.
Hunter, Archibald M. *Paul and His Predecessors*. London: Nicholson & Watson, 1940.
Hurst, Lincoln D. "Christ, Adam, and Preexistence Revisited." In *Where Christology Began: Essays on Philippians 2*, edited by Ralph P. Martin and Brian J. Dodd, 84-95. Louisville: Westminster John Knox, 1998.
Irwin, William. "The Aesthetics of Allusion." *The Journal of Value Inquiry* 36 (2002) 521-32.
———. "Against Intertextuality." *Philosophy and Literature* 28 (2004) 227-42.
———. *Intentionalist Interpretation: a Philosophical Explanation and Defence*. Westport, CT: Greenwood, 1999.
———. "What Is an Allusion?" *The Journal of Aesthetics and Art Criticism* 59 (2001) 287-97.
Jauhiainen, Marko. *The Use of Zechariah in Revelation*. WUNT 2/199. Tübingen: J. C. B. Mohr, 2005.
Jeansonne, S. P. "The Old Greek Translation of Daniel 7-12." *CBQMS* 19 (1988) 96-99.
Jellicoe, Sidney. "Prolegomenon." In *Studies in the Septuagint: Origins, Recensions, and Interpretation*, edited by Sidney Jellicoe and Harry M. Orlinsky, xiii-liv. New York: KTAV, 1974.
———. *The Septuagint and Modern Study*. Oxford: Clarendon, 1968.
Jenny, Laurent. "The Strategy of Form." In *French Literary Theory Today: a Reader*, edited by Tzvetan Todorov. Translated by R. Carter, 34-63. Cambridge: Cambridge University Press, 1982.
Jeremias, Joachim. "Zur Gedankenführung in den paulinischen Briefen." In *Studia Paulina in honorem J. de Zwaan*, edited by J. W. Sevenster and W. C. van Unnic, 146-54. Haarlem: Bohn, 1953.
———. "'Ηλ(ε)ίας." In *TDNT* 2.928-41.

Jewett, Robert. "Conflicting Movements In The Early Church As Reflected In Philippians." *NovT* 12 (1970) 362-90.
Jobes, Karen H. "Jerusalem, Our Mother: Metalepsis and Intertextuality in Galatians 4:21-31." *WTJ* 55 (1993) 299-320.
Jobes, Karen H., and Moisés Silva. *Invitation to the Septuagint*. Grand Rapids: Baker, 2000.
Johnson, Aubrey R. *Sacral Kingship in Ancient Israel*. Cardiff: University of Wales Press, 1967.
Kahle, Paul. *The Cairo Geniza*. Oxford: Blackwell, 1959.
Kaiser Jr., Walter C. *The Uses of the Old Testament in the New*. Chicago: Moody, 1985.
Käsemann, Ernst. "A Critical Analysis of Philippians 2:5-11." Translated by A. F. Carse. *JTC* 5 (1968) 45-88.
Keefer, Donald. "Reports of the Death of the Author." *Philosophy and Literature* 19 (1995) 78-84.
Keesmaat, Sylvia C. *Paul and his Story:(Re)Interpreting the Exodus Tradition*. JSNTSup 181. Sheffield: Sheffield Academic Press, 1999.
Kennedy, George A. *New Testament Interpretation through Rhetorical Criticism*. Chapel Hill: University of California Press, 1984.
Kennedy, H. A. A. *The Epistle to the Philippians*. London: Hodder and Stoughton, 1903.
Kilpatrick, George D. "ΒΛΕΠΕΤΕ, Philippians 3:2." In *Memorium Paul Kahle*, edited by Matthew Black and Georg Fohrer, 146-48. Berlin: Töpelmann, 1968.
Kittel, Gerhard., ed. *Theological Dictionary of the New Testament*, Vols. 1-10. Translated by Geoffrey W. Bromiley. Grand Rapids: Eerdmans, 1964-1976.
Klijn, A. F. J. "Paul's Opponents in Philippians III." *NovT* 7 (1965) 278-84.
Kline, Meredith G. *The Structure of Biblical Authority*. Grand Rapids: Eerdmans, 1972.
Koch, Dietrich-Alex. *Die Schrift als Zeuge des Evangeliums: Untersuchungen zur Verwendung und zum Verständnis der Schrift bei Paulus*. BHT 69. Tübingen: J. C. B. Mohr, 1986.
Köster, Helmut. "The Purpose of the Polemic of a Pauline Fragment." *NTS* 8 (1961-62) 317-32.
———. "σπλάγχνον." In *TDNT* 7.548-59.
Koole, Jan L. *Isaiah III*. Translated by Anthony P. Runia. Leuven: Peeters, 1998.
Koperski, Veronica. *The Knowledge of Christ Jesus My Lord: The High Christology of Philippians 3:7-11*. Kampen: Kok Pharos, 1996.
Kramer, Werner. *Christ, Lord, Son of God*. Naperville, IL: A. R. Allenson, 1966.
Kraus, Hans-Joachim. *Theology of the Psalms*. Translated by K. Crim. Minneapolis: Augsburg, 1986.
Krentz, Edgar M. "Epideiktik and Hymnody: The New Testament and Its World." *BR* 40 (1995) 50-97.
———. "Military Language and Metaphors in Philippians." In *Origins and Method: Towards a New Understanding of Judaism and Christianity. Essays in Honour of John C. Hurd*, edited by Bradley H. McLean, 105-9. JSNTSup 86. Sheffield: Sheffield Academic, 1993.
Kreitzer, Larry J. "Resurrection." In *DPL* 805-12.
———. "'When He at Last is First' Philippians 2:9-11 and the Exaltation of the Lord." In *Where Christology Began: Essays on Philippians 2*, edited by Ralph P. Martin and Brian J. Dodd, 111-27. Louisville: Westminster John Knox, 1998.

Kristeva, Julia. *Desire in Language: a Semiotic Approach to Literature and Art*, edited by Leon S. Roudiez. Translated by Thomas Gora, Alice Jardine and Leon S. Roudiez. New York: Columbia University Press, 1980.

———. *La révolution du langage poétique*. Paris: Éditions Du Seuil, 1974.

———. "Revolution in Poetic Language." In *The Kristeva Reader*, edited by Toril Moi, Oxford: Blackwell, 1986.

———. "Word, Dialogue and Novel." In *The Kristeva Reader*, edited by Toril Moi, Oxford: Blackwell, 1986.

Kruse, Colin. *2 Corinthians*. Leicester: InterVarsity, 1987.

Kugel, James L. *The Idea of Biblical Poetry: Parallelism and its History*. New Haven, CT: Yale University Press, 1981.

———. "Some Thoughts on Future Research into Biblical Style." *JSOT* 28 (1984) 107–17.

Laato, Antti. *The Servant of YHWH and Cyrus: A Reinterpretation of the Exilic messianic Programme in Isaiah 40–55*. CBOTS 35. Stockholm: Almqvist & Wiksell, 1992.

Lack, R. F. "Intertextuality or influence: Kristeva, Bloom and the *Poésies* of Isidore Ducasse." In *Intertextuality: Theories and Practices*, edited by Michael Worton and Judith Still, 130–42. Manchester: Manchester University Press, 1990.

Lacocque, Andre. *The Book of Daniel*. Translated by David Pellauer. London: SPCK, 1979.

Landy, Francis. "Poetics and Parallelism: Some Comments on James Kugel's *The Idea of Biblical Poetry*." *JSOT* 28 (1984) 61–87.

Lane, William L. *The Gospel of Mark*. Grand Rapids: Eerdmans, 1974.

Lane-Mercier, Gillian. "Quotation as a Discursive Strategy." *Kodikas* 14 (1991) 199–214.

Lattke, Michael. *Hymnus: Materialen zu einer Geschichte der antiken Hymnologie*. NTOA. Göttingen: Vandenhoeck & Ruprecht, 1991.

Laub, Roger M. "The Poetics of Literary Allusion in the Early Fictions of William Makepeace Thackeray." PhD diss., University of Kansas, 1978.

Leddy, Michael. "Limits of Allusion." *British Journal of Aesthetics* 32 (1992) 110–22.

Leupold, Herbert C. *Exposition of Daniel*. Grand Rapids: Baker, 1969.

Lightfoot, J.B. *Saint Paul's Epistle To The Philippians*. CCL. Grand Rapids: Zondervan, 1961.

Lim, Timothy H. *Holy Scriptures in the Qumran Commentaries and Pauline Letters*. Oxford: Clarendon, 1997.

Lincoln, Andrew T. *Ephesians*. WBC Vol. 42. Dallas, TX: Word, 1998.

———. *Paradise Now and Not Yet*. SNTSMS 43. Cambridge: Cambridge University Press, 1981.

Lindars, Barnabas. *New Testament Apologetic*. London: SCM, 1961.

———. "The Place of the Old Testament in the Formation of New Testament Theology." *NTS* 23 (1976-7) 59–66.

Loh, I-Jin, and Eugene A. Nida. *A Translator's Handbook on Paul's Letter to the Philippians*. Stuttgart: UBS, 1977.

Lohmeyer, Ernst. *Kyrios Jesus: Eine Untersuchung zu Phil. 2,5–11*. SHAW.PH. Heidelberg: Carl Winter Universitätsverlag, 1928.

Longenecker, Richard N. *Biblical Exegesis in the Apostolic Period*. Grand Rapids: Eerdmans, 1983.

———. *Galatians*. WBC Vol. 41. Nashville: Thomas Nelson, 1990.

———. *New Wine Into Fresh Wineskins: Contextualizing the Early Christian Confessions.* Peabody, MA: Hendrickson, 1999.

———. "'Who is the Prophet Talking About?' Some Reflections on the New Testament's Use of the Old." *Themelios* 13 (1987) 4–8.

Losie, Lynn Allan. "A Note on the Interpretation of Phil 25," *ExpTim* 90 (1978) 52–53.

Louw, J. P., and Eugene A. Nida. *Greek-English Lexicon of the New Testament Based on Semantic Domains Volume 2.* New York: UBS, 1989.

Lowth, Robert. *De Sacra Poesi Hebraeorum Praelectiones Academicae Oxonii Habitae.* Oxford: Clarendon, 1753.

Lüdemann, Gerd. *Opposition to Paul in Jewish Christianity.* Translated by M. E. Boring. Minneapolis: Fortress, 1988.

Lucas, Ernest C. *Daniel.* AOTC 20. Leicester: InterVarsity, 2002.

Lust, Johan, et al. *A Greek-English Lexicon of the Septuagint Part I.* Stuttgart: Deutsche Bibelgesellschaft, 1992.

———. *A Greek-English Lexicon of the Septuagint Part II.* Stuttgart: Deutsche Bibelgesellschaft, 1996.

Mach, Michael. "Concepts of Jewish Monotheism During The Hellenistic Period." In *The Jewish Roots of Christological Monotheism: Papers from the St. Andrews Conference on the Historical Origins of the Worship of Jesus*, edited by Carey C. Newman, et al., 21–42. Leiden: Brill, 1999.

Mack, Burton L. *Rhetoric and the New Testament.* Minneapolis: Fortress, 1990.

Mackay, B. S. "Further Thoughts on Philippians." *NTS* 7 (1960–61) 161–70.

Macquarrie, John. "The Pre-existence of Jesus Christ." *ExpTim* 77 (1965–66) 199–202.

Mai, Hans-Peter. "Bypassing Intertextuality: Hermeneutics, Textual Practice, Hypertext." In *Intertextuality*, edited by Heinrich F. Plett, 30–59. Berlin: Walter de Gruyter, 1991.

Maile, John F. "Exaltation and Enthronement." In *DPL* 275–78.

Malherbe, Abraham J. *Social Aspects of Early Christianity.* London: Louisiana State University Press, 1977.

Marchal, Joseph. A. *Hierarchy, Unity, and Imitation: A Feminist Rhetorical Analysis of Power Dynamics in Paul's Letter to the Philippians.* Atlanta: SBL, 2006.

Marcos, Natalio F. *The Septuagint in Context.* Translated by Wilfred G. E. Watson. Leiden: Brill, 2000.

Marshall, I. Howard. *The Epistle to the Philippians.* EC. London: Epworth, 1992.

Marshall, John W. "Paul's Ethical Appeal in Philippians." In *Rhetoric and the New Testament: Essays from the 1992 Heidelberg Conference*, edited by Stanley E. Porter and Thomas H. Olbricht, 357–74. Sheffield: Sheffield Academic, 1993.

Martin, Ralph P. *2 Corinthians.* Dallas, TX: Word, 1986.

———. *Carmen Christi: Philippians 2:5–11 in Recent Interpretation and in the Setting of Early Christian Worship.* Grand Rapids: Eerdmans, 1983.

———. *Philippians.* NCBC. London: Marshall, Morgan & Scott, 1980.

———. *Philippians.* TNTC. Leicester: InterVarsity, 1987.

Mays, James L. *The Lord Reigns: A Theological Handbook to the Psalms.* Louisville: Westminster John Knox, 1994.

McKenzie, John, ed. *Epistle to the Philippians (New Testament for Spiritual Reading).* London: Sheed and Ward, 1971.

McLay, R. Timothy. "Daniel." In *NETS*, edited by Albert Pietersma and Benjamin G. Wright, 991–1022. Oxford: Oxford University Press, 2007.

———. *The OG and Th Versions of Daniel.* SBLSCS 43. Atlanta: Scholars, 1996.
———. *The Use of the Septuagint in New Testament Research.* Grand Rapids: Eerdmans, 2003.
McLean, Bradley H. *Citations and Allusions to Jewish Scripture in Early Christian and Jewish Writings Through 180 C.E.* New York: Edwin Mellen, 1992.
McLean, Paul D., and Bernard A. Taylor. "2 Reigns (Old Greek) 1–2." In *NETS*, edited by Albert Pietersma and Benjamin G. Wright, 271–96. Oxford: Oxford University Press, 2007.
Mearns, Chris. "The Identity of Paul's Opponents at Philippi." *NTS* 33 (1987) 194–204.
Meeks, Wayne A. *The First Urban Christians: The Social World of the Apostle Paul.* New Haven: Yale University Press, 1983.
Metzger, Bruce M. "A Reconsideration of Certain Arguments against the Pauline Authorship of the Pastoral Epistles." *ExpTim* 70 (1958) 91–94.
———. *A Textual Commentary on the Greek New Testament.* Stuttgart: United Bible Societies, 1975.
Meyer, Frederick B. *The Epistle To The Philippians.* London: The Religious Tract Society, 1906.
Meyer, Heinrich August Wilhelm. *Critical and Exegetical Handbook to the Epistles to the Philippians and Colossians.* Edinburgh: T. & T. Clark, 1875.
Michael, J. Hugh. *The Epistle To The Philippians.* MNTC. London: Hodder and Stoughton, 1928.
Michel, Otto. *Paulus und seine Bibel.* BFCT 2.18. Gütersloh: Bertelsmann, 1929.
———. "ὁμολογέω." In *TDNT* 5.199–220.
Michaelis, Wilhelm. "πάσχω." In *TDNT* 5.904–39.
Miller, Arthur B. "Rhetorical Exigence." *Philosophy and Rhetoric* 5 (1972) 111–18.
Miller, Ernest C. "Πολιτεύεσθε in Philippians 1:27: Some Philological and Thematic Observations." *JSNT* 15 (1982) 86–96.
Minear, Paul S. "Singing and Suffering in Philippi." In *The Conversation Continues: Studies in Paul & John in Honour of J. L. Martyn,* edited by Robert T. Fortuna and Beverly R. Gaventa, 202–19. Nashville: Abingdon, 1990.
Miner, Earl. "Allusion." In *The Princeton Encyclopedia of Poetry and Poetics.* Enlarged edition. Edited by Alex Preminger. London: MacMillan, 1975.
Minn, Herbert R. *The Servant Songs: Excerpts from Isaiah 42–53 Introduction Translation and Commentary.* Christchurch: Presbyterian Bookroom, 1966.
Moo, Douglas. *The Epistle to the Romans.* Grand Rapids: Eerdmans, 1996.
Moore, George Foot. *Judaism in the First Centuries of the Christian Era: The Age of the Tannaim, Vol. 1.* Cambridge: Harvard University Press, 1927.
Morgan, Robert. "Incarnation, Myth, and Theology: Ernst Käsemann's Interpretation of Philippians 2:5–11." In *Where Christology Began: Essays on Philippians 2,* edited by Ralph P. Martin and Brian J. Dodd, 43–73. Louisville: Westminster John Knox, 1998.
Morgan, Thaïs E. "Is There An Intertext In This Text? Literary And Interdisciplinary Approaches to Intertextuality." *American Journal of Semiotics* 3 (1985) 1–40.
Morris, Leon. *1 Corinthians.* TNTC. Grand Rapids: Eerdmans, 1985.
Motyer, J. Alec. *Isaiah.* Leicester: InterVarsity, 1999.
———. *The Message of Philippians.* BST. Leicester: InterVarsity, 1984.
———. *The Prophecy of Isaiah.* Leicester: InterVarsity, 1993.

Moule, C. F. D. "Further Reflexions on Philippians 2:5-11." In *Apostolic History and the Gospel*, edited by W. Ward Gasque and Ralph P. Martin, 264-76. Grand Rapids: Eerdmans, 1970.

———. *An Idiom Book of New Testament Greek*. Cambridge: Cambridge University Press, 1953.

Moule, H. C. G. *The Epistle Of Paul The Apostle To The Philippians*. CBSC. Cambridge: Cambridge University Press, 1903.

———. *Philippian Studies*. London: Hodder and Stoughton, 1897.

Moulton, James H. *A Grammar Of New Testament Greek, Vol. I, Prolegomena*. Edinburgh: T. & T. Clark, 1985.

Moulton, James H. and George Milligan. *The Vocabulary of the Greek Testament Illustrated from the Papyri and Other Non-Literary Sources*. London: Hodder and Stoughton, 1930.

Moyise, Steve. *Evoking Scripture: Seeing the Old Testament in the New*. London: T. & T. Clark, 2008.

———. "Intertextuality and Historical Approaches to the Use of Scripture in the New Testament." *Verbum et Ecclesia* 26 (2005) 447-58.

Moyise, Steve, and Maarten J. J. Menken, eds. *Deuteronomy in the New Testament*. London: T. & T. Clark International, 2007.

———. *Isaiah in the New Testament*. London: T. & T. Clark International, 2005.

———. *The Psalms in the New Testament*. London: T. & T. Clark International, 2004.

Müller, Jac J. *The Epistles Of Paul To The Philippians And To Philemon*. NICNT. Grand Rapids: Eerdmans, 1955.

Müller, Mogens. *The First Bible of the Church: a Plea for the Septuagint*. Sheffield: Sheffield Academic Press, 1996.

Mullins, Terence Y. "Disclosure. A Literary Form in the New Testament." *NovT* 7 (1964) 44-50.

Murphy-O'Connor, Jerome. "Christological Anthropology in Phil. II:6-11." *RB* 83 (1976) 25-50.

Nagata, Takeshi. *Philippians 2:5-11: A Case Study in the Contextual Shaping of Early Christology*. Ann Arbor: University Microfilms International, 1981.

Neumann, Peter H. "Das Eigene und das Fremde: Über die Wünschbarkeit einer Theorie des Zitierens." *Akzente* 27 (1980) 292-305.

Newman, Robert. "כוכב." In *NIDOTTE* 2.609-14.

Nickelsburg, George W. E. *A Commentary on the Book of 1 Enoch Chapters 1-36; 81-108*. Minneapolis: Fortress, 2001.

Niehaus, Jeffrey J. "Deuteronomy: Theology of." In *NIDOTTE* 4.537-44.

North, Christopher R. *The Second Isaiah: Introduction, Translation and Commentary to Chapters XL-LV*. Oxford: Clarendon, 1964.

Oakes, Peter. *Philippians: From People to Letter*. Cambridge: Cambridge University Press, 2007.

———. "Re-mapping the Universe: Paul and the Emperor in 1 Thessalonians and Philippians." *JSNT* 27 (2005) 301-22.

O'Brien, Peter T. *The Epistle to the Philippians*. NIGTC. Grand Rapids: Eerdmans, 1991.

O'Day, Gail R. "Jeremiah 9:22-23 and 1 Corinthians 1:26-31: A Study in Intertextuality." *JBL* 109 (1990) 259-67.

Oepke, Albrecht. "ἀπόλλυμι." In *TDNT* 1.394-97.

———. "κενοδοξία." In *TDNT* 3.659-62.

Ogden, Graham S. "Literary Allusions in Isaiah: Isaiah 44.28–45.13 Revisited." *BT* 54 (2003) 317–25.
Olbricht, Thomas H. "Classical Rhetorical Criticism and Historical Reconstruction: A Critique." In *The Rhetorical Interpretation of Scripture: Essays from the 1996 Malibu Conference*, edited by Stanley E. Porter and Dennis L. Stamps, 108–24. Sheffield: Sheffield Academic, 1999.
Olbricht, Thomas H., and Jerry L. Sumney. *Paul and Pathos*. Atlanta: SBL, 2001.
O'Neill, John C. "Goethe and Philippians 2:6." *ExpTim* 110 (1999) 359.
———. "Hoover on Harpagmos Reviewed, with a modest proposal concerning Philippians 2:6." *HTR* 81 (1988) 445–49.
Oppenheimer, Fred E. "Literary Allusion in the Novels of Theodor Fontane." PhD diss., University of Wisconsin, 1961.
Orr, Mary. *Intertextuality: Debates and Contexts*. Cambridge: Polity, 2003.
Osiek, Carolyn. *Philippians Philemon*. Nashville: Abingdon, 2000.
Oswalt, John N. *The Book of Isaiah: Chapters 40–66*. NICOT. Grand Rapids: Eerdmans, 1998.
Otto, Randal E. "'If Possible I May Attain the Resurrection from the Dead' (Phil. 3:11)." *CBQ* 57 (1995) 324–40.
Palmer, D. W. "'To Die is Gain' (Philippians i 21)." *NovT* 17 (1975) 203–18.
Park, M. Sydney. *Submission within the Godhead and the Church in the Epistle to the Philippians: An Exegetical and Theological Examination of the Concept of Submission in Philippians 2 and 3*. LNTS 361. London: T. & T. Clark, 2007.
Patton, John H. "Causation and Creativity in Rhetorical Situations: Distinctions and Implications." *The Quarterly Journal of Speech* 65 (1979) 36–55.
Perelman, Chaim, and Lucie Olbrechts-Tyteca. *The New Rhetoric: A Treatise on Argumentation*. Translated by John Wilkinson and Purcel Weaver. Notre Dame: University of Notre Dame Press, 1969.
Perri, Carmela. "On Alluding." *Poetics* 7 (1978) 289–307.
Perriman, Andrew C. "The Pattern of Christ's Sufferings: Colossians 1:24 and Philippians 3:10–11" *TynBul* 42 (1991) 62–79.
Peterlin, Davorin. *Paul's Letter To The Philippians In The Light Of Disunity In The Church*. New York: Brill, 1995.
Pfister, Manfred. "How Postmodern is Intertextuality?" In *Intertextuality*, edited by Heinrich F. Plett, 207–24. Berlin: Walter de Gruyter, 1991.
Pfitzner, Victor C. *Paul and the Aegon Motif: Traditional Imagery in the Pauline Literature*. Leiden: Brill, 1967.
Pietersma, Albert, and Benjamin G. Wright, eds. *NETS*. Oxford: Oxford University Press, 2007.
———. "Psalm 2." In *NETS*, edited by Albert Pietersma and Benjamin G. Wright, 548. Oxford: Oxford University Press, 2007.
———. "Septuagint Research: A Plea to Return to Basic Issues." *VT* 35 (1985) 296–311.
Pilhofer, Peter. *Philippi. Vol. 1: Die erste christliche Gemeinde Europas*. WUNT 87. Tübingen: J. C. B. Mohr, 1995.
Plato: *The Republic*. Translated by Desmond Lee. London: Penguin, 1974.
Plett, Bettina. *Die Kunst der Allusion: Formen literarischer Anspielungen in den Romanen Theodor Fontanes*. KS 23. Köeln: Böhlau, 1986.
Plett, Heinrich F. "Intertextualities." In *Intertextuality*, edited by Heinrich F. Plett. Berlin: Walter de Gruyter, 1991.

Plummer, Alfred. *A Commentary on St. Paul's Epistle to the Philippians*. London: Robert Scott, 1919.
Pobee, John S. *Persecution and Martyrdom in the Theology of Paul*. JSNTSup 6. Sheffield: Sheffield Academic, 1985.
Pogoloff, Stephen M. *Logos and Sophia The Rhetorical Situation of 1 Corinthians*. Atlanta: Scholars, 1992.
Pollard, T. E. "The Integrity of Philippians." *NTS* 13 (1966–67) 57–66.
Polycarp. "Epistle to the Philippians of Saint Polycarp Bishop of Smyrna and Holy Martyr." In *The Apostolic Fathers Vol. 1*. Translated by Kirsopp Lake, 280–81. LCL. London: Heinemann, 1912.
Portefaix, Lilian. *Sisters Rejoice: Paul's Letter To The Philippians And Luke-Acts As Received By First-Century Philippians Women*. CBNTS 20. Stockholm: Almqvist and Wiksell International, 1988.
Porter, Stanley E. "Further Comments on the Use of the Old Testament in the New Testament." In *The Intertextuality of the Epistles*, edited by Thomas L. Brodie, et al., 98–110. Sheffield: Phoenix, 2006.
———. "Paul and His Bible: His Education and Access to the Scriptures of Israel." In *As It Is Written: Studying Paul's Use of Scripture*, edited by Stanley E. Porter and Christopher D. Stanley, 97–124. Atlanta: SBL, 2008.
———. "Paul as Epistolographer *and* Rhetorician?" In *The Rhetorical Interpretation of Scripture: Essays from the 1996 Malibu Conference*, edited by Stanley E. Porter and Dennis L. Stamps, 222–48. Sheffield: Sheffield Academic, 1999.
———. "The Use of the Old Testament in the New Testament: A Brief Comment on Method and Terminology." In *Early Christian Interpretation of the Scriptures of Israel*, edited by Craig A. Evans and James A. Sanders, 79–96. JSNTSup 148. Sheffield: Sheffield Academic, 1997.
Porter, Stanley E. and Thomas H. Olbricht, eds. *The Rhetorical Analysis of Scripture: Essays from the 1995 London Conference*. Sheffield: Sheffield Academic, 1997.
———, eds. *Rhetoric and the New Testament: Essays from the 1992 Heidelberg Conference*. Sheffield: Sheffield Academic, 1993.
———, eds. *Rhetoric, Scripture and Theology: Essays from the 1994 Pretoria Conference*. Sheffield: Sheffield Academic, 1994.
Porter, Stanley E., and Dennis L. Stamps, eds. *Rhetorical Criticism and the Bible*. Sheffield: Sheffield Academic, 2002.
———, eds. *The Rhetorical Interpretation of Scripture: Essays from the 1996 Malibu Conference*. Sheffield: Sheffield Academic, 1999.
Poythress, Vern S. "'Hold Fast' Versus 'Hold Out' In Philippians 2:16." *WTJ* 63 (2002) 45–53.
Pucci, Joseph. *The Full-Knowing Reader: Allusion and the Power of the Reader in the Western Literary Tradition*. New Haven, CT: Yale University Press, 1998.
Rahlfs, Alfred, ed. *Psalmi cum Odis. Septuaginta: Vetus Testamentum Graecum Auctoritate Societatis Litterarum Gottingensis Vol. 10*. Göttingen: Vandenhoeck & Ruprecht, 1967.
———. *Verzeichnis der griechischen Handschriften des Alten Testaments*. Göttingen: Vandenhoeck and Ruprecht, 1914.
Räisänen, Heikki. *Paul and the Law*. Philadelphia: Fortress, 1986.
Reed, Jeffrey T. *A Discourse Analysis of Philippians*. Sheffield: Sheffield Academic, 1997.
Rengstorf, Karl. "δοῦλος." In *TDNT* 2.261–80.

———. "γογγύζω." In *TDNT* 1.728–37.
Reumann, John. *Philippians: A New Translation with Introduction and Commentary*. The Anchor Yale Bible Series 33B. New Haven, CT: Yale University Press, 2008.
Riesenfeld, Harald. "ὑπέρ." In *TDNT* 8.507–16.
Riffaterre, Michael. "Compulsory Reader Response: The Intertextual Drive." In *Intertextuality: Theories and Practices*, edited by Michael Worton and Judith Still, 56–78. Manchester: Manchester University Press, 1990.
———. "Interpretation and Undecidability." *New Literary History* 12 (1981) 227–42.
———. "Interview." *Diacritics* 11 (1981) 12–16.
———. *Semiotics of Poetry*. London: Methuen, 1980.
———. "Sémiotique intertextuelle: L'Interprétant" in *Rhétoriques, sémiotiques: Revue d'esthétique 1–2*, 128–50. Paris: Union Générale d'Editions, 1979.
———. "La Trace de l'intertexte." *La Pensée* 215 (1980) 4–18.
Robinson, Donald W. B. "We are the Circumcision." *AusBR* 15 (1967) 28–35.
Robuck, Thomas D. "The Christ-Hymn in Philippians: A Rhetorical Analysis of its Function in the Letter." PhD diss., Southwestern Baptist Theological Seminary, 1987.
Rosner, Brian S. *Paul, Scripture, & Ethics: A Study of Corinthians 5–7*. Grand Rapids: Baker, 1994.
Ross, Stephanie. "Art and Allusion." *The Journal of Aesthetics and Art Criticism* 40 (1981) 59–70.
Sacchi, Paolo. *Jewish Apocalyptic and its History*. Sheffield: Sheffield Academic, 1990.
Sanders, E. P. *Paul, the Law, and the Jewish People*. Minneapolis: Fortress, 1983.
Sanders, Paul. *The Provenance of Deuteronomy 32*. Leiden: Brill, 1996.
Sandmel, Samuel. "Parallelomania." *JBL* 81 (1962) 1–13.
Sandnes, Karl O. *Paul: One of the Prophets*. Tübingen: J. C. B. Mohr, 1991.
Schaar, Claes. *The Full Voic'd Quire Below: Vertical Context Systems in Paradise Lost*. Lund: CWK Gleerup, 1982.
———. "Vertical Context Systems." In *Style and Text: Studies Presented to Nils E. Enkvist*, edited by Håkan Ringbom, 146–57. Stockholm: Språkförlaget, 1975.
Schmid, Wolf. "Sinnpotentiale der diegetischen Allusion: Aleksandr Puškins Posthalternovelle und ihre Prätexte" In *Dialog der Texte*, edited by Wolf Schmid and Wolf-Dieter Stempel, 141–87. Vienna: Wiener Slawistischer Almanach, 1983.
Schmithals, Walter. *Paul and the Gnostics*. Translated by J. E. Steely. New York: Abingdon, 1972.
Schneider, Johannes. "μετασχηματίζω." In *TDNT* 7.954–58.
Schoon-Janssen, Johannes. *Umstrittene "Apologien" in den Paulusbriefen: Studien zur rhetorischen Situation des 1. Thessalonicherbriefes, des Galaterbriefes und des Philipperbriefes*. GTA 45. Göttingen: Vandenhoeck & Ruprecht, 1991.
Schrenk, Gottlob. "βίβλος." In *TDNT* 1.615–20.
———. "διαλογισμός." In *TDNT* 2.93–98.
Schüssler-Fiorenza, Elizabeth. *The Book of Revelation: Justice and Judgment*. Philadelphia: Fortress, 1985.
———. "Rhetorical Situation and Historical Reconstruction in 1 Corinthians." *NTS* 33 (1987) 386–403.
Schweizer, Eduard. *Lordship and Discipleship*. London: SCM, 1960.
———. "πνεῦμα." In *TDNT* 6.389–455.
Selwyn, Edward G. *The First Epistle of St. Peter*. London: Macmillan, 1961.

Silva, Moisés. "Discourse Analysis and Philippians." In *Discourse Analysis and Other Topics in Biblical Greek*, edited by Stanley E. Porter and D. A. Carson, 102-6. Sheffield: Sheffield Academic, 1995.

———. "Old Testament in Paul." In *DPL* 630-42.

———. *Philippians*. BECNT. Grand Rapids: Baker, 2005.

———. "Philippians." In *Commentary on the New Testament Use of the Old Testament*, edited by G. K. Beale and D. A. Carson. Grand Rapids: Baker, 2007.

Smith, D. Moody. "The Pauline Literature." In *It is Written: Scripture Citing Scripture. Essays In Honour of Barnabas Lindars*, edited by D. A. Carson and Hugh G. M. Williamson, 265-91. Cambridge: Cambridge University Press, 1988.

Smith, Gary. "לִין." In *NIDOTTE* 2.780-82.

Snodgrass, Klyne. "The Use of the Old Testament in the New." In *New Testament Criticism & Interpretation*, edited by David A. Black and David S. Dockery, 409-34. Grand Rapids: Zondervan, 1991.

Sommer, Benjamin D. *A Prophet Reads Scripture: Allusion In Isaiah 40-66*. Stanford: Stanford University Press, 1998.

Stagg, Frank. "The Mind In Christ Jesus: Philippians 1:27-2:18." *RevExp* 77 (1980) 337-47.

Stählin, Gustav. "ἴσος." In *TDNT* 3.343-55.

Stamps, Dennis L. "Rethinking The Rhetorical Situation: The Entextualization of the Situation in The New Testament Epistles." In *Rhetoric and the New Testament: Essays from the 1992 Heidelberg Conference*, edited by Stanley E. Porter and Thomas H. Olbricht, 193-210. Sheffield: Sheffield Academic, 1993.

———. "The Theological Rhetoric of the Pauline Epistles: Prolegomenon." In *The Rhetorical Interpretation of Scripture: Essays from the 1996 Malibu Conference*, edited by Stanley E. Porter and Dennis L. Stamps, 249-59. Sheffield: Sheffield Academic, 1999.

———. "The Use of the Old Testament in the New Testament as a Rhetorical Device: A Methodological Proposal." In *Hearing the Old Testament in the New Testament*, edited by Stanley E. Porter, 9-37. Grand Rapids: Eerdmans, 2006.

Stanley, Christopher D. *Arguing With Scripture: the Rhetoric of Quotations in the Letters of Paul*. London: T. & T. Clark, 2004.

———. *Paul and the Language of Scripture: Citation Technique in the Pauline Epistles and Contemporary Literature*. SNTSMS 69. Cambridge: Cambridge University Press, 1992.

———. "Paul's 'Use' of Scripture: Why the Audience Matters." In *As It Is Written: Studying Paul's Use of Scripture*, edited by Stanley E. Porter and Christopher D. Stanley, 125-55. Atlanta: SBL, 2008.

———. "'Pearls Before Swine': Did Paul's Audiences Understand His Biblical Quotations?" *NovT* 41 (1999) 124-44.

Stanley, David M. "Become Imitators of Me: The Pauline Conception of Apostolic Tradition." *Bib* 40 (1959) 859-77.

———. *Christ's Resurrection in Pauline Soteriology*. Rome: Pontifical Biblical Institute, 1961.

Stauffer, Ethelbert. *New Testament Theology*. Translated by J. Marsh. London: SCM, 1955.

———. "ἀγών." In *TDNT* 1.134-40.

———. "ἀθλέω." In *TDNT* 1.167-68.

Stenschke, Christoph W. *Luke's Portrait of Gentiles Prior to Their Coming to Faith*. Tübingen: J. C. B. Mohr, 1999.

Sternberg, Meir. "Proteus in Quotation-Land: Mimesis and the Forms of Reported Discourse." *Poetics Today* 3 (1982) 107-56.

Stowers, Stanley K. "Friends and Enemies in the Politics of Heaven: Reading Theology in Philippians." In *Pauline Theology Volume 1: Thessalonians, Philippians, Galatians, Philemon*, edited by Jouette M. Bassler, 105-21. Minneapolis: Fortress, 1994.

Stierle, Karlheinz. "Werk und Intertextualität." In *Das Gespraech*, edited by Karlheinz Stierle and Rainer Warning, 139-50. München: Fink, 1984.

Strimple, Robert B. "Philippians 2:5-11 in Recent Studies: Some Exegetical Conclusions." *WTJ* 41 (1979) 247-68.

Suleiman, Susan R. "Introduction: Varieties of Audience-Oriented Criticism." In *The Reader In The Text*, edited by Susan R. Suleiman and Inge Crosman, 3-45. Princeton: Princeton University Press, 1980.

Sundberg, Albert C. *The Old Testament of the Early Church*. Cambridge: Harvard University Press, 1964.

Swete, Henry B. *An Introduction to the Old Testament in Greek*. Cambridge: Cambridge University Press, 1914.

Swift, Robert C. "The Theme and Structure of Philippians." *BSac* 141 (1984) 234-54.

Talbert, Charles H. "The Problem of Pre-existence in Philippians 2:6-11," *JBL* 86 (1967) 141-53.

Taylor, Vincent. *The Person of Christ*. London: Macmillan, 1958.

Tellbe, Mikael. *Paul between Synagogue and State: Christians, Jews, and Civic Authorities in 1 Thessalonians, Romans, and Philippians*. ConBNT 34. Stockholm: Almqvist & Wiksell, 2001.

Tetzeli von Rosador, Elizabeth. "Kunst im Werke George Eliots: Anspielungen, Figuren, Thematik." PhD diss., München, 1973.

Theissen, Gerd. *The Social Setting of Pauline Christianity: Essays on Corinth*, edited and translated by John H. Schütz. Philadelphia: Fortress, 1982.

Thielman, Frank. *Paul & the Law: A Contextual Approach*. Downer's Grove, IL: InterVarsity, 1994.

Thomas, D. Winton, ed. *Documents from Old Testament Times*. London: T. Nelson, 1958.

Thomson, J. A. *Deuteronomy*. TOTC. Leicester: InterVarsity, 1974.

Thomson, Michael B. *Clothed with Christ*. JSNTSup 59. Sheffield: Sheffield Academic, 1991.

Thurén, Lauri. *The Rhetorical Strategy of 1 Peter: With Special Regard to Ambiguous Expressions*. Åbo: Åbo Academy, 1990.

Tov, Emanuel. *The Greek and Hebrew Bible: Collected Essays on the Septuagint*. Leiden: Brill, 1999.

———. *The Text-Critical Use of the Septuagint in Biblical Research*. Jerusalem: Simor, 1981.

Tyson, Joseph B. "Paul's Opponents at Philippi." *Perspectives in Religious Studies* 3 (1976) 82-95.

Van Dam, Cornelis. "אבד." In *NIDOTTE* 1.223-25.

VanGemeren, William A, ed. *NIDOTTE*, Vols. 1-5. Carlisle: Paternoster, 1997.

Van Pelt, Miles V., and Walter C. Kaiser Jr. "ירא." In *NIDOTTE* 2.527-33.

Van Spanje, T. E. *Inconsistency in Paul? A Critique of the Work of Heikki Räisänen.* Tübingen: J. C. B. Mohr, 1999.
Van Wolde, Ellen. "Trendy Intertextuality?" In *Intertextuality in Biblical Writings: Essays in honour of Bas van Iersel,* edited by Sipke Draisma, 43–49. Kampen: Kok, 1989.
Vatz, Richard E. "The Myth of the Rhetorical Situation." *Philosophy and Rhetoric* 6 (1973) 154–61.
Vincent, Marvin R. *Epistles To The Philippians And To Philemon.* ICC. Edinburgh: T. & T. Clark, 1897.
Voelz, James W. "Multiple Signs and Double Texts: Elements of Intertextuality." In *Intertextuality in Biblical Writings: Essays in Honour of Bas van Iersal,* edited by Sipke Draisma, 27–34. Kampen: Kok, 1989.
Vos, Geerhardus. *The Pauline Eschatology.* Grand Rapids: Eerdmans, 1961.
Wagner, J. Ross. *Heralds of the Good News: Isaiah and Paul "In Concert" in the Letter to the Romans.* Leiden: Brill, 2002.
Wakefield, Andrew H. *Where to Live: The Hermeneutical Significance of Paul's Citations from Scripture in Galatians 3:1–14.* SBL 14. Atlanta: SBL, 2003.
Walter, Nicholas. "Die Philipper und das Leiden. Aus den Anfängen einer heidenchristlichen Gemeinde." In *Die Kirche des Anfangs: Festschrift für Heinz Schürmann,* edited by Rudolph Schnackenburg, J. Ernst and J. Wanke, 417–34. Leipzig: St. Benno, 1977.
Walvoord, John F. *Daniel: The Key to Prophetic Revelation.* Chicago: Moody, 1971.
Watson, Duane F. "The Contributions and Limitations of Greco-Roman Rhetorical Theory for Constructing the Rhetorical and Historical Situations of a Pauline Epistle." In *The Rhetorical Interpretation of Scripture: Essays from the 1996 Malibu Conference,* edited by Stanley E. Porter and Dennis L. Stamps, 125–51. Sheffield: Sheffield Academic, 1999.
———. "The Integration of Epistolary and Rhetorical Analysis of Philippians." In *The Rhetorical Analysis of Scripture: Essays from the 1995 London Conference,* edited by Stanley E. Porter and Thomas H. Olbricht, 398–426. Sheffield: Sheffield Academic, 1997.
———. "The New Testament and Greco-Roman Rhetoric: A Bibliography." *JETS* 31 (1988) 465–72.
———. "A Rhetorical Analysis of Philippians and Its Implications for the Unity Question." *NovT* 30 (1988) 57–88.
Watson, Francis. *Paul and the Hermeneutics of Faith.* London: T. & T. Clark, 2004.
Watson, Wilfred G.E. *Classical Hebrew Poetry: A Guide to its Techniques.* Sheffield: JSOT, 1984.
———. "A Review of Kugel's Idea of Biblical Poetry." *JSOT* 28 (1984) 89–98.
Weber, Beat. "Philipper 2, 12–13: Text—Kontext—Intertext." In *Biblische Notizen* 85 (1996) 31–37.
Wegener, Mark I, "Philippians 2:6–11—Paul's (Revised) Hymn to Jesus." *CTM* 25 (1998) 507–17.
Weima, Jeffrey A. D. "The Pauline Letter Closings: Analysis and Hermeneutical Significance." *BBR* 5 (1995) 177–98.
Wenham, Gordon J. *Genesis 1–15.* WBC Vol. 1. Waco, TX: Word, 1987.
Westermann, Claus. *Isaiah 40–66.* OTL. London: SCM, 1969.
———. *The Living Psalms.* Translated by J. R. Porter. Edinburgh: T. & T. Clark, 1989.

Wevers, John, ed. *Deuteronomium. Septuaginta: Vetus Testamentum Graecum Auctoritate Societatis Litterarum Gottingensis Vol. 3.2*. Göttingen: Vandenhoeck & Ruprecht, 1977.

———. "The Earliest Witness to the LXX Deuteronomy." *CBQ* 39 (1977) 240–44.

———. *Notes on the Greek Text of Deuteronomy*. SBLSCS 39. Atlanta: Scholars, 1995.

Wheeler, Michael. *The Art of Allusion in Victorian Fiction*. London: Macmillan, 1979.

White, James R. "Beyond the Veil of Eternity: The Importance of Philippians 2:5–11 in Theology and Apologetics." *CRJ* 22 (2000) 31–38.

Whybray, Roger N. *Isaiah 40-66*. NCBC. Grand Rapids: Eerdmans, 1981.

Wichelns, Herbert A. "Some Differences between Literary Criticism and Rhetorical Criticism." In *Historical Studies of Rhetoric and Rhetoricians*, edited by Raymond F. Howes, 217–24. New York: Cornell University Press, 1961.

Wierzbicka, Anna. "The Semantics of Direct and Indirect Discourse." *Papers in Linguistics* 7 (1974) 267–307.

Williams, Demetrius K. *Enemies of the Cross of Christ: The Terminology of the Cross and Conflict in Philippians*. London: Sheffield Academic, 2002.

Williams III, H. H. Drake. "Review of Christopher D. Stanley, Arguing With Scripture: The Rhetoric of Quotations in the Letters of Paul." *Review of Biblical Literature* (Online: http://www.bookreviews.org) 2005.

———. *The Wisdom of the Wise: The Presence and Function of Scripture within 1 Cor. 1:18–3:23*. Leiden: Brill, 2001.

Witherington III, Ben. *Friendship and Finances in Philippi*. Valley Forge, PA: Trinity International, 1994.

Worton, Michael, and Judith Still, eds. *Intertextuality: Theories and Practices*. Manchester: Manchester University Press, 1990.

———. "Introduction." In *Intertextuality: Theories and Practices*, edited by Michael Worton and Judith Still, 1–44. Manchester: Manchester University Press, 1990.

Wright, Christopher J. H. *Deuteronomy*. NIBCOT. Peabody: Hendrickson, 1996.

Wright, N. T. *The Climax of the Covenant*. Edinburgh: T. & T. Clark, 1991.

Wuellner, Wilhelm. "Greek Rhetoric and Pauline Argumentation." In *Early Christian Literature and the Classical Intellectual Tradition: In Honorem Robert M. Grant*, edited by William R. Schoedel and Robert L. Wilken, 177–88. Paris: Éditions Beauchesne, 1979.

———. "Paul's Rhetoric of Argumentation in Romans: An Alternative to the Donfried-Karris Debate over Romans." *CBQ* 38 (1976) 330–51.

———. "Where is Rhetorical Criticism Taking Us?" *CBQ* 49 (1987) 448–63.

Yule, George U. *The Statistical Study of Literary Vocabulary*. Cambridge: Cambridge University Press, 1944.

Ziegler, Joseph, ed. *Isaias. Septuaginta: Vetus Testamentum Graecum Auctoritate Societatis Litterarum Gottingensis, Vol. 14*. Göttingen: Vandenhoeck & Ruprecht, 1967.

———, ed. *Susanna, Daniel, Bel et Draco. Septuaginta: Vetus Testamentum Graecum Auctoritate Societatis Litterarum Gottingensis, Vol. 16.2*. Göttingen: Vandenhoeck & Ruprecht, 1954.

Zimmerli, Walther. *I am Yahweh*. Edited by Walter Brueggemann. Translated by Douglas W. Stott. Atlanta: John Knox, 1982.

Author Index

Abasciano, Brian J., 25, 30, 37
Aichele, George, 68, 81
Albright, William F., 204
Alexander, Loveday, 8
Allen, Graham, 60, 62
Allen, Leslie C., 21
Alter, Robert, 69, 77, 79, 81, 194
Anderson, Robert A., 219
Aquinas, Thomas, 95
Aune, David E., 11

Baker, David L., 248
Bakken, Norman K., 130
Baldwin, J. G., 219
Balz, Horst, 186
Barclay, John M. G., 216
Barnes, A., 218
Barnett, Paul, 182
Barr, James, 18
Barth, Gerhard, 2
Barth, Karl, 93, 96, 106, 122, 126, 129, 180, 227–28
Barthes, Roland, 25, 60–61, 63–64, 68, 71, 81
Barton, John, 223
Basser, Herbert W., 203
Bateman IV, Herbert W., 136
Bauckham, Richard, 173
Beale, G. K., 3, 219, 223
Beale, Timothy K., 60, 66
Beare, Frank W., 94, 103, 164, 179, 200–201, 208–9, 215
Beker, J. Christiaan, 2, 6, 11, 31–33
Bell, Richard H., 201, 203
Belleville, Linda, 208

Ben-Porat, Ziva, 8, 12–13, 27, 39, 43, 46, 69–73, 76–78, 84–86, 89, 161–63, 167–69, 176–78, 183–84, 188, 193, 207, 211, 219, 225, 244–45
Bentzen, Aage, 195
Berger, Klaus, 113
Bertram, Georg, 193, 203
Betz, Hans D., 140
Bitzer, Loyd F., 10–13, 51–56, 58–60, 88–89, 99, 130–31, 140, 170, 172, 175, 189, 194, 209–10, 246, 252
Black, David A., 101, 103
Blevins, James L., 8
Bloom, Harold, 25, 69, 86
Bloomquist, L. Gregory, 51, 60, 90, 98
Bockmuehl, Markus, 3, 106, 125–26, 131, 139, 151, 153, 166–67, 169, 187, 195, 200, 213–14, 218, 227–29
Booth, Wayne C., 57
Bormann, Lukas, 9–10, 12, 48, 161, 197, 247
Bostock, Gerald, 164
Brand, Myles, 80
Brand, Peg Zeglin, 80
Brant, Jo-Ann A., 157
Bratcher, Robert G., 168
Braumann, Georg, 125
Brawley, Robert L., 148
Brenton, Lancelot C. L., 16, 18, 201
Brett, Makk G., 48
Brewer, David I, 4
Brewer, Raymond R., 91
Brinton, Alan, 53–54

Brock, Sebastian P., 22
Brown, Colin, 117, 183
Bruce, F. F., 11, 20, 90, 95, 97, 139, 219, 221, 230
Brueggemann, Walter, 173, 175
Büchsel, Hermann, 93, 107
Bultmann, Rudolph, 212, 226, 239
Burton, Ernest De Witt, 92

Caird, G. B., 118, 139
Callow, Kathleen, 90
Calvin, John, 94
Campbell, J., 80
Capes, David B., 121-22
Carpzov, Johann G., 24
Castelli, Elizabeth A., 157
Chandler, James K., 65, 78
Chapple, Allan L., 177
Charles, R. H., 20-21, 218
Charlesworth, James H., 22
Childs, Brevard S., 168, 232-36, 241
Chrysostom, John, 95
Ciampa, Roy E., 3, 25, 30, 141-42, 150, 232
Clark, Herbert H., 38
Clarke, Andrew D., 157
Clarke, W. K. Lowther, 114
Clayton, Jay, 60, 64-65, 68, 86
Clements, Ronald E., 170-71
Coats, George W., 134
Cohen, Ted, 83, 86
Collange, Jean-François, 103, 132, 164, 168, 179, 200, 213, 238
Collins, John J., 21, 216, 219
Combs, J. H., 39, 69
Consigny, Scott, 54
Conte, Gian B., 69, 80-81, 83
Conzelmann, Hans, 215
Craddock, Fred, 94, 209
Craigie, Peter C., 191, 195-96, 204, 209
Cross, Frank M., 15
Croy, N. Clayton, 148
Culler, Jonathan, 25, 64, 66, 101

Dahood, Mitchell, 191
Dailey, Thomas F., 148
Dalton, William J., 136

Davila, James R., 185
Davis, Casey W., 60
Day, J., 21
Deissmann, Adolf, 140
De Lacey, Douglas R., 171
Delling, Gerhard, 108, 147-48
De Silva, David A., 146
De Vogel, Cornelia J., 148
De Vos, Craig S., 3
Dibelius, Martin, 2
Di Lella, Alexander, A., 21, 219-21
Dines, Jeniffer M., 14-18, 22
Docherty, Susan E., 22-23
Dodd, C. H., 4
Donfried, Karl P., 91
Driver, G. R., 21
Driver, Samuel R., 204
Duncan, G. S., 8
Dunn, James D. G., 124, 127, 129-30, 152, 165, 171, 189
Durham, John I., 184

Eaton, John H., 191, 195
Eckman, Barbara, 114
Ehrhardt, A. A. T., 124
Elam, H. R., 60, 67
Ellis, E. Earle, 5, 25, 33, 35
Eriksson, Anders, 47, 51
Evans, Craig A., 25, 31

Fee, Gordon D., 1, 6-7, 86, 90, 92, 94-96, 99, 101-4, 107-9, 113, 117, 123, 129, 135, 137-38, 151, 164-69, 173, 180-83, 213-15, 226, 230, 239
Feinberg, Paul D., 128-29
Fields, B. L., 60
Fitzmyer, Joseph A., 23, 114
Foerster, Werner., 127, 172
Fortna, Robert T., 95
Fowl, Stephen E., 19, 47-48, 92, 101, 113, 129, 132, 169
France, R. T., 172
Friedman, S. S., 60
Fung, Ronald Y. K., 141
Furness, J. M., 124
Furnish, Victor, 137-38

AUTHOR INDEX

Gamble, Harry Y., 38, 40–42
Garland, David E., 95, 137, 139, 145, 149
Genette, Gérard, 64, 68, 81
Geoffrion, Timothy C., 60, 90, 92–93, 98
Gerrig, Richard, J, 38
Glasson, T. Francis, 127
Gloer, W. Hulitt, 114
Gnilka, Joachim, 2, 5, 100, 102, 155
Goldingay, John E., 218–19, 221, 224, 234
Grant, Robert M., 118
Gray, George B., 114–15
Grayston, Kenneth, 136
Green, Joel B., 148
Greenlee, J. Harold, 147
Grundmann, Walter, 91, 217
Gudas, Fabian, 83
Gundry, Robert H., 114
Gundry Volf, Judy M., 151–53, 179

Hagner, Donald A., 75, 172
Hanhart, Karl, 148
Hanson, Anthony T., 4, 5, 34
Hanson, Paul D., 232
Harnack, Adolf von, 2
Harris, J. Rendel, 35
Harris, William V., 38
Harrington, Daniel J., 113
Hartman, Louis F., 21, 219–21
Hatina, Thomas R., 60, 67–68
Hauck, Friedrich, 138, 227, 230
Hawthorne, Gerald F., 8, 94, 104, 156, 164–66, 180, 193, 212–13, 228
Hayes, J. H., 190
Hays, Richard B., 3, 5, 23, 25–33, 42–43, 46, 66–69, 82, 84, 132, 176, 178, 200, 232, 247–49
Hebel, Udo J., 73–74, 77–78, 84–85
Hellerman, Joseph H., 166
Hendricksen, William, 96
Hengel, Martin, 113–14, 118, 198
Herklots, Hugh G. G., 139
Hermerén, Göran, 69, 79
Hezser, Catherine, 40
Hickling, C. J. A., 35
Hofius, Otfried, 114

Holladay, Carl R., 136
Hollander, John, 26–27, 29
Holleman, Joost, 223
Holloway, Paul A., 55–56, 60, 98
Hooker, Morna D., 110, 124, 136, 241
Hoover, Roy W., 127
Houlden, James L., 95, 210
Howard, George, 113, 124, 130
Hübner, Hans, 5, 14, 16, 25, 28, 32–33, 69, 163, 183, 187, 215
Hunsaker, David M., 54
Hunter, Archibald M., 113, 118
Hurst, Lincoln D., 129

Irwin, William, 8, 12–13, 39, 60, 63, 69, 76, 78–80, 82–87, 145

Jauhiainen, Marko, 30–31, 42–44, 46, 80, 162, 187
Jeansonne, S. P., 221
Jellicoe, Sidney, 14, 17
Jenny, Laurent, 66
Jeremias, Joachim, 75, 113–14, 129
Jewett, Robert, 136, 138
Jobes, Karen H., 16, 25
Johnson, Aubrey R., 191

Kahle, Paul, 16
Kaiser Jr., Walter C., 25, 187
Käsemann, Ernst, 122, 129, 192–93
Keefer, Donald, 60
Keesmaat, Sylvia C., 25, 30
Kennedy, George A., 13, 51, 55–56
Kennedy, H. A. A., 93, 132
Kilpatrick, George D., 142
Klijn, A. F. J., 136
Kline, Meredith G., 204
Koch, Dietrich-Alex, 4, 24, 35–37
Köster, Helmut, 104, 143–44
Koole, Jan L., 176, 231, 233, 235
Koperski, Veronica, 153–54
Kramer, Werner, 171
Kraus, Hans-Joachim, 191–92, 195
Krentz, Edgar M., 92, 94, 97–98, 113
Kreitzer, Larry J., 17, 167, 219
Kristeva, Julia, 25, 60–61, 64, 66, 68, 71
Kruse, Colin, 182
Kugel, James L., 113–18

Laato, Antti, 232
Lack, R. F., 66
Lacocque, Andre, 218, 220
Landy, Francis, 116-18
Lane, William L., 75
Lane-Mercier, Gillian, 38
Lattke, Michael, 113
Laub, Roger M., 74
Leddy, Michael, 69, 75-76, 183
Leupold, Herbert C., 219
Lightfoot, J. B., 99, 103, 107-8, 132, 139, 212
Lim, Timothy H., 24
Lincoln, Andrew T., 91, 144, 157, 182
Lindars, Barnabas, 4, 33
Loh, I-Jin, 90, 92, 99-100, 105, 106, 132, 200
Lohmeyer, Ernst, 8, 102, 111, 114, 116-17, 163, 183
Longenecker, Richard N., 4, 114, 141
Losie, Lynn Allan, 122
Lührmann, Dieter, 212
Louw, J. P., 147
Lowth, Robert, 114-16
Lüdemann, Gerd, 136, 144
Lucas, Ernest C., 218

Mach, Michael, 172
Mack, Burton L., 54
Mackay, B. S., 137-38
Macquarrie, John, 128
Mai, Hans-Peter, 60-61
Maile, John F., 192
Malherbe, Abraham J., 35
Marchal, Joseph. A., 60
Marcos, Natalio F., 16-17, 22-23
Marshall, I. Howard, 101
Marshall, John W., 59
Martin, Ralph P., 110-11, 113-14, 118, 126-27, 130-31, 182, 193, 198-99, 229
Mays, James L., 192
McKenzie, John, 88
McLay, R. Timothy, 14-16, 18-22, 215, 217, 220
McLean, Bradley H., 5, 44, 187
McLean, Paul D., 191
Mearns, Chris, 136

Meeks, Wayne A., 35
Menken, Maarten, J. J., 3
Metzger, Bruce M., 112, 167
Meyer, Frederick B., 164, 226
Meyer, Heinrich August Wilhelm, 92, 95, 105, 107
Michael, J. Hugh, 92, 96, 164, 200, 209
Michel, Otto, 4, 172
Michaelis, Wilhelm, 97, 100
Miller, Arthur B., 53
Miller, Ernest C., 91
Minear, Paul S., 113
Miner, Earl, 69
Minn, Herbert R., 231
Moo, Douglas, 165, 189
Moore, George Foot, 4
Morgan, Robert, 123
Morgan, Thaïs E., 62, 66
Morris, Leon, 182
Motyer, J. Alec, 153, 234-35
Moule, C. F. D., 129, 141, 164, 206, 226
Moule, H. C. G., 132
Moyise, Steve, 3, 60
Müller, Jac J., 97, 128, 132, 140
Müller, Mogens, 14
Mullins, Terence Y., 238
Murphy-O'Connor, Jerome, 125

Nagata, Takeshi, 111, 173
Neumann, Peter H., 74
Newman, Robert, 216
Nickelsburg, George W. E., 185
Nida, Eugene, A., 90, 92, 99-100, 105-6, 132, 147, 200
Niehaus, Jeffrey J., 204
North, Christopher R., 232, 234

Oakes, Peter, 98, 101, 166, 173-74
O'Brien, Peter T., 91-92, 94-95, 99, 101-6, 110, 123, 132, 139, 153-55, 157, 165-66, 168-69, 173, 179-80, 187, 199-200, 203, 213-15, 218, 226-28, 230
O'Day, Gail R., 25
Oepke, Albrecht, 108, 195, 227
Ogden, Graham S., 176
Olbrechts-Tyteca, Lucie, 56
Olbricht, Thomas H., 51, 54, 60

O'Neill, John C., 127
Oppenheimer, Fred E., 74
Orr, Mary, 60, 65, 68–69, 81
Osiek, Carolyn, 154
Oswalt, John N., 177, 232, 234
Otto, Randal E., 152–54

Palmer, D. W., 148
Park, M. Sydney, 131, 145, 151, 156, 173
Patton, John H., 54
Perelman, Chaim, 37, 56
Perri, Carmela, 39, 69, 77–78, 83
Perriman, Andrew C., 150, 154–55
Peterlin, Davorin, 9, 95–96, 101, 108, 209
Pfister, Manfred, 64, 68, 81
Pfitzner, Victor C., 92
Phillips, Gary A., 68, 81
Pietersma, Albert, 15, 191
Pilhofer, Peter, 2
Plett, Bettina, 74
Plett, Heinrich F., 66, 72
Plummer, Alfred, 95, 132, 238
Pobee, John S., 92, 239
Pogoloff, Stephen M., 12
Pollard, T. E., 95, 136
Polycarp, 139
Portefaix, Lilian, 3, 69
Porter, Stanley E., 3, 29–30, 42, 51, 60
Poythress, Vern S., 214
Pucci, Joseph, 80

Rahlfs, Alfred, 14, 22
Räisänen, Heikki, 59
Reed, Jeffrey T., 6, 169
Rengstorf, Karl, 134–35, 187–88
Reumann, John, 5–7, 9, 48, 169, 200, 226, 247
Riesenfeld, Harald, 97, 164
Riffaterre, Michael, 8–9, 12–13, 44–46, 61–68, 73, 78, 80–82, 84–85, 88–89, 156, 194, 242, 247
Robinson, Donald W. B., 136
Robuck, Thomas D., 60
Rosner, Brian S., 13, 25, 30
Ross, Stephanie, 69, 79
Rothstein, Eric, 60, 64–65, 68, 86

Sacchi, Paolo, 222–23
Sanders, E. P., 4
Sanders, J. A., 25
Sanders, Paul, 204
Sandmel, Samuel, 63, 79, 149
Sandnes, Karl O., 232
Schaar, Claes, 78
Schmid, Wolf, 9
Schmithals, Walter, 54, 142–47, 149
Schneider, Johannes, 157
Schoon-Janssen, Johannes, 9
Schrenk, Gottlob, 133, 217
Schüssler-Fiorenza, Elizabeth, 12, 54, 56–57
Schweizer, Eduard, 103, 181
Selwyn, Edward G., 91
Silva, Moisés, 2–3, 16, 96, 99, 101–3, 105, 140, 164–165, 179–80, 201, 203–4, 207–9, 213–15, 230, 238
Smith, Craig, R., 54
Smith, D. Moody, 2
Smith, Gary, 134
Snodgrass, Klyne, 3, 75
Sommer, Benjamin D., 67
Stagg, Frank, 95
Stählin, Gustav, 126
Stamps, Dennis L., 42, 51, 55, 58, 90
Stanley, Christopher D., 2, 22–24, 33–42, 72, 77, 119–21, 157, 167, 176, 246, 249
Stanley, David M., 113
Stauffer, Ethelbert, 92, 94, 130
Stenschke, Christoph W., 41
Sternberg, Meir, 38
Stowers, Stanley K., 8, 86
Stierle, Karlheinz, 74
Still, Judith, 60, 62, 64
Strimple, Robert B., 124
Suleiman, Susan R., 57
Sumney, Jerry, L., 51
Sundberg, Albert C., 15
Swete, Henry B., 14, 201
Swift, Robert C., 8–9

Talbert, Charles H., 113, 123–24, 130
Taylor, Bernard, A., 191
Taylor, Vincent, 118
Tellbe, Mikael, 11, 90, 92

Tetzeli von Rosador, Elizabeth, 74
Theissen, Gerd, 35
Thielman, Frank, 6, 12
Thomas, D. Winton, 174
Thomson, J. A., 206
Thomson, Michael B., 30
Thurén, Lauri, 51
Tov, Emanuel, 14, 16, 22
Tyson, Joseph B., 136

Van Dam, Cornelis, 195
Van Pelt, Miles V., 187
Van Spanje, T. E., 59
Van Wolde, Ellen, 68
Vatz, Richard E., 53
Vincent, Marvin R., 92, 95, 132, 139, 154, 179, 181, 212, 226, 238
Voelz, James W., 66
Vos, Geerhardus, 190

Wagner, J. Ross, 25, 30
Wakefield, Andrew H., 25, 44–48, 86, 89, 156
Walter, Nicholas, 99, 177, 206
Walvoord, John F., 219
Watson, Duane F., 51, 55, 58, 60, 90, 131, 136

Watson, Francis, 203, 216
Watson, Wilfred G. E., 115–17
Weber, Beat, 1, 197
Wegener, Mark I., 130
Weima, Jeffrey A. D., 140
Wenham, Gordon J., 184
Westermann, Claus, 171, 174–75, 177, 190–91, 234
Wevers, John, 22, 201
Wheeler, Michael, 74
White, James R., 130
Whybray, Roger N., 231, 234, 236
Wichelns, Herbert A., 59
Wierzbicka, Anna, 37
Williams, Demetrius K., 55–56, 60
Williams III, H. H. Drake, 25, 29, 40, 133
Witherington III, Ben, 51, 60, 200
Worton, Michael, 60, 62, 64
Wright, Christopher J. H., 204–5
Wright, N. T., 128
Wuellner, Wilhelm, 56

Yule, George U., 112

Ziegler, Joseph, 19–20, 22, 167
Zimmerli, Walther, 173

Ancient Document Index

OLD TESTAMENT

Genesis

1	48
1–3	125
1–15	184
1:14	212
1:16	212
1:26	124
2:7	124
3:22–24	124
9:2	184
12:3	44
15:6	44
17:1	6
18:10	199
18:14	199
22	116
22:12	116
24:20	128
31:44	251

Exodus

6:9	176
15:16	180, 184–85, 187
15:24	135
16:2	134
16:3	135
16:7	134, 209
16:7–12	134
16:8	134–35, 209
16:9	209
16:12	5–6, 209
17:2	134
17:3	134
23:22	93
32:32	217, 251
32:33	217

Leviticus

18:5	44–45
26:20	227

Numbers

14:1	135
14:2	5, 134
14:11	134
14:27	134
14:27–29	134–35
14:29	134
14:35	134
16:3	134
16:11	134
16:41	134
16:41–49	135
17:5	134
17:6	134
17:7	134
17:10	134
17:20	134
20:2	134
27:3	134

Deuteronomy

2:25	180, 184
3:26	209
3:27	209
4:21	209
4:22	209
7:16	207
8:19	207
11:25	180, 184
21:23	44
27:26	44
31:2	209
31:7	204
31:8	204
31:14	209
31:16	204–9
31:17	204
31:21	204
31:23–26	209
31:27	209
31:29	209
32	205, 211
32:1–4	204
32:1–5	200
32:1–43	200, 202, 204–5, 209, 211
32:1–45	201
32:3	206
32:3–4	206
32:4	206
32:5	1, 5–6, 24, 66, 163, 198–204, 206–8, 211, 244
32:5–6	205
32:6	203, 207
32:6–14	205–6
32:6b-14	207
32:6b-18	205–6, 208
32:15–18	205
32:15	203, 205
32:16–17	205
32:16–18	207
32:19–26	205
32:20	207
32:26–27	205
32:28–30	205
32:31–43	205
32:43	210
32:48–52	209
33:29	211
34:9	204

1 Samuel

26:12	116

2 Samuel

7:12–14	191
14:15	151–53

2 Kingdoms (Reigns)

7:12–14	191

1 Kings

20:31	152

2 Kings

2 Kgs	152

3 Kingdoms

21:31	152–53

4 Kingdoms

18:13	152–53

2 Chronicles

24:11	128

Job

1:12	27, 133
2:3–6	133
2:6	27
2:9	229
2:9b	229
4:14	184
13	27
13:16	26–27, 132–33, 200, 251
20:18	229
38–41	27
39:16	229

Psalms

2	72, 184, 186–94, 196–98, 244, 250–51
2:1–2	186–87, 250
2:1–3	196
2:1–5	192
2:2	189, 192
2:2–3	195
2:6	188, 191–94, 198
2:6–9	192
2:7	189, 191–94, 198
2:8	191–93, 198, 250
2:9	191–93, 198
2:10	186–87, 196, 250
2:11	1, 5, 23, 66, 72, 111, 163, 178, 180–84, 186–88, 192, 194, 196–98, 244, 249–51
2:12	188, 191–92, 195–96
16	190
18	191
20	191
21	191
22	75–76
22:1	75
22:1–18	75
22:18	75–76
23	116
45	191
54:6	180, 184
69:28	217, 251
72	191
77:7	207
77:40	134
77:41	134
78:40	134
78:41	134
89	191
94:11	133
101	191
109	190
109:13	217
109:14	217
110	191, 251
132	191

Proverbs

3:9	251
11:30	251
13:2	251

Isaiah

19:16	180, 184, 187
29	40
29:8	227
29:14	39
40–55	231–38, 240, 242
40–66	171, 174–75, 177, 231–32, 234, 236
41–48	233
41:8–13	233
42:1	233–38
42:1–4	231–35
42:6	235–37
42:18–19	233
42:18–25	233
42:19	233
42:20	233
42:24	233
43:1–13	233
43:10	233
43:22–24	233
44–47	233
44:1–5	233
44:21	233
44:22	233
44:24	233
44:24—45:8	171, 174
44:24—45:25	175
45	170–73, 176–77
45:1	174
45:1–5	174
45:1–23	175
45:1–25	170–72, 174, 178
45:1b-3	174
45:3	172–73
45:4b	174
45:5	172
45:6	172
45:6–7	173
45:7	172
45:8	172
45:9–11	175
45:9–13	170, 176, 236
45:11	173

Isaiah (continued)

45:13	173
45:14	172–73
45:15	171
45:16	170
45:17	171
45:18	172–73
45:18–24	167
45:19	173
45:20	170–71, 177
45:20–25	171
45:21	165, 170–72
45:21–22	170
45:22	170–73
45:22b	165
45:23	1, 5, 7, 17, 23, 36–37, 66, 74, 110–11, 119–22, 163–71, 173–78, 183, 196, 198, 224, 240, 244, 249, 251
45:24	120, 170
45:24a	165
46:3–13	233
46:4	171
46:13	171
48	233, 236
48:4	233
48:8	233
48:16	234
48:16b	233
48:20	233, 236
49	236, 240–41
49:1	230
49:1–3	238
49:1–4	233
49:1–6	230–35
49:2	236
49:3	234, 241
49:4	1, 5, 24, 66, 163, 226–32, 235–37, 239–42, 244, 249
49:4b	235
49:5	230, 234, 237, 241
49:6	230, 234–35, 237, 241
49:6–7	240
49:6c	235
49:6d	235
49:7	235, 237, 241
49:8	230, 234–35, 237, 241
49:8–13	234–35
49:13	235
49:14	235–36, 240
49:15–23	236
49:18	230
49:23	173
49:24	236, 240
49:25–26	236
50:1	236
50:1–3	236
50:2	236
50:3–4	238
50:4	236
50:4–5	236
50:4–9	231, 235–36
50:5–6	241
50:6	236, 239
50:6–7	235
50:7	235, 237, 239
50:9	237
52–53	251
52:13	235, 241
52:13—53:12	231
52:13—53:12c	235
52:14—53:2	241
53	241
53:2–12	234
53:3	21, 125, 235
53:3–4	241
53:4	237
53:4–6	237–38
53:5	241
53:6	237
53:8	125, 241
53:11	21
53:12	125
54:14	184
56:7	251
60:2	212
65:23	5, 6, 227, 229–30

Jeremiah

1:5	230
6:29	227
9:22–23	25
9:23	226
14:2	128
15:9	128

28	153
28:8	152
28:58	229

Ezekiel

20:41	251

Daniel

3	220
4:19	184
4:30a-37	250
4:37	184, 186, 250, 251
4:37b	250
7–12	221
10:11–12	184
10:12	184
11:21–35	219
11:30	221
11:31–35	221
11:32	217
11:33	220, 224
11:36–45	219
12	220
12:1	19, 219, 221–23
12:1–3	223
12:1–4	18, 221–22
12:1d	217
12:2	154, 217–19, 221–22
12:2–3	217
12:2–4	222
12:2b	217
12:2b–3b	217
12:3	1, 5–6, 16–18, 21, 24, 163, 208, 212, 214–25, 244, 249, 250
12:3a	18
12:3b	19, 214, 217
12:4	19–21, 217
12:4c	20, 221

Amos

6:12	251
8:12	20

Habakkuk

1:12–17	205
2:4	36, 44–45

Zechariah

1	43
1:8–17	43
6:1–8	43

Malachi

3:16	217

APOCRYPHA

Judith

2:28	184
15:2	185

1 Maccabees

1:20–64	219
1:41–52	221
7:18	185
13:2	185

2 Maccabees

4:5	109

4 Maccabees

	92
2:15	108
4:10	185
6:10	92
7:15	147
9:22	157
9:23	92
11:20	92
13:15	92
17:12	92

Odes

1:16	184–85
2	201
2:5	201

Sirach

43:7	212
50:19b	147

Tobit

3:6	251
11:17	251

Wisdom of Solomon

1:6	251
2:23	125
3:7	216
4:16	147
10:2	92
13:2	212

PSEUDEPIGRAPHA

Syriac Apocalypse of Baruch

	223
51:10	216

Ethiopian Enoch

	217, 223
1	185
1:5	185
13:3	185
14:13	185
47:3	217
104:1	250
104:2	216, 250
104:2–6	216
104:5	250
104:6	250

4 Ezra

	223

Testament of Abraham

16:1	185

NEW TESTAMENT

Matthew

1:21	172
5:14	214
5:16	214
24:27	212
27:11	75
27:35	76
27:39	76
27:42–43	76
27:46	70, 76
27:46–49	75

Luke

13:17	93
13:32	147–48
21:15	93

John

3:16	212
7:12	134
12:46	212
13:3–17	193
18:36–37	75
18:37	75
19:14–15	75
19:19–21	75
19:19–22	75
19:24	75–76
19:30	148

Acts

6:1	134
8:28	35
13:16	189

13:22	189
13:23	189
13:30	189
13:33	189
13:34	190
13:37	189–90
13:47	230, 232
16:22	95
16:22–23	95
16:23	95
18:1–11	41
20:24	148
21:12–14	148
22:3	13
24:15	154
27:12	151–53

Romans

1:1–4	189
1:3–4	192
1:5	178
1:7	121
1:10	151–52, 154
1:13	41
1:15	41
1:17	36
1:21	133
2:7	118
2:8	108
4:14	128
5:19	178
6:16	178
6:17	178
7:13	212
8:16	199
8:21	199
8:31	118
8:32	97
9:2–4	208
9:7	34
9:8	199
9:16	227
10:1	226
10:9–10	172
10:16	178
10:19	202
11:14	151–52

11:33–36	118
12:16	107
12:19	202
13:4	226
14:1	133
14:1–12	165
14:11	37, 74, 111, 119, 120–22, 165, 167, 183, 230
15:5	107
15:10	202
15:18	178
16:12	227
16:19	178, 199
16:26	178

1 Corinthians

	5, 56–57, 124, 146
1:3	122
1:8	226
1:11—14:21	57
1:17	128
1:18	118
1:19	39
1:26–31	25, 118
2:3	180, 182–83
2:12	97
3:20	133
3:21	196
4:5	196
4:7	143
4:10	118, 143
5:2	143
8:6	121
9:9	4
9:15	128
9:24	227
9:26	227
10:10	134–35
10:12	196
10:23	118
11:33	196
12:4–6	118
13	118
14:1	238
14:5	238
14:22	226
14:39	196

1 Corinthians *(continued)*

15:1–12	57
15:10	227
15:20	153
15:23–28	223
15:25	190
15:27	34
15:40–42a	216
15:58	196
16:5–11	57
16:9	93
16:16	227

2 Corinthians

2, 4, 39, 108, 143–44, 149, 150

1:2	121
1:14	226–27
3:4	143
3:12	208
4:2–5	143
4:12	179
5:1	153
5:11–15	143
5:12	149
5:19	212
5:20	152
6:1	227
6:2	230
6:4	118
7:5	94–95
7:8	182
7:15	180, 182–83
8:1	95
8:2	95
8:4	152
8:9	129
9:3	128
9:6	118
9:21–29	118
10–13	145
10:4–5	143
10:5	178
10:6	178
10:12	143
10:12–17	149
11:12—12:9	149
11:13	143–44, 149
11:13–15	144
11:18	149
11:21	149
11:23–30	142
11:25	95
12:11	143
12:20	108
13:7	212

Galatians

1:3	121
1:9	138
1:13	141
1:14	13
1:15	230, 232
1:16	230
1:23	141
2:2	227, 230
3	2
3:1–14	44–46, 89
3:6	44
3:6–13	44
3:8	45
3:8–13	45
3:10	44
3:11	36, 44
3:12	44
3:13	44
3:18	97
4:8–11	230
4:11	227, 230
4:12	152
4:21–31	4
5:7	227
5:13	107
5:17	93
5:20	108
5:26	108
5:29	138
6:11	141
6:11–13	142
6:11–18	140, 142
6:12	141
6:12–14	141
6:12–17	141
6:12–18	140–41, 145, 149

ANCIENT DOCUMENT INDEX

6:12c	142
6:13	141
6:14	141
6:14–17	142
6:15	141
6:16	141
6:17	141–42
6:17b	141

Ephesians

6:5	180, 182–83
6:7	182
6:11	91
6:13–14	91

Philippians

1:1	209
1:2	121
1:4	105, 139
1:5	95, 104
1:6	106, 179, 206, 223, 226
1:7	95, 104
1:8	251
1:10	223, 226
1:11	251
1:12	238
1:12–14	90
1:12–26	10, 90, 237, 240
1:13	97, 222
1:14	238
1:15–17	26, 109, 209, 238
1:16	98, 231, 239
1:17	105, 108
1:17–18	140
1:18	99, 105, 133
1:18–20	239
1:19	26–27, 123, 132–33, 172, 200, 237, 239, 241, 251
1:20	157, 222–23, 235, 239
1:20–23	210
1:20–26	238
1:21	157, 211, 218, 223
1:21–24	210
1:21–25	140
1:21–26	148, 156
1:23	148, 157, 211, 218, 251
1:23–24	148
1:25	149
1:26	149, 226
1:27	92–93, 178, 180, 195, 197–98, 210, 214, 230
1:27–28	97–98, 172
1:27–29	94, 100
1:27–30	49, 90, 95, 98, 100–101, 103, 105, 109, 123, 132, 136, 149–50, 158, 167, 194, 206, 222
1:27—22:18	90
1:27—23:21	12, 33, 47, 89, 158–59, 170, 178, 213, 220, 236, 246
1:27—24:3	252
1:27a	90, 91
1:27c–28a	94
1:28	91, 93, 96, 123, 165, 179, 187, 195, 222–23
1:28–30	96
1:28a	93
1:29	94–95, 97–99, 103–5, 131–32, 155, 158, 166, 175, 178, 224, 231, 237, 241
1:29b	99
1:29c	99
1:30	94–95, 98, 148, 158
2:1	101, 103–6, 109
2:1–3	109
2:1–4	49, 101–4, 109–10, 123, 131–32, 136, 158, 167
2:1–5	145
2:2	103, 107, 109, 133
2:2–4	104, 106
2:2c	106–7
2:3	101, 103, 106–7, 109, 214
2:3–4	106–7
2:3–5	107
2:3–13	145
2:3a	107
2:3b	108
2:4	101, 107–9, 123
2:5	106, 166, 214
2:5–8	130–32, 156, 166, 210, 228
2:5–11	7, 49, 101, 109–11, 113, 122–24, 131–32, 136, 158, 164–65, 173, 180–81, 193–94, 228
2:6	123, 127–29, 164

Philippians (continued)

Reference	Pages
2:6–7	129
2:6–8	91, 107, 110, 123, 125, 130–31, 163, 166, 173, 196
2:6–11	1, 17, 93, 97, 102, 106, 110–15, 117–19, 122–24, 129–30, 145, 150, 163, 168–69, 175, 177, 179, 181, 192–93, 196, 198, 206, 210, 224, 241, 249, 251
2:6b	125
2:7	126, 129, 187
2:7a	129
2:7b	123, 129
2:7c	129
2:8	117, 149, 157, 173, 179–80
2:9	97, 122, 155, 157, 164, 166, 173–74, 187, 191, 193–94, 198, 222, 237
2:9–10	106
2:9–11	110, 113, 121–22, 130–31, 163, 165–67, 171–75, 178, 192–94, 196, 223, 228, 231
2:9a	112, 193
2:9b	193
2:9c	193
2:10	17, 36, 74, 122, 164, 171, 218
2:10–11	1, 5, 7, 23, 36–37, 74, 110–11, 119–21, 163, 166–69, 171–74, 176, 178, 193, 196, 198, 244, 251
2:10–16	1, 2, 5–10, 25, 33, 43, 45–50, 66–67, 85–86, 89, 122, 158–59, 161, 167, 170, 220, 243–44
2:10a	193–94, 198
2:11	36, 74, 112, 164, 174
2:12	1, 5, 7, 23, 72, 84, 111, 163, 172, 178–79, 181–84, 186–88, 192, 194, 196–98, 205, 208, 210, 226, 241, 244, 251
2:12–13	1, 178–81, 197
2:12–16	1, 5, 181, 228, 230, 237
2:12–18	6, 123, 200, 208
2:13	179, 206
2:14	6, 49, 101, 136, 158, 199
2:14–15	6
2:14–16	6
2:15	1, 5, 16–18, 21, 24, 135, 163, 195, 198–203, 207–8, 211–12, 215–18, 223, 225, 244
2:15a	198
2:15b	198
2:15c	18, 214
2:15c–16a	19, 212, 215
2:16	1, 5, 24, 163, 215, 217, 223, 226–31
2:16a	217
2:16b	226
2:16b–c	226–27, 231
2:16c	226
2:17	105, 139–40, 148–49, 210, 223–24
2:17–18	133, 228, 237
2:18	90, 139–40
2:20–21	145
2:21	109, 123
2:24	148
2:25–30	137
2:27	211, 251
2:27–30	140
2:28	139
2:29	139
2:30	145, 149, 156–57, 210, 223
3	9, 142–46, 149–50, 214
3:1	137–41
3:1–2	137
3:1–14	146
3:1–20	147
3:1–21	1, 49, 101, 136–37, 141, 158, 167, 207
3:2	136, 140, 142–45, 149, 195, 200, 204, 206, 222
3:2–5	149
3:2–9	145
3:2–11	145–46
3:2b	143
3:3	141, 144, 146, 226, 251
3:4	141, 144
3:4–6	149
3:4–10	156
3:4–11	136, 145, 150–51, 156, 224
3:4–14	147

3:4–16	156	4:3	12, 92, 217, 251
3:4–21	142	4:4	133
3:5	141	4:5	223
3:5–6	13	4:10	154, 238
3:5–8	156	4:14	158
3:6	141, 199	4:15–18	238
3:7–10	222	4:18	196, 251
3:7–11	132, 141		
3:8	157–58		
3:8–11	157		

Colossians

1:28–29	230

3:9	141, 153, 155–56		
3:10	97, 104, 149, 153–55, 158, 210–11, 223		

1 Thessalonians

3:10–11	143, 149		
3:10–14	157–58	1:1	121
3:10–21	222	1:5	212
3:11	145–46, 150–52, 218	2:2	94–95
3:11–14	142, 146, 155–56, 214	2:8	212
3:11–16	150, 156	2:10	199
3:12	141, 145–49, 152–54	2:19	226–27
3:12–14	136, 142–44, 146, 149, 155	3:3	239
3:12–15	143	3:5	227
3:12–16	144–46, 156–57	3:8	91
3:13	149	3:10	152
3:14	141, 227	3:13	199
3:14–16	143	4:16–17	223
3:15	107, 144–45	4:18	196
3:15–17	123	5:12	227
3:15–21	136	5:23	199
3:16	141, 156		
3:17	156, 214		
3:17–21	156		

2 Thessalonians

3:18	137–38, 141, 157, 195, 208	1:8	178
3:19	165, 223	2:4	93
3:19–21	222	3:14	178
3:19d	141		
3:20	93, 123, 171–72, 197, 211, 223		

Philemon

3:20–21	172, 223	3	121
3:20a	91, 197	22	97
3:20b	91, 197, 223		
3:20c	91, 197		

Hebrews

3:21	141, 157–58, 195, 210, 218, 223, 241	1:13	190
3:21b	198	2:6–9	190
3:21c	223	5:5	190
4:1	133	11:40	147
4:2	11–12, 99, 107, 109, 209		

1 Timothy

1:10	93
5:14	93

2 Timothy

2:5	92
4:6	148, 154
4:6–8	148
4:7	92, 148

James

3:14	108
3:16	108

1 Peter

4:9	134

Revelation

2:26	190
6	43
6:1–8	43
21:11	212

DEAD SEA SCROLLS

1QSa. 2.11–12	190
4QFlor. 1.10–14	190
4Q119	14
4Q122	14
7Q1	14

GRECO-ROMAN WRITINGS

Aristotle

Probl. 11, 906a	185

Diodorus Siculus

2.19.2	93
17:34.6	93

Dionysius Halicarnassus

Ant. Rom. 5.54.2	185

Euripides

Rhesus	185

Hippocrates

Flat. 8	185

Homer

Il. 22, 136–37	185

Papyri

P.Oxyrh 3522	14

Plutarch

Vit. 175	93
Mor. 449a	186

JEWISH HELLENISTIC WRITINGS

Philo

Flacc. 176	185
Leg. 3 (45)	147
Sobr. II.9	202
Sobr. III.10	202

EARLY CHRISTIAN WRITINGS

Ignatius

Pol. 6:1	92

Polycarp

Phil. 3.2	139

www.ingramcontent.com/pod-product-compliance
Lightning Source LLC
Chambersburg PA
CBHW061431300426
44114CB00014B/1640